GOVERNING THE SUBURBS

GOVERNING THE SUBURBS

by Charles E. Gilbert

Indiana University Press · Bloomington and London

To the memory of

WILLIAM H. BROWN, JR.

CONTENTS

MAPS

TABLES

PREFACE

This book began in conversations with PENJERDEL (The Pennsylvania, New Jersey, Delaware Project, Inc.) in 1962 about a study of suburban governments that would complement work then in progress at the Fels Institute of Local and State Government and the Pennsylvania Economy League. I have leaned heavily on those studies (and others), especially in Section V, while emphasizing different aspects of local government.

In particular, this inquiry deals with counties more than with munici-palities and with politics more than with management. It is confined to the Pennsylvania section of the Philadelphia region partly for lack of ways to study a large area in depth, partly for better comparison of local political systems within one state's governmental context.

I have tried to write for the general reader as well as for academic specialists because the questions of governmental reorganization that I ultimately reach are everyone's concern. I hope all readers will be alert to the opportunities for personal bias in a work of this sort. For instance, the importance I attach to politics (as distinct from social and market forces or public administration) affects not only the focus of the study but some of its conclusions. Another issue stems from the relations between social status and political style, which numerous studies have illuminated. These made it difficult, at points, to avoid an invidious tone in the discussion because the concepts involved are, to most of us, intrinsically invidious. Because this study is implicitly critical of some local governments and perhaps especially of my own county, I should acknowledge some minor personal involvement in Delaware County Democratic politics and civic activity. Finally, an observer's biases ap-pear in his geographical perspective, which may vary from regional to local. I have tried to compromise between a bird's eye view and a worm's eye view of the subject, i.e., to keep my feet on the ground.

The pace of metropolitan change soon outmodes the details of any study. Still, some detail is needed to support analysis of developmental tendencies on which evaluations are based. My written account stops at the end of 1963, though I have taken note of subsequent events in the last revision. I have retained as evidence of basic tendencies the narrative of past events.

This study rests heavily on interviews with several hundred people who were gracious and patient and whom I wish I could thank individually. It is a pleasure to acknowledge my debt to PENJERDEL, sponsor of the study, and especially to John Bodine, president, and Barbara Terrett, research coordinator, for their encouragement and assistance in all stages of the work. Next I have to acknowledge the leading roles of Cyril Roseman (now of San Francisco State College), Stephen Decter and Jon Van Til (then graduate students in political science and sociology, respectively), who were my close associates in aspects of the research that are described in the Appendix, together with Glenn Coven, Jr., Robert Lyke, and Richard Poole, who participated as Swarthmore College undergraduates under a Ford Foundation Public Affairs grant. Robert Hawkinson, also a Swarthmore student, allowed me to use some survey data he had gathered for a senior thesis. The manuscript was read in draft and criticized in detail by Mitchell Hunt of the Pennsylvania Economy League, Morton Lustig of the Fels Institute of Local and State Government, and Professors Cyril Roseman and David G. Smith. My colleagues, Frederick Tolles and George Von der Muhll, read sections of it, as did several local informants. The final revision was improved by the advice of Professors Charles S. Hyneman and York Willbern of Indiana University. Swarthmore College gave me leave from teaching duties during part of the study, and James Maginnis of the Drexel Institute of Technology kindly made computer time available. My wife, Annalee Gilbert, was not content with the long-suffering domestic role so commonly acknowledged by scholars; she assisted critically in several parts of the research, including administration of a sample survey. To all those named and to many others who helped I am deeply grateful. I gladly accept full responsibility for the result and specifically acquit PENJERDEL of all save financial aid and personal encouragement.

Swarthmore, Pa.   C. E. G.

GOVERNING THE SUBURBS

1

Introduction

The Pennsylvania section of the Philadelphia metropolitan area contains five counties, Philadelphia included. Less than half that region's residents now live in the central city; less than half the labor force works there. Population, employment, and transportation patterns changed rapidly after World War II and raised new issues of suburban governance and regional management.

This book is a study of suburban governmental development. It emphasizes the last decade together with the institutional lags and historical factors affecting recent measures. It is focused on three counties—Bucks, Montgomery, and Delaware—adjoining Philadelphia, and on selected municipalities within them. Each of the counties is large in population or area or both: two exceed half a million persons, and two are so extensive that communications and sectionalism raise serious problems. All display significant social diversity, though in suburban rather than urban dimensions. Two counties have long traditions of local industry, and all now combine an industrial base with rapid residential and commercial growth. All are now third class Pennsylvania counties with similar powers but different politics.[1]

Briefly, Bucks County burgeoned in a decade from a bucolic retreat into a new society with a two-party, competitive political system in which county government was used energetically to promote, control, and accommodate development. Montgomery's population increase did not so drastically change that county's social character, but it broke up the old political organization, and county government began a modicum of innovation. Delaware County long reposed on an urban, industrial base and boasted a strong political organization substantially untroubled by public competition and resistant to new public policies. The seventeen municipalities studied here were also chosen to represent

3

presumably critical similarities and differences in social, political, and governmental character.

In both counties and municipalities the study's theoretical objective is to explain variations in public policy and performance; its method combines comparison with analysis of change and relies heavily on narrative and description. In both jurisdictions the practical purpose is to assess the implications of comparison and change for metropolitan organization. Most citizens are far more interested in municipalities than in counties, but the latter are emphasized in this study: there is more reason to believe that political choice and organization affect policy and performance at the county level, and the counties are more likely to change in the future.

Two broad concerns are explored at both levels of suburban government. These may be termed political democracy and governmental adequacy. The first primarily relates to the theoretical side of the inquiry, the second to the practical side. But the two concerns are closely related because, to many persons, the standards for evaluating them are inseparable. This study is not primarily normative, and no specific standards are suggested until the concluding chapter. Not defining *democracy* and *adequacy* leaves room for implicit bias, but early definition may equally induce a kind of dogmatic blindness to local context. Political democracy is the concern more heavily emphasized in this study both because it is too often neglected in discussions of metropolitan organization and because (to the author) the more interesting theoretical issues of political science lie on that side of the governmental equation.

These theoretical issues have to do with the effects of political structure, broadly construed, on governmental action. Political structure here has two main aspects: (1) electoral organization and competition, and (2) patterns of socioeconomic pluralism or, conversely, "power structure." These are the principal factors studied as possible explanations of governmental action; one would expect them to be closely related. Because the theoretical issues about effects of political competition and power structure and the methodological issues about how to study them are difficult to summarize precisely, those most relevant to this study are discussed in the appendices, and a general statement is attempted here to justify the content of the research and the course of the argument. (Appendix A parallels in more detail the argument of this chapter.)

Electoral competition is commonly thought to undermine oligarchy and equalize advantage. Two-party competition is alleged to do so especially by providing (1) popular majorities based on shifting coalitions, (2) party labels by which voters can distinguish incumbents and opponents, and (3) continuing organizations with incentives both to cultivate and to compromise popular differences. Because of its counterbalancing tendencies toward provocation and moderation the mechanics and effects of party competition are not entirely clear, even in theory. At the *local* level, moreover, there may be a less pluralistic base for shifting coalitions, party labels may be chiefly relevant to *national* alignments, and party organizations may be rudimentary and mere extensions of social or economic structure.

In general, however, party competition in the suburban counties should tend to undermine established power structures and promote innovation and inclusiveness of policy; in rendering government more broadly accountable it should tend to discourage corruption. Short of two-party competition, factionalism within a single, open party organization should provide the same benefits in less degree. Primary election competition is not so broadly based as general election competition, and party loyalty may narrow its scope. The relatively closed, electorally unchallenged organization has fewer incentives to innovate and may sense disincentives in the growth of broader public interest, the threat of governmental professionalism to political careerism, and the transfer of loyalty from leadership to policy. As for corruption, the close organization usually affords more opportunity for it—and may even come to depend on it—but one must recognize that *corruption* is about as hard to define as it is to discover.

So far, ignoring several necessary qualifications, the more electoral competition the more innovation, inclusiveness, and integrity in government. But the qualifications are important. They include questions already noted about the extent of socioeconomic pluralism, range of local issues, and nature of party organization. They probably also include the level of popular interest and morality on one hand and, on the other, the standards of the politically active minority.[2]

The chief methodological problem in studying the effects of competition stems from the fact that competition normally depends on socioeconomic diversity. Because such diversity is commonly slight in small areas, because national alignments often override local issues, and perhaps because local organization sanctions are sometimes more salient than grass roots issues, party competition is the exception in American local government. Where both social diversity and political competition exist together it is difficult to show empirically that competition (rather than direct governmental response to diversity) is a determinant of policy—that, as an intervening variable, competition has an independent effect. Opportunities for direct access to government by individuals and groups are probably greatest at the local level. The relative informality of local government makes it difficult to distinguish the effects on policy of party organization and social power structure or of political competition and social pluralism. Thus the theory of political competition may be both harder to demonstrate and less applicable in counties and municipalities.

Some scholars feel that social forces are always more influential than political arrangements, but especially so at the local level, where the latter are less distinct. In many communities, they add, private power structures—cohesive social or economic elites—dominate policy and direct it in their own interests. Other scholars dispute this view. Two positions have thus developed, which may be termed the structuralist and the pluralist positions. Sociologists have leaned toward the first and political scientists toward the second, but the concepts and methods at issue are common to both disciplines.

Structuralists tend to think of power as inhering in basic, pervasive relations like class and status; political power is thought to be derived from economic control or social prestige. Pluralists are impressed with the variety of resources that may be used to influence public policy, and with the breadth and independence of their distributions (at least in American society). At the extremes, one approach is categorical, the other statistical. Pluralists add that latent political resources are often poorly exploited in our affluent society: "If a man's major life work is banking, the pluralist presumes he will spend his time at the bank, and not in manipulating community decisions."[3] Some structuralists argue, however, that important community decisions are *entailed* in the banking business. Others say that certain socioeconomic "structures" have high potential for power that their incumbents *may* employ according to their motives, and they note that some of this potential may be self-fulfilling based in local beliefs or ideologies. Pluralists stress critical differences in the settings and significance of business decisions and official decisions. They distinguish potential from actual power, and acknowledge only what can be empirically demonstrated.

Thus the issue becomes one of research methods. Structuralists have studied people's reputations for influence and have inferred power from the positions men hold. Pluralists have insisted that influence must be demonstrated in explicit decisions between contending forces. Pluralists, then, propose a test for the existence of a ruling elite that is best applied under pluralistic conditions, while the structuralists' methods tend to predetermine their conclusions. These are the extremes. All investigators study the distribution of resources, the occupants of top positions, and the histories of decisions, however defined.

Recently some scholars have argued that, even if the pluralists' criticism of structuralist methods is correct, their own emphasis on specific individuals and discrete decisions neglects two vital considerations. One of these is the institutional and ideological *context* of decisions; the other is that policy is often a matter of "nondecisions," which are implicitly conditioned by this context. That is, prevailing procedures and beliefs create a "mobilization of bias" that predisposes policy.[4] Conservative mobilizations of bias tend to produce nondecisions by limiting alternatives or by making it more difficult for some interests to organize. In such cases structuralists would say that policy is manipulated by a self-interested minority; pluralists would argue that no one cares enough to contest the decision. The middle ground is that the context of policy may have so raised the price of effective action for many people that their effective demand for an alternative decision is slight. In other words, the threshold to perception and accomplishment of alternative policies is too high. This would be the case if, for example, there were few social organizations to raise an issue, no strong political opposition to adopt it, no competing doctrine to support it.

Thus, in analyzing the effects of political structure on governmental action one must look both to electoral organization and to socioeconomic forces. One must be alert to mobilization of bias, which includes the reciprocal effect of both the role and the form of government on social and political factors.

Therefore, this volume deals with three broad variables: (1) the socioeconomic context of policy, (2) political (electoral) organization, and (3) governmental functions and structure. These are treated in this order in the first three sections of the book. Then several subjects of policy are examined so as to assess the influence of political structure, broadly construed, on policy. This is possible because the three counties differ significantly in both politics and policy. After that the effects of political structure are separately studied in seventeen municipalities. In the final section an evaluation of political democracy and governmental adequacy in the suburbs is attempted.

The first three sections of the book pose an organizational problem because of the close interdependence of their basic variables. No single order of discussion seems wholly satisfactory. The present order was adopted as most chronological if not most logical. In general, the sections on "Society" and "Government" are more synoptic and analytical; those on "Politics" and "Policy and Performance" are more narrative and descriptive. Policy differences among the counties cannot simply be explained by abstract comparisons. The reciprocity among basic variables means that narrative description of policy decisions, with all the risks this admittedly entails, may help identify critical relations.

In summary, several questions are asked about political democracy at both the county and the local levels. These have to do in general with relations among the three main variables termed socioeconomic forces, electoral organization, and governmental structure and functions, and in detail with specific aspects of these relations. The principal focus is on the sources and consequences of electoral organization, and especially on the effects of electoral competition of various kinds, but one cannot assume that electoral organization is always the most relevant aspect of political structure for the policy and performance of government. At the municipal level the question of civic participation is also emphasized.

The questions asked about local governmental adequacy are not so systematic: there is, for example, no rigorous analysis of unit costs or

efficiency. Issues considered include the ability to tax, plan, act effectively, and relate problems and policies creatively and constructively.
The adverbs suggest the practical, judgmatic nature of the inquiry.

This study has some relevance to suburban government in general—
a subject not extensively studied. But its conclusions about both political democracy and governmental adequacy rest on some peculiarities of
the Philadelphia region, perhaps especially on the strength of party
organization in Pennsylvania and on existing transportation and utilities
systems in greater Philadelphia. In this writer's view, as metropolitan
studies accumulate they should enhance appreciation of local differences
and of their relevance to reform proposals. These points are emphasized
in this study, in particular by attention to local history as it has affected
institutions and interests.

PART I. SOCIETY

2

Three Centuries of Settlement

Social structure, political structure, and governmental structure are intimately linked in the suburban counties. In this study they are discussed in the order just mentioned, without meaning to imply priority in determining county policy and performance.

Four social factors particularly affect suburban governmental action: the historical patterns of settlement that still condition government today, the elements of unity and division in the counties considered as bodies politic, the interests that give rise to policy issues, and the apparent distribution of private political influence. A chapter is devoted to each of these.

The suburban counties' histories consist far more in trends of development than in recorded events. Four stages of growth are noteworthy: the eighteenth-century agrarian pattern with its cultural diversity (in two counties), dispersed population, and decentralizing pressures; the rise of industrial concentrations beginning at mid-nineteenth century; suburban residential settlement (in two counties) at the end of that century; and recently, the role of the automobile and of a regional economy in renewing dispersal at higher densities.

1. *Early settlement.* There were three original counties in William Penn's colony: Philadelphia, Bucks, and Chester. Present-day Montgomery was a city hinterland until its separate establishment as a county in 1784, and five years later the separation of Delaware from Chester County occurred. Penn's first settlements took place along the river, and the later suburban counties were rapidly surveyed and sold off in large tracts. By the end of the seventeenth century the whole of present-day

11

THE SHADED MUNICIPALITIES ARE THOSE
THAT APPEAR IN PART Ⅴ OF THIS BOOK

ALLENTOWN   BETHLEHEM

QUAKERTOWN

NEW JERSEY

BUCKS
COUNTY

PERKASIE
SELLERSVILLE

NEW
HOPE

POTTSTOWN

MONTGOMERY
COUNTY

LANSDALE

YARD-
LEY

TRENTON

MORRIS-
VILLE

HATBORO

LANGHORNE

MIDDLETOWN

PHOENIXVILLE

NORRISTOWN

BRYN
ATHYN

BRISTOL
TWP

BRISTOL
BORO

UPPER
MERION

CHESTER COUNTY

RADNOR

LOWER
MERION

CHELTENHAM

PHILADELPHIA

NEW JERSEY

WEST CHESTER

MARPLE

MT. HOLLY

DELAWARE
COUNTY

YEADON

MEDIA   SPRING-
FIELD

ALDAN

COLLINGDALE

CAMDEN

MIDDLETOWN

SWARTHMORE   RIDLEY

COLEN-

ASTON

CHESTER

WOODBURY

DELAWARE

THE
PHILADELPHIA
SUBURBS

WILMINGTON

N

0   4   8   12   16   20

SCALE IN MILES

12

Delaware County and more than half of Bucks were spoken for and sparsely settled; negotiations with the Indians held off settlement of upper Bucks until the late eighteenth century. The result of such rapid settlement was remarkable cultural homogeneity in lower Bucks and, to a lesser extent, in Delaware County. In the latter Swedes and Finns were already settled in small sections along with later holders from the Duke of York before the advent of the Friends, but one of Bucks' historians noted that his county "enjoys the unique distinction of exhibiting the social product of the 'divine experiment' unmodified by early foreign influences. Nowhere was loyalty to William Penn so marked, fidelity to the tenets of the Society of Friends so general, the simplicity of manners and sobriety of life . . . so long preserved."[1] In the early eighteenth century Welsh Friends reached central Bucks County; the Scotch-Irish arrived a decade later; then the Germans followed the Perkiomen Creek from the west and had settled widely in central and upper Bucks by 1750. Hence the situation described a century later:

> Between this [German] class and the successors of the early Quakers there is a natural but friendly contest for supremacy in the public control, the issue of which is by no means certain. There is not a wide difference between the habits of thought in the two people here. Society as a whole is conservative rather than radical, and practical rather than experimental or inventive.[2]

Bucks' early cultural unity was thus short-lived: by mid-eighteenth century the dominance of Quaker ways was reduced by immigration of other nationalities and denominations and competition from more indulgent religions; and the Friends' political influence was diminished by their refusal to support recourse to arms in the French and Indian War.

Bucks' later cultural diversity came from Montgomery County, where it had existed from the beginning. The Welsh settled the later "Main Line" on land purchased from William Penn. Most of their acreage was in the subsequent townships of Lower and Upper Merion, and Radnor and Haverford in Delaware County, where their place names still predominate.* Penn's first county line, laid out in 1685, divided the lands of the Welsh against their desire, for they had wanted one municipal government. English settlement began in Cheltenham and spread through the present York Road region. Germans settled between these two sectors, developed the outer county, and crossed into Bucks. By 1740, when Montgomery County was largely in farmland, the Germans were a majority. Thus Bucks and Montgomery Counties contained mixed

---

* Many of the Main Line place names, however, "were chosen from a gazetteer by a nineteenth century president of the Pennsylvania Railroad looking for distinctive names for his suburban stations." Frederick B. Tolles, "The Culture of Early Pennsylvania," *Pennsylvania Magazine of History and Biography*, 81, 120.

populations from the eighteenth century. Delaware County was easily the least diverse of the three and was the county in which Quaker influence persisted longest; it declined, however, in the nineteenth century with urbanization and the Irish migration.

Besides cultural diversity, the even distribution of people was an early characteristic of the counties that was apparent in the census of 1790. Population concentrations occurred in the nineteenth century from industrial and "dormitory" development, but these suburban counties were first agrarian counties. Philadelphia was the center of colonial government, but primitive transportation and growing urban-rural differences, together with the imperatives of agriculture, tended to limit outlying residents' interest to the counties and, indeed, to the townships. As the main roads radiating from the city were laid out most went *through* the surrounding counties rather than to them. Civic, commercial, and cultural ties to the central city were tenuous.[3]

The distribution of population and difficulty of communication soon led to decentralization of government, separation of counties, and the removal of county seats. Bucks' county court was established at Falls, the first settlement, then shifted to Bristol in 1705, northward to Newtown in 1724, and finally to Doylestown in 1810. Each move, on order of the provincial or state assembly, was a response to the demands of an advancing population. After the court's establishment at Doylestown there was a movement to split the county and call the southern section "Penn"; one of the prime movers had bought the old county buildings at Newtown, where he proposed to locate the county seat. Property speculation and political ambition sometimes prompted removal and separation efforts in the early period, but social differences also contributed. In Bucks separation projects recurred, were resisted by the north in the legislature, and died out after the Civil War.*

Montgomery, meantime, had separated from Philadelphia right after the Revolution. Location of the county seat at the later site of Norristown for the benefit of back-country farmers caused the early suburbanites of Germantown and Chestnut Hill to stick with Philadelphia; their region remained a salient in Montgomery County later tending to separate the Main Line and York Road sections. Unsuccessful attempts to split the county and attach the outer part to Chester or Berks occurred in the middle of the nineteenth century, some promoted by the Democratic Party, which was stronger in the northern German regions.

Delaware County's dismemberment from Chester County in 1789 and the later courthouse removal from Chester Borough to Media were intense political issues. Removal dominated county politics until 1845. Separation from Chester County left Delaware less than half the size of Montgomery, less than a third the size of Bucks, thus adding compact-

---

* In 1954, after the rapid settlement of Levittown, residents of Falls and Bristol townships petitioned for removal of the county seat to the south, but the county solicitor held that removal would be illegal without specific legislative provision.

ness to its early cultural homogeneity and arbitrarily contributing to its later density of settlement.

In 1800 Philadelphia was larger, at 80,000 population, than our three suburban counties combined—but only because of the division of Chester, then the largest outlying county, and its omission from this account. By mid-nineteenth 'century the city's population was double that of the four surrounding counties and in 1900 it was treble that of the suburbs—a measure of increasing urban concentration. By 1950 the central city–suburban ratio had receded to 2:1, and a decade later to 4:3. Two aspects of this population change are especially interesting. Most apparent is the long-run trend of urban concentration and its later reversal with suburban dispersion. Less evident is the steady increase of Delaware and Montgomery Counties through the nineteenth century (averaging around twenty percent per decade) and the slower growth in agrarian Bucks and Chester Counties, which began the century with the largest outlying populations because of their larger land areas. As Table 2:1 shows, differences among the surrounding counties set in with the second half of the nineteenth century: growth in Montgomery and Delaware increased as it diminished in Chester and Bucks. Two factors largely determined this pattern: first, the industrial development of Montgomery and Delaware, and later the suburban extension of Philadelphia to the west and northwest. Northeast Philadelphia, adjoining Bucks, was not much improved until mid-twentieth century; thus Bucks' dramatic postwar growth began outside Philadelphia in an area with rural instead of suburban traditions.

TABLE 2:1

Population Growth in Southeastern Pennsylvania Counties

	Bucks		Chester		Delaware		Montgomery		Phila-delphia	
	N	%*	N	%*	N	%*	N	%*	N	%*
1800	27,496		32,093		12,809		24,150		81,009	
1850	56,091	104	66,438	107	24,679	93	58,291	141	408,762	405
1900	71,190	27	95,695	44	94,762	284	138,995	138	1,293,697	216
1950	144,620	103	159,141	104	414,234	337	353,068	154	2,071,605	60
1960	308,567	113	210,608	32	553,154	34	516,682	46	2,002,512	−3

* Percent of growth in 50 years.
Source: U.S. Census.

From all this a crucial point emerges for modern comparison of the three counties: Bucks was a rustic county until recent times; Montgomery by this century was a mix of rural, suburban, and industrial uses; and in Delaware the independent city of Chester and the absence of a spacious hinterland produced a different mix with high overall density (ranging from urban to rural), heavy industry, and a larger ratio of suburban to rural development.

These trends affected governmental development. Public forms were

fixed before suburban growth began. In the few counties (like Montgomery and Delaware) where growth surpassed natural increase it was
associated with concentrations in industrial boroughs and commuting
townships. The Pennsylvania borough, incorporated for higher density
and service levels, was sufficient for the first concentrations, and the
later establishment of first class townships took care of suburban needs.
By and large municipal, not county, government responded, adapted,
and contained the effective community. The county remained an agency
for more remote and occasional concerns.

2. *Industry and early suburbs.* The growth of Delaware and Montgomery that began in the middle of the nineteenth century was uneven.
The trend toward concentrations appears in tax returns and census data.
Table 2:2 shows populations of the counties' industrial enclaves and of
the municipalities contiguous to Philadelphia as percentages of total
county population, and illustrates the cumulations that took place with
industrial and residential growth. In all counties industrial centers
preceded residential development in time, though in different sections.
Industry began along the rivers and main railways, residential growth
along a wider range of rail and trolley lines. After World War II a new
order set in: the automobile spread residential densities, and now turnpikes, taxes, and new technology are scattering light industry more
widely in their wake. Hence the return to dispersion, though at higher
densities, known today as sprawl.

TABLE 2:2

Population Concentrations in the Three Suburban Counties
(High density areas as percentage of total county population)

Region	1800	1850	1900	1930	1950	1960
Bucks						
Bristol area	12	13	17	25	25	36
Doylestown area	13	14	13	11	10	7
Delaware						
Chester area	9	13	39	23	18	14
Darby area	7	5	10	13	13	13
Ridley area	6	6	7	8	9	11
Upper Darby area	5	8	10	24	27	22
Montgomery						
Abington–Cheltenham area	7	5	9	15	17	19
Lansdale area	8	6	7	7	7	7
Merion area	10	12	16	20	20	17
Norristown area	4	13	17	15	13	11
Pottstown area	..	6	11	9	9	7

The distribution of natural resources influenced industrial growth.
Bucks' up-river location was least fortunate: Bristol lay above Chester
and Philadelphia, and tidewater stopped at Trenton-Morrisville. Farther
up the river was not fast enough for milling operations; neither were

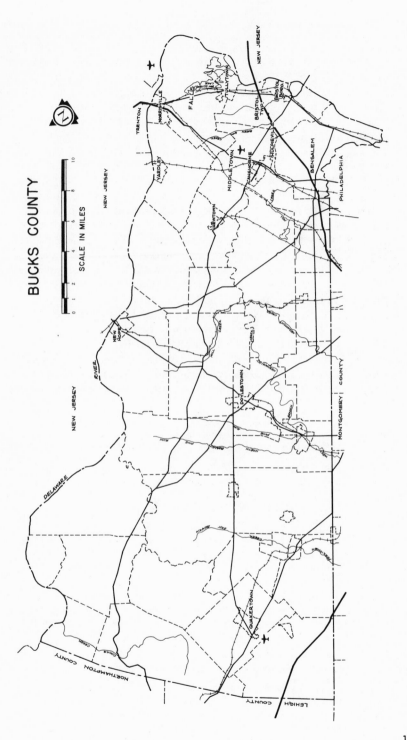

BUCKS COUNTY

SCALE IN MILES

0 1 2   4   6   8   10

17

the county's main streams, the Neshaminy in the south and the Perkiomen in the north. What Bucks had was highly arable land, plus rich clay and gravel deposits. Today the latter support the region's largest construction materials company, which has existed for a century and a half. Most of Bucks' industries, however, were light industries in dispersed locations: seed farms, shad fisheries, boat building, lumber milling, clock making and pottery, cigars in the northern German boroughs, and textiles in Bristol. Several were in serious decline by the time of the Great Depression.

Only Bristol gave real promise of breaking with Bucks' rural character. In the early nineteenth century canal, turnpike, and railway development were followed by textile mills and iron foundries, and the Bristol Improvement Company, organized in the 1870's, promoted more of the same. One of the company's principals, William Grundy, was a Quaker descendant of original settlers, whose woolen mills were Bristol's leading industry.* On William's death in 1893 the mills and later the family banking interests passed to his son, Joseph Grundy, who became the county's political leader and, as founder and eminence of the Pennsylvania Manufacturers' Association, a pillar of the state's Republican and protective traditions. Yet Bristol remained a small manufacturing enclave of no more than 10,000 inhabitants. And Bucks remained a rural and small-town society in a local economy interspersed with light industry, modified in time by truck farming and tourism, but substantially unaffected by scattered Philadelphia commuters and New York exurbanites.

TABLE 2:3

Summary of Manufacturing Census for 1880

County	Manufacturing Establishments	Capital	Total Employed	Annual Wages	Materials	Product
Bucks	591	$ 3,039,014	3,609	$ 904,915	$ 4,033,627	$ 6,208,209
Delaware	416	14,256,720	11,442	3,839,838	11,262,964	19,601,493
Montgomery	840	13,789,461	11,639	3,596,208	13,189,707	20,656,993
Philadelphia	8,567	187,148,857	185,527	64,265,966	˙ 199,155,477	324,342,935

Adapted from Theodore W. Bean, *History of Montgomery County,* Philadelphia: Evarts and Peck, 1884, p. 574. Total employed column includes female and child labor.

Minerals and waterways gave Montgomery County a more diversified economy. A limestone belt in the south was tapped for building materials in the eighteenth century, fertilizer in the nineteenth century, refractories in the twentieth century, and still supports prominent enterprises. Copper mining and marble quarrying were important in the nineteenth century. Manufacture of iron and steel began near Pottstown

* William Grundy was descended from the Hulmes, large landholders who owned the Newton public buildings and promoted the concept of "Penn County" earlier in the century.

TABLE 2:4

Percentage of County Residents Employed in Various Industry Groups,
1950 and 1960*

	BUCKS		DELAWARE		MONTGOMERY	
	1950	1960	1950	1960	1950	1960
Agriculture	9.5	2.8	0.1	0.7	1.9	1.6
Mining	0.4	0.3	0.1	0.1	0.3	0.3
Construction	7.9	7.3	6.2	5.3	6.3	5.1
Manufacture	42.4	41.7	37.0	35.1	39.6	38.5
Furniture, lumber	2.3	1.7	1.3	1.2	1.6	1.5
Primary metal	4.7	12.6	6.2	4.3	12.5	9.2
Fabricated metal	8.7	13.7	3.3	7.5	8.2	11.6
Machinery	5.6	9.2	7.5	12.7	7.1	8.7
Electrical machinery	7.0	9.5	9.3	8.0	5.3	13.0
Motor vehicles	4.4	2.7	3.8	2.4	4.0	2.8
Transportation equipment	2.8	2.1	10.2	8.1	0.9	1.5
Other durable goods	10.7	10.2	3.4	3.3	11.5	11.4
Food	4.6	5.6	4.7	6.1	4.6	6.6
Textiles	13.5	4.0	11.5	3.6	15.4	5.2
apparel	14.4	7.1	2.9	3.5	9.9	6.7
Printing	2.4	4.3	7.3	9.5	3.8	5.0
Chemical	8.7	8.0	7.6	9.4	3.2	6.1
Other nondurable	9.8	9.2	20.1	20.6	10.6	11.4

* Employment outside county of residence is included.
Source: U.S. Census.

early in the eighteenth century, and establishment of steel mills by
John Wood (1832) and Allen Wood (1856) at Conshohocken commenced
the county's heavy industrial development. At the end of the Civil War
there were ten blast furnaces and twelve rolling mills along the Schuylkill River at Conshohocken, Norristown, and Pottstown. Several of the
region's earliest railways—the first Main Line and routes from Philadelphia to Reading and Bethlehem—ran through the county, and the
Reading route engendered more commerce and industry in the centers
along the Schuylkill. The industrial clusters grew rapidly after the Civil
War, while others began along the railways. Light industries, like those
in Bucks were widely scattered in small towns. Mines and factories
spread through the lower end of the county.

Suburban growth followed with railway, trolley, and highway development. The Main Line and York Road promotions are famous in local
social history.[4] As the Pennsylvania Railroad improved its Main Line
service (to Pittsburgh) in the 1860's it first developed summer resorts
along the route; then it bought large tracts to protect its right of way,
which it subdivided and sold under its own zoning regulations. The era
of Main Line estate building began in the 1890's, paced by the Pennsylvania's higher management, who have lived on the Main Line ever since.
Development of the York Road section by Peter Widener and William
Lukens Elkins (gas and traction magnates) occurred in the same period.
As these two wealthy quadrants grew in this century they gradually

MONTGOMERY COUNTY

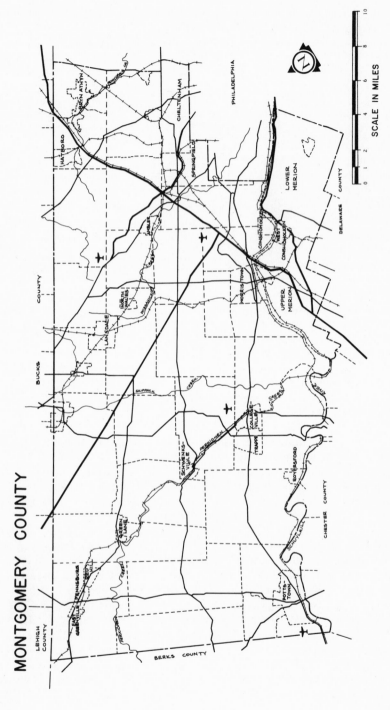

SCALE IN MILES

accumulated nearly half the county's population and contributed a larger portion of its taxes, but they remained distinct sections along different routes of communication with the central city, largely disoriented from the center of the county and from its rural and industrial areas. After World War II the Pennsylvania Turnpike spread new industrial growth and higher suburban densities across the lower end of the county, which enlarged and reoriented the older sections and may in time diminish their distinctiveness.

Delaware County's history is like Montgomery's in its progress from industrial to residential growth, but the pattern differs in the greater influence of heavy industry, its high concentration around a single city, and the smaller size (higher density) of the county. The industrial growth of Delaware County took place in four stages. From the late eighteenth century milling was widely established on the county's several creeks. In the 1840's the real estate development of Chester began and was carried forward by the founders and scions of the county's leading families; by mid-century mills were moving to Chester for labor and transportation, and this movement quickened after the Civil War.

A third phase of growth thus followed the Civil War with the rapid expansion of original Chester industries and their diversification, including introduction of heavy industry. By 1870 Chester was the nation's greatest shipbuilding center. The Roach shipyards were the city's leading industry and largest employer, and their closing at the turn of the century was a heavy setback—yet Chester's high diversification, based on the river and railways, carried it through. Despite shipbuilding, oil, tools and engines, and steel, the city's thirty textile mills still led the area in value of production.

In the fourth stage of growth, beginning with the twentieth century, heavy industry came to dominate in lower Delaware County: in this phase established firms built large plants in the Chester vicinity—Sun Oil (1901), Baldwin Locomotive (1906), Scott Paper (1908), American Viscose (1911), Sun Shipbuilding and Drydock (1916), and later Ford Motors and Westinghouse Electric. World War I was a forcing influence: "The development of the industrial area between Philadelphia and Chester was almost unbelievable. Steel plants and arms factories sprang up as if by magic, and along the Delaware the magnitude of shipbuilding enterprises was the most extensive ever known."[5] Delaware County held more industrial jobs during the First World War than at any time thereafter.[6] The later effects of the Depression were equally forceful, while World War II and the postwar riverfront recession again made clear the county's dependence on federal contracts. Chester's population doubled between 1890 and 1920 and grew but little thereafter; then suburban growth drastically altered the county's population balance.

Some early suburban growth stemmed from Chester and occurred in the south-central part of the county, but outward pressure from

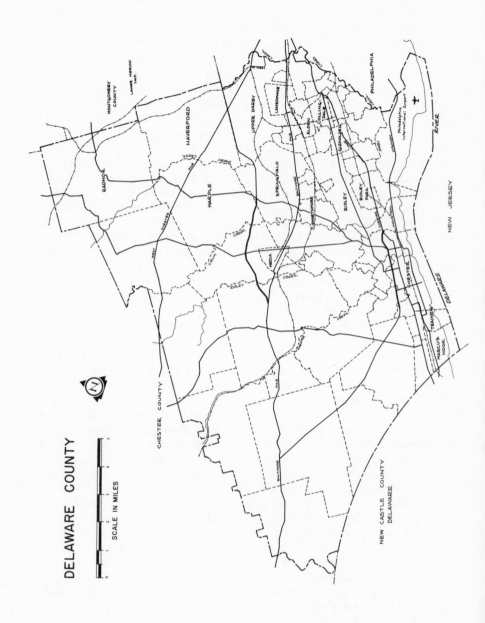

DELAWARE COUNTY

SCALE IN MILES
0 1 2 3 4 5

22

Philadelphia soon became dominant. The first developments occurred after the Civil War on the realigned route of the Philadelphia-Chester-Wilmington-Baltimore Railway, and, as in the wealthier Main Line, the first subdivisions were summer residences. Full-time suburban development ensued, and in the 1890's Darby Township, a nineteenth-century textile center, was split into the several boroughs that divide that section today; its population has steadily grown since 1890. The dramatic growth of Upper Darby and lower Haverford Township occurred in the 1920's with the lengthening of trolley lines and advent of the automobile. This region forms a western extension of Philadelphia's Market Street, and a county historian, writing in 1932, observed that "the visitor to Philadelphia finds it a difficult matter to distinguish the point at which the city limits are reached and those of Upper Darby Township begin."[7]

After the hiatus of the 1920's population pressure continued due west of the two Darbies. In the postwar era Ridley, Springfield, and Marple grew dramatically, though at lower densities toward the north, where high incomes and tight zoning prevailed. Farther north large family tracts, earlier Main Line subdivisions, and social pressures lowered densities and raised values still higher. Despite the small size of the county, semidistinct regions thus developed: the riverfront industrial area; the Darby-Ridley district, where suburban growth began; north of that the densely settled Upper Darby region; west of it the central county suburbs, most recently developed; north of those the Main Line, least socially identified with Delaware County. Generally speaking, income levels and property values increased from south to north and densities decreased from east to west as well as south to north. The relatively high densities of some Delaware suburbs are partly the result of earlier development there than in the other counties; when clustering about commuter railway stations was the rule, this trend was later reversed by changing preferences and transportation patterns.[8] There remain the central and western municipalities, some now burgeoning and some still rural, and what Baltzell has termed the "Swarthmore suburbs" and styled "intellectual"—the boroughs of Swarthmore and Rose Valley and parts of Nether Providence Township, whose gradual, rather exclusive growth began late in the nineteenth century along the route of the West Chester local.[9] Baltzell points to this region and the Main Line as most closely connected to old Philadelphia society, but the "Swarthmore suburbs" were partly settled by old Chester families and are still the residence of many Chester businessmen and professionals. As in Montgomery, the new suburban residents are less oriented to county affairs than are people employed in Chester or living in the old central and western sections.

3. *Recent regional growth.* Except for transportation routes and capital sources on occasion, the suburban counties' industrial histories were largely independent of Philadelphia, though their residential devel-

opment was not. Regional economic connections are more apparent today in two perspectives.

In national perspective greater Philadelphia has lost ground since the Second World War. Relocation and alterations in national demand have affected such local industries as iron and steel specialties, textiles, electrical and transportation equipment. The region's recovery from the Depression was slow by national standards, and its sensitivity to wartime demands has been marked since the American Revolution.[10] One social characteristic of the regional economy has been its concentration in small, conservatively managed family firms. The chief regional gainers in the postwar period have been large plants in petroleum, chemicals, and paper, but rapid automation in those industries has diminished employment. In ways to be described later the region's relative economic concentration on manufacture (rather than service) of intermediate (rather than consumer) products by family firms, many in nationally declining industries, may give a conservative cast to politics today in the counties that have long been industrialized.[11]

A second perspective is that of change *within* the region: industrial and commercial dispersion combined with financial centralization. In 1940 69 percent of southeastern Pennsylvania's employment was in Philadelphia; in 1950, 58 percent; in 1960, 48 percent. Responding to residential preferences, transportation routes, and new site requirements, the decentralization affected some industries and counties more profoundly than others.

Bucks' development was most striking because it occurred on the smallest base and was most autonomous. It began with wartime industry in Bristol and a ribbon of growth along Route 1 from Trenton to Philadelphia. The United States Steel works came in 1950, with satellite industries and communities. In the next decade Lower Bucks was transformed as large tracts of spinach and asparagus were subdivided and Levittown spread through four municipalities, leveling off at some 70,000 souls. Lower Bucks was distinct from the rest of the county; and its development, from east to west, was detached from the central city. Despite the slow close-out of Bristol's wartime Kaiser plant and some old textile mills, manufacturing employment doubled in Bucks between 1940 and 1960, based on steel, paper, textiles, and chemicals. Yet unemployment also grew after the Korean War and troubled the county.

Industrial employment in Montgomery and Delaware nearly doubled in the World War II–Korean War decade. After that these counties' paths diverged. The opening of two Pennsylvania Turnpikes through Montgomery attracted new branch plants and laboratories and outweighed closings or declines in older firms. In the next decade Montgomery's industrial employment increased most rapidly in the region, while Delaware lost jobs through secular decline in textiles and transportation equipment, automation in petroleum and chemicals, and lack of new industry to supplement its few large firms.

The dispersal of industry and population was followed by commercial dispersion in shopping centers and professional services. Most suburban banks became branches of city banks, and Philadelphia department stores established suburban branches. Yet regional decentralization was not so much directed from Philadelphia as it was a response to market forces carrying central city institutions in their wake.

The trends just discussed appear in Table 2:5, which shows the proportion of income earned in the counties from each of several sources and relates each county's roles as source of income and as residence of income earners. The balance between the two roles roughly measures a county's economic autonomy; a close balance shows that most people probably reside and produce in the same place. Despite the striking contrast between Philadelphia and the outlying counties as sites of employment and residence respectively, several contrasting trends are evident.

TABLE 2:5A

Percent of Total Income at Source

	Penn-sylvania	Bucks	Delaware	Mont-gomery	Phila-delphia
Manufacture					
1929	23.0	26.4	33.7	28.5	20.3
1940	25.5	33.7	34.5	31.4	22.4
1960	29.0	39.1	33.0	35.0	23.3
Trade					
1929	10.6	6.5	9.9	9.2	13.7
1940	10.6	6.7	12.1	8.5	13.7
1960	11.1	9.8	9.6	11.4	13.7
Finance, Insurance, Real Estate					
1929	2.9	1.0	3.1	2.4	5.0
1940	2.8	2.0	2.4	2.2	5.0
1960	2.7	1.4	2.4	1.9	4.6
Transportation, Communication, Utilities					
1929	7.6	4.2	6.3	5.5	8.0
1940	7.3	3.4	5.2	5.6	6.5
1960	6.1	2.6	6.2	4.1	6.5
Services					
1929	5.4	3.3	1.3	8.7	7.3
1940	5.5	3.9	5.4	8.0	7.0
1960	6.5	4.8	5.8	7.7	7.6
Government					
1929	4.5	1.3	2.8	2.4	7.3
1940	9.0	3.7	7.7	6.8	11.8
1960	8.2	6.2	7.2	5.7	11.2
Proprietary Income					
1929	24.2	23.8	28.8	25.2	26.0
1940	16.9	19.8	16.6	19.5	18.3
1960	13.6	13.2	13.8	12.2	14.0

TABLE 2:5B

Personal Income by Source as Percentage
of Personal Income by Residence

	Bucks	Delaware	Mont-gomery	Phila-delphia
Manufacture				
1929	65.9	66.4	88.7	116.1
1940	67.0	67.5	90.2	118.1
1960	67.9	68.3	91.3	119.5
Trade				
1929	65.3	62.3	93.1	122.1
1940	66.6	63.5	95.0	125.0
1960	67.6	64.5	96.4	126.4
Finance, Insurance, Real Estate				
1929	36.5	33.7	46.3	142.6
1940	36.8	35.0	48.0	147.9
1960	39.0	37.0	50.8	156.5
Transportation, Communication, Utilities				
1929	50.0	57.4	80.5	125.3
1940	38.3	56.7	80.0	135.8
1960	36.7	57.3	80.1	141.8
Services				
1929	58.0	12.9	89.6	128.9
1940	59.5	50.6	91.9	132.5
1960	60.8	51.8	94.1	135.1
Government				
1929	50.0	54.0	83.1	118.0
1940	52.1	56.2	86.4	122.8
1960	52.8	57.0	87.5	124.4
Proprietary Income				
1929	95.4	77.3	50.1	95.9
1940	105.7	102.5	70.1	80.0
1960	114.6	85.0	67.7	96.4
Total				
1929	69.7	62.1	73.4	115.0
1940	68.3	66.9	86.4	117.0
1960	68.9	66.2	87.7	111.0

Source: Pennsylvania Department of Internal Affairs, *Pennsylvania's Personal Income, 1929-1960* (Harrisburg: 1962).

There is some growth in suburban self-sufficiency, especially in Montgomery. The historical role of industry in the suburban counties is apparent, but so is growing diversification in financial, commercial, and service activities. If *suburbanization* means anything economically it would seem to be this growing diversification, which does not necessarily result in autonomy.

That the trend toward autonomy is slight can be seen in Table 2:6, derived from 1960 census data on place of employment of county residents. Two temporal shortcomings of the data are the absence of comparable figures for the past, and the possibility that rapid growth since 1960 has substantially altered the proportions shown. The figures confirm what has already been described: Bucks' diverse orientations to

TABLE 2:6

Place of Employment of County Residents, 1960

		Percentage of county's labor force employed in:				
Home county	*Bucks*	*Dela-ware*	*Mont-gomery*	*Phila-delphia*	*Rest of SMSA**	*Out of SMSA**
Bucks	52.8	0.3	8.1	19.3	2.6	13.1
Delaware	0.2	51.0	4.4	34.3	2.5	3.7
Montgomery	2.1	1.4	60.9	26.5	2.7	2.6
Philadelphia	0.7	1.6	2.6	86.3	1.8	1.0

Source: U.S. Census.
* Standard Metropolitan Statistical Area (Greater Philadelphia, in Pennsylvania and New Jersey).

other cities, eastern Delaware County's dormitory characteristics and heavy central city commutation, Montgomery's substantial autonomy and attraction of workers from other counties, and Philadelphia's declining primacy as a place of work. There was little evidence in 1960 of reverse commutation by Philadelphia's labor force, but this seems to be growing as decentralization and diversification increase. The result is likely to be a "regional," rather than a "metropolitan," economy.

4. *Summary.* On the verge of mid-twentieth-century dispersion heavy industrial concentrations were prominent in Delaware and Montgomery, but not in Bucks. The same statement holds for residential development. Urban and suburban living were most advanced in Delaware and least in Bucks; Montgomery was intermediate because of its rural hinterland and its lack of a city like Chester. With regional diffusion all the counties achieved more diversified economies and societies, but their politics were affected by earlier paths of development. Delaware and Montgomery contained important old industries and communities and social ties to Philadelphia, while Bucks' growth was more independent and explosive.

Some social characteristics of the counties appear in Table 2:7. Bucks' lower median incomes reflect both its rural–small-town sector and its wealthy entrepreneurs and professionals. Montgomery affords contrasts among affluent suburbs, small towns in its rural districts, and industrial boroughs. Delaware's population is more evenly distributed across ethnic and religious, income and occupational spectra than that of either of the other counties; its diversity is most nearly that of the mid-century city. One would probably expect the heaviest demand for public services in Bucks, from its rapid growth and the urban origins of its new residents, and in Delaware from its density and urban diversity. Mont-

TABLE 2:7
County Socioeconomic Profiles and Comparisons, 1960

	Bucks	*Delaware*	*Mont-gomery*
Population growth in decade (percent)	113.4	33.5	46.3
Percent rural nonfarm	22.3	3.9	19.3
Percent rural farm	2.5	0.1	1.2
Percent foreign born	4.4	5.4	5.6
Percent foreign stock	15.4	18.3	17.7
Percent nonwhite	1.9	7.1	3.8
Percent elementary school children in private school	29.4	41.9	31.5
Percent under 18 years of age	40.6	35.6	34.3
Percent over 64 years of age	6.1	8.2	9.0
Median school years completed	11.6	12.0	12.1
Percent in white collar employment	41.9	52.7	51.3
Percent in manufacturing employment	41.7	35.1	38.5
Percent unemployed	3.6	3.8	2.5
Percent work outside county	43.4	45.0	35.6
Percent of family incomes $10,000 and over	19.0	25.4	30.7
Percent of family incomes under $4,000	14.1	13.7	12.6
Median family income	$ 6,182	$ 7,289	$ 7,632
Median value of owner-occupied housing	$12,000	$13,500	$15,000

Source: 1960 U.S. Census.

gomery's small towns and wealthy suburbs should be more self-sufficient and conservative. When conventional measures of dispersion (range and standard deviation) are applied to the Census data (incomes and occupations), the suburban counties show only a little less socioeconomic diversity than does Philadelphia. Trends in the relative diversity of central city and suburbs are extremely hard to identify, but the present heterogeneity of the counties holds potential significance for their political systems.

The political implications of aggregate population data depend, however, on how social attitudes are organized and oriented. The data form profiles of the counties, but they do not yield full portraits. The suburban county may amount to a polity without a community, or even without a society in any effective sense. The main factors bearing on this issue are discussed in the following chapter.

3

The County as Society and Community

Although the county is primarily a governmental unit, social ties may derive from it. There is little historical evidence of trends in the counties' social roles, so this chapter explores contemporary factors shaping publics for county affairs. Three competing orientations come to mind; these may be termed localism, sectionalism, and regionalism. Patterns of mass communication make a fourth factor.

1. *Localism.* The counties' most obvious competitors for civic loyalty are the municipalities. In a survey of six townships, residents were asked:

> Which would you say is most interesting and important to you: the Philadelphia area generally; _____ county; _____ township; or your own particular neighborhood?

The results are mixed, and the counties are not eclipsed in most localities. Radnor Township's indifference to Delaware County no doubt reflects its historic Main Line ties. Its residents' high interest in the township is like that in Springfield Township and is consistent with other evidence of civic satisfaction in those two communities, which happen to be those of highest social status. There is a suggestion (discussed in Part V) that civic satisfaction and community attachment increase with income and social status, and there is also strong evidence that neighborhood-mindedness at the expense of municipalities is negatively linked with respondents' social rank (education and occupation). *Regional* identification, on the other hand, is positively associated with social rank in this sense, perhaps in part because central-city commuters tend to score high on educational and occupational scales. Thus in all

TABLE 3:1

Orientations to Official and Social Areas

PERCENT OF RESPONSES

Township	Phila. Area	County	Township	Neighbor- hood	Don't Know
Radnor	42.2	6.6	42.2	6.6	2.2
Marple	22.0	28.0	24.0	18.0	8.0
Springfield	23.5	25.4	41.1	9.8	0.0
Ridley	31.1	26.6	11.1	28.8	2.2
Bristol	16.0	24.0	26.0	32.0	2.0
Middletown (Bucks)	27.0	21.6	24.3	24.3	2.7
Glenolden	22.0	40.0	24.0	12.0	2.0
Swarthmore	42.0	12.0	32.0	2.0	8.0

communities the tendency was for more highly educated, professional and executive people to favor the region or their municipality, while the counties or neighborhoods were more likely to be named by respondents of lower social rank. Although the six townships involved are all large ones with relatively distinct neighborhoods, a later survey that included two small boroughs (Glenolden and Swarthmore), of low and high social rank respectively, indicates that size of municipality was less a factor in geographic orientations than were social rank and place of employment.*

Expressions of interest are one thing, information is another. Citizens display little knowledge of county affairs. When asked "What do you feel are the most important things the county does?" some 60 percent mentioned functions (such as highways) not performed by the counties. Despite the recent, rapid governmental changes in Bucks, nearly two-thirds of those interviewed there did not respond when asked, "What do you think have been the main changes or innovations in things done by the county in recent years?" In Delaware County three-fourths failed to respond. In comparison, the question, "What would you say are the main issues facing the township?" drew but 20 percent "Don't know" and a relative profusion of informed and informative answers, which, with other evidence on involvement in local affairs, are reviewed in Part V.

There are financial and functional bases for civic indifference to the counties. Some municipalities tax more heavily than counties, and their commonly congruent school districts spend much more. On this argument, a modest increase in county expenditures, together with school district consolidation (lately mandated by state law), might reduce localism substantially. Still, municipalities perform the more visible regulatory and service functions (e.g., zoning, police, local roads), and are rightly viewed as vested interests: to the extent that county expan-

* The methods used in the surveys, and tests of their validity, are discussed in Appendix B.

sion absorbs or threatens local functions the municipal lobbies in Harrisburg and local politicians in the county are effective counterforces.

Local devotion is said to rest on two foundations. One is a putative ideology, image, or Jeffersonian residue in American life that favors the small community.[1] A second alleged source is the municipalities' socioeconomic distinctiveness. To the degree that it exists, this suburban differentiation may prompt a desire to retain it for the sake of community feeling or to preserve social and economic advantages against a more random and leveling distribution. Thus the impulse may be a selfish opposition to the redistribution of real income or invidious resistance to the commingling of cultural characteristics, or homogeneity may be prized for its reduction of the costs of consensus and its enrichment of social and civic life.[2]

The literature of local government abounds in such interpretations, for all of which the evidence is mixed. A recent Fels Institute study of the southeastern Pennsylvania counties distinguished "suburbs" (primarily residential units with population densities above 500 per square mile) from rural townships, old towns, and industrial enclaves, and found more "specialization" and "differentiation" among the new, commuter suburbs than among the other municipal types.[3] Prevailing age, income, and social status of residents were differentiating features, with evident effects on local policy. Among these factors it appeared that social rank (status) outweighed wealth (class) in determining residential preferences and public expenditure patterns in the suburbs.[4] Municipal policies seemed to be reflecting cultural attitudes, not economic calculations primarily, life styles instead of fiscal pressures.

Differentiation *among* local units implies specialization within them; yet overall measures of differentiation may obscure the extent to which municipalities vary in diversity-homogeneity.[5] In Part V the governments and politics of seventeen municipalities are discussed in some detail, and the census data there (Tables 21:2, 22:1, 22:2) indicate that suburbs vary significantly in degree of specialization with respect to class and status, at least as these are reflected in the census. There is, however, no wholly satisfactory way to measure or compare municipal diversity, even on a single variable. By some indices of dispersion, such as range and standard deviation, several suburban communities show nearly as much diversity as Philadelphia, though most are more homogeneous.[6] In general, the municipalities that are largest in area contain the most social diversity (measured by educational and occupational distributions), and logically, those with the highest median incomes have the widest range of incomes, but some large jurisdictions are more homogeneous than a few small ones. Most large, wealthy townships (especially older ones) contain substantial low income pockets, while newer, less affluent communities are less diverse in this respect, but social (occupational) and economic (income) diversity, as reflected in the census, are imperfectly correlated. Incidentally, survey data in Part V show that residents are well aware of the variations in local diversity that appear in the census data.

Suburban differentiation surely tends to divide the counties even if, on census indices, many municipalities are as diversified as counties. Possibly the categorical factors in social stratification are declining in salience while more subtle, subjective, and perhaps less invidious distinctions are increasing. Or local tastes and traditions may be more responsive to a community's *modal* population than to its range of variation or to certain relations between these two. Moreover, the strength of local attachment seems to depend in some part on the quality of local government, which partly depends in turn on ability to pay for it and on sufficient social homogeneity to support it. These relations are more fully discussed in Part V.

Three further survey questions bear on the incidence of localism, homogeneity, and exclusiveness. Inhabitants of the six townships were asked to express the extent of their agreement or disagreement with the following statements:

1. Local governments like townships and boroughs should be combined and consolidated for more efficiency wherever this would result in lower costs.
2. It's a good thing for most people in a township or borough to be the same type of people, so far as income and social background are concerned.
3. Local government should use zoning laws to keep out of this community the type of people who usually build cheaper houses on smaller lots.

TABLE 3:2

Social and Economic Attitudes Toward Local Government

| | CONSOLIDATION | | | HOMOGENEITY | | | EXCLUSIVE ZONING | | |
	Favor	No Opin.	Op-pose	Favor	No Opin.	Op-pose	Favor	No Opin.	Op-pose
Radnor	48.8	6.6	44.3	19.9	6.6	73.3	62.2	6.6	31.0
Marple	58.0	8.0	34.0	30.0	10.0	60.0	58.0	10.0	32.0
Springfield	45.0	0.0	54.8	35.2	3.9	60.7	76.4	9.8	13.6
Ridley	77.7	8.8	13.2	35.4	6.6	57.6	53.3	13.3	33.3
Bristol	90.0	6.0	4.0	32.0	0.0	78.0	62.0	10.0	28.0
Middletown	83.7	5.4	10.8	24.3	10.8	64.8	64.8	10.8	24.3

Answers to the first question (on consolidation) varied most distinctly among communities: those of least wealth and lowest social rank were most approving of consolidation—especially in the new communities of lower Bucks County. Differences *among* townships were more significant than differences *within* them based on cross-tabulations of individuals' answers with such characteristics as income, occupation, or education. It should also be noted that majorities in most municipalities (excepting only the two of highest local morale) favored consolidation, at least in the hypothetical terms of the question.

Substantial majorities in all municipalities *disagree* with the second statement; they favor diversity. Disagreement increases with respondents' income and occupational level, and such individual differences are greater than community differences. Conversely (perversely, it seems), like majorities in all jurisdictions *agree* with protective zoning policies. Except for one especially exclusive (and highly homogeneous) community, municipal differences were not significant, nor was individual income or social rank, save for a tendency to disagree as educational level increased.

Thus, consolidation and social diversity are favored by substantial majorities of the sample, but when diversity is put to a hard test, opinion tends to go the other way. Neither communal nor exclusive values are dominant. The supposed ideology of localism and homogeneity is not widespread, but residents respond to specific threats to community character and, perhaps, to municipal autonomy. Significantly, those who have lived in the township longest are most inclined toward both localism and homogeneity, while social rank has ambiguous effects on such orientations.

No doubt politicians are more opposed to consolidation than are rank and file residents. Previous surveys in the region have found this so.[7] Community leaders (both political and civic) interviewed in the present study were more likely than others to identify with their municipality (cf. Table 3:1)—political leaders most of all. Among plain residents, however, members of local civic organizations were more likely to identify with the *region* than were nonjoiners. This suggests that localism is more a function of vested interest in formal position than of active attachment to community life and that it is largely a matter of leadership.

Finally, one would expect acceptance of county consolidation to vary with municipal self-sufficiency. Montgomery County's largest, most politically influential townships are among its oldest and wealthiest (those in the Main Line and York Road sections), while the large jurisdictions of lower Bucks are less rich in resources and tradition, less self-reliant. Delaware County contains units of both types. In considering the public for county activity, therefore, one must look to political structure, population, and income distribution as well. These factors vary among the three counties, and their likely effects are discussed later.

2. *Sectionalism.* Historically, settlement patterns and topographical factors tended to section the counties, especially Bucks and Montgomery. Industrial development and local differentiation sometimes cut across the older divisions and sometimes reinforced them; socioeconomic characteristics have tended to cluster in contiguous townships.

Today Bucks County is mentally divided into three parts; upper, middle, and lower; its business and civic organizations are also trisected. Montgomery's several districts include the Main Line; the York Road; the suburbs intervening between those two; the Norristown industrial region; the Lansdale–North Penn complex; the central low density, small-town area; the Pottstown industrial region; and the northeast hinterland. In each county such organizations as chambers of commerce and community funds have tended to follow these lines, if only because travel to luncheons and evening functions has been difficult on any other basis—especially in Bucks, the largest and most elongated of the counties. Even smaller Delaware County contains distinct sections that were described in the preceding chapter. But no corner of Delaware County is more than a half hour drive from the courthouse; and for this reason, together with the earlier predominance of Chester, organizations are more integrated in Delaware.

Any growth in county activity or political competition would probably accentuate sectionalism, at least initially. Different urban densities, industrial tax burdens, drainage basins and water tables, and distinctions in income and social status might all be increased in relevance and salience. In most of these ways—even, in subtle, noncensus terms, the socioeconomic—the counties are more diverse than localities (partly because of the latter's existence); emphasis on local home rule has been a method of dodging distributive issues and cultural differences.

3. *Regionalism* also competes with the counties and localities, at least potentially. The Philadelphia region is ill defined and intangible. For some purposes it is Southeastern Pennsylvania, and for others it is an eleven-county, tristate district promoted as the "Delaware Valley." County lines do not mark it socially or economically. It is intangible because it is uninstitutionalized:

> There has never been much serious talk about "metropolitan government" in the Philadelphia area. Throughout the United States, academics (particularly political scientists) and citizen reform groups have sparked the effort to "rationalize" local government. Certainly, there is no scarcity of either kind of group in the Philadelphia area. However, none has shown interest in adapting the literature of metropolitan integration to the Philadelphia scene, and none has devoted time to the invention of new schemes of area-wide government.[8]

Organizations for regional planning and public relations have in the past filed their reports with little effect. The interstate agencies that manage river crossings and water resources are rigidly functional and define the region by different criteria.

There are two sources of area-wide concern. One is professional and intellectual, centered in universities and nonprofit institutions. Liaison is close within it, but no common program has evolved and its Philadelphia emphasis has only reinforced the suburbs' natural indifference. In general, this circle favors regional consolidation.

The other source is economic. Both utilities and finance have slowly undergone consolidation in southeastern Pennsylvania: railways late in the last century; transit, electricity, telecommunication, and water supply during the present century; and banking since World War II. Gradual decentralization of heavy industry in the first third of this century was followed by rapid residential and business dispersion after World War II, and then by attempts at central city regeneration. The two historical forces of dispersion and regeneration are organized in the Delaware Valley Council and the Greater Philadelphia Movement, respectively. The first tends to represent utilities, petroleum refining, and contracting, while finance, old Philadelphia law firms, and merchandising predominate in the latter. Banking and retailing have increasingly hedged on this issue as mergers and dispersion have continued.

The regional problem most widely recognized is transportation, but it is at the core of the foregoing conflict of interest: mass transit appeals to the center city, highway construction to the suburbs, while terminal facilities and road locations generate still narrower rivalries. Highways are primarily a state and federal responsibility, and county planners spend hours negotiating with these higher powers. River ports possibly and airports certainly depend on federal and state participation, but the initiative is primarily local and the financing partly so. Mass transit has traditionally been privately run, but it is now in transition (see Chapter 18). In 1958 the Penn-Jersey Transportation Study (a federal-state-local agency) was created to make a long-range transportation plan for the region. In 1965, as more federal grants were conditioned on establishment of a regional planning body, Penn-Jersey became the Delaware Valley Commission—a general purpose planning agency governed by delegates from the counties. Transportation thus may become the fulcrum for regional planning, at least in a consultative sense. As this is written DVC is interpreting its transportation research and assessing political support for alternative transportation plans and administrative schemes. In these plans and mechanics two concepts must be adjusted: "metropolitanism," or the predominance of the central city; and "regionalism," or radical dispersion.

Federal pressure today is producing some rudimentary regional institutions. Governmental initiatives in specific functions may in time create regional publics. However, differences between city and suburban perspectives and between intellectual and entrepreneurial interests remain acute, if increasingly confused. In particular some economic powers are primarily concerned with the salvation of Philadelphia, others with regional development. Neither group has felt a need for formal institutions. Perhaps the most ubiquitous interests, long-established and with well-mended fences, would prefer not to tear down the fences. In the meantime, in each of the suburban counties—especially Delaware and

Montgomery—men of high stature and capacity who are leaders in the city are lost to the counties, and there are others—especially new industrialists—whose outlook is regional from rational business interests and lack of local roots. In these ways the city and the region stretch across the counties; "metropolitanism" and "regionalism" compete in them.

4. *Mass communications.* The county is no more a natural area for mass communications than it is an object of individual attention. Journalism reflects the forces of localism, sectionalism, and regionalism.

The county seat newspapers in Bucks, Montgomery, and Delaware began as weeklies in the federal period and became dailies late in the nineteenth century. Doubtless their circulation declined sharply with distance from the county seat, but they did emphasize county affairs. They were edited in the polemical style of the time: in Doylestown and Norristown there was, for most of the nineteenth century, a paper for each political party. The Chester papers were almost always Whig and Republican. There were also numerous small-town weeklies.

Distribution is similar today. There are three dailies in Bucks County (one in each major section), three in Montgomery County (in Norristown, Lansdale, and Pottstown), and Chester has the *Delaware County Daily Times*. There are many weeklies—some sectional, some municipal. Like the dailies, the larger sectional weeklies give prominent coverage to county as well as local events, but the dailies also aim at full-scale coverage of world affairs. Many weekly newspapers are owned in "strings"; and in Montgomery County most of those in the lower end of the county have come under two chains owned by or close to prominent county politicians.

The Philadelphia press with its metropolitan orientation has heavy circulation in Delaware and Montgomery counties. Suburban decentralization has sharply challenged the city papers; they have responded with more regional reportage, special suburban inserts of county and municipal news, and some editorial attention to the counties. Paid circulation figures may understate the impact of the metropolitan dailies because of commuter purchases. Their circulation is heaviest in the populous, inlying areas, while the county dailies are concentrated in their home sections. Overall, city papers overshadow the county press in Delaware and Montgomery, but not in Bucks.

Circulation patterns of the city and county dailies (Table 3:3) reflect Bucks' relative remoteness from Philadelphia and relative self-consciousness despite its sectionalism. In all three counties local dailies effectively rival the Philadelphia press *in their own sections*. Chester's *Delaware County Daily Times* claims to enter roughly half the households in an area with slightly more than half the county population; the daily published at Montgomery's county seat has a heavier distribution in a smaller area. But the lower Bucks paper reaches nearly two-thirds of the households in its city and retail trade zone, which contains almost

TABLE 3:3
Percentage of Households Reached by Daily Newspapers

County	County Dailies	Philadelphia Evening Bulletin
Bucks	70	35
Montgomery	38	58
Delaware	30	55

Source: Certified Circulation Audits, 1963.

three-quarters of the county population; it also owns the *Doylestown Intelligencer*, with a similar distribution in middle Bucks. Trenton, Allentown, and Easton papers enter Bucks County in some volume, but the local dailies compete energetically and effectively.

An early signal of social and political change in Bucks was Joseph Grundy's sale of the *Bristol Courier* and the *Doylestown Intelligencer* in 1954. The new owners were not newspapermen: they came from the accounting business, and they aimed to make the papers pay. Their method was to reach the new, youthful, responsive population and to boost county growth. They were aggressive in circulation, progressive in civic affairs, partisan in county politics. Local politics received front page treatment, the expansion of county government had steady editorial backing, and all politicians acknowledged the newspapers' influence. Some of the sense of county among the elites and some of the impetus for governmental progress in Bucks may have stemmed from these policies—even if the policies were in turn a response to the rapid growth and relative self-sufficiency of the county.*

If the sense of county is less acute in Montgomery and Delaware (as it seems to be despite Bucks' length and sectionalism), newspaper distribution probably has something to do with it. But in these counties, too, the local dailies are emphasizing the county more heavily. Thus the *Chester Times* recently became the *Delaware County Daily Times*, and the weekly *Upper Darby News*, the *News of Delaware County* in attempts to broaden circulation as neighboring sections reached higher densities. Competition between metropolitan and county papers has produced more suburban news and growing confusion of focus among locality, municipality, county, metropolis, and region, but there seems to have been a relative increase in county intelligence.

* The effect of lower Bucks County's daily paper is indicated in survey returns. Respondents in the four Delaware County and two lower Bucks County municipalities were asked whether, in the daily paper, they were most likely to read national or international news, county and local, both, or neither. The percentage of readers responding to county and local *and* both in Bucks County was far higher than in Delaware County (89.6 percent against 53.4 percent). On the other hand, about 65 percent of the Delaware County respondents said they regularly read a local, weekly paper as against 10 percent of Bucks. Evidently Bucks' respondents get their local news in the Bucks County daily—though Philadelphia papers probably account for some of it.

4

Interests

Despite its limitations as a community or a society, the suburban county is a focus for numerous provincial interest groups. Their interaction is more particularistic than pluralistic because broad county policies and publics are lacking. The reasons for these deficiencies are at least as much governmental as social and are discussed in Part III. This chapter is an attempt to characterize the chief interests in county policy and to compare their importance in the three counties. Some receive special attention because of their relevance to theoretical issues in this study or their distinctiveness to the region.

1. *Occupational and economic organizations.* The venerable professions of medicine and law are organized on county lines, and, as to government, are interested respectively in hospitals and public health, judicial appointments and administration. Professional traditions, emphasis on personal contact and counsel, and accumulated community ties probably predispose both groups to conservatism. Politically, this is most important among lawyers, who, in the judicial tradition, are often arbiters of public action. Pennsylvania was until recently the only state in the nation where legal practice (except by local courtesy) was limited to one county. This fact may strengthen the conservatism of both bench and bar by insulating them from urban influence, intensifying personal interactions in a narrow sphere, reinforcing the traditions of family firms, and limiting alternative avenues of practice for nonconformists. The last point may also increase lawyers' sensitivity to political sanctions and incentives.*

* The county closed-shop rule, which the state supreme court had upheld for a century, was ended by that court late in 1965 at the urging of big-city lawyers and over the resistance of suburban county bar associations. Delaware County's courts, among others, said they would continue to abide by the old rule.

Organized agriculture and labor are of minor importance except in Bucks County. Farm groups petition for county appropriations; labor is routinely represented in welfare activities but looks to the state for legislative benefits. In Montgomery labor unions are dispersed among industrial boroughs and outweighed by suburban and small-town forces; in Delaware their leadership has long been divided. In lower Bucks a strong CIO activist tradition, continuity of leadership, and dominance of a few large plants, combined with political competition, have enhanced labor's influence. There its leadership has pressed for political recognition and joined in civic action for county health and welfare programs, but its participation has nevertheless been episodic.

Three business interests—real estate, commerce, and manufacturing —stand out in the counties. The first and most specific of these includes land developers, builders, and brokers. Their interests are not wholly consistent: developers' pressures for change occasionally undermine community values important to local brokers; large operators differ from small contractors in their desire for standardization of building controls. Developers are more loosely organized than brokers, but neither group often confronts county government collectively because of the counties' limited powers over land use. The largest builders are based in Philadelphia. Some suburban builders operate in several counties, but local contractors are still important in the building industry. Only in Bucks, which alone among the suburban counties has a health department with serious sanitation regulations, have the builders organized for county action. Real estate dealers are often politicians—they have a logical interest and expertise in municipal policy, a local base and personal contacts, and business opportunities in advertising, appraisals, finder's fees, and insurance commissions. Holding such sensitive and lucrative local offices as justice of the peace, assessor, or tax collector is entirely consistent with the brokers' business. With developers they frequently serve on the most relevant county agencies—planning, housing, redevelopment, utilities authorities—a fact that raises subtle issues of public purpose and personal advantage. Yet in polities that chiefly regulate real property such involvement is surely natural, and its prohibition would be unnatural.

Suburban chambers of commerce are sectionally oriented. Bucks County, predictably, has three, and Montgomery still more. Delaware County's single chamber has slowly evolved from the nineteenth-century Chester Board of Trade and, despite its more ecumenical title, is still centered in Chester. Sectionalism may be a more serious problem for suburban than for city chambers; merchants in the several centers are implicitly in competition and are provincial from self-interest. The most successful chambers are those in manufacturing areas with industrial membership. The Lower Bucks County Chamber of Commerce, Central Montgomery County Chamber of Commerce, and the Chamber of Commerce of Delaware County and Chester have thus emphasized county industrial development and have sought county aid for promotional and transportation facilities. Banking is dealt with in the following chapter.

2. *The manufacturers.* The Pennsylvania Manufacturers' Association was founded by Joseph Grundy of Bucks County in 1909. It was a response of vulnerable industries to threatened state regulation of wages, hours, and working conditions. Most of the founders were textile manufacturers in southeastern Pennsylvania and heavy employers of female and child labor; their action continued a long state tradition of industrial politicking for protection.[1] But PMA's tactics were distinctive, stemming from Grundy's personal ascendency. Grundy was president, 1909-1930; chairman, 1930-1948; and he always appointed the executive committee. He first stressed personal lobbying in Harrisburg for a free hand in labor relations in a low-cost, low-state-tax economy.[2] Then he encouraged formation of county affiliates in order to influence state legislators where they were elected.[3] Chapters were formed in Montgomery (1912) and Delaware (1914); none was active in Bucks, and perhaps none was needed, since Grundy was that county's political leader. Later, in response to unfavorable legislation, PMA developed such membership services as fire and casualty insurance, safety information to lower workmen's compensation costs, and labor relations data for collective bargaining purposes.

But the PMA was not merely a pressure group. Gradually it became a faction in the state Republican party, strongly conservative in policy, stressing local organization rather than public relations in politics. These were logical tactics in the period of Republican dominance in Pennsylvania that followed the election of 1896. Grundy was their promoter and exemplar. He began as the lieutenant of Bois Penrose and became the patron of later state party leaders. Much of his influence was based on the campaign funds he raised from industrialists for their own protection. Yet Grundy was also a dedicated Republican who regularly worked at the polls in his home precinct.

For many years textiles led in PMA's membership, followed by such industries as brewing, metals, paper, glass, and clay that faced western or foreign competition and were frequently in decline. Thus small family firms predominated. After the Depression and World War II the complexion changed as larger firms in more dynamic fields subscribed. Most of Delaware County's heavy industry belonged to the association from the very beginning (which coincided with the county's greatest period of industrial growth); the same is true today in Montgomery, though it has not always been so.

The county organizations in Delaware and Montgomery are *industrial* associations, neither broadly civic nor commercial in intent. Thus the Montgomery County Manufacturers' Association early decided that:

> Manufacturers have specific interests which do not always run along lines of others' interests; for instance: during the Manufacturers' fight against unfair legislation in the employment of women and chil-

dren, the Chamber of Commerce of Philadelphia could not support our position, lest it should drive customers away from the retail dealers. This position was taken especially by the large department stores.[4]

As membership diversified, the Association's public stands diminished. Labor relations and taxes are the principal legislative interests today. For the most part they require state action, but they may also be locally promoted. In 1917 the Montgomery County secretary wrote a prospective member of "frequent meetings, at which matters of local interest, especially regarding labor conditions, are discussed, and an endeavor made to treat each other with proper decency as to taking each others help."[5] The concern with local wage levels has continued. County tax levels and individual plant assessments have become another major interest in which Manufacturers' Associations formally represent their members.

The Delaware and Montgomery Associations are closely allied to the Republican Party; the financial ties are individual, but the organization cultivates state legislators. Neither association takes public stands in elections, but both are private fund-raising vehicles. In Montgomery County a small group of established, affluent industrialists, known locally as the manufacturers, are financial standbys for the county Republican Party and active state Republican "angels." In these one-party counties, where native industrial leadership remains active, the Grundy tradition contributes a protective, conservative cast to county politics. The recent advent of branch plants and transient management has somewhat diluted this tradition.

Industrial tax consciousness takes shape in county affiliates of the Pennsylvania Economy League, which provide research and counsel to local governments. Dating from 1932, with branches in Pennsylvania's most important counties, PEL has been described as "essentially a taxpayer organization . . . handsomely financed by big business."[6] This description does not precisely fit the Philadelphia region, where, for a decade, PEL has been merged with the Philadelphia Bureau of Municipal Research, in which the middle class tradition of municipal reform was combined with commercial and professional board membership. The suburban branches have their own boards but also report to the Philadelphia office, where the main intellectual resources are located.

PEL's suburban branches vary in devotion to pure economy. This may depend on the local strength of the Manufacturers' Associations—for there is substantial overlap of boards in Delaware and Montgomery, but no manufacturers' association in Bucks. The Bucks County office has emphasized advice to the burgeoning municipalities of lower Bucks. County liaison is closer in Montgomery, where the staff man serves as critic of courthouse budgets and capital projects, constant watchdog at commissioners meetings, and advocate of reforms in county housekeeping.

Delaware County's Branch of PEL broke away in the 1940's and became the Committee of Delaware County Industry. This happened when the Philadelphia office criticized the branch's lack of research and preoccupation with low taxes. Since the break, as before, the Committee has been run from the office of the county's leading corporate-tax lawyer, who is also general counsel to the Manufacturers' Association. At quarterly luncheon meetings of the membership he reviews county expenditures and local fiscal conditions. There are no other staff and no formal reports, but the lawyer communicates the Committee's views to the county political leaders. This he can easily do, since he has been the chief political leader's personal attorney for more than a quarter century. As a member of one of Chester's oldest commercial and political families and a descendant of three former mayors, the lawyer's textbook qualifications for influence are exceptional. His conservatism is impeccable. As counsel in most industrial assessment cases and self-appointed conservator of public funds, his public and private interests are entirely consistent.

3. *Conservation.* PMA's protective tradition is one distinguishing facet of Pennsylvania Republicanism. Another is the progressive, Gifford Pinchot tradition of conservation of natural resources and government reform. The state's one-party politics in the first half of the twentieth century favored incorporation of both traditions in the majority party structure. Both remain socially strong in the suburbs. The Pinchot legacy supports civic organizations for open space and conservation, which are most active in Bucks County, where protectionism now is weakest.

The tradition's embodiment in Bucks is the Delaware Valley Protective Association, which dates from 1933, and whose progenitor, the Friends of the Delaware, was organized in 1920. Membership of DVPA is both organizational and individual, including municipalities and politicians; its center of gravity is in middle and upper ("old") Bucks County. Its base remains the individuals of means and the local groups who can be mobilized for conservation in the twin senses of history and amenity; much of DVPA's effectiveness stems from its focus on a stretch of the Delaware that is rich in both. DVPA has demonstrated its ability to mount legislative campaigns and has developed a capacity for negotiation with the nest of governmental agencies in the river basin. It operates through committees on specific subjects, but its driving force for many years has been the man who serves as director and deploys its activities from his home in Doylestown. Its traditional antagonist has been the state Highway Department, its ally the Department of Forests and Waters. As the county has launched new programs DVPA has kept a weather eye on them: mosquito control has jeopardized wild fowl; land development has threatened open space. Governmental liaison is DVPA's usual method (its director belongs to the county park board), but DVPA does not stick at public campaigns. For its most devoted members conservation is a way of life and action for the cause comes naturally in the tradition of Theodore Roosevelt and Gifford Pinchot.

The historic role of Delaware County's transecting creeks has already been noted. The other two counties show a contrasting pattern: in the north, a number of major streams—the Tohickon, Perkiomen, and Skippack—flow east and west to join the Delaware and Schuylkill Rivers, while the inlying areas are drained and dominated each by a single large creek. In Bucks, the Neshaminy begins near Doylestown and empties into the Delaware near Bristol. It is a long, slow-moving, low-lying stream, with broad flood plains, which wrought costly destruction of new subdivisions in the fall hurricanes of 1955. In the next year the Neshaminy Valley Watershed Association was organized; it was fostered by the County Planning Commission and Park Board and by INCODEL —a confederation of federal, state, and local agencies formed after World War II to study the future use and control of water resources in the entire Delaware River basin affecting four states.

NVWA covers the whole water resources front. Its membership consists of some 300 individuals and 50 organizations, including industries and municipalities. Like DVPA, NVWA depended heavily on the energy and dedication of one knowledgeable citizen as catalyst and planner, but it also retained as its salaried executive a professional in the water resources field. Unlike DVPA and some conservationists, the Neshaminy group emphasized information and agency coordination, eschewing political action, preserving its federal tax exempt status, stressing technical and administrative concerns, and avoiding ideological and electoral activity.

Thus when the Corps of Army Engineers proposed a major reservoir on the Neshaminy, NVWA argued that flood control and low-flow augmentation also belonged in the proposal. It sought state aid and stimulated the county commissioners to form a soil conservation district and helped to organize rural support for it in order to qualify for federal assistance under the small-watershed program. Later, when Bucks and Montgomery Counties applied for federal aid, NVWA became their liaison with the federal agencies and local municipalities—carefully reserving its right to future criticism. Federal flood control studies and state recreational studies were completed as this account was being written, and further work then depended on federal appropriations. In the meantime, NVWA provided flood-risk maps of the lower Neshaminy Valley, made by an INCODEL engineer and paid for by the affected boroughs and townships; ultimately all of the latter were supplied with maps for use in zoning and building controls. The Corps of Army Engineers then agreed to do the same for the Upper Neshaminy.

Through its expertise and initiative NVWA had brought about federal, state, and local studies of the creek valley and was on the verge of witnessing construction. Its relations with county government were complex: it supplemented and supported the professionals and built public pressure for county programs; like DVPA, it received a small county subsidy. State and regional agencies perceived it as a civic base. It was in several ways a vital, private ingredient in governmental action.

Watershed organizations find support in conservation as an ideology, in attachment to locality, and in existing governmental agencies that badly need coordination and support in local projects. The foregoing are established rural concerns, but small-watershed associations like Montgomery's Wissahickon Valley Watershed Association (see Chapter 15) have ingeniously adapted them to suburban living. In Delaware County no single stream stands out, and the conservation interest has been merged with other civic concerns.

4. *Civic and charitable interests.*   Although conservation has been their dominant concern, citizens' councils in Delaware and Montgomery Counties have sought a broader focus. As it had earlier counseled during lower Bucks' growing pains, the Philadelphia Housing Association in the midfifties stimulated and briefly staffed housing and planning councils in Montgomery and Delaware, modeled loosely on PHA itself and its sister organization, the (Philadelphia) Citizens' Council on City Planning.[7]

The history of Delaware County's council illustrates the difficulties of general purpose civic action, though the highly organized inertia of this county was a special problem. In the spring of 1954 a small group from Baltzell's "Swarthmore suburbs" and the Main Line met to discuss formation of a housing and planning organization. They lived in settled, gracious communities threatened by residential sprawl. With their invitation to some 250 local improvement groups Delaware's Housing and Planning Council began as a federation of civic agencies; some forty were represented at the first meeting. By the middle of 1955 the Council had two dozen organizational members and less than a dozen individual members; it was staffed by the PHA and operated through committees on housing, planning, and stream valley preservation.

For several reasons the last committee, though least related to the Council's founding purposes and Philadelphia stimulus, turned out to be the tail that wagged the dog. Its members' aggressiveness and the longstanding interests of some local conservationists and horticulturalists plus a few rural aristocrats (called the "fox-hunting set" by Philadelphia "housers") were important reasons, but so was the available focus on the county planning commission's proposed creek valley preservation program (see Chapter 15). Soon the Council, with the county planning director's encouragement, began a separate organization, the Citizens' Creek Valley Association, to support the commission's proposal, sharing its part-time staff with the new movement. After the creek valley plan failed the two groups joined forces in the Citizens' Council of Delaware County. This organization developed a structure of committees encompassing open space, transportation, water supply and pollution, industrial development, and planning. Initially its officers emphasized close relations with the county commissioners, but publicity and visible results seemed necessary to stimulate membership, and CCDC's tactics vacillated between liaisons and crusades. Within its implicit focus on the physical environment, objectives were hard to define because of occasional rivalry between esthetic and economic interests: between amenity and development, conservation and change. Yet CCDC did have a program: it sought more county action on open space, industrial development, mass transit, redevelopment, and comprehensive planning; and it fought the state over highway locations. Its implicit priority was open space: that committee was most enthusiastic and most influential in state and county decisions. In one bitter fight over location of an expressway through the center of the county, commercial interests among the leadership tangled with rank-and-file open-spacers, and in membership votes at special meetings, the conservationists were victorious—after which most business representatives quietly left the organization.

CCDC's history illuminates several aspects of county government, politics, and society. The occasional nature of county action made it difficult to focus on priorities, as did absence of the comprehensive planning and capital programming that exist in the city. Without a stream of public policy available for comment, CCDC had either to react to isolated county, regional, and state initiatives; to try to cover the municipalities as well, or to sponsor a program of its own. CCDC lacked a natural geographical base: the zoning and locational issues that are staples of local civic associations raised conflicts within CCDC precisely because it was a county organization, since county policy is often high in sectional content. The organization and powers of county government itself were not live issues, and they potentially conflicted with localism.

CCDC's problems were especially difficult in Delaware County. Its initiatives implicitly challenged the ruling political structure, but its public was narrowed by social and political limits already noted. Partly because its membership was entirely individual, CCDC overrepresented upper income districts and interests in a county with a large working-class population toward which the political organization was solicitous. The council's "cosmopolitan," intellectual members alienated some "local" businessmen and professionals. Because it sought more county action, it may have forfeited the financial support of tax-conscious, politically sensitive industries. Without large-scale financial backing it lacked professional staff and public relations, and fell back on civic enthusiasm. In all these respects CCDC's situation differed in degree from those of counterpart organizations in Philadelphia. In the absence of political competition only CCDC (and the Health and Welfare Council) would urge county innovation, but lack of competition was preserved by county response to forces that were local and conservative. In

this mobilization of bias CCDC kept its concerns alive and served as an
outlet for civic energies, but its roles as both initiator and critic were
played in a relative vacuum.

5. *Health and welfare organizations* probably stem from more specific,
religious, and personal instincts than does civic activity. The voluntary
tradition in both fields is lively, if not vital; especially in health. Pennsylvania has a history of general county welfare organization sponsored at
the state level first by private sources (the Public Charities Association
early in this century) and later (in the 1920's) by state government.
The purpose in each case was to provide critics and constituents for
public welfare services (especially poor relief), but no trace remains of
these agencies in the suburbs except in Delaware County. For the present study the contemporary funds and coordinating councils are most
important, but they are also conventional, differing little from those
around the country.* Businessmen—especially large firms—are most
heavily represented in the funds. The county planning councils are
favored by member agency executives, professional men, and an active
distaff contingent. The articulate county welfare constituency consists
far more of helpers than of helped, held together by professional
workers employed by funds, councils, and governments. Charity and
character building still rival institutional welfare in its philosophy. The
constituency's unity and activity varies among the counties.

When U.S. Steel arrived in Bucks, the existing community services
were appropriate to a small-town society: scouting and youth groups,
isolated clinics, and selective charities; there were no general family or
children's agencies, though the county's progressive school administration provided partial public substitutes. When U.S. Steel was approached for a separate contribution, it urged consolidation; industry
in lower Bucks, with social and political leaders in the rest of the county,
set up a United Services Federation within which were lodged a United
Fund and a Community Services Council.† By 1953 the machinery was
in existence. In time the typical voluntary agencies developed, but

* In the field of public health the county Tuberculosis and Health Associations are
also important. They are long established agencies, independently financed from
Christmas seal sales, and linked to state and national direction. Their main resource
is staff, and the county boards tend to be *pro forma*. On their history, see Esther G.
Price, *Pennsylvania Pioneers Against Tuberculosis* (Washington: National Tuberculosis Association, 1952), and Richard H. Shryock, *The National Tuberculosis Association, 1904-1954* (Washington: The Association, 1957).

† During World War II a national organization to aid defense-impacted areas operated in the county (the United Community Defense Council), and in the early
fifties it provided staff and a small grant to get the county's health and welfare
organization under way. The Philadelphia Housing Association also provided personnel assistance. Late in 1952, when the first fund drive began, its chairman stated:
"Never before has a primarily rural county established a community chest. Our chest
is unique, but so is our county and [so are] our problems." *Delaware Valley Advance*,
November 12, 1952.

county-wide planning and financing took hold slowly because of local and sectional traditions. Gradually a division grew up in which lower Bucks County industry and labor dominated the United Fund, while the planning council was manned by women from central Bucks assisted by professionals from the County's health and education agencies. Relations between the two groups were affected by these sectional and occupational differences; most of the money came from large firms in lower Bucks, businessmen tended to prevail in the fund allocations, and the council's budget was small, but its social constituency in central Bucks was important. The Fund's offices were in lower Bucks, the Council's in Doylestown.

In Delaware and Montgomery the social planning councils are county divisions of the Philadelphia Health and Welfare Council and are largely financed by the Greater Philadelphia United Fund. Both counties have closer regional connections than does Bucks, but sectionalism in Montgomery has separated residential retreats and industrial boroughs, while Delaware's social agencies are more nearly county-wide and its social problems more apparent. There are eight smaller community funds in Montgomery and only one (for Chester and vicinity) in Delaware; however, Delaware's planning council is older and more fully staffed than Montgomery's. Both councils have pressed hard for more county services in child welfare, recreation, and health.

5. *Summary.*   Banfield and Wilson have written that:

> Nothing in small-town politics is as important . . . as the preservation of peace and harmony and the maintenance of easy personal relations. . . . To put the matter more generally, the function of politics in the small town is less to resolve issues than, by suppressing them, to enable people to get along with each other while living together in very close contact.[8]

On the other hand, in writing of cities, they argue that most public issues arise from the "maintenance and enhancement needs" of organizations, i.e., from their self-concern with survival and growth.[9] The suburban counties seem to fall between these extremes.

The counties are weaker than the city in associations for *general* and nonprofit objectives. The city housing movement connects residential amenity to social welfare and even, under urban renewal, to fiscal and economic concerns, but these interests are more discrete in the suburbs. The county citizens' councils have attempted to extend Philadelphia's strong tradition of civic action in planning and improvement, but have been hampered by the lack of governmental endeavor, by business indifference, and by rivalry from the older, naturalistic conservation ideology. Also lacking in the counties is the organized interest in official rectitude and reform that is so common in cities. Suburban tax-consciousness does not encompass governmental structure and procedure

—perhaps because reform is more apt to lead to more expenditure than to less. There are active Leagues of Women Voters in prestigious communities, but they have largely ignored the counties; League organization at that level is only a formality, and the Leagues are thus busiest in the most congenial local environments. In summary, the city organizations missing from the county scene are those whose interests are broadest in scope. Where these exist in the counties they lack professional staff and rely heavily on the dedication of a few members.

The range of voluntary endeavor is narrowed by the specificity of public functions and their division among governments. The traditional private interests in the counties can be described as business, charity, and conservation. Economic interests are expansive or protective, depending on local circumstances. Welfare organizations are the best professionalized and most closely linked to social distinctions. The conservationist concern is perhaps the most socially aristocratic, but all three county-wide interests are pretty much limited to the upper middle class except for *pro forma* labor participation in welfare. Still, class orientations are not uniform among the counties; they appear to vary with prevailing economic and political conditions, competitive or protective. Also, in Montgomery and Delaware Counties the three principal interests involve different people almost entirely, whereas in Bucks there has recently been some overlap. Thus the counties are characterized by particularism—low participation for limited purposes—though Bucks has evolved a bit toward pluralism in the sense of concurrent membership. The county with the most electoral competition and governmental innovation has the most overlapping private leadership, though this is clearly less than a concerted elite. The rapid development of Bucks seems to have made the relations among interests more pressing and visible, but some of these relations are competitive.

There are other differences among the suburban counties in their patterns of organized interests. One has to do with the relations of groups to government. In Bucks the Neshaminy Valley Watershed Association has attained a quasi-official position, and the county-sponsored Industrial Development Corporation (see Chapter 17) has acted as a pressure group for new projects and programs. This kind of relationship is less developed in Montgomery and Delaware.

Few civic participants in Delaware and Montgomery are active in party politics, though local businessmen, especially those in the PMA, contribute financially. In Bucks County some politicians have joined conservation groups and chambers of commerce, but business, civic, and political leadership remain distinct.

Another important difference is in business participation, which is dominantly expansionist in Bucks, protective in Delaware, and mixed in Montgomery. Most of Bucks' major industries are recent arrivals and absentee owned. Delaware is at the opposite end of this spectrum in age and ownership, and Montgomery's old manufacturers are now rivaled by recent development. Despite Joseph Grundy's personification of the PMA, that organization has no branch in Bucks County today, but it is active in Montgomery and Delaware. County development programs should help lessen the public visibility and fiscal vulnerability of Bucks' large industries; Bucks' autonomy from Philadelphia has bolstered local commercial growth. These interests are weaker in the other counties. Intercounty differences in business involvement thus stem from concrete incentives. They parallel differences among the counties with respect to political competition, which suggests a close relation between economic and political structures. This possibility is further discussed in the next chapter.

5

Influence

The distribution of influence over county policy cannot be measured or even described precisely. Structural and historical factors affecting it are discussed in this chapter. The conclusion is that local industry and old families have until recently held high potential for influence but that county political organizations normally exert still more control. There are subtle intercounty differences in this respect.

Close relations among such possible bases of power as established local industry, old family ascendency in the professions, and one-party politics are now most apparent in Delaware, somewhat less so in Montgomery (more decentralized, sectionalized, and factionalized), and negligible in Bucks—except that in each county some notables stand high in legal practice and Republican politics. The most striking intercounty differences today are in business and politics: in each case, pluralism of interests, or competition, increases from Delaware through Montgomery to Bucks, and in each case the difference is larger between Bucks and Montgomery than between the latter and Delaware.

The infirmities of county government (described in Part III), its limited tax base, relative lack of redistributive expenditures and regulatory functions, and the restricted nature of county society in either a formal or a functional sense all suggest an implicit mobilization of bias rather than a tested structure of power. Such a mobilization is, by definition, systematic, involving not simply individual favoritism but a cast of policy. If it exists, then the protectiveness of old industry and the several conservative interests of entrenched political organizations should be served in complementary ways by existing public institutions with minimal functions, and reinforced by judicial and custodial doctrines of the legal profession to be described later.

Many community studies have emphasized industry's political influence. Yet sociologists have also noted that nationally oriented managements tend to reduce industrial participation in community affairs to the most noncontroversial (e.g., United Funds). They suggest that the large corporation may be devitalizing local government through its engrossment and neutralization of natural leadership.[1]

In the suburban counties several factors probably condition the political action of industrialists: degree of tax sensitivity, public relations policies, extent of management's local versus national orientation, the availability and community balance of organization and other resources, and the personal interests and ideologies of some free-wheeling entrepreneurs and executives. Each of these factors is complex. Although industry in general is not directly affected by most local or county programs, its limited interest in taxes leads to an indirect concern with all policies. This interest varies among firms or plants according to factors discussed in Chapter 13 (together with the mechanics of taxes); only a few are intensely interested, but none are indifferent. As for public relations, the most rational element in a corporation's policy appears to be whether its market is public or industrial; makers of consumer products are normally more public relations-conscious and reluctant to seem to intervene privately in local government.

The familiar distinction between local and absentee ownership needs refinement, so far as management's attention to the counties is concerned. The major suburban employers include (1) old, local firms still exclusively based in one county although their business may be international; (2) equally well established plants now merged with national firms though still under the old, local management; (3) national firms whose original installations or home offices are housed in one of the counties (Some home offices are in Philadelphia.); (4) old branch plants of absentee firms; and (5) new branch plants.* In general, the managements of the first three types are most evidently sensitive to taxation, most active in county Manufacturers' Associations and in state Republican finance and factionalism. Bucks County's industries are predominantly in the last two categories, Delaware's in the first four, and Montgomery's diversified through all five. Significantly, Delaware and Montgomery have active Manufacturers' Associations, while Bucks does not. Montgomery's more numerous industries, with their greater variety, sectional distribution, and new additions suggest that industrial mobili-

---

* Some illustrations are (1) the G. and W. Corson Company in Montgomery County in lime, concrete, and building materials; (2) the American Encaustic Tile Company of Lansdale or the American Viscose Company of Marcus Hook; (3) the Scott Paper Company of Delaware County or the Sun Oil Company in Delaware County (the latter having its home offices in Philadelphia and its refineries in Marcus Hook); (4) Westinghouse Electric Company's Steam Turbine Division in Delaware County; (5) branches of national firms newly established such as those of General Electric, Philco, and American Can Company in Montgomery County or U.S. Steel in Bucks County.

zation for political influence may be growing more difficult there than in Delaware despite the activity, wealth, and reputation for power of the minority known as the manufacturers.

The formal organization of industry is important in concerting its legislative objectives and local fiscal concerns, but large-scale party finance—probably the chief industrial sanction—is the province of a few wealthy entrepreneurs. These men continue a pattern more common in the past, and most are deeply conservative. About half a dozen figure in Montgomery's county politics, fewer men reportedly spend less in Delaware, and none are now mentioned in Bucks. The financial sanction's effectiveness, so far as it can be estimated, is discussed in Part II, but it has been most important in Montgomery.

Family ties still connect industry and politics occasionally in Delaware, less frequently in Montgomery. Family standing is still a political, commercial, and professional resource in the remaining rural and small-town areas, which are most important in Bucks and least so in Delaware. In general, the social nexus seems to have loosened in suburban politics for several reasons: the disjunction and diffusion of industrial ownership and control, the rapid growth and fragmentation of the suburban counties, the dominance by Philadelphia of formal society, and the city's role as a cultural and institutional center.

It will be helpful to place these factors in historical perspective, since traditions contribute to mobilization of bias. A useful frame of reference is provided by Robert Dahl's study of New Haven, in which he argues that society and polity there have progressed from cumulative to dispersed inequalities (i.e., that disproportionate control of one political resource, such as wealth, prestige, or legality, no longer forcefully implies a like share of other resources), and that public office-holding has gravitated since colonial times from social "patricians" to economic "entrepreneurs" to "ex-plebs" (politicians from undistinguished or minority socioeconomic backgrounds).[2] The comparison with New Haven should be useful despite the social and governmental fragmentation of the suburbs and low salience of the counties compared with cities. Information about the background and attributes of county officials and politicians is limited, but a few trends are evident, although they are less distinct than those in many cities.[3]

The limited applicability of Dahl's patrician pattern to the three counties in the colonial period has already been noted. In the early nineteenth century each county had its surviving landed elite, which frequently filled the higher offices. Several factors combined to limit its hold on public affairs, including Pennsylvania's intense partisanship and extensive patronage, the force of Republican ideology (most influential in Montgomery and least in Delaware), and long-standing cultural diversity and Protestant nonconformity (most pronounced in Montgomery and least in Delaware).[4] These factors, part of southeastern Pennsylvania's colonial and revolutionary heritage, took effect before the early industrial growth of Delaware and Montgomery Counties. With this growth, entrepreneurs appeared more commonly in public office—most frequently in Delaware County, where milling was most widespread and often combined with farming, banking, and real estate as a source of wealth. But many early industrialists had neither time nor taste for politics, and in none of the counties did manufacturers predominate in office. The entrepreneur-politicians sought wealth, prestige, and responsibility in commerce, agriculture, real estate, or law, often in combination. Some (especially those in the Jefferson-Jackson tradition) chose politics as the primary field that contributed to commercial or professional success, instead of conversely; such men were Samuel Ingham of Bucks, John Sterigere of Montgomery, and others on a lesser scale. In the post-Civil-War period men with military records were commonly nominated and elected.

In all counties up, say, to the time of the Civil War there was an observable concentration of office-holding in the so-called civil lists: whoever held one place was likely, later, to hold others. There was an office-holding hierarchy: successful businessmen and lawyers tended to enter public life at higher levels (state legislature and county bench); local and county positions were typically filled by political careerists, or, in contrast, by reputable farmers, who probably served more from a sense of civic obligation that they did from ambition. Some of those who ran for higher office were scions of important county families, but most were self-made men. Of the latter some advanced economically through political activity; most turned to politics from other endeavors. One thing many had in common was banking. Beginning in the second decade of the nineteenth century the county bank boards connected the successful in industry, commerce, agriculture, real estate, law, and politics. Prominent politicians typically held bank directorships, and in this way the public and private direction of development fell to the same men. Business and political competition, however (including banking competition), doubtless served to dilute this early power elite.[5]

Certain differences obtained among the three counties in the same period. There were more early industrialists in politics and public office in Delaware County than in Bucks and Montgomery: milling was most advanced in Delaware and, as industry and politics developed, industrialists tended to be Whigs, while Bucks and Montgomery voters were preponderantly Democratic. Another (predictable) contrast derived from county settlement patterns: Delaware County officeholders in the early nineteenth century were predominantly of English and Quaker background. In time the Scotch-Irish joined them in business, politics, and such society as existed, but the first Quaker families were heavily represented throughout the period. Montgomery County, was most diverse: Germans, Welsh, Scotch-Irish, Huguenots, Quakers, and occasional Anglicans all held office, but men of German background were a clear plurality in county politics throughout the nineteenth century and, in the early period, contributed heavily to the prevailing Republican sentiments. The leading Republican-Democratic politicians of the early period were such men as Jonathan Roberts (Welsh), Nathaniel Boileau (Huguenot), and John Sterigere (German), all from Protestant sects or nonconformist background. The rivalry and regional divisions in Bucks among the English (especially the Quakers), the Germans, and the Scotch-Irish have already been described. Socially and politically, Delaware was most homogeneous and Montgomery most competitive.

The relations between local politics and economics began to change after the Civil War and especially by the 1880's. It is convenient to comment on a period with ragged edges beginning sometime between the Civil War and the turn of the century and declining by the Great Depression. By the late nineteenth century the counties, especially Delaware and Montgomery, developed socioeconomic patterns that superficially favored class control of politics.

Four trends contributed to the new pattern. One was the growth of industries more centrally affecting employment and more sensitive to state labor legislation and local taxation. A second, related development was scattered urbanization: greater densities and social differences with industrialization and immigration. A third factor was the gradual establishment by the early entrepreneurs of family traditions in business and politics. Finally, there was the rise of a new Republican ideology after the Civil War, successor to the old Republican doctrine of the early nineteenth century. In Bucks and Montgomery the new Republican faith led to political realignment; in Delaware it confirmed the conservative politics of a county that had been solidly Whig and had exhibited strong Quaker sympathies for the antislavery cause.

The four trends worked together. Differences of class and status were enhanced by industrialization and immigration respectively. These trends peaked in the early twentieth century. They were most prominent in Delaware, where Chester dominated economic, social, and political life. In Montgomery the effect was dispersed among industrial boroughs (including the county seat) and somewhat diluted by the size of the county.[6] The development of Bristol in Bucks was a lesser version of the Chester story, but in the twentieth century Bucks' political leadership was firmly lodged in Bristol. In each county the connections among industry, family, and politics were potentially closer with the growth of notable families—especially those in the legal profession. And the new Republican ideology helped establish one-party dominance in all three counties by about the turn of the century. In all these respects the urban centers of the suburban counties came to look (at least in retrospect) like pyramidal power structures.

Yet two trends worked the other way in county politics. One was the suburban settlement—i.e., commuter settlement—that soon followed industrial development. This enhanced the fragmentation of Montgomery and Delaware because it occurred in different sections than did industrial development. The new suburbanites strengthened the Republican Party, but few cared about county politics or policy. Socially, localism, sectionalism, and regionalism were intensified. Formal society was oriented to the city: most county notables did not belong to it, and few Philadelphia socialites were active in provincial affairs. Thus social fragmentation reinforced jurisdictional divisions. The county was not enough of a polity to provide direct confrontations between elites and plebes or among group interests. Indirectly this situation mobilized bias, but probably it was directly advantageous to a few individuals and families more than to interests and classes in general.

Another countervailing trend was the formal separation of political and business management, especially in industry. Twentieth century political leaders were not industrialists; the more usual combinations continued to be with real estate and banking. Bucks' Grundy was exceptional in his union of industrial and political control, but his county was closer to the old entrepreneurial culture, and Grundy's business interests were diverse. In the other counties a division of labor developed between industry and politics as each field became more organized and specialized. Corporate leaders and their lawyers rarely held local or state legislative office, nor did business and professional men who worked in Philadelphia. Some political leaders, too, eschewed public office, concentrating on the organization that new population densities made possible. These political developments are discussed in Part II; here it is enough to note that urbanization and suburbanization gave politicians an electoral base potentially independent of industry, while state and county patronage created financial independence. On the other hand, industrial jobs and contributions were convenient assets for politicians, while control of state legislators was especially important to industry. Thus, despite the new division of labor, some local industrialists—ideological conservatives—remained politically active in Delaware and Montgomery. Their interests were usually consistent with those of the county political leaders, and relations between them were normally close. The details, intercounty variations, and change over time of these relations are discussed in the following chapters. But it does appear that in the most rural county (Bucks) the union of politics and industry, based in Bristol, was most complete; that in the most urban county (Delaware) the distinction between them was clearest; and that the larger population concentrations favored specialized political leadership at the same time that large industry required the full attention of management.

In the period after World War II some of the foregoing trends continued in ways that again changed the bases of political organization and influence. In politics, if not in policy, the trend emerged that Robert Dahl termed the rise of the "ex-plebes." By the time of the Depression it was at work in some industrial boroughs where Irish and Italian populations were important. In the postwar years recognition began to

be accorded on county tickets—even to judgeships in relatively urbanized Delaware County—as suburban subdivisions varied over a wider
range of income and social rank. But tribal politics was much less significant in the suburbs than in the city: it was confined by municipal
lines and, except in Bucks, by lack of outright party competition.

There were still more significant effects from postwar industrial and
residential development. New industrial growth meant an increase in
branch plants of absentee corporations and in a new breed of mobile
managers and professionals. Residential growth strained local governments and probably strengthened interest in public action at all levels;
it altered the electoral bases of county politics and introduced a few
competing social and cultural interests in county policy. Both trends
together generated business interests in development that sometimes
conflicted with established interests and put pressure toward innovation on government. These interests were most evident in Bucks and
least so in Delaware because of different growth rates.

Some of the new business interests were regional in scope: an economic regionalism followed social metropolitanism to the counties as
a fragmenting force. Most striking were decentralization in retailing
and the high rate of bank mergers replacing the old local directorates.[7]
Financial concentration was rapid in the postwar period. By 1960 all
Delaware County's banks but one had combined with Philadelphia firms.
(The remaining bank was the county's oldest, which was controlled
by the Pew family of Sun Oil and Sun Ship, and was still an important
local institution.) In the other counties merger had not gone so far:
roughly a dozen banks remained in Montgomery, including the oldest
and most prestigious, and in Bucks County there were more than two
dozen independent banks. Significantly, few of the independents were
able to finance large development projects. Thus the nexus of county
industry, commerce, and politics in local banking and of these with old
families was loosened—though not wholly dissolved—most completely
in Bucks, and least so in Delaware.

A related postwar development occurred in the field of real estate,
traditionally a local business with close political connections and direct
relevance to policy. Large Philadelphia firms increased their holdings
in the counties, primarily in land marked for large-scale development.
This trend, however, was less pronounced than the metropolitanization
of banking. Local land developers continued their participation in
county civic and political affairs as they had for at least a century and
a half.

The inquiry into power structure is still incomplete, but the historical
background has been explored. The secular movement from so-called
cumulative to dispersed inequalities occurred in the three counties
somewhat as Dahl conceived it in New Haven, but much less distinctly.
No doubt the gradual separation of status, property, and ethnicity as
political resources was less perceptible in the counties because differ-

ences on each dimension were less pronounced, public functions were more primitive, and public offices less visible, than in the city. Both social differences and governmental activities were divided by borough and township boundaries. Beside these factors, the lack of electoral competition in the twentieth century must have narrowed the range of political resources available. Until recently the largest private concentrations of political concern and resources belonged to local industry. Yet, as Part II suggests, political leaders were advantaged *vis-à-vis* these concentrations by urban and suburban growth and by the structure of government.

To summarize: social, cultural, economic, and political leadership were perhaps most closely combined in a few individuals during the colonial period, when socioeconomic differences in the suburbs were evidently not intense. There followed a reordering in the social aftermath of the Revolution—the rise of party organization, of the early Republican ideology, and of business-cum-political entrepreneurs. This reordering, a function of cultural diversity, was most effective in Montgomery County and least significant in Delaware.

With urbanization there developed more division of labor between industry and politics, with more formal organization and centralized resources on each side. The legislative situation stimulating the PMA was described in the last chapter; the conditions of county political consolidation are discussed in the next. Both occurred within one-party political systems. Party and factional finance was industry's principal counter, local taxation and state legislation its principal concerns. Strength of political organization in primary elections determined the balance of power, but a more important point was the two sides' substantial identity of interest and ideology in a conservative, parsimonious polity. There were few other organized interests. Residential and industrial growth have recently produced more interests and political competition in two of the counties, and the old mobilization of bias is altering in all of them.

PART II. POLITICS

6

The Old Organizations

County politics is deeply conditioned by the social structure described above and by the governmental structure to be discussed below.* It is also affected by the state framework. Together, these factors have produced hardy, deep-rooted political parties.

The state's role in policy and patronage is critical in county politics. Not only are counties and municipalities creatures of the state, but most public benefits and regulations stem directly from state law and administration. If, therefore, one seeks effective support or protection one turns to state politics.

At this point a seeming paradox occurs: state politics is highly decentralized, and one of the most effective routes to influence is through the county political organization. The county is the molecular unit of state politics. Legislators are elected in counties or large sections thereof; counties are the basic state senatorial districts.† The state party committees are composed of county delegates. And at least two other governmental factors favor political decentralization. One of these is the relative weakness of the governor, who is elected on a moderately long ballot and cannot succeed himself. The other is Pennsylvania's abundant

---

* As background to these political chapters it need only be noted that the counties are governed by three county commissioners (of whom one must represent the minority party), by several independently elected row officers (e.g., controller, district attorney, recorder of deeds) for specific functions, and by the locally elected judges of the county courts (which are really state agencies). Commissioners are elected concurrently to four-year terms, row officers and judges at various times to four- and ten-year terms respectively. County elections are held every odd-numbered year, together with municipal elections.

† In 1965 state legislative reapportionment altered this pattern, creating smaller, single member districts for both chambers. Its effects on electoral competition are not readily predictable: most districts will be more socially homogeneous; but candidates of the minority party may be better able to capitalize on their reputations in smaller areas.

patronage: some two-thirds of all state positions are unclassified by law, and there is virtually no local civil service. Patronage is a potential weapon of the governor, but in practice it works the other way: it must be used to satisfy county organizations that influence legislative votes and gubernatorial nominations; it is bargained for budgets and legislative confirmation or appointments; and it lends itself to political careerism and local organization control, thus discouraging a more issue-oriented, executive-centered type of politics and administration.

In this situation counties with large legislative delegations and heavy voting populations are especially favored. "Safe" counties have at least as much leverage as competitive counties; their legislators build seniority buttressed by gerrymandered, multimembered districts; and they dominate primary elections. The suburban counties of Montgomery and Delaware are crucial Republican units in state-wide elections; they offset urban Democratic majorities and contain them at the city line.

In relations with municipalities, as with the state, the political role of the county tends to outweigh and overshadow its governmental role, especially in well-organized, one-party counties. The county organization as dispenser of patronage and intercessor with the state has more sanctions than the local organization—*if* the county organization is already strong and the local politicians are interested in patronage. The county organization's bargaining power is probably strengthened by the tendency of rank-and-file residents to ignore the county in favor of municipal concerns: local politicians have only their personal interests to promote before the county organization and lack primary electoral sanctions to support them; in general elections their fortunes are tied to the county organization's. In some counties, however, certain large municipalities carry great weight, or the county organization may largely amount to a coalition of a few populous localities. The structure and strength of the county political organization thus depend in part on settlement patterns and on the distribution of party sympathies, both of which may change. In these respects the three counties differ sharply: the recent sea-change in Bucks County politics was centered in a few large lower Bucks municipalities; Montgomery's politics was long dominated by a few townships and industrial boroughs, as Delaware County's was by Chester, but in recent years population dispersion has been altering organization patterns in both counties.

At the county level several factors favor a low-pressure politics centered on careerism and organization loyalty. The absence of any civil service means that county jobs may be used for disciplinary and financial purposes: the larger counties, like Delaware and Montgomery, have 1,000 or more county positions, or roughly 1 to every 500 residents, not including state and municipal patronage. (State patronage is unstable and varies in size with state installations in the counties, but the average number of state jobs controlled by the county organization in each suburban county is over 500.) Most county jobs are nonprofessional and freely available for politics; they are neither demanding nor remunerative, but they afford time for political activity, psychic rewards for party loyalty, bargaining power over local organizations, and financial support: consider the return from assessing more than 1,000 employees an average of $100 annually, as is done in Delaware County. There is thus every incentive for overstaffing county government and every evidence of it in the more politically organized counties; on the other hand, the practice is not especially costly at existing pay scales, and conservatives, concerned for the tax rate, are probably right in preferring political careerism to professional enterprise.

Factors noted in preceding chapters abet political organization. Localism, regionalism, and particularism imply limited publics for county affairs—lawyers, realtors, welfare workers, and certain local businesses—and for these people the political party has such restraints and incentives as appointments, permits, contracts, assessments, appropriations, and a few county programs plus numerous state sanctions, sinecures, and emoluments when Harrisburg is in friendly hands. The effectiveness of these counters is enhanced by lack of publicity and of professional standards: people may easily believe conformity is requisite to reward and play it doubly safe, especially when they are competing for individual rather than group advantage.

Finally, there is the matter of state tradition. Pennsylvania politics has long been strongly partisan. The first political cleavages (which soon declined) involved distinct interests and ideologies, and partisanship was doubtless strengthened by the later prevalence of the Jeffersonian-Jacksonian, republican-democratic ideology, and the great importance of state and local patronage.[1] In the twentieth century organized industry and labor directed their political action into opposing party channels, thus reinforcing the tradition. The roots of party organization go deep and partisanship is the prevailing orientation to public affairs.

Thus the county turns out to be a vital political unit; its political importance often overshadows its governmental role. If a power structure is based in industry or society it is likely to manifest itself in party activity, but party organization or leadership may emerge as an independent base of power. There are sufficient resources available for the support of party organizations—including both partisan attitudes and material benefits and penalties—so that purely organizational ends are likely to bulk large in public policy; a highly programmatic politics would not be predicted. Moreover, where the socioeconomic and cultural bases of party cleavage are relatively weak the county organizations have the wherewithal to limit political competition if they are ably led and amply exploit their resources.

These tendencies have prevailed in all three counties in the past, but in light of recent changes they are not unalterable. Today traditional organization politics no longer exists in one of the counties and has been subtly undermined in another; in the third it is virtually unchanged. The changing relations of political structure to social and governmental factors may be seen in the following review of the counties' political histories.

1. *Electoral history.* Until the Civil War the party that began as Republican and converted to Democracy was dominant in Pennsylvania. This dominance was probably more a matter of ideology than of class cleavage by the early nineteenth century. By that time the eastern aristocracy had largely retired from public life. The local Republican party began as a group of conservatives who opposed the popular Constitution of 1776 and achieved its revision in 1790. Its leadership was hardly radical after national alignments developed; state politics tended to be sectional, personal, and oriented to the pork barrel. In southeastern Pennsylvania the Quakers were typically Federalists; the Scotch-Irish, Republicans; and the Germans divided, though preponderantly Republicans; merchants and manufacturers (especially those oriented to Philadelphia) tended to be Federalists, and farmers to be Republicans. Class and nationality were more important political determinants in and around Philadelphia, where colonial distinctions lingered and urban-rural differences were most evident.[2]

Counties differed politically. The Republican-Democratic ideology and leadership were strongest in Montgomery. Several Jeffersonian leaders in that county, like Jonathan Roberts and Peter Muhlenburg, came from prominent colonial families, and the later Jacksonian politicians were able organizers. The Republican doctrine appealed to the county's nationalities and denominations, and the rural German Democratic majority, once established, was especially dependable because of its linguistic insulation. Up to the Civil War the county was dominantly Democratic in national elections, though Whigs occasionally won state or local office when the majority divided.

Bucks County was more closely competitive. There the first party divisions bore traces of regional and cultural differences in colonial times; the up-country Germans and the Scotch-Irish shared Republican tendencies, but the English population still formed a majority. Federalism therefore remained in effective force in Bucks for a decade after its decline in most counties, and the party balance remained close throughout the nineteenth century because it retained its early regional-cultural bases.

The most conservative, least competitive county was Delaware, where English stock predominated and Quaker influence lasted longest. In the presidential election of 1808 Delaware was the only Pennsylvania county in the Federalist column. It remained a Federalist stronghold for the life of that faction, and then became Whig. Jackson's majority there was paper-thin in the four-way election of 1824 and disappeared thereafter; no national candidate styled Democrat ever carried the county until President Lyndon Johnson did so in the Goldwater debacle of 1964.

Only Delaware displays such unbroken electoral continuity; politics in Bucks and Montgomery reflected national events that ultimately turned them Republican early in the twentieth century. The first event was the Civil War and the realignments connected with it; from that time Delaware was more heavily Republican than it had been Whig; Democratic strength declined slightly in Bucks and substantially in Montgomery, so that, for the rest of the nineteenth century, both were tightly competitive counties. The new Republican ideology, allied to military action and emancipation, was doubtless more contagious than the old Whig doctrine and preserved some old Republican principles; antislavery sentiment only confirmed the leanings of most Friends, but it helped convert the Scotch-Irish, while German cultural isolation declined. Some Democratic political leaders like Simon Cameron (whose career began in Bucks County) changed sides and carried others with them.

Thus Bucks and Montgomery, like Pennsylvania, moved from the Democratic to the "doubtful" column. Their emergence as safely Republican units, like Pennsylvania's, dates from the presidential election of 1896. The landslide effects of that election persisted.[3] As in the Civil War period, at least a few county leaders and prominent families changed sides. These effects were reinforced in Delaware and Montgomery Counties by the suburban growth that began in that period. The high-income residential settlement in Montgomery and the small-scale industrial concentration in lower Bucks combined with the persisting realignment of 1896 to offset decisively the rural German habit of voting Democratic in upper Bucks and outer Montgomery. From 1896 to 1964, with one exception, the three counties went Republican in presidential elections.[4] In the off-year local elections Democrats were never a serious threat to the strong Republican county organizations that developed once Republican electoral dominance was established by national party alignments, state patronage, and local population movements.

2. *Organizational history.* The Federal forms of county politics endured into the twentieth century. These were the local caucus and county convention: party loyalists met in townships or election districts to name delegates to the county committee, which nominated candidates for office. From the beginning the county was the basic political unit. "In many cases," writes an historian of the system's origins, "these [county] committees were permanent bodies holding power until new ones were chosen," and he adds that local meetings for the election of delegates were "ill-attended and were dominated by officeholders."[5] Both local meetings and county conventions were often held in taverns and were commonly intemperate. The system lent itself to personal

leadership and often to organization control; but not inevitably so—anyone could play the game, and organized opposition to a personal following could at least hope to enter local meetings on roughly equal terms.

We know little about nineteenth-century local politicians and their methods. Partisanship was keen and the press was intensely political. In Bucks and Montgomery Counties political journalism was imported and supported by the leaders of the Jeffersonian Republican party. Pennsylvania's franchise was broad under the Constitution of 1790 (virtually universal manhood suffrage), which doubtless stimulated electoral organization. Patronage was critical. The Constitution placed most of it in the hands of the governor, who appointed all judicial officers and many others in the counties. Until this situation was changed by the 1838 Constitution a prime incentive for county political organization was to reach the candidate for governor and participate recognizably in his election to office; later, more positions became elective or directly available in the counties, but access to the governor and legislature remained a principal objective of county political control.

Patronage and electoral organization produced new politicians: in Montgomery the local aristocracy retired from politics early in the century, as the pursuit of office quickened in accord with Republican doctrine and method. This retirement was less observable in Bucks and Delaware, where old English families still dominated the principal towns, but the nineteenth-century county politicians are better classified as entrepreneurs than as patricians. Few were full-time professionals; the field of county politics was too small for that, and state or national preferment too uncertain. Probably John B. Sterigere of Montgomery most closely approached professional status: emerging from rural German origins, "He organized his supporters in every district of the county, thus creating what was later called a machine whereby his will could be executed."[6] Sterigere was successively justice of the peace, state legislator, congressman, and county Democratic chairman; he studied law while in Congress and ultimately made his living as a lawyer-politician in Norristown. For most county leaders politics was combined with law or business, as by Ingham in Bucks or the Eyres of Chester in Delaware County. Organization control was slippery and shifting. Philip Klein describes the situation in the 1830's, when state party lines were blurred and party labels lost their luster, when local improvements and patronage, rather than state or national policy, were the issues:

> It was almost impossible to create even a lasting county organization built on patronage, much less a state machine. Independent candidates by the score threw their hats into the ring in opposition to the settled tickets. So weak was the "organization" [the county convention] that a year after their bolt they were back in the party and more than likely secured a place on the "regular" ticket. Independent vot-

ing, too, was easy before the days of straight tickets. As the voter had the ballot for each office separately, splitting tickets was much more common than now. When members of one party purposely elected candidates of the other, it was not held disloyalty to the party but merely a rebuke to particular individuals. Bolters usually supported all their party slate save the two or three candidates fixed upon as focal points of protest, and these they ousted in favor of their political opponents.[7]

Change came with the direct primary required by law in 1913, which broadened the popular base of nominations and probably increased the advantages of county-wide organization and the incentives for maintaining it.[8] The earlier system combined patronage and personal ascendency as the principal tools of the political trade. Primary elections required some impersonal organization and party finance. At the same time state law was changed to facilitate straight-ticket voting in general elections.

There were other, supporting sources of political consolidation. One was denser settlement of industrial centers and residential suburbs, and perhaps especially the working-class wards of industrial boroughs. The decline of party competition in the counties and the state at large was doubtlessly equally important. Political control in the counties was easier with the lapse of competition in general elections; it also became more important to participate in the nomination of governors and other state officers, since the perquisites of state office now belonged to one party alone. In time, county leaders combined in leagues to influence state nominations, and influence was measured in part by the size and security of the county vote in primary and general elections. Still another element was the increasing political consciousness of industry, manifest in the PMA. By the twentieth century industrialists rarely entered politics directly, but their concern with state policies, resting in part with nominations and elections in the counties, had increased, and their financial backing was most important to local organizations.

For these reasons, it seems, political structure changed at the turn of the century. In mid-twentieth century other forces altered it again. The rise and decline of the old organizations in Bucks and Montgomery are described in the rest of this chapter; Delaware County's remarkable machine is reserved for later analysis.

3. *Bucks County.* For nearly half a century Bucks County's affairs were managed by the Republican organization of Joseph Grundy, textile magnate, banker, publisher, and founder of the PMA. Grundy entered politics in his native Bristol late in the last century and assumed control of the county by 1910. For more than forty years he was a power in state politics and a symbol of industrial protection; he was appointed to fill an unexpired term as United States Senator in 1929. Most of Grundy's activity was directed beyond the county boundaries, and his local organization was almost a sideline. Bucks' break with nineteenth-century

society was not so sharp as the other counties', and political control was not difficult. Opposition was hard to concert in its large, sparsely settled confines. By the 1920's party registration was heavily Republican, so general elections were no problem. The traditionally Democratic German registrants in upper Bucks were conservative, so no policy differences arose. Grundy himself looked after Bristol, the principal center of population, in primary elections. Available perquisites were carefully shared with business and the bar; ordinary patronage was of limited importance because the county was run so parsimoniously. Grundy is reported not to have employed his extensive state influence in Bucks because he preferred to see patronage used where it was more needed. In short, Bucks was a low-pressure political system where a few resources went a long way.

It thus appears that from 1920 to 1950 Grundy's control was all but complete. The local political committees were screened by him and the county chairman, his lieutenant in Doylestown. County meetings and nominations were run according to plan, and the plans were laid— sometimes the speeches were written—in Grundy's Bristol office. The leading newspapers, of longest standing, were Grundy's Doylestown *Intelligencer* and Bristol *Courier;* they covered most of the county, apart from upper Bucks, and were the only dailies in their areas to survive the Depression. Their political reporting was highly biased: in the rare Republican primaries no notice was taken of opponents while organization candidates' pictures graced the front page on election eve; when Roosevelt carried Bucks in 1936 the disaster was reported on the back page of the *Intelligencer.* Business and politics were tightly interlaced: legal and political advertising went to Grundy's papers; public and party printing contracts went to Grundy's press. Grundy's county chairman was the Doylestown insurance agent who handled the local governments' accounts.

As in many well-run county organizations, tenure in office was carefully regulated to govern ambition and dissension. Row officers were allowed one term and county commissioners two; candidacy was a reward for long service on local committees. Regular financial contributions, local political activity, and organization loyalty were expected of appointed job-holders.* The two majority commissioners in effect served staggered eight-year terms, thus providing for experience and the natural selection of a chairman by seniority. Grundy's principal concern in county policy was the tax rate and, in the custodial tradition, there

---

* It was Grundy's custom to balance the three sections of the county in selecting row-office candidates. For commissioner, the county was divided slightly below Doylestown and a candidate was picked from the north and one from the south. The system was extolled to the author by one of Grundy's former county commissioners, who said that the one-term tradition promoted both honesty in office and loyalty to the organization, and that the long political apprenticeships obviated the young officeholder, who was most likely to yield to temptation and corruption.

was little more to policy than that. The commissioners meticulously checked the budget with Grundy, who sometimes suggested alterations.

In time, in this environment of conservatism and political success, one of the leader's chief resources was the personal respect he inspired. Old-timers still speak in awe of Mr. Grundy, who ran the party at a respectable distance. For most local politicians an audience in Bristol was an occasion, and many party loyalists never knew him well enough to speak to him. His conservatism, incorruptibility, plain Quaker speech, and local philanthropy were county legends. His rural organization, unlike some baroque suburban counterparts, was remarkable for economy and simplicity. Thus, when Grundy in his late eighties sold his businesses and retired from politics at the time of Bucks' spectacular midcentury growth, nothing remained of the organization save the old local committeemen in areas unaffected by immigration. Then Bucks' political break with the nineteenth century began.

4. *Montgomery County*. At the end of the century Montgomery's nominal leader was James B. (Dutch) Holland, a Norristown lawyer who became a federal district judge in 1904. Party leadership then passed to Holland's nominee, Charles Johnson, who converted his growing suburban Republican vote into county offices and his courthouse control into a strong political organization. Montgomery became a banner Republican county, and an important one because of its size and the wealth of its residents.

Johnson was successively county sheriff, state insurance commissioner, secretary of state, and secretary of revenue. Though he was a partner in a large real estate firm and board chairman of the Peoples Bank of Norristown, he was primarily a politician, not a businessman. Those who knew him well say he loved power and the approbation of state leaders for his large county majorities. He spent most of each week in Harrisburg, but his Saturday schedule began with the weekly meeting of the bank board, followed by audiences in his office with local politicians and petitioners and an afternoon tour of some part of the county. His habit was to visit the hotels, where voters were apt to congregate on Saturday afternoons. In this easy communication system the innkeepers were a vital network, and their liquor licenses were issued by the county court.

Neither oratory nor autocracy was part of Johnson's style; his was a careful system of consultation and avoidance of issues; he was legendary for his reluctance to give his word and for his loyalty in keeping it. His leadership in the later Johnson period rested heavily on arrangements with strong local leaders, especially in the large townships of Cheltenham and Lower Merion and in individual wards of such industrial boroughs as Ambler, Conshohocken, and Norristown, and on his skillful relating of county nominations, patronage, and local electoral support reflecting the limited interests of each level in the affairs of the other and the *amour-propre* of local politicians. Johnson's courthouse organization was tight; despite his fiscal conservatism, county employment was increased and used, with state patronage, for disciplinary purposes though reportedly not for fund-raising. (One of his requirements was that jobholders contribute to the relief of fellow public servants who suffered misfortune.)

Johnson's conservatism was deep-seated. He began the strong tradition of parsimony in Montgomery County government by retiring the bonded debt, refusing to borrow money (except at short term from local banks), and reducing the tax rate over the course of his leadership. His relations with Joseph Grundy and the PMA were close, and the county Manufacturers' Association was his main surce of financial support.

Johnson's organization rested partly on electoral success and business financial backing—these were available then to whoever led the Republican party, but were probably enhanced by Johnson's philosophy and ability. His own ascendency was based on control of the courthouse jobs and of candidacies. This organizational economy was maintained by carefully consulting and supporting strong local leaders in large population centers, strictly disciplining jobholders, shrewdly anticipating and often co-opting challengers, and quietly avoiding unnecessary issues. Johnson rarely lost a primary election.

Toward the end of his tenure he is said by oldtimers to have erred in several decisions. One was nonsupport of Governor Pinchot, which for the first time in years placed the county in the Democratic column. Another was his nomination of an in-law to a county judgeship; the nominee proved unpopular with the county bar and was defeated for a second term by a member of an old county legal and political family running as an ad hoc Democrat. In the same year Fred Peters, then a state legislator, defeated an incumbent county commissioner, Johnson's son-in-law, in the primary. Johnson's mistake appears to have been his growing family solicitude; by the time of these election defeats he was declining physically and retiring politically, and in 1937 he died.

In the interregnum that followed Fred Peters held a strong position. Peters grew up on a farm near Lenox, Massachusetts, and studied forestry and landscape architecture at the University of Massachusetts. Moving to Montgomery in 1908, he began pruning trees on the large estates of Lower Merion and later established his own landscaping business. A lifelong bachelor, he lived for several years in the Ardmore YMCA; he enlisted in the Army in World War I and shared in the 82nd Artillery's citation for unrelieved front-line duty. After the war Peters entered politics and successively became local committeeman, state legislator, and county commissioner. By then he was aiming at county leadership. He began with a group of personal followers, a legacy from his legislative career, and with the few county jobs he could dispose of as an individual commissioner. After Roosevelt's inroads in 1936 the

Peters group began a campaign with businessmen and local politicians to restore the Republican party's standing. In the upper part of the county he argued that the old organization had slighted that area in its reliance on the large municipalities. Peters backed primary winners in 1937 and 1938, and in 1940 persuaded the county court to appoint his candidate to a vacant commissionership. His man was Foster Hillegas, an up-county newspaper publisher and banker.

How the leadership was won is hard to say: certainly the successive primary victories helped, but control of the courthouse jobs clinched it. In the scramble for Johnson's mantle Peters had beaten the established county organization, which had the strong support of the county Manufacturers' Association and the PMA wing of the state party. His leadership thus began with some estrangement from the PMA. During his long county rule, however, he received important support from local industrialists, and it was during this period that the subtle distinction developed in Montgomery County between the county's manufacturers and the PMA.

Peters' organization differed from Johnson's primarily in greater reliance on courthouse workers, rather than business, for financial support. Workers were required to contribute fixed percentages of their salaries to the party, though the obligation could be lifted by personal hardship (an implicit commutation to personal loyalty). Some oldtimers refer to the courthouse in that period as a family, but Peters was an austere father figure. Job applicants were screened with extreme care to ensure maximum political mileage from the jobs, and unswerving loyalty was required in primary contests. Lest elected row officers develop their own organizations, new positions created by the county salary board were often placed directly under the commissioners. Primary contests were rare and candidates were carefully groomed. Opposition was co-opted or backfires were strategically lighted. A two-term limit applied to all offices save county commissioner. Peters relied on loyal advisors and lieutenants, and on arm's-length alliances with certain local leaders and industrialists. Courthouse and candidate assessments covered normal expenses, but business giving was not neglected. In its prime, Peters' machine ran an annual surplus, which was later dissipated.

Although less a businessman and more exclusively a politician than Charles Johnson, Peters took pride in New England parsimony and continued Johnson's policy of the lowest county tax rate in the state. Despite political levies on county jobholders, Peters sternly resisted pressure for salary increases, and the traditional Christmas bonus was usually held to $100. When the local Pennsylvania Economy League told him he could lower taxes no further without committing "false economies" he lowered them anyway. Peters' critics later accused him of penny wisdom and pound foolishness, declaring that he let the courthouse facilities run down without repair, wrongly resisted long-run management improvements because of short-run costs, and borrowed excessively at short term from banks rather than budgeting for a prudent surplus.* (Clearly the county's record low tax rate rested heavily on its large personal property tax receipts, mandated by state law.) Yet Peters did innovate marginally in county programs: he began the county park system by shopping for property at Depression-bargain rates, paying cash, and accepting donations, and he established a planning commission. He was proud of these accomplishments and later explained them as natural outgrowths of his background in landscape architecture. He also installed a police radio system and bookmobile system for suburban and rural benefit, respectively.

Peters' administration was run from the front office. Its logic hinged on public satisfaction (or indifference) and thoroughgoing courthouse control—i.e., on the conduct of the county commissioners. Fred Peters and Foster Hillegas thus served throughout Peters' party leadership, despite personal differences that developed as time went on. An important feature of the system was acquiescence of the minority commissioner. Peters later put it simply: "We picked him." In 1939 Raymond Mensch, an automobile dealer from the German area, became chairman of the moribund Democratic machinery. Most party registrants lived in his part of the county; they were deeply conservative and their Democratic registration was simply traditional. Mensch kept local committee posts vacant, filling them with his friends before the county committee meetings and ensuring his nomination for county commissioner; organized "cutting"† in both parties decided his election; the award of a few county jobs and Mensch's own conservativism encouraged his cooperation with the majority.

Like Johnson, Fred Peters developed a yen for state influence, which in turn could be employed at the county level. It was a logical desire: Montgomery's large population produced lopsided majorities and harbored influential party financiers; Philadelphia's stature in Republican affairs was declining by the 1950's, when the city fell to the Democrats. Early in the forties Peters joined with leaders of Delaware, Chester, and Lancaster Counties against the dominant PMA state faction backed by Joseph Grundy. By 1950 three more nearby county leaders adhered to what was termed the Blue Bell Conference for its meeting

---

* The economy program had its tangible political effects: thus Peters used the county highway department to build roads in municipalities, with the county contributing 60 percent of the cost and the municipality contributing some of the help. As Peters reminisced about it later, he could reduce county taxes himself; but to hold down local levies, he entered this expensive program directly, while creating jobs in the municipalities.

† Under Pennsylvania law each party nominates two candidates for the three commissioner positions, and voters may vote for two; thus one minority member is assured of election, and this frequently leads to party divisions and "cutting"—i.e., voting for only one candidate by minority registrants or for a picked minority party candidate by enough majority registrants to ensure his election.

place in Montgomery County. They backed James Duff for senator and John Fine for governor against the PMA group's gubernatorial choice, Jay Cooke, who was also supported by Joseph Pew. In a hot primary that severely tested the county organization the Duff-Fine ticket carried the state. Lloyd Wood, Peters' county chairman, became lieutenant governor.* In 1954 John Fine, then governor, swung his support to the PMA choice (Pennsylvania's governors cannot succeed themselves.), and Peters, now nearly a king-maker, pressed Lloyd Wood on the Blue Bell Conference and carried him through the primary—only to see the state go Democratic in the general election for the first time since the Depression. One result was Peters' ruination: he had heavily importuned the county's industrialists in the hard-fought campaign (having consumed the party's treasury in Wood's nomination), yet had not produced a winner; Wood's gross, old-fashioned political image (especially on television) was widely blamed for the party's defeat by a youthful opponent; impatient postwar newcomers to the county were now openly challenging Peters in their quest for office; and some old, reliable organizations (including the Lower Merion bastion) were breaking under this pressure. Peters saw the writing on the wall and in 1955 retired to be collector of customs of the Port of Philadelphia, shortly before the expiration of his fifth term as county commissioner. A new interregnum began and lengthened through two county administrations without the emergence of a new leader of the old character.

5. *System and method.* Viewed as systems of incentives and sanctions, the old organizations emphasized income-producing and loyalty-inducing counters: jobs, contracts, retainers; vanity, privity, power. They dealt with individuals, not with publics; with benefits, not with policies. And they operated in the broad ideology of conservative, business-oriented Republicanism in tradition-minded counties where agriculture and industry—not suburban residence merely—had long been leading modes of life.

One class of sanctions and incentives was and still is largely reserved for the licensed professions and local businessmen: the host of state

* By this time state Republican politics had become badly factionalized—a development in which the constitutionally weak governorship was doubtless a factor. There were personal feuds over succession and United States Senate seats among the top politicians, plus a split between Grundy's PMA and several county leaders. Chester, Delaware, Lancaster, Montgomery, Berks, Dauphin, and Northampton Counties adhered to the Blue Bell Conference. During the century three basic forces had developed in the party: the county leaders and organization professionals; the PMA and conservative business ideologues; and the progressives and reformers, beginning with Governor Pinchot and Philadelphia city reformers in the Progressive era. These loose groups were all-important in the populous southeastern counties. In 1950 the contest was between the first two, with Jay Cooke (who lived in Montgomery County) in the second group this time, though historically he belonged to both.

and local retainers for attorneys; finders' fees and tax sales for realtors; loans and contracts for bankers, brokers, suppliers, and contractors; tax assessments on everyone, most important to the least mobile. The list, if not infinite, is better illustrated than catalogued. The number affected in most businesses and professions is and was a distinct minority (though enough perquisities and prospects are available to reach in some way the majority of the members of a county bar association). Clearly, one need not enter politics to make a living, and characteristically the best livings are made without direct political activity. But *if* one commits time to politics, then the sanctions and incentives operate most effectively. The other main class of inducements and disciplines is employment and recognition for the political professionals. As to all of them three observations are in order: this sort of currency remains valid and, indeed, has increased absolutely though not relatively; organizations seem to have differed in the extent to which their resources were employed, but failure to centralize them leads to dissension, and they evidently favor centralization in one-party counties.

Certain occupations—especially law and real estate—have long been associated with political activity. For this there are several reasons: their close business and professional connection with local and county government and policy; the relatively unregulated time and extensive personal contacts they afford; their practitioners' common interest in conserving local values and institutions. One aspect of political recruitment seems remarkable, though its actual incidence is hard to measure: that is the role of inheritance. In the old organizations both elected officials and the local committeemen were often descended from political forebears; recent immigration and competition have diminished this tendency. In stable communities it is hardly surprising that a taste and capacity for politics should be passed on with the family name, local connections, and sometimes the family profession; its effects are less obvious. Probably the tendency favored careerism, conservatism, and organization loyalty if only because connections and activities were simply inherited rather than self-consciously pursued and acquired.

The most striking characteristic of the old organizations was the personal ascendancy of the leader. Formal position was not necessarily a factor: Charles Johnson was actually county chairman during most of his leadership, and Fred Peters was county commissioner; in Bucks and Delaware, on the other hand, Joseph Grundy and John McClure (see Chapter 9) held neither party nor public office. Significantly, each of the last two leaders had extensive business interests that were effectively integrated with politics, albeit in different ways. Grundy's newspapers conferred public influence as well as private gain. If no man's control is complete and any man's rests on the acquiescence of others, it still appears that Grundy's ascendancy in Bucks surpassed that of the Montgomery County leaders because of his economic preeminence and the shortage of political resources in other hands in a rural county.* Montgomery leaders were more severely tested, and financially they relied in some degree on the business community instead of in large part embodying it.

Each county had three main elements of political organization. One was dominion of the courthouse—of jobs and nominations. No one could be county leader without, at the minimum, control of the county commissioners and, for surefire job regulation, of most row officers. With courthouse control went the sanctions and incentives implicit in county government. And allied to courthouse control—its logical extension—was control of nominations to state office and of state patronage through the party headquarters. Since independence might tempt elected officeholders, leaders had to win primary elections when put to the test, and to this capacity job control was critical.

Courthouse supremacy was the leader's own source of strength, and it often rested heavily on his personal attributes. But there were two other aspects of county organization to be reckoned with: one was the business community; the other was the municipal leaders. *Business community* meant industrialists primarily, who were deeply interested in state legislation and county assessments and who, on their side, had personal wealth and private job control. Thus, in Montgomery County, half a dozen manufacturers could easily defray half the cost of general election campaigns. They rarely used their wealth to threaten the county leadership, and they carefully avoided participation in local primary elections. Their very regularity may have diluted their ultimate influence, but they were always consulted on legislative candidacies. Unlike Charles Johnson, Fred Peters sought to maintain independence of the Montgomery industrialists by financing primary elections entirely from courthouse assessments. Commercial influence on party organizations was, and is, less important than industrial influence because the service trades had to compete for county patronage and had less income to offer in return.

The third element was strong local leadership in a few populous municipalities. Both industrial boroughs and suburban subdivisions were important, though their organization for primary control was different. By the twentieth century the uneven distribution of population made possible a few influential local organizations with high voting power in primary and general elections and a modicum of local patronage. Where these organizations developed (and they were not inevitable; some large boroughs and townships were perpetually divided) the desirability of *quid pro quo* arrangements with the county organization

---

* Fred Peters, in an interview, spoke with something like awe of Grundy's arrangement: "He had everything in that county . . . ." He thought that leadership must have been easier in this state of imbalance. Peters, on occasion, was opposed in state primaries by the county's leading papers and some business leaders.

was obvious. The county could offer jobs, nominations, recognition, and some financial highway aid to local leaders; the leaders could offer electoral support. Unless local leaders formed alliances, as they sometimes did, the balance of bargaining power probably rested with the county organization; there were clear gains for each party from a quiet liaison with well-defined spheres of influence and cogent risks in intervention or disagreement.

In these terms the emergence of strong individual leaders seems understandable, even apart from the decline of party competition in Bucks and Montgomery. With larger populations and primary elections, politics was more nearly a full-time occupation. Courthouse control became more important with primary elections and the rise of large local organizations. Industrial concern with state policy increased, and county industrial organizations found it convenient to work with stable political organizations. From everyone's standpoint, stability was most likely to occur where consultation and control of the main bases of politics were centralized. There were sufficient resources to ensure stability, but only if someone related them. This the leaders did in a utilitarian fashion, but the function required talent and timing, since contenders were always in sight.

This organizational economy was facilitated by two contextual factors. One was the Republican dominance that, save for a brief Depression interlude, endured in Pennsylvania from the beginning of the century till its midpoint, and that enhanced the influence of county organizations on state policy and patronage, thus enlarging their political resources. The ruling party was heavily influenced by business, especially industries and utilities, in finance and philosophy, though divisions occurred in the Pinchot period and increased after the Depression. The other, related, factor was the conservatism of the counties —especially in the rural German areas, the business and the professional community, and the affluent suburbs. There were few publics for county policy; only the tax rate commanded attention. In this context the political organization quietly flourished as a nearly closed economy of inducements and contributions.

Thus the county developed more highly as a political than as a governmental unit, with its governmental functions heavily weighted toward limited political ends.

7

Bucks County

In the foregoing analysis of the old organizations one can see what kinds of contextual changes might have undermined them. Indeed, it is perhaps too easy to discover a few broad trends and to extrapolate these to a radical new future for county politics. In brief, what happened in Bucks and Montgomery was rapid population and economic growth. These produced new interests in competition, and reduced the old mobilization of bias. The growth rates were greatest in Bucks and least in Delaware.

Bucks' population influx after 1950 has already been described, together with its distinguishing characteristics of youth and blue-collar status in a suburban county. Many new families came from Philadelphia, and a number from Pennsylvania's economically declining coal counties. They brought new attitudes toward politics and government; many of them were Democrats. They swiftly altered the electoral balance in lower Bucks: by 1953 the Democrats carried some municipalities there and threatened others. By 1954 nearly half the county vote was cast in lower Bucks—the region south of Newtown—whose new state legislative seat fell to the Democrats. The county registration margin narrowed from about 3:1 Republican in 1951 to 2:1 in 1955 (by 1961 it reached 5:4). Since in the suburban counties Democratic votes usually exceed Democratic registrations substantially, the trend was upsetting.* In the gubernatorial election of 1954 Lloyd Wood (a weak candidate) won only 51 percent. That election had a galvanizing effect on both parties.

* The disparity between registration and election ratios probably means that normally Democratic voters register Republican for one or more of several reasons: social conformity, concern about sanctions like tax assessments, or a desire to participate in the local primaries of the dominant party, perhaps especially in school board elections. The difference between ratios is usually most marked in state and national elections and in counties where the registration ratio is most one-sided; as that ratio narrows the reasons for registering Republican are less operative.

Democrats sensed a new majority; Republicans sought to reorganize, and their new county chairman declared the next day: "This means to me that there has to be a generous shakeup in county row-office employees who have been working for years on the same job and turning in very few votes at election."[1]

In late 1954, as both parties looked ahead, the new electorate was of overriding importance, but organization was also a serious problem. Before the great immigration the Democratic party had contained roughly a quarter of the county's registrants, concentrated in rural, German upper Bucks and urban, industrial lower Bucks. The Germans were conservative, while industrial Bristol was the center of a strong CIO labor organization that began with the wartime Kaiser plant and later assimilated the Fairless steelworkers. Bucks' labor movement was one of the first in the nation to fulfill the 1954 AFL-CIO merger at the local level; its membership was loyal and was actively led by men who sensed new opportunities. From Doylestown (middle Bucks) these disparate elements were led in the postwar period by John Welsh, a native real estate dealer of Irish Catholic descent, then in his late thirties— dedicated Democrat, devoted Bucks Countian, complete politician. These attributes are emphasized because all informants agree on them; Welsh's party leadership became controversial, and his governmental role is important in this study. In 1954 Welsh was minority county commissioner as well as county Democratic chairman; in a close race for the former post in 1951 he had barely defeated a Bristol labor leader— a sign and minor incitement of tensions to come.

In 1951 Grundy's Republican organization faced its first primary fight in years. Neither of Grundy's county commissioner candidates hailed from lower Bucks, and an opposition slate appeared emphasizing its lower Bucks affinity. The organization won easily, but temporarily. By 1953 several lower Bucks municipalities were involved in tough factional battles between newcomers and oldtimers—and even among newcomers. Personal ambition was not the only issue; sharp differences often emerged over services, taxes, and patterns of community development. Old local organizations based on friendship, tradition, and inertia were easily broken up as political substance and style changed radically.

Joseph Grundy was ninety in 1953. He sold his mills and withdrew from banking; in 1954 he sold his newspapers and in September—before the gubernatorial election—resigned from the Republican county committee. Death and infirmity prevented his old lieutenants from succeeding him.

The new county chairman was considered an outsider and opportunist. An ex-vaudeville performer and theatrical agent, he had come to Bucks County in 1937 and opened a roadside stand which became a nightclub, El Rancho. He began as Republican committeeman and justice of the peace (significantly, a fee-producing office). In 1951 Grundy slated him for county coroner; by 1954 he was also treasurer of the county campaign committee and was busily collecting committee proxies in upper Bucks before the party reorganization. With these proxies and some support in the executive committee Russell Ferris won the chairmanship without open opposition. This slipshod succession soon brought short-term disaster to the party in the county election.

Predictably, both parties faced primaries in 1955. The Democratic opposition turned out to be negligible, though its source was significant: a lower Bucks labor leader, with the public support of most of his colleagues, challenged John Welsh and his lower Bucks running mate, but secured less than 20 percent of the light primary vote.*

The Republican contest was more exciting. Late in 1954 the county's longtime president judge retired, and the bar association sent the governor its customary list of acceptable aspirants. Passing over these suggestions, the governor named the counsel for the corporation that developed Fairless Hills. He was a newcomer to the county and lacked the experience of trial work that is traditional among rural and suburban lawyers. In the outraged conjecture over the appointment the new county chairman bore much of the censure together with the burden of supporting the new judge in the primary election. One of the neglected candidates was slated by the Democrats in the general election. The lawyers' committee formed to support him included the retiring county judge, most leaders of the county bar, and a coterie of young lawyers then just entering Republican politics—in all, three-fourths of the bar association's seventy-eight members. The county bar included many social notables, and its members were proud of the quality of its court, which the lawyers felt had been respected by the old political order. When a write-in effort in the Republican primary failed most lawyers campaigned for the Democratic candidate, confining their rebellion to the judgeship.† They campaigned hard and even hired a New York public relations man; the venture was a formative influence on several future political careers.

In the fall election the Democrats emphasized the judgeship issue in a platform new to county politics, one that pledged a specific list of programs and reforms in county government.‡ Six weeks before the election they played their trump card: they accused the Republican

* Adolph Andrews, Welsh's running mate, was to serve two terms as county commissioner. He listed himself as a "time study engineer," had completed his education at Bensalem High School, and had lived in Bucks County for twenty-seven years.

† In Pennsylvania judicial candidates—but no one else—may enter both party primaries. The rule permits observation of the sitting-judge principle.

‡ Democratic advertising promised (1) to elect qualified judges free of political obligations, (2) to promote industrial expansion so as to maintain high employment, (3) to establish bipartisan representation on all commissions, (4) to clean out political "drones" and reform and automate the courthouse, (5) to reorganize completely the county assessor's office and to speed the tax equalization program, (6) to establish county parks and recreational facilities; (7) to expand the mental health program with emphasis on early childhood difficulties. The Republicans emphasized economy and continued good government.

county chairman, Ferris, as county coroner, of embezzlement through false expense accounts. The district attorney—an impeccable Republican from an old county family—opened an investigation and asked state police assistance. Ferris resigned the party chairmanship to fight the charges; soon he was arrested and indicted, and he finished his campaign for reelection while free on bail. He was later convicted. He and the incumbent judge both lost the election by 2:1 margins, and the Democrats narrowly carried both their commissioner candidates and two of the five row offices at issue.

Despite heavy ticket-splitting it seems unlikely that the Democrats could have won without the Ferris scandal. In electing two county commissioners by a hair's breadth they achieved a Democratic administration, though Republicans controlled most row offices. Bucks' business, professional, social, and civic leaders were still overwhelmingly Republican, but the 1955 election made party competition at least a temporary reality. This changed the pattern of county politics, reflecting local socioeconomic changes.

In reviewing events since 1955 two themes will be pursued alternately: the conduct of politics and the conduct of government. The relation between them is left for later discussion. Two contextual factors in Bucks' development bear emphasis. First, the county was becoming a new society: many of its businessmen, professionals, and politicians, and its leading newspaper publishers, were new men. In the lower Bucks boom they sensed large opportunities; these stimulated a more free-wheeling, less-inhibited pursuit than had obtained in the old order, and they provoked conflicts of value, as well as of interest, affecting the conduct of politics. Second, in the conduct of government the old order was already responding to change, as Joseph Grundy gradually loosened his political hold. The administration of 1952-56 had hesitantly begun programs that later were much enlarged: the planning commission, the park board, a new county courthouse, real property reassessment. By referendum in 1953 a county health board was established, and the commissioners built a juvenile detention home and began expansion of the county home for the aged. In that administration John Welsh served as minority commissioner and stimulated some of these beginnings. His experience provoked the Democratic platform of 1955.

The new administration could fairly be termed the Welsh administration. Its acts were implicitly the chairman's, reflecting his convictions about county government. Welsh cooperated with the working press, and his administration was cordially reported, though he also stripped the old Grundy papers of county printing and advertising contracts—a move that brought retaliation later. He early announced reappointment of several Republican employees, including the chief clerk; a salary raise for all courthouse workers; cancellation of the county's insurance policies; and a new method of awarding the business. He followed a bipartisan policy in appointments to boards and commissions. Within

two weeks of taking office the commissioners (of whom two were holdovers: Welsh and the minority member) announced an increase in the
estimated budget of more than 25 percent. Health board and private
hospital appropriations were nearly doubled, and the park board budget
went from $10,000 to $110,000; Welsh observed that these increases followed platform commitments. The county solicitor was set to exploring
state law on industrial development, and the first county promotional
agency in the state was appointed in the summer of 1956. Later that year
the mosquito-control program was enlarged, and a library board was
appointed to administer a new bookmobile operation. These programs
substantially raised county expenditures, and a new courthouse drastically increased the bonded debt. Nevertheless per capita operating expenditures increased by only a third, little more than the previous
administration's increase. Population growth, large state aids, and new
assessments meant that per capita taxes did not increase in the Welsh
administration, nor did the county tax rate.

Two projects inherited from the old administration were expanded
and soon clouded in controversy. John Welsh was devoted to both of
them. One was the new county courthouse. Joseph Grundy had opposed
the project, favoring purchase of an old inn across the street as an annex
to stave off the cost of construction. This transaction required judicial
sanction, and the county court appointed a grand jury to consider it.
Welsh, as minority commissioner, badly wanted a new courthouse and,
over the lukewarm opposition of his majority colleagues, persuaded the
grand jury to veto the alternative. An architect's contract for a new
courthouse was let, but the location was yet to be decided when Welsh
became chairman. This point required the advice (though not the approval) of the planning commission. The planning staff preferred a new,
open location at the edge of Doylestown for parking accommodations
and architectural compatibility; Welsh strongly preferred the existing
site, which was surrounded by lawyers, brokers, bondsmen, and other
businessmen whose pressure he must have felt. The Philadelphia archi-
tects sided with Welsh. Despite recommendations of the grand jury and
planning commission, numerous editorials, and a taxpayer's suit, Welsh
commenced test borings and later placed the new courthouse in the
old location. Before its completion the original estimates were several
times overrun and Welsh incurred severe criticism for it throughout his
administration; but he proudly took credit for the courthouse.

The other hot potato was tax equalization, i.e., resassessment. In 1951
Bucks, as a fifth-class county, came under a general legislative mandate
to commence reassessment of its property rolls by 1957. (Third class
counties, including Delaware and Montgomery were not included in the
law.) Bucks' commissioners delayed action for nearly the length of their
term, although Welsh, sensing an issue for the minority, kept goading
them. In the spring of 1955 the first stage began with a contract for
aerial photographic maps. Early in the Welsh administration the second

phase followed with a contract for reassessment of the entire county. To critics of the contractual approach Welsh replied that it had entailed no county debt or increased millage. Under steady pressure from the administration the project was nearly finished by the 1959 election— when it became a serious political liability.

By the 1959 election the Republicans, in opposition, had achieved some unity; the Democrats, with their administration and state patronage, were deeply divided. In the Republican party an alliance of younger elements and several county-squire lawyers grew from the 1955 campaign divisions and soon forced from power the supporters of Russell Ferris—a group identified, through Grundy, with the old-fashioned PMA faction in the state party. A new county chairman was selected, the executive committee was enlarged, reporting and publications were begun, and the list of financial contributors was expanded. A modern party, more broadly based and public relations conscious, was established on the county level, while the precinct work was taken over in lower Bucks by comparative newcomers and continued elsewhere by oldtimers. The Eisenhower presidential election of 1956 provided a lift after the local defeat of 1955. In 1957 the party beat back a primary challenge from the oldtimers and scored a clean sweep of the county row offices. Two loose factions remained: the old county officers and holdovers from the Grundy era, and the youthful group based in lower Bucks County. Conflict was tactfully managed by delegation to regional chairmen and by relatively open primaries. Factional lines could not long be clearly drawn in terms of new versus old; contrasts in political style cut across the early division and would later become acute.

Differences in political style are hard to analyze uninvidiously. They afflicted the Democrats, also, in a long fight for party control between regulars and insurgents. The division had an obvious base in conflicting ambitions: for many Democrats in lower Bucks politics was an avenue of social advancement in an environment more malleable than the city or the coal counties; yet, despite state patronage and local fee-paying elective offices, there were not enough remuneration and recognition to go around. John Welsh, for his part, took a dim view of Johnny-come-latelies. As he saw it, the party was his party, maintained in lean years by his devotion; newcomers should demonstrate their loyalty and wait their turn. However understandably Irish his reaction, friends and foes agreed about Welsh's autocracy, his tactlessness in expressing it, and his adeptness at reaching into insurgent ranks to pick out weak sisters for slating or patronage. Issues of program and organization compounded conflicts of ambition. One hard core of insurgency developed around a group of newcomers from Philadelphia who emphasized liberalism and activism, public relations and participation as the bases of the party. Welsh's conservatism and old-fashioned organization philosophy antagonized this group; his blunt resistance to the claims of labor leaders spread alienation further. Regional and cultural differences overlay these divisions: in the conservative north and urban south an Irish Catholic politician, Jewish liberals, and ambitious labor leaders reflected different constituencies and traditions.

Conflicts of policy and ambition were mixed in the tax assessment of U.S. Steel in Falls Township. Until 1962, when Bucks became a third-class county, the commissioners served as a tax board. When the Fairless plant was first built they provisionally assessed it at $3 million while the Falls Township assessor valued it at $14 million; when the township appealed a compromise was reached at $8 million while construction continued. As the plant neared completion the county reassessed it at about $21 million, and the township again appealed. Welsh alone, as minority commissioner then, supported its appeal for a $30 million figure. The 1955 election that produced the Welsh administration also installed a Democratic majority in Falls Township and an evenly divided local school board. When in 1956 the new school board confidently carried a fresh assessment appeal to the new county commissioners, they were dismayed to learn that Welsh had changed his mind; their appeal was denied. Here the narrative rests on conjecture about motives. Welsh says he still felt $30 million was about right, but that the appeal should await the county's overall professional assessment and completion of the Fairless plant. He was concerned lest seeming harassment of the steelworks slow further industrial development, and he was advised by his county solicitor that state law sustained the exemptions sought by U.S. Steel. For their part, Falls Democrats were committed to an increase because they had long campaigned for it: they argued that calculations of the State Tax Equalization Board set a higher valuation on the township than the county did, thus reducing state school subsidies, while the county was reducing tax assessments, and they privately suspected a deal between Welsh and the steel company.

Thus the township continued its appeals to the county, and in the 1955 primary Falls Democrats entered their own man for commissioner, who lost. Then the insurgents faced the question of whether to support Welsh in the general election. They approached him and, it appears, obtained his agreement to an assessment increase in return for electoral support. When reports of this hit the newspapers Welsh repudiated any suggestion of a deal; Falls Democrats then made a deal with the Republicans and organized a "cut" of Welsh in the general election. The cut, revengeful or not, was effective, and Welsh was retired from county office.

In the 1959 election campaign, as reported in the press, policy issues were more heavily emphasized than ever. The Democratic platform hailed the new county services and facilities, and the administration's experience. The Republican platform, strongly backing county parks and industrial development, charged extravagance against experience: it promised a hard look at spending (especially by the health board) to reduce county taxes and to make room for rising local expenditures; at the same time it proposed adding an historical commission, a tourist bureau, and an industrial exposition to the county's promotional resources, and a police radio system and traveling-registrar program to its custodial activities. One may doubt the public impact of written programs but still accept them as specific pledges and bids to limited publics. Platforms in Bucks were at least briefly acquiring the significance of being carried out; this held good after the Republican victory in 1959 as it had in the preceding administration.

In retrospect the Republican victory seems more to have been expected than to be explained. By 1959 party registration had stabilized at about 55 to 45 in the Republicans' favor, and the election produced the same ratio. Nevertheless, the Democrats' rejection in lower Bucks was surprising. Three reasons were commonly cited. One was the Democratic divisions and organized labor's open lack of support. Another factor was an emerging scandal in Bristol Township's Democratic school board (the sale of promotions) at a time when rising school taxes were raising concern; that township then cast one sixth of the total county vote, and the Democrats lost it despite a large registration majority. Later the cause that seemed most important to many was the tax assessment program and its treatment in the newspapers. One Republican candidate repeatedly charged that the administration had completed the assessment but was holding up notices until after the election; Welsh replied that final figures remained under study and would be released, as promised, in January. Whatever the state of the assessment review, the Bristol *Courier* gave the campaign charges a careful buildup and on the day before the election it headlined an exclusive report, leaked from the courthouse, that county taxes—not simply assessments —were due to increase one-third: later the paper took credit for ousting the administration, and many politicians in both parties agreed.

Thus the legend and perhaps the fact of this paper's influence in Bucks County politics was begun. Under new ownership in 1955 it had not played a large role in that year's elections; since then its circulation had increased five times, far outstripping the population increase. Though vigorously Republican, it had backed Welsh's new county programs, sharing credit for them with the county. Angered by deprivation of county advertising and anxious to reassert the paper's old Republican influence, the publisher gave an order to "pull out all the stops" in the 1959 campaign.

Having won the election, the Republicans soon divided, like the Democrats, into rival camps, producing what a discerning journalist termed Bucks' four-party system. The new administration contained one holdover Democrat and two new Republicans. Where upper, middle, and lower Bucks had all been represented, there were now two lower Bucks men and a Doylestown lawyer, John Justus Bodley. Then forty-three, Bodley had been raised in Doylestown and returned there to practice after a stint with the FBI and legal work in Philadelphia. A conservative, he had sought office in the past with the backing of the old PMA faction, and in 1959 he was PMA's counsel in Bucks County.

The dominant figure, however, turned out to be Edward B. Boyer of lower Bucks. "Eddie" Boyer moved to Levittown from Philadelphia in 1951; like the Falls Township Democratic insurgents, he was one of the first Levittowners. In time, as his income and political prospects improved, he removed from the lower-priced home in Tullytown to a "country clubber" in Middletown, complete with swimming pool, but he remained within Levittown. Salesman for an office supply firm, Boyer was genial and energetic; he entered politics immediately and was soon a political force in lower Bucks with a large personal following. By 1955 he was president of the Lower Bucks Republican Club; in the 1956 reorganization he became regional party chairman for lower Bucks and was generally credited with the party revival there. By 1959 he was clearly in the small group that most nearly controlled the party and probably closest of any to the county chairman. When Boyer sought the commissionership in 1959 it seemed entirely appropriate, and he accepted "Jus" Bodley as his running mate.

Boyer and Bodley did not hit it off. Although Bodley acknowledged Boyer's claim to chairmanship of the commissioners, he refused to move it at their first meeting and left Boyer to do so himself. After the initial displacement of Democratic jobholders and board members Boyer gradually allied with the lower Bucks minority commissioner, isolating Bodley in votes on patronage and county programs, and controlling the salary board, tax board, and strategic developmental authorities. The intraparty division took in both personnel and policy. The Boyer administration raised salaries of selected employees and increased courthouse personnel. Nonetheless, the economy pledge was honored in some fields, and there was a perceptible shift in policy from the preceding administration: spending for parks and planning was reduced at first (later increased); industrial development and infrastructure were emphasized. The county established an historical and tourist commission, a soil conservation district, a water and sewer authority, an airport authority, and a redevelopment authority; began study of a port authority; and joined a regional mass-transit subsidy system. (Several of these initiatives stemmed from pressures and studies begun in the Welsh administration.) It worked responsively with the Industrial Development Corporation, involving its officers and directors in new county programs. Some projects were opposed by Bodley on philosophical grounds—e.g., that full legal sanction for a water and sewer authority was doubtful and its sectional emphasis inequitable and that redevelopment was an unwarranted extension of an urban emergency program reflecting the myth that federal funds are free. Yet he favored transportation and terminal projects with federal subsidies, and Boyer coolly noted that Bodley was counsel for a Doylestown airport seeking county aid. Bodley stressed the same side of Boyer's progressive projects: the susceptible solicitors and engineers taken on by authorities, the opportunities for developers, contractors, and consultants—the bases for patronage and financial gain.

That attention should center on motivation of the new measures was nearly inevitable, for most of them were undertaken after the break between Boyer and Bodley was completed by an astonishing incident. Toward the end of the administration's first year Eddie Boyer was indicted for extorting political funds from lower Bucks discount houses in return for police neglect of Sunday blue-law violations. Jus Bodley supplied information that helped establish the charges. In the sensational trial that followed Boyer was acquitted, but the Republican district attorney made no secret of his disappointment in the outcome. When Boyer's announced retirement from active politics proved temporary a deep breach opened in the party organization; for nearly everyone remembered 1955.

As in 1955, there were two reactions: one to close ranks and repair the damage, the other to clean house. Fred Ziegler, county chairman since 1956, took the first line. Some younger elements were more militant, demanding extirpation of all Boyer influence in the executive committee. They formed a reforming Alliance and were in turn fired from party office. There followed an all-out primary fight between the Alliance and the organization. Both Bucks' daily newspaper publishers and lower Bucks' most influential weekly backed the Alliance together with most old county families and professional leadership. On the organization's side were the county committee, many local committeemen of implicit organization loyalty, half the courthouse row officers, and a few important local leaders. Here again, in high degree, was a contest of party organization against public relations. The Alliance won decisively, and the daily papers were generally held responsible. The district attorney was elected county chairman. The party was again reorganized: executive committee posts were made elective rather than appointive; the county was redistricted to split lower Bucks and enlarge upper Bucks' representation. The Boyer-Ziegler faction went into opposition and, for a time, retained its hold in the courthouse and a few municipalities. Eddie Boyer continued as chairman of the county commissioners in coalition with the minority member, but he did not run for reelection the next year and the candidate of his dwindling faction was defeated in the primary. The Alliance victory then seemed complete.

For some Alliance leaders the party division was a straight-forward question of ethics; they feared enrichment of a few politicians and promoters from the new county agencies and their municipal counterparts. For others it was a subtle matter of style; they disliked Boyer's covert Philadelphia connections, his urban approach to party organization, the favoritism and inefficiency in the courthouse. For a few it was a simple exercise in political survival; Boyerism meant defection and defeat. For most old organization hands the question of style was uppermost, and other issues smacked of vindictiveness or opportunism; they placed organization loyalty above public relations. Although both sides saw the issue in personal terms, the Boyer faction remarked some social and policy divisions, too. They observed that central Bucks was the primary election's critical battleground, claiming a preponderance of committee support for the old organization in upper and lower Bucks, where the new politicians of lower social standing and the old Grundy elements predominated. Central Bucks, they argued, was the region of the county's social elite, which, allied with the all-powerful newspapers, had turned the organization out. This interpretation, in which regional and social divisions were partly tied to cleavage over political style, appears sound from an analysis of the personnel on both sides. To this the Boyerites added that their opponents were mainly conservatives resisting progress and innovation in county policy—a less accurate interpretation. There were conservatives and progressives on both sides, although people most directly interested in industrial development and infrastructure (which the Boyer administration was emphasizing) for the most part either inclined toward Boyer or were neutral, and those with interests in fields like planning, open space, residential amenity, and health and welfare were more likely to be found in the Alliance. Orientations toward substantive policy and political style were loosely related.

During most of the Boyer administration divisions within the two political parties were more bitter than were interparty differences. The Democrats could hardly capitalize on Republican differences, for their own county commissioner had collaborated with Boyer—and their own differences soon resulted in a trial by jury.

When the Democrats left county office their feuding increased. "Johnny" Welsh's handpicked party chairman from lower Bucks began to listen to others once county patronage was lost; state patronage, after all, belonged to the county chairman. Entreaties from state headquarters held the party together for a time; then Welsh declared war. In the spring primary of 1962—while the Republicans were locked in struggle —Welsh also overturned his party organization and reassumed the chairmanship. Thus in both parties incumbent organizations were beaten; in both, the forces based in central Bucks had divided and defeated populous lower Bucks.

Control of state patronage proved Welsh's undoing. In the fall, at a meeting of state turnpike workers, Welsh discussed the coming election and the financial needs of the party in frank and, some felt, threatening terms. His opponents had, in anticipation, brought a Philadelphia newspaperman to the meeting; the next morning the county chairman's remarks were public knowledge. Pressure mounted on the district attorney to prosecute his personal friend and partisan counterpart for illegal "macing" (obtaining political contributions by coercion). With evident reluctance and with urging from the state Republican party, the prosecution began; Welsh was indicted two years (nearly to the day) after "Eddie" Boyer. In a highly publicized trial he was acquitted of utterances that technically constitute "macing." His defense was heavily based on character witnesses widely drawn from the county's social, professional, and business leadership—most of it Republican. Many of these testimonials came from people who deeply admired Welsh's work as county commissioner and believed in his loyalty to Bucks County.

Welsh's trial precluded his candidacy for county commissioner in 1963 had he wished to run. The party endorsed two principled, liberal insurgents from lower Bucks. (Cynics said Welsh expected to lose the election.) In the primary they defeated the incumbent minority commissioner and the president of the AFL-CIO council. The Republican organization nominated the titular head of the Alliance to run with "Jus" Bodley. In the fall campaign both sides criticized the conduct of the Boyer administration while generally accepting its works. Few new programs were proposed and economy was promised; by this time most county options had been exercised and local taxes were a salient issue in lower Bucks. The Republicans won with a margin equal to their registration advantage of 55 percent.

In this election labor's official disaffection from the Democratic leadership was completed: its joint council endorsed the Republican candidates, though individual leaders protested and went their own way. Prospects for healing the Democratic rift appeared dim because personal differences seemed irreconcilable; yet it prevented the organization effort essential to victory in lower Bucks or an effective appeal to marginal voters throughout the county. Compromise seemed impossible; but the party would probably lose, too, if either group vanquished the other, for its base would then be too narrow. With registration, the press, and Democratic divisions in their favor the Republican position was strong but not impregnable. Bucks could still be termed competitive.

Before leaving office the lame-duck Boyer coalition took two controversial steps in public welfare: it let expensive contracts for a large medical extension of the county home for the aged, and it accepted the proposal of a citizens' committee for a professional child care agency. With these measures it perversely continued to innovate—perhaps because the Republican candidates had pledged similar measures together with economy. Some of the economy, like the innovation, appears to have been factionally motivated: the new commissioners drastically pruned the operating budgets of old Boyer authorities (sewer and water, industrial development, urban redevelopment, even the park board, whose spending and condemnations were becoming unpopular in tax-conscious lower Bucks), and stressed professional qualifications in replacing Boyerite courthouse incumbents. The substance of the old programs remained, however, and a few new ones were undertaken, of which the most expensive was a two-year community college.

Population change in Bucks County brought party competition. The early advent of a Democratic administration, based on the political accidents of 1955, enhanced it and—it will be argued later—enlarged its influence on county government.

More broadly, the new population induced *political* competition— rivalry for position within the parties and an emphasis on elections, both primary and general. This altered party organization. Each party, but especially the Republican, sought to broaden representation of the rank and file, though both failed to control factionalism. In the Republican party the financial pattern changed to one of reliance on a large number of contributors; in neither party was financial support highly centralized or dependent on corporate or union giving.*

In both parties state and county jobs remained important for finance and discipline in primary elections. But both parties—especially the Republican—found supporters and participants to offset the patronage. Such activists were of critical importance in the upset primary elections of 1962. Political leaders in the large municipalities were also influential —but in the largest communities of lower Bucks these leaders faced rivalry and party competition. Thus both parties were as much county structures as leagues of local leaders. The broadening of party finance, the lack of secure local organizations, the emergence of circles of party activists offsetting the jobholders and of rivalry for office and party position all undermined the old foundations and reinforced public competition.

In this competition there were persisting, cross-cutting divisions within the parties besides the intense ambitions of individuals. One was regional—the recognition of lower Bucks and the fear of neglect in upper Bucks. Another was rivalry between old and new elements for status and influence. A third was cultural: implicit social differences between new urban minorities and some business, professional, and publishing men who formed something of a social elite despite the absence of exclusive institutions or an organized establishment. The question of what type of person was appointed to county boards and commissions reflected this social dissonance, though conventional ethical issues were also involved. In the Democratic party labor's dissatisfaction with Welsh's personal leadership was a continuing irritation. And there were

* In each party the annual budget ran around $50,000. Roughly half the Republican budget came from givers in the $100-$500 range (the Century Club), the remainder from small contributors (including jobholders) and a few heavy givers. The Democrats relied more heavily on fund-raising affairs and on state jobholders (up to 1963); they received little direct aid from labor unions, and as noted above, indirect union aid was probably of small value. Both parties received some assistance from the state organizations, chiefly in state and national campaigns.

different conceptions of political style—between patronage and public relations—that were enlarged by enthusiasts to moral differences. None of these divisions overlapped exactly, and alignments often shifted, but it is clear that some cleavages reenforced one another and that all of them existed in both parties.

Contrasting views of public policy were not directly involved in the divisions between or within the parties. In the Democratic party some of the insurgents thought of themselves as authentic liberals and of Welsh as a conservative, but these views mostly referred to political style and national policy. Welsh saw himself as a fiscal conservative, but his county administration made the sharpest break with the past, and when two liberal, erstwhile insurgents ran for commissioner in 1963 they emphasized economy. Republican factionalism was no more consistent. The two instigators of the anti-Boyer Alliance were a labor-endorsed state legislator and a Goldwater backer. It does appear, however, that most members of the Alliance were more interested in things like physical amenity and social welfare than was Boyer, who empha-sized industrial development and utilities—fields in which social progress and private profit were complementary.

As political competition developed in Bucks it had more directly to do with personal advancement and party position than with public policy. It was intraparty as much as interparty. It took in sectional and social differences. It occurred in a developing context of limited-interest groups pressing for action in spheres like conservation, indus-trial and commercial growth, and public welfare. Several of these interests were either created or encouraged by governmental action— e.g., Bucks' Industrial Development Corporation. Some persons were active in several spheres of policy—but there was no evidence of a single-peaked power structure. Instead, there was a constellation of private interests in development, more often individual than institu-tional, more commercial than industrial, together with residents and professionals who pressed for more emphasis on amenity and welfare as relatively neglected public interests, and who won some attention for them. Once competition and selective interest in county action began, the newspapers' potential for influence was enhanced because public information became more important; the papers sought leadership and readership for business reasons. Thus Bucks came to a system of political competition, interest group organization, and mass communica-tion focused on county government. Activists were drawn from most regions, interests, and social conditions. They remained a small enough group so that, in a large county, most of the leaders knew one another and, in collaboration or competition, could communicate directly.

8

Montgomery County

Politically and geographically Montgomery County stands between Bucks' change and Delaware's stasis, shortly to be described. Montgomery remained a one-party county, sociologically and electorally the most Republican of the three. But over a decade a modicum of competition developed within the majority party, and county government altered perceptibly.

Two factional episodes in Fred Peters' reign betokened future competition. In 1945 Peters broke with the long-time political leader of Lower Merion, supporting a rival primary candidate for treasurer and (implicitly) leader of the county's largest township. Peters won the fight, but Lower Merion—really a host of communities—was never wholly reunited and later became a potent source of county political divisions. In 1950 Peters faced a serious primary challenge when the "Blue Bell boys'" state ticket was opposed by the late Jay Cooke of Montgomery, a prominent party financier. Cooke, in his campaign for the governorship, attracted most of Peters' early opponents for the county leadership plus some newcomers seeking to break in. One such newcomer was young Elkins Wethérill, whose wealth and impeccable social connections seemed to make him a natural for Montgomery County politics. Peters beat back the challenge and, characteristically, adopted Wetherill —who would, however, challenge the regulars again.

By Peters' retirement in 1955 the trend toward competition was confirmed: there was more erosion of local control, more pressure from the next generation. Most of Montgomery's growth occurred in well-to-do suburban areas where its main effects were to alter local leadership and the county-wide balance among municipalities. Most county contestants still had deep roots in their communities. This company included minorities—especially Italians—from the old industrial boroughs who, as businessmen and professionals, put heavy pressure on the party for nomination. With wealthy new residents—especially Jews in the York Road region—they later formed their own leagues and councils for greater party influence. Their constituencies were subject to Democratic inroads.

There were also important continuities. Several of the old local leaders remained in command, usually grouped in loose regional alliances; and the manufacturers maintained their financial support, if more cautiously than before. Political differences centered on recognition, not policy. The largest, most influential localities were the most affluent and self-sufficient; the heaviest individual contributors were conservative.

In the administration that followed Peters' in 1956 the dominant figure was Walter Hammonds, whom Peters had earlier elected treasurer of Lower Merion Township. Hammonds sought control of the party organization, but lacked the strength to elect a county chairman. Instead, as county commissioner, he fought with party chairmen over courthouse patronage and incited primary contests in Lower Merion and the county. His first antagonist was the county's Congressman (also from Lower Merion), who, as a compromise, "harmony" chairman, enlarged the party's executive committee to recognize all regions and factions—unsuccessfully. The next chairman was James Staudinger, a York Road insurance man and political leader of Abington Township, which would soon succeed Lower Merion as the county's largest municipality. Staudinger tried to restore control by *reducing* the size of the executive committee. Courthouse discipline had badly lapsed by then, and Lower Merion's factionalism was obstinate. There seemed no way to repair the foundations until the end of the administration and Hammonds' anticipated retirement to Florida.

In policy the Hammonds administration was largely negative. Its principal actions were the emasculation of county planning (described in Chapter 12) and its leadership in defeating a proposed county health department (described in Chapter 16). It did establish a redevelopment authority and a tentative industrial development committee and authorized a soil-conservation district, but all these agencies were inactive. It sustained the county's traditions of low taxes and local autonomy, responding to its fundamental forces of rural conservatism, old industries, and rich suburbs. Nevertheless, the political events preceding its retirement appeared at the time to mark at least a minor turning point.

In 1959 party slate-makers faced continuing factionalism. Chairman Staudinger concluded he would have to be county commissioner to help restore party discipline. This meant replacing Hammonds' cohort, who, like Staudinger, hailed from the York Road region, and Hammonds responded with a threat to fire large numbers of courthouse jobholders. Traditionally one commissioner had represented Lower Merion—which paid nearly half the county taxes—but Lower Merion could not agree on a candidate. In this tangle, Staudinger's slate-making committee of elder party statesmen temporized; by and large they nominated themselves, including Staudinger for county controller. The ticket posed three outstanding omissions: Lower Merion had no commissioner; the incumbent district attorney, an Italian, was dropped; and Elkins Wetherill, then county treasurer and legally ineligible to repeat, was not on it either.

The district attorney was an interim appointee who had antagonized party leaders by flamboyant statements about gambling in the county; he was strongly supported by his staff of young Republican lawyers just beginning in county politics. He filed for the primary. So did Elkins Wetherill, who had been groomed for higher office by Peters and Hammonds. As a candidate for commissioner Wetherill could call on inherited social connections and an acquired political background in Harrisburg and Norristown. Joining with Lower Merion's principal candidate for commissioner, he compiled his own slate of "modern Republicans," endorsed the incumbent district attorney, and ran for election.

The modern Republican campaign was not about policy, but neither was it solely a quest of dissidents for office. It seems to have been a brief confrontation of social constituencies. Against the organization the moderns mobilized two small but important forces. One was a group of young, politically ambitious lawyers and businessmen angered by the mediocrity and decrepitude of the organization slate; this group furnished the energy and personnel. Another was a coterie of county families tied to the Philadelphia financial community, rather than to local industry; this group furnished the money. It included Jay Cooke, with whom Wetherill had campaigned for governor against Fred Peters in 1950.* The two groups, young and old, were united by Cooke's son-in-law, who served as campaign manager. Both personnel and money were used hard: every poll in the county was manned on election day, and some $50,000 were raised and spent—spectacular achievements in a primary campaign. In the outcome, Wetherill edged out one organization commissioner candidate, and a single row office was won; the Italian district attorney, who was loosely identified with the modern Republicans, defeated the organization with strong support from the Protestant pulpits, neutralizing some organization elements. The moderns ran best along the Main Line (especially Lower Merion) and in the newer residential sections.

The primary seemed a personal victory for Wetherill but was not itself decisive of party control. In the aftermath the young moderns looked to Wetherill to build a more effective organization. Wetherill,

* Cooke was the great-grandson of Jay Cooke (1821-1905), the financier of the Civil War. A Philadelphia investment banker who later moved to Montgomery, he was for a time in the 1930's the principal angel of the state Republican party and later, like his father, a member of the Republican National Committee. In 1950 when he ran for governor against the Duff-Fine ticket endorsed by Fred Peters, he lost Montgomery County by a narrow margin. He died in 1963.

looking to gubernatorial prospects for 1962, turned his attention instead to county policy and state politics and thus arrived at a *modus vivendi* with the county chairman. Moderns were not installed in the organization, though Wetherill's running mate became county solicitor. Courthouse discipline was not restored, and local leaders were neither challenged nor conciliated. It developed that Wetherill had neither taste nor time for political detail: he emphasized public relations and image-making, and he declined to sacrifice weekends to political meetings. His closest allies sadly described him as a nine-to-five politician.

Wetherill thus remained one force among several in the county organization. Within a year another force emerged when Richard Schweiker, scion of a Lansdale tile manufacturer, scored an upset primary victory over the county's conservative congressman from Lower Merion. Schweiker's campaign was modeled on the moderns'— but few members of that faction supported him because they still considered themselves members of the organization. He also ran best in the most rapidly growing regions. When Wetherill's bid for the gubernatorial nomination failed, Schweiker as Congressman and Staudinger as county chairman became the party's chief decision-makers in a loose alliance. Each maintained close ties with the manufacturers, Staudinger through party finance, Schweiker through family. Staudinger's strength depended heavily on relations with local leaders, especially in the York Road area, and on the state patronage regained in 1963; Schweiker assiduously developed his electoral base and saw to the reward of his loyal supporters.

Party control was thus decentralized. In slate-making the chairman required the support of a few local leaders (from at least two or three large municipalities) and of Schweiker. In finance, something like a third of the normal party budget came from a small group of manufacturers (of whom a half dozen were paramount), another third from a much larger list of regular contributors, about a sixth from courthouse assessments, and another sixth from candidates. In an important respect slatemaking and finance were separate realms, for the manufacturers appear never to have intervened in the former or in primary elections (though they maintained an implicit interest in state and national candidates) and their giving was virtually automatic.* As for patronage, chairman Staudinger had, by the party change in Harrisburg in 1963, achieved enough stature to control effectively all but a few state appointments of the roughly 600 available, though local leaders were recognized in the allotment. County jobs, however, were still poorly controlled; courthouse discipline was almost nonexistent in the important 1960 primary election, and again in 1963, when Fred Peters challenged the organization in an abortive comeback. Most important, perhaps, for

* One characteristic of party finance has been its occasional reliance on loans of as much as $25,000 from one or more of the manufacturers. All these loans are said to have been repaid despite the expressed willingness of the lenders to cancel them.

this account was the absence of any pronounced intraparty cleavage over county policy and the failure of a clearly identifiable modern Republican faction to emerge after 1959. All the main forces in the party could fairly be labeled conservative.

Nevertheless, the Wetherill administration broke new ground in policy. It was marked by three phases. The first departed sharply from tradition but was short-lived. With the momentum of the moderns' limited victory and his own aspirations Wetherill moved to vitalize county government and modernize the party by holding periodic meetings of all row officers (with the state legislators sometimes included). He spoke experimentally of ultimate structural reforms of county government. In the background was a major scandal that, while reflecting past practices, might also deflect Wetherill's state candidacy. With the new administration two row officers and the minority commissioner demanded an audit. It was the first in county history, and it unearthed enough so that the state attorney general investigated and one county official committed suicide. The principal difficulty was deficient accounting and missing funds in the fee-collecting offices. The principal scandal occurred in the prothonotary's office, where legal fees were lost in large amounts, but several other fee offices were found deficient in accounting. Gradually the scandal died down, and so did discussion of governmental structure—to which the political environment was plainly hostile.

Meantime the Wetherill administration was considering the substantive programs that marked its second phase. The industrial development committee was changed from a study group to a functioning promotional organization. A county-wide water resources study, authorized but unsupported by the Hammonds administration, was begun, under strong local pressure, for one drought-prone sector. An appropriation was made for a federal flood-control project in a major creek valley, and subsidies were made to municipalities for mosquito control. One county park was prepared and another projected, and a grant-in-aid program was begun for municipal open-space acquisition. The planning commission was expanded, a county budget and purchasing office was instituted, and a capital budget discussed. A citizens committee was appointed to study the county's role in child welfare; when it recommended enlargement (and acceptance of state grants and standards), an advisory committee was appointed to counsel on implementation. Of all the administration's designs and new departures, however, the most dramatic was its championing of the Southeast Pennsylvania Transportation Compact (SEPACT) for the improvement, with federal aid, of regional mass transit. The story of SEPACT is told in Chapter 18, but it should be noted here that Elkins Wetherill was its political sponsor in the suburban counties and that the first rail commuter arrangement to be made was in Montgomery County.

It would be easy to overstate the innovations made during Wetherill's tenure. The two most publicized programs, SEPACT and open space, emphasized regional action and local participation respectively—concepts favored by Fred Peters. Most others, like child welfare and water resources, were studies that stopped short of implementation. SEPACT and open space, while applauded in the metropolitan press, found their chief local backing in Wetherill's personal circle and the professionals in county government. The others resulted from intense pressure and perseverance by the county's few organized interests; some studies were undertaken reluctantly and delayed as counterpressures apparently developed.* County priorities thus tended to favor the growing, well-to-do, commuting suburbs.

All the innovations were first considered and at least tentatively begun when Wetherill was seeking the gubernatorial nomination, working closely with the planning commission staff, county solicitor, and his own public relations aides. After the nomination was lost the pressures against county action strengthened, too, since the transportation and water resources projects appeared to favor specific regions at a time when expenditures were rising anyway and threatening the county's penurious tradition.† By 1963 the total county tax rate, still the state's lowest, had doubled over the last decade. In the administration's four years combined expenditures had increased 75 percent (per capita, about 33 percent), though the bulk of the increase occurred in conventional fields like courthouse administration and correctional and welfare expenses.

Thus, in the third phase of the Wetherill administration few new projects were initiated, and contact with the county planners (a fruitful source of initiative) was less close. Wetherill assumed a state position and left county office shortly before his term ended, but he first provided for the nomination of a modern Republican colleague for commissioner. Privately, he maintained that enough had been done for one Montgomery County administration, though he voiced some priorities for the future. The chief accomplishments were in physical planning and facilities

* The child welfare study was pressed on the commissioners by the League of Women Voters and the Health and Welfare Council; the North Penn water resources project by a regional organization largely composed of local industries. The Industrial Development Committee was originally favored by the county planning commission and the Central Montgomery Chamber of Commerce, but the Manufacturers' Association was cool to the idea, as was Elkin Wetherill. A sharp conflict of private forces brought the matter of a county airport to public attention but forestalled any county action. Budgetary reforms were proposed in detail by PEL. SEPACT and open space were ardently backed by the Citizens Council of Montgomery County, a new group of untested effectiveness.

† On the regional distribution of taxes and benefits, note Wetherill's remarks about the Wissahickon Creek project: "When you are going to spend county money you have got to be careful. You have got Lower Merion and the York Road area to consider. Those people pay a good percentage of the tax income and many of them might not even care about the Wissahickon watershed." Philadelphia Evening Bulletin, November 22, 1960. Two years after these remarks the county agreed to participate in the project.

(especially open space and mass transit), but administrative changes and action in health and welfare had at least been mooted and might later be pursued. Perhaps most important, county government had responded to some group importunities and professional suggestions, in full awareness of the county's conservative tradition.

In 1963 Fred Peters, then in his early eighties, tried a comeback, running for commissioner with a ticket pledged to economy, but he lost the primary decisively. The next administration contained a balance of modern and conservative, one commissioner being Wetherill's protégé and the other the county chairman's, while the controller was the county's leading protagonist of localism. All were loyal organization men.

The conservative tradition was endemic in the German country and small towns, in local industry and the PMA, and in large, luxurious suburbs oriented to Philadelphia and able to provide for themselves. For each of these interests the county's low tax rate and assessment ratio on real property were important, and the regional impact of county programs was apparent to each. Outlying areas had no interest in suburban problems, and they had long resisted consolidated government. Old industries hardly welcomed new competition. Increased expenditures raised the spectre of property reassessment, most serious to some old, declining businesses and extractive industries. The redistributive nature of county expenditures was less apparent in the few wealthy suburbs, where most of the personal property valuation was located: more than half of the combined county budget was defrayed from the securities tax (see Chapter 13), and more than half the real property duplicate was based in those suburbs.* Of the three interests, the first—rural Montgomery—was but routinely represented in party councils and public office, but the other two were crucial in finance and elections. The county had few low-income suburbs and little unemployment in its manufacturing centers. The interest groups that were most evident to officeholders were the Manufacturers' Association and the Economy League (the first in the party, the second in the courthouse).

The principal manufacturers did not belong to civic and charitable organizations; some of them sat on county boards and commissions, where they resisted innovations; they were financially active Republicans and intensely conservative. In these respects they differed at least in degree from the most active men of affairs in Bucks, who were as likely to be bankers and brokers as industrialists and, as the latter, were managers of absentee-owned installations or owners of small firms. No precise measure of the manufacturers' influence is available because there were no direct confrontations over county policy; they helped

* The duplicate is a record of the tax liabilities of real property parcels. In 1961, three large suburbs—Lower Merion, Cheltenham, Abington—contained 33 percent of the county's assessed real property valuation and paid 60 percent of the personal property tax, with 30 percent of the county population.

condition party attitudes toward innovation and expenditure, but they did not control nominations to county office. Their expressed preferences (usually after the fact) did not prevail in several specific policies: e.g., SEPACT, open space, airport development. During the conservative Hammonds administration relations between courthouse officeholders and party organization, commissioners and manufacturers, were neither close nor cordial. More recently, at least two failing, old county industries sought specific assessment relief and failed to gain it.

There were also elements of change. New transportation routes produced commercial interests in development. Some new industries and new suburbanites alike were interested in land planning and regional action. Conservation and welfare found growing social constituencies. Several proposals for county action met evident physical needs for urban redevelopment, mass transit, open space, water supply. New politicians came forward and found support in these quarters, the county planners persevered, and a few interest groups emerged. These developments occurred as the old political leadership declined, permitting intraparty competition, especially in prosperous residential areas.

Intraparty competition was not a salient factor in policy change. By 1960 Democratic leadership was no longer domesticated, but the party was not a threat in county elections. Between 1948 and 1962 its registration disadvantage fell from 4:2 to 3:1; its percentage of the presidential vote varied between 30 and 40 with no perceptible trend. It was strongest (though rarely a majority) in the old industrial boroughs and the German rural areas, but the county's largest vote and the chief forces of change lay in the residential suburbs. This fact—together with rivalry for the minority commissioner post—fostered division between organization Democrats and intellectual Democrats, something like the difference between the Republican organization and Elkins Wetherill. The minority commissioner in Wetherill's administration adhered to the latter faction.

Montgomery's history indicates that the emergence of only a modicum of socioeconomic pluralism and of electoral competition may suffice for policy change despite survival of the old ideologies and interests. Whether pluralism or electoral competition alone would have sufficed is unclear; in fact, the two were loosely related in that the limited publics for policies could also be involved in primary elections. The principal forces for innovation were the ambitions of a few politicians, backed by county planners and specific civic interests. The principal forces of conservatism were the political organization and its more tax-conscious financial supporters. This tension between immediate participants, within a context of amorphous public attitudes, has continued since the Wetherill administration. Gradual implementation of the Wetherill beginnings and modest innovations have been combined with the old job-conscious, tax-conscious politics.

9

Delaware County, I

Montgomery's Fred Peters described Delaware County's political leader to this writer as the state's ablest. He added that Delaware posed special problems for Republican control, but that its political organization was the region's most efficient. Its leader prevailed for nearly half a century and died in 1965.

Delaware is the most densely settled and heavily industrialized of our three counties. Its governmental issues are both social and physical. Its old manufacturing base along the river and its close family ties have suggested to many that a socioeconomic power structure is linked to the political machine. In the normal absence of outright competition this possibility is hard to explore except in historical perspective. Legend plays a large role in county government and politics, and firm information about either is closely guarded. Yet the county affords a study of solid organization politics at a time when policy issues are more pressing than they were for other old county organizations. These conditions may justify a more detailed account of Delaware.

In the late nineteenth century three common-pleas judges served in turn as formal county leaders in the decentralized, low pressure political environment of the time. They were succeeded by William Cameron Sproul, who graduated from Swarthmore College, married into the Roach shipyard family, acquired controlling ownership of the Chester *Times* and, later, extensive local interests in banking, shipping, steel-casting, and land development. In 1895, at age 25, he was elected state senator, and in 1918 he became governor. The county's modern political history begins with that event. Its principal elements were the city of Chester and the McClure family.

Chester's development has been described. Here the point is the city's rapid access of political influence with its population increase after the Civil War. Its numerical preponderance peaked at the time of John

TABLE 9:1

Chester City Population as Percentage of
County Population by Decades

1850	.07	1890	.27	1930	.21
1860	.15	1900	.35*	1940	.19
1870	.25	1910	.32	1950	.15
1880	.26	1920	.33	1960	.11

* Some annexations figure in this increase.

McClure's emergence as city leader in 1919 and county eminence in the 1920's. Soon after his establishment the suburban settlements of the twenties altered the balance; but in 1921, when McClure began to extend his control to the county seat, Chester held one-third of the county population and often cast a majority of the Republican primary vote. This decisive fact, together with urban organization, offset the later population balance. Thus the origins of the county organization lay in Chester and were grounded in its social conditions: the heavy industrial base that was completed during World War I, the ethnic minorities susceptible of precinct control, and the residential removal from the city of its old civic leaders after the turn of the century.

The first John J. McClure, a Presbyterian carpenter, emigrated in 1840 from County Donegal "and for several years was in the railroad employ in bridge building and construction work, holding authority over others and prospering," acquiring farm land on the outskirts of Chester, assuming the new Republican faith, and ultimately settling in Chester.[1] Of his seven sons at least two were politically inclined. William J., father of the late county leader, was born into comfortable circumstances, attended Chester Academy, and began his career as a clerk in a dry-goods store. In 1872 he opened a cigar and tobacco shop in Chester's Old South Ward, which is said to have expanded into Chester's largest; later he entered the manufacture of cigars. He established a liquor store, to which he later added a brewery, which also became Chester's largest. He evidently prospered on men's minor vices, but he was remembered for two related qualities: his gift for organizational detail (and, evidently, for vertical integration), and his loyalty and generosity to friends, of whom he had many. He early entered politics and became tax collector of the old South Ward, then City Controller; but he was more a party than a public man:

> His skill was in planning campaigns, perfecting the details, and as an organizer of men there was no superior in the county. His lieutenants were in all parts of the county and at all stages of the campaigns ... he kept in close touch with the men who manned the precincts. . . . He is said to have been one of the ablest political leaders the county has produced.[2]

Thus the elder McClure combined business and politics. He was an important force in Chester's South Ward (which later became the city's principal low-income, ethnic section) and in some sections of the county, but he was not the acknowledged single leader of either precinct. He was prominent in fraternal organizations, president of the Delaware County Subway Company and the Consumers' Ice Company, and a director in two of the county's leading banks.

One fact is essential to understanding William McClure's blend of business and politics: liquor licenses were then awarded by the county court. A man who stood well with the judge would at least be thought to influence franchises, and it would be best to purchase beer from his brewery. William McClure's first excursions into county politics occurred in judicial contests, which were bitter campaigns. Add to this business fact the social importance of beer and liquor in politics: taverns were political meeting places throughout the county, and some political clubs, especially in the city tenderloin, were primarily drinking places. Early in this century county reformers and prohibitionists began strenuously to reprobate the connection between publicans and Republicans. It was in this situation that William McClure served as head of the county wholesale liquor dealers association, which was thought to be his most important position. On his untimely death of typhoid in 1907 hotels throughout the county closed for the funeral.

William's son, John J., left Swarthmore College in his sophomore year to assume control of the family interests under the tutelage of his uncle, also a banker, businessman and politician. Oldtimers say that John inherited his father's business and political acumen without his warmth or generosity. He seems to have elevated his father's informal methods to principles; by about 1910 the McClures' operation became known as "the corner": starting with the brewing monopoly, they established a bonding firm that cornered the beer-bonding business, and added a real estate holding company that owned a long string of licensed hotels that were leased to keepers who bought their beer at the right brewery.* The entire operation rested on at least the reputation for control of licenses and thus of judges (Influence with the district attorney would have been helpful, too.), but the actual extent of this influence remains a matter for speculation. However that may have been, "the corner" did not long persist in its original form. As the forces of prohibition increased, John McClure, with sure prescience, shifted into the lines of politically relevant business that became his mainstays: the Chester Construction and Contracting Company was organized in 1916, the McClure Company for Bonding and Insurance in 1919. With politics, boosterism, and wartime prosperity there were lots of building and public improvement in Chester.

* "The corner" was originally a geographical expression for William McClure's store, a frequent political meeting place. The Chester *Times* in this period strongly opposed the whole operation and argued that it was illegal under decisions of state courts invalidating retail liquor licenses to establishments owned or controlled by brewing companies or wholesale liquor dealers.

Thus McClure had ample incentive to extend his influence in the city. By 1918 he was alleged to control both its commissioners and the school board; his strength was said to rest in the slum wards and especially in the Negro wards. With its riverfront traditions and immigrant communities, the city supported a core of slum and segregated districts and of intensive business in gambling, liquor, and prostitution. (The most notorious of these districts survived with little change from the late nineteenth century until 1960, when it was displaced by a prominent industry's parking lot.) In these areas leadership rested on primitive sanctions (and often in turn on McClure's still-rumored control of liquor licenses); registration and election fraud were common.

McClure's accumulation of influence was infrequently contested in city primaries (which he usually won), though it was strongly opposed by the Chester *Times*, of which William C. Sproul was half owner. The paper had long opposed liquor in politics, and Sproul, as a candidate for governor in 1918, declared for prohibition. With his removal to Harrisburg the division with McClure came to a head in three primary elections. In 1919 McClure's man beat the incumbent mayor (and Governor Sproul) by seventy-nine votes.* The *Times* charged that votes were bought for as much as eight dollars; the incumbent mayor sought the county sheriff's assistance on election day because he mistrusted the city police, and the county court declined to inspect alleged false ballots. Out in the county McClure's candidates—the incumbent commissioners, who were pledged to build a new county jail—were defeated by an organization called the Republican League, forerunner of the "independent" groups that sporadically contested primaries with McClure for the next forty years. In 1920 Governor Sproul backed a winner for the state senate against McClure's candidate, but he is then reported to have said he could no longer stand the expense of electoral competition with the Chester machine. And in 1921 McClure defeated the League in a crucial county primary, carrying to a third term the octogenarian president judge whom he and his father had long supported.

The 1921 primary established McClure, at thirty-four, as the chief political force in the county, and the decentralized pattern of county politics gradually declined in the 1920's. From his base in Chester and its extensions in the county McClure could dominate primary elections. He seems to have concentrated on the selection of sheriffs, but at least one county commissioner regularly came from Chester. In the mid-twenties unfriendly governors appointed three new judges: McClure later slated them all, and with his support, they sat through the 1930's.†

* The victorious candidate was a long-time McClure employee, a leader in fraternal organizations who, after his second term as Mayor, was convicted of embezzling over $200,000 in city funds.

† Governors Sproul (1919-1923), Pinchot (1923-27, 1931-35), and Fisher (1927-31) were all Republicans at odds with McClure for reasons of principle and state and county factionalism; Governor Earle (1935-39) was a Democrat.

An "independent" opposition continued in both city and county: in Chester there were persistent charges of malversation in contracting and protection of crime; in time these complaints spread to neighboring sections of the county. County government spent freely for improvements in the booming twenties. As political control tightened in Chester, primary margins widened.

Late in the 1920's McClure developed the centralizing device that has since characterized Delaware County politics and is thought by insiders to explain its continuity. Known officially as the Board of Supervisors and informally as the War Board, it was a small group of sectional leaders picked by McClure to represent sections or large municipalities. Its three original members were Upper Darby's congressman, a Chester Pike contractor-politician, and an out-county farmer-politician. It grew naturally from the existing distribution of voting strength, but in time its rules were formalized: McClure named the supervisors, who were then accepted in their areas. The trick was to pick a man who could win local acceptance and who would maintain loyalty. Beginning with three members, it grew with the county to its present fourteen—though significantly its numbers never were fixed nor the sections permanently defined. This group nominally decided matters of slating and patronage, though not normally by voting. McClure seems to have controlled it by the organized force of his precincts, by personal strength and sagacity, by seeming not to seek to dominate, and by virtue of the value of unity and the futility of individual challenge. One of the War Board's strengths —especially later in an era of rapid change—was its strictly limited centralization in accordance with prudence and local sensibility. It was not a device for interfering in local political affairs but only for consolidating the perquisites of county organization. In this form it was actually a method of decentralizing controversy and thus of isolating and insulating it.

In 1920 McClure was elected state senator. Evidently a natural leader and adept legislator, he quickly won the chairmanship of the Senate's finance committee and became a specialist in taxation and utility regulation. (He offered legislation reducing taxes on the shipbuilding industry.) As a power in state politics, he supported Joseph Grundy and opposed Governor Pinchot, who was a stern prohibitionist. Later McClure himself became a prohibitionist and, as such, was nearly nominated for United States Senator in 1932. Though not a publicity-minded public man, he attracted important industrial support within the party and a larger career was clearly in prospect when Prohibition intervened.

In June 1933 John McClure and ninety-five colleagues were indicted for conspiracy to violate the prohibition laws. McClure was named leader of the operation, which was said to include at least seven of Chester's eleven ward leaders, several city, county, and local officeholders, the county's chief of detectives, and McClure's personal secretary. The federal government further charged some defendants with intimidation of witnesses and, later, with jury tampering. At the trial in federal district court witnesses testified that provision of liquor and protection of sales were highly organized, that a Sun Oil tanker captain had often by-passed his Marcus Hook berth to unload "rum" at a Chester pier secured by city police, that local constables regularly executed "knock-off lists" of nonpaying, nonparticipating public houses, and that these monopolistic operations were personally directed by John McClure. No defense was offered to this testimony, the defendants proposing to attack the trial itself on appeal. All were convicted and sentenced without serving; while their appeal was pending, the Presidential amnesty that ended Prohibition took effect. Four days after the conviction Governor Pinchot signed the bill that created state liquor control: there would be no more local licensing.

The thirties were a time of trouble for McClure, who faced the aftermath of scandal, the population shifts of the twenties, and the New Deal Democratic trend. The personal scandal hurt: in 1935 a Democrat was elected county sheriff by forty votes. In 1936 McClure lost his senate seat: with strong support from the local industrial community, he handily won the primary against the independents; then his primary opponent accepted Democratic fusion support and edged into office on Roosevelt's coattails.* In that election the president narrowly carried Chester, but not the county. It was McClure's misfortune to run in a presidential year. In all local elections Chester held firm, preserving the county leadership. Its fidelity depended on the usual machine methods, especially with the depressed and segregated wards at the city's core.

Equally serious were the county's population changes. By 1930 the Upper Darby region exceeded the Chester section in size; the growth there unsettled local organizations, thus provoking local aggrandizement at the county level. The county's congressman attempted, from his expanding Upper Darby base, to extend his influence out the Main Line and down the Chester Pike, but the suburban unsettlement worked both ways, and McClure held the allegiance of some Upper Darby leaders. The first sharp contest came in 1937 over election of an orphans' court judge. The Upper Darby region supported a local resident; McClure adopted the incumbent Democrat (just appointed by a Democratic governor), a native of Chester's Old South Ward. McClure carried his man by winning

---

* McClure is believed by many to have entered bogus candidates in the primary to divide the opposition; certainly there was a large field. The ultimate winner was Weldon Heyburn, son of a former state legislator, nephew of a former county sheriff, and scion of old county Quaker stock, who served until 1948, when he was elected State Auditor General. The fusion effort included not only the Republican independents and the Democrats, but the Royal Oak Party of Father Couglin, whose members—especially the railroad brotherhoods—played a large role in the campaign (Coughlin's vice-presidential candidate was an attorney for the Brotherhoods.) Later, state law was changed to prevent the loser of a primary from filing for the general election, except in the case of judgeships.

Chester 10:1 while losing the rest of the county 2:3. Upper Darby was held at bay, but it had clearly superseded the perennial "independents" from the old "intellectual" suburbs as the main challenge to McClure. Four years later the two forces reached an accommodation with appointment of the defeated orphans' court candidate to common pleas and his later slating for a full term.

With this arrangement in 1941 the complexion of the county court began to change. In the twenties McClure accepted three gubernatorial appointees to the county bench. (One of which cleared his way to the state senate.) Their reslating must have conciliated men who cherished their positions, and their relations with McClure were normally cordial. In 1941 the leader's first selection to a judicial place was challenged by a Chester "independent," then assistant district attorney, who made a strong race in the primary and was later appointed to a judicial vacancy by a governor opposed to McClure. The new jurist was perforce accepted and later became the county's president judge. In 1947, when McClure faced his most serious primary fight for courthouse control, he dumped an incumbent in order to slate a man from the Upper Darby region. After that court appointments went to political regulars; two were War Board members, two were McClure's own attorneys.

The legal work in which the two future judges figured is known in the county as the Chester Water Scandal, and it led to McClure's second trial. In 1939 the city commissioners bought the local water company (previously owned by New York City interests), and John McClure received $1 million for stock purchased shortly before for $750,000. Then a city lawyer and civic reformer brought a taxpayer's suit and showed that McClure and an associate each took $85,000 of the profit, McClure's two lawyers $20,000 each for legal services, while the remainder went to a Philadelphia lawyer and a Chicago bonding firm. This disposition was not denied, but it was held in the court that a "confidential relationship" with the city fathers had not been made out, and the State Supreme Court affirmed on appeal.

The water scandal betokened adversity for McClure in the forties as the "rum" scandal had in the thirties. In the 1936 senatorial election McClure had enjoyed the public support of most local industries, and industrial patronage was an asset in the Depression. After 1936 the new state senator, Weldon Heyburn, became the center of anti-organization forces in the county. These included the old "independents" and new factions in Upper Darby, which, for most of the forties, were financially backed by the elder of the politically active Pew family of Sun Oil and Sun Ship. McClure's industrial support was thus divided, and he was again detached from the state Republican leadership, which then included Pew and Heyburn; the latter's gubernatorial prospects were a factor in the local challenge to McClure. The reasons for Pew's break with McClure are unclear, but shifting state alignments and personal liking for Heyburn were evidently important; differences with McClure over money and morals are also reported. Pew's financial support of the local opposition was generous but undependable.

Four hard primary engagements were fought, beginning in 1945. In the first McClure dislodged an interim orphans' court appointee, Wallace Chadwick, who had been named to the vacancy by McClure's enemy, Governor Martin, and sponsored by Joseph Pew. In 1946 Chadwick ran for Congress, backed by the state organization and the Heyburn-Pew faction; he beat the organization by 300 votes, narrowly carrying the divided Upper Darby region and capturing 30 percent of the Chester vote. (The federal government sent FBI agents to Chester to check election irregularities; they found city policemen working the polls in some precincts but brought no prosecutions.) It was the beleaguered Mc-Clure's first serious primary defeat. In 1947 the new faction ran a full slate for county offices but lost a close primary: they closed the gap in Chester, where their top candidates were prominent, but lost the Upper Darby region, where McClure's top candidates resided. In 1948 the organization turned Chadwick out of Congress and defeated the rest of the "independent" slate; a one-time Radnor "independent" ran against Chadwick and, despite Pew's generous backing, as Chadwick later put it, "Every time I spent a dollar McClure spent two." With this incident, the most serious challenge since Sproul's reconciliation abated. It had been fought most intensely over local control of the large townships of Haverford and Upper Darby and over state gubernatorial nominations; in both fields McClure emerged with conditional victories. With the Blue Bell Alliance in 1950 the Pew-PMA candidate for governor was defeated and the state patronage regained; state and county jobs were used to the hilt to swing the balance in Upper Darby.

The precarious Chester–Upper Darby balance was the chief postwar fact in the county's political geography. By midcentury there were, besides Chester and its satellites, a half dozen populous townships; a dozen large, low-density settlements to the north and west; and the congeries of small jurisdictions in the southeast corner dating from the late nineteenth century. Upper Darby alone was larger than Chester. With its natural extensions in Haverford and Springfield it made a third of the county population, roughly 40 percent lived in the Chester-Ridley-Darby region (see map on p. 19) of lower incomes and higher densities, and the remainder inhabited the part of the county destined from then to grow most rapidly. The second region, the southeast quadrant, contained a population more sensitive to organization sanctions than the rest of the county. Socially, it included parts of Upper Darby, which ranged from the 69th Street extension of Philadelphia and the old milling centers to the Drexel Hill suburbs; Upper Darby's social differences reinforced its political divisions.

As the old factional leaders died or retired McClure sought a reliable satrap who could stabilize Upper Darby. In succession the recognized leaders defected over local offices (especially tax collector) and divided county primaries. With the defeat of the Pew-Heyburn faction, Sam Dickey a new leader, long a power in the core area, took control of the township commissioners in a decisive primary in 1951. Perforce, McClure accepted Dickey as the man to bargain with in Upper Darby. Like the county leader, Dickey occupied no office and shunned publicity, but Upper Darby received increased courthouse recognition, including the post of county personnel director.

In the 1950's, during which Delaware County grew by one-third, tight political order returned. Republican registration margins declined somewhat (to 3.5:1 in 1961) and Democrats threatened some boroughs in the Ridley-Darby region. John Kennedy made heavy inroads in that region in 1960, thus encouraging the minority party. In the midfifties the Democrats broke loose from McClure's control and elected their own minority commissioner, but county government was unaffected by these developments. Instead, in the early 1960's tight county control was threatened by Republican divisions, which, predictably, started in Upper Darby.

Like most of the old organizations, the War Board had a two-term rule for county officeholders. This led to slating difficulties when vacancies occurred in posts occupied and sought by Upper Darby's organization. Albert Swing, county commissioner and Radnor Township leader, feared extension of Sam Dickey's influence along the Main Line; he opposed Dickey's candidates and argued for men who would improve the party's image. Matters were further complicated by McClure's health; during the 1960 election campaign the leader fell in his home, broke his hip, and endured three years of intermittent hospitalization. Inevitably the prospect of succession arose. Swing circulated in the War Board a petition to vest party leadership temporarily in the chairman of the county commissioners rather than the formal party chairman.* This move, too, was aimed at both image and sectional balance: the county chairman was Mayor of Chester, and his courthouse personnel director was Sam Dickey's man. The move was averted when a Chester–Upper Darby coalition intervened with McClure's family. In turn, the coalition invoked against Swing a recent War Board rule that no man might hold two income-producing positions (in this case, county commissioner and township tax collector). The coalition feared a take-over, and its members reacted personally to Swing's talk of image improvement; Swing saw himself faced with a nascent Chester–Chester Pike–Upper Darby axis of urban, organizational elements that would be hurtful in suburbia, but he held some high cards as county commissioner. As

* "We the undersigned Republican political supervisors of Delaware County hereby elect G. Robert Watkins the temporary Republican political leader of Delaware County to take the place of John J. McClure as such leader until that time when John J. McClure recovers his health and is able to resume the leadership. This leadership is to involve all political patronage and policy matters." *Main Line Times,* November 10, 1960.

the rift widened, he allied himself with the minority commissioner, deposed the old chairman, and took over county administration, both policy and patronage. Several issues discussed elsewhere in this volume were affected by the division, which occurred at a time when new departures in policy were being urged on the county, but the interlude was too brief for much innovation. Soon Swing was through, dismissed from the War Board, defeated in the primary election, legislatively evicted from county office in events described in Chapter 13.

To almost everyone but Albert Swing it seemed clear that he could not expect renomination, for he had conspired with the opposition and refused or removed the organization's men. Swing went to McClure and recanted; it seemed to him that the leader was noncommittal. It is said that at the slate-making War Board meeting in 1963 McClure simply handed down the ticket; Swing was dumped, and so was Watkins for his unfortunate part in the quarrel; Mayor Eyre was demoted to a county row office. Watkins was quoted in the press: "Senator McClure put me in . . . and he took me out. That's politics. . . . I will support the organization ticket down the line."[3] (The following year he was nominated for Congress when the incumbent was dumped.) On the ticket for county commissioner were a Media retailer, a War Board member, formerly sheriff and personally devoted to McClure; and the son-in-law and assistant to Upper Darby's largest real estate developer and rentier (who was also father-in-law of the county judge elected in 1959), an Irish Catholic with no political background. Both commissioners would be sound, conservative businessmen. As usual, McClure had given careful thought to the ticket.

For three years McClure, from varying degrees of hospital and home confinement, had received selective intelligence and issued occasional directives, resolving crises he could not or would not avert. Late in 1963 his physician devised a brace that relieved his pain and his disabling need for heavy sedation. At seventy-seven years the leader resumed full direction of party affairs on a limited schedule of appointments. His return lent perspective to the past two years in which certain aspects of the organization stood out.

One was the problem of succession: none of the old county political leaders ever developed a successor, and McClure was no exception. (He was obviously proud of his organization but not evidently concerned about its future.) When the problem arose, McClure's leadership was found sufficiently awesome so that no logical candidate was publicly eager to assume it, though each was anxious to prevent others' doing so.

The spectre of succession heightened regional rivalries that had first divided the War Board. These, too, were inevitable: strong local leaders felt heavy pressures to assert their strength in the county courthouse, especially from 1955 to 1963, when the Democrats controlled state patronage. In Upper Darby's case it was important not to lose positions that were won in the period of stabilization. With growth in the county pressure increased on the constant number of top elective jobs.

With McClure's removal the role played by individual leadership in the War Board was partly revealed. It turned out that some supervisors disliked one another personally (which McClure well knew) and that regional rivalries involved differences of interest and style that were likely to increase with county growth both north and south of the Baltimore Pike. Albert Swing's newness to countywide politics was also a factor in the division. In these circumstances the supervisors suddenly had to communicate directly about urgent matters, and they sometimes did not understand one another's interests and intentions very well. Apparently collective leadership worked less well than personal leadership: a single center helped to make the communication of interests continuous instead of intermittent, to avert direct confrontations, to divert emerging and merging issues, to construe the intentions of parties and interpret them to one another, and to adjudicate claims and guarantee future compensations. Through a single nerve center interests could best be altered in the process of adjustment, related carefully one to another, rendered incremental and noncumulative, and viewed in large enough context to maximize satisfactions. The Republican machine was carefully contrived, with rules and balances of power, but it probably could not run for long unattended; like the other old organizations, it was designed for an operator.

John McClure died in the spring of 1965 after more than half a century's dominance of Chester politics and after serving nearly as long as Delaware County's leader. His funeral, said to be the largest in Chester's history, was attended by Republican leaders from throughout the state. The chairman of the county commissioners was elected McClure's nominal successor as head of the War Board. A year later there were no visible changes in county politics or policy: patronage was still centralized and innovation still resisted. In view of trends described in the next chapter, however, primary election divisions, though not inevitable, seemed likely to develop.

10

Delaware County, II

Delaware County's political structure belies the suburban stereotype. Its stability and adaptability are nearly unique. This chapter supplements the previous narrative with an analysis of its distinctive attributes and a comparison with the other counties.

1. *The leader.* John McClure himself was one distinctive attribute. Like most of the old leaders, he was a man of personal moderation and imperturbability, reserved rather than affable, hard as nails when necessary.[1] His ability to outwait adversity and willingness to co-opt opponents were notable if not exceptional among county leaders. He carried two characteristics to extremes. One was his methodical, cerebral approach to politics: he claimed to have studied closely many other organizations and to have adapted the best in all of them, he came to emphasize rules and procedures, which only he could interpret or waive, and he kept voluminous files on patronage and election performance in precincts and maintained close contact with his Chester committeemen during campaigns. With this approach went the view that politics was a branch of business and vice versa: "Politics must be conducted by a firm business organization on a firm business foundation—as much as the Pennsylvania Railroad or the shoemaker down the street."[2] In this version, his views conformed to the conservative business ideology that he espoused and whose support he sought, but there was more to it than this. One of his sometime opponents, equally conservative with deep roots in Chester, said his main complaint was that McClure ran politics essentially as a branch of his business. His business methods were sometimes unorthodox, but as times changed he came to emphasize honest county government as good suburban politics.

2. *The War Board.* McClure's chief innovation was the Board of Supervisors, which helped him to control the county from his base in

Chester as the city's electoral weight declined. The device was more effective than efforts in other counties to recognize local and sectional interests, in part because its origin antedated several sectional pressures. It began as an advisory group and, after expansion, its independent status remained ambiguous. Some of its genius lay in this careful ambiguity: meetings were called by McClure, members were chosen by McClure; local committeemen then elected McClure's nominee to represent them, so the organization could be democratically interpreted.

The War Board's limited centralization was also important: it controlled only the crucial perquisites, decentralizing troublesome issues. It placed the leader at one remove from local pressure, yet preserved his accessibility; it allowed the recognition and co-optation of local leaders and their exposure to a larger view of policy and patronage, while isolating sectional representatives by its voting rules; it provided the leader with allies against factional attacks on the organization's common interests; it obscured formal responsibility. The county organization rarely intervened directly in municipal divisions; McClure simply waited and recognized the victor, transferring the county patronage if necessary. The postwar maneuvers to stabilize Upper Darby—a crucial township—are the chief modern instance of local intervention.

Supervisors dispensed patronage in their districts and kept the political peace. Collectively the War Board made party rules and nominated candidates, but its chief function was oversight of campaigns. Normally the War Board met once a month at McClure's home or office; during campaigns it met weekly or oftener. McClure himself said that he emphasized teamwork, collaboration, and tactical flexibility in the board. More than a sounding board, it was a means of avoiding drift and inertia; it was a pliable cabinet. It maintained standing committees on county and party problems (e.g., party finance, personnel vacancies) and normally proceeded by majority vote. However, McClure sometimes settled crucial issues himself, and his personal decisions about patronage and policy were always accepted. In particular, all significant appointments were his decisions. The Board's suggestions about county policy were not strictly binding on the majority commissioners (who were automatically members), but it regularly reviewed the county budget with special attention to salary scales and sometimes held hearings on departmental estimates.

With the population shifts of the 1950's a subtle difference appeared in the War Board: some of the new men representing large residential townships were able, authentic local leaders, while the senior members (old courthouse hands) derived from smaller jurisdictions and more clearly owed their stature to McClure. The older group constituted a majority, making McClure's control possible, but it was probable that the balance would change with continued growth of the larger townships. Sectional rivalries and social differences might increase and centralization decline.

3. *Sinews of war.* The War Board's ambiguity of function and limited centralization can be seen in its principal rules and procedures. Elective offices were filled by the Board; appointive positions required sponsorship of the sectional supervisor. Patronage was formally allocated by dollar (salary) value to sections and municipalities on the basis of election returns, though it was informally biased toward the lower-income districts by recognizing vested interests in positions. Job tenure was carefully regulated, and fifteen years' county residence were required for nomination to elective office. Row-office candidates contributed 10 percent of their four-year salary in advance, and courthouse jobholders were assessed on a set, progressive scale and expected to pay up by the spring primary.* The total courthouse levy was more than $100,000 annually. This relieved the organization from heavy reliance on large contributors or contractors through its subsidy by county taxpayers (assuming that some of the "tax" on officeholders was passed on).

Major county contracts were cleared through McClure's office, which also acted as county insurance agent. Architectural and engineering work were concentrated in two concerns, the latter in a firm whose partner served two elective terms (without salary) as county surveyor. Construction contracts and county advertising were bid and broadly distributed, but certain small suppliers seem to have been favored. Thus such politically sensitive interests as insurance, contracting, and the press were usefully conciliated with local and county business—though there was nothing unique to Delaware in this. (The major county daily paper lost official advertising in its periods of opposition.) The same was true of lawyers: there were about 125 local and county appointments distributed among some 75 of the county bar's 200 members, in addition to the state positions that were normally available. The prospect of such emoluments and the hope of high elective office normally served to deter opposition from the most likely professional source, though some ambitious lawyers publicly bucked the organization in order to win its recognition later.

4. *The urban base of Delaware County politics.* The existence of Chester distinguishes Delaware County politically. Though smaller alone than Montgomery's industrial boroughs combined, this city of 60,000 is different in kind from any other suburban municipality—perhaps especially in the size of its depressed and Negro populations and in its independent political existence as a third-class city. Even in recent years the ratio of registered voters to adult population in Chester has been at least as high as it is in the rest of the county, and though the registration ratio

* The scale varied according to salary. In 1963 it was 2 percent on salaries up to $4,500, 4 percent on $4,501 to $5,500, 6 percent above $5,500. Two years earlier the rates were 3, 5, and 7 percent; they were reduced after an across the board county pay increase. Chester *Times*, August 8, 1962.

has declined, it remains lopsidedly Republican. Turnout in local and county primary elections is typically higher in Chester than in the county at large. In general elections the city turnout is about the same as that of the remainder in county elections, but it has been lower in presidential elections, all but two of which have been lost by the Republicans since 1936. Despite the trend to Democratic dominance of large eastern cities and the erosion of Republican control of most small Pennsylvania cities, Chester has remained decidedly Republican in local elections. In underprivileged areas the organization's sanctions are impressive and its methods pervasive: registration and election fraud are frequently reported; police commonly have manned the polls and periodically have disciplined the Negro population; patronage and political sensitivity are extensive throughout the city government, including the school system, police, and the minor judiciary, and are at least believed in the Negro quarter to extend to private employment and community leadership; the Democratic party structure frequently has been infiltrated.*

Bucks County has suburbs of low social rank and Montgomery has something like cities, but Delaware County has both. Nearly 40 percent of its population lives in the high-density, low-income region south of Baltimore Pike. Outside of Chester, the rate of growth in this section has recently been slower than that farther north, though it has been steady throughout the century. This has probably assisted the absorption of newcomers by the party organization. Patronage and election day activity are critical in this region, which also has somewhat smaller election districts on the average (and thus more elected party workers) than the newly settled, low-density sectors, despite the equalizing requirements in state election laws. The region is heavily represented in the War Board and the county courthouse.

Delaware County's politics thus range from those of the city machine through the job-centered and solidary politics of the Chester Pike to the status-based Republican voting habits of northern sections of the county. But—as will be seen below—several large municipalities (especially Upper Darby) contain income ranges and pockets of urbanism that also favor organization politics at local and county levels. And one should not suppose that patronage is without influence in upper-income suburbs. In both Montgomery and Delaware, county jobs provide distaff and retirement income for straitened families in prestigious townships. Some large municipalities also have a number of blue-collar jobs. Politically, the larger, more prosperous townships are slightly unbalanced microcosms of the counties, with elements susceptible to job control, some lawyers and businessmen alert to state and county opportunities,

---

* Several city policemen, including their chief, are known to be party committeemen; the school board president is vice-chairman of the party committee; Republican registration is normally required of city residents who teach in the schools and man the police force.

and natural Republican majorities interested simply in adequate, economical government.

5. *Illegality*. The political history of the county and especially of Chester suggests the question of whether crime is important in city and county politics. The question is not in the usual line of academic inquiry, and it cannot be answered by social science. Factually it is either a matter of legal conviction or of surmise, morally it is often a matter of class and cultural differences, and its discussion almost inevitably inflicts some personal or political damage. One would thus prefer to avoid it— but the question does bear on the nature of political organization and the conduct of county government, and it has been commonly discussed in the county.

A useful approach is that of Daniel Bell, whose observations on crime in recent decades appear to fit Delaware County.[3] Bell argues that syndicated gambling and labor racketeering logically followed repeal of Prohibition as alternatives to bootlegging for specialists in illegal activity. This kind of specialty was a natural upward path for new urban minorities, especially where the Irish already monopolized politics and contracting. Vice and gambling, in turn, through taxation or protection, became financial bases for city politicians at a time (during and after the Depression) when other inducements and contributions were failing. The persistence of vice and gambling has also been favored by governmental factors: acceptance in some cities of the theory of "controlled" crime, by which a degree of illegality is tolerated on the ground that total enforcement would be costly and self-defeating; and the metropolitanizing of crime, through inadequate law enforcement in the suburbs and satellite cities. Nonetheless, Bell argues, some types of crime are in decline: industrial racketeering in most fields has been outmoded by labor legislation, and prostitution by changes in sexual morality; gambling has fallen off from the easy-money, wartime era and is somewhat curtailed by more effective federal regulation. In particular, Bell contends that cultural and economic changes have reduced the middle-class market for gambling and vice and that crime has, therefore, not increased in recent decades.

In Chester, gambling, prostitution, and the illegal sale of liquor were evidently well established by the turn of the century and enhanced by the wartime industrial boom at the onset of Prohibition. The McClures' alliance of liquor and politics began on a paralegal basis and continued under Prohibition along different lines. During the 1920's the newspapers carried frequent reports of protection and extortion of gambling and bootlegging in Chester, culminating in the trial and unenforced conviction in 1933. There was also a history of racketeering in Upper Darby's core area, on the Philadelphia border (known as Little Cicero, after Cicero, Illinois, once the home of Al Capone) during the twenties and early thirties. The township's current political leader was active in

liquor traffic and gambling there in that period, and his careful avoidance of publicity since then continues to arouse suspicion without, however, any evidence of complicity today.*

Before the repeal of Prohibition, protection, centered in Chester, was
perhaps the most important resource of the county political organization. For the next two decades gambling flourished in the county's urban
pockets, but protection was probably informal and decentralized. At
midcentury there was no public evidence connecting political leaders
in the county's two largest centers to rackets, though there remained
the disquieting circumstance of their personal associations. In Chester
men convicted in 1933 served as ward leaders and city officials into the
1950's, and one of the most important was convicted in the 1940's of
other offenses; in Upper Darby a public land purchase scandal in 1957
stemmed from the appointment of a recently convicted violator of the
liquor revenue laws as director of sanitation.†

Several facts of the last decade are relevant to illegality. One is that
John McClure undertook a clean-up of Chester in the early 1950's at the
urging of some influential supporters: a special assistant to the mayor
(at $5,000!) was recruited from the state police and led a three-year
campaign against gambling establishments before leaving for lack of
support. At the same time the county hired a special investigator, assigned to the district attorney and appointed by the court. Interviews
indicate that McClure was concerned lest the gamblers (who were
mostly his old associates) take over Chester with outside alliances and
support from Upper Darby and that this threat, if it existed, was broken
in the fifties. Petty, independent gambling and prostitution continued

---

* In a rare interview he was quoted as saying: "I am proud that I have never been
a hypocrite. I was a hundred percent rackets man when I was in the rackets. Never
did I pose as a pious, good living individual. I am back now in decent society. I am a
hundred percent for good but just and human government." In the interview he
explained that he had been in bootlegging until the repeal of Prohibition and then
went into bookmaking. He invested heavily in Upper Darby real estate and entered
politics in the 1940's, at which time he apparently left illegal activity. Philadelphia
Evening Bulletin, March 7, 1954. During the 1940's Upper Darby police assigned a
detective to watch him; when he became township political leader, the chief of
police was demoted and a dossier of several years was destroyed.

† The scandal began when the sanitation director's trash collection firm was
charged with sending unlicensed trucks to Philadelphia to extort business. Then
the township contracted to purchase as an incinerator site a tract of land without
clear title; although who owned the land was never disclosed, the suspicion was that
the sanitation director had an interest in it, and it was known that the township's
political leader was present at the commissioners' caucus when the decision was
made to purchase the land. After the county grand jury heard charges and recommended that further action be taken, the district attorney (an Upper Darby man)
dismissed the proceedings for lack of evidence. It might be added that trash collection has been an occasional focus of illegal operations because it is characterized by
payments in cash, because the temptation to organize bidding is acute, and because
the trash collectors can provide empty liquor bottles to operators of unlicensed
stills.

in Chester to an extent that suggests some toleration and domestication, but it seems unlikely that the county political leader was directly involved: his method was to use an outsider to prune the threatening excesses without disturbing the root system of city politics.

Evidence of *syndicated* crime is understandably hard to come by, despite plausible stories of outside connections. The question is of obvious concern to politicians. Albert Swing charged in his primary campaign (as have the Democrats) that the county was threatened by an Upper Darby–Chester axis linked to syndicated gambling, and the county's president judge has warned against the outward pressure of organized rackets through Upper Darby: "It takes a strong minded cop at $35 a week to refuse to turn his back." Salaries of municipal police and of county detectives are indeed low. Widespread public concern would almost certainly harm the majority party, the political organization, or both, but mere suspicion may work the other way. Some insiders acknowledge Chester's history and culture and rely on the "controlled" crime theory. One of the county's most highly placed lawyers expressed it:

> There is something about the principle of a political machine that I don't believe in, that rubs me the wrong way. But break down the political machine—like they broke down the Vare machine in Philadelphia—and what have you got? You've got chaos and scandal and more filth and dirt. This is no time in our national life to have chaos anywhere.[4]

In summary, it seems unlikely that crime has increased in Chester or the county in the past quarter century. There is little evidence of highly organized depravity or violence. Most evident are the legacy of local politicians' illegal associations and marginal activities left over from Prohibition, and the gambling that flourishes in urbanized areas, including Montgomery County's industrial boroughs and lower Bucks County. Delaware County, with its riverfront tradition, seems to have the highest suburban concentration of crime. County politicians commonly point to Philadelphia as the source of their crime problems, but the technical and financial connections that some suburban operators maintain in the central city are not necessarily syndication in the ominous, national sense.

6. *The Democratic party* has never been an active factor in Delaware County. As in the other counties, business and civic elites are overwhelmingly Republican. The traditional voting alignments of urban minorities should aid Delaware's Democrats, but suburban residence itself may well be altering these alignments. More than 40 percent of the county's population is Roman Catholic, but this group (both Irish and Italian) has recently been recognized by Republican judgeships and has long won lower organization posts. More than 40 percent of the county's population lives in municipalities that fall in the bottom quarter of the

Fels Institute's social-rank scale for the metropolitan area and that contain blue-collar majorities.[5] The two groups overlap heavily in the lower end of the county. However, that is the region most susceptible to job-centered politics and, perhaps, to appeals to its social distinction from Democratic Philadelphia, from which many of its younger residents are recent emigrants. Democratic presidential voting has lately increased in this region, which also was closely contested during the depression. Kennedy's confessional appeal produced a majority there in 1960; Johnson slightly increased this majority in 1964, but these margins have not obtained in off-year, local elections. In the late 1950's a few municipalities fell to the Democrats, but the trend was sharply reversed in the early 1960's, when the organization campaigned hard on charges of Philadelphia annexation (based on an imperialistic congressional redistricting plan of the Democratic city machine) and played subtly on the fears of a Negro invasion.*

Republican leadership has been alert to possible softness in the southern region, and this threat may be a consolidating force in its organization. If Chester alone went Democratic the county balance would not be seriously affected, but close competition for county office would follow from a Democratic trend in the Ridley-Darby region as well.

By at least the late 1930's McClure's organization normally controlled the minority county commissioner and enough of the Democratic Party to elect him. Equally disabling was the invisibility of control, giving rise to constant bickering and suspicion. As Democratic prospects improved in the early 1950's a coalition was formed, and in a series of hard primaries, it broke the older elements' hold and rendered the party independent. But a chronic division persisted between the urban, organization Democrats to the south and east and the urbane, intellectual Democrats in the north and west: the first group, when it held together, could win primaries, but did not appeal to independent voters. This division, and others within it, depressed both party competition and attention to county issues.

7. *Old family*. Montgomery County politics has been heavily financed by local industrialists, and in Bucks some gentry are influential Republican lawyers and elder statesmen. Delaware County has notables of both types. Their contemporary role stems from the independent status

* In 1961 Negroes were brought into some communities on the Sunday before election day to look at houses, and local committeemen then made their rounds to drive the point home. Recently Republican congressional candidates have made known their opposition to national fair-housing legislation. Thus the civil rights issue at all governmental levels seems likely to hurt the Democratic party in suburban areas where it is in the minority by dividing its social constituency and reinforcing some of the more exclusive Republican associations of suburban residence. In this way place of residence may still compete with social rank as a factor in popular party identification, as it once did when urban-rural differences were more important.

of Chester, where most of the old family fortunes and connections began in the last century, and from leisurely growth in the county's central and western sections, where such families now tend to reside. Several of the largest law firms in Chester and Media are at least second-generation firms, with old family names in the partnership. Scions of nineteenth-century clans are important in the political organization: as of 1963 Chester's mayor (also party chairman) bore the names of two of Chester's founding families; the county sheriff stemmed from one of these families plus at least three others of equal antiquity. During the confused party leadership situation of 1961-63 two men were said by political lieutenants to be centers of decision or deferral in matters of county policy, though their influence cannot be clearly assessed. One was the president judge, tied by wedlock and descent to Chester society and industry. The other was general counsel for the Manufacturers' Association and John McClure's personal attorney (both for more than twenty-five years), and a direct descendent of three mayors of Chester, the last of whom was a close associate of McClure.

Despite the surface role of genealogy in Delaware's political arrangements, population growth and economic competition have eroded its importance. There is no formal county society. Civic and political leadership tend to represent different sections of the county. Of notables in the organization, those with high offices or reported influence are men whose professional ability has been independently tested; others lack stature. John McClure sensitively employed local reputation as a political resource. This currency is difficult to appraise, but it almost certainly declined in value with settlement of the county and narrowing of its realm of circulation.

8. *Industry.* McClure's control was often said to rest on heavy industry. Delaware County's economy does have distinguishing features: its geographical concentration, the PMA tradition of direct Republican participation, and the political ties of some industrialists through personal interest and family connection. Such corporations as Scott Paper, American Viscose (division of FMC Corporation), Sun Oil, and Sun Ship have home plants and top management in the county; their officers are long-time county residents, leaders in the Manufacturers' Association, loyal Republicans, and at least occasional participants in politics and governmental appointees. Thus the break with the nineteenth-century entrepreneurial pattern is not complete. When John McClure was challenged in the primary of 1936 most local bankers and industrialists organized by PMA's county attorney supported him strongly. Employment in some plants was used as patronage in the Depression. Local industrialists enjoyed close personal association with Senator McClure as long as he lived.

Yet the common attribution of predominance to industry is probably wrong. Industry's principal interests appear to be two: taxes and backing in Harrisburg; concrete local governmental programs and projects are only occasional concerns. Both interests are less negotiable now than they were before modern federal taxation and state electoral competition. Organization control of local assessors and state legislators is tight, but industry's interest in them has diminished. Both interests appear to favor politicians with stronger sanctions than industry's, which also would seem to be two: the threat of removal of the industry (with its effect on jobs and profits) and political contributions, i.e., control and wealth.

In general, industrial job control has been reduced by automation and upgrading. Moreover, threats of locally owned industries to remove are rarely credible; on this score absentee-owned plants would seem to be favored. Threats of directing expansion elsewhere might carry more weight in a more growth-oriented county, but they have figured in tax bargaining by the Manufacturers' Association in the past. Since McClure's death the county commissioners have, in private, referred to this as an implicit consideration in county policy, especially with respect to expanding, absentee-owned plants, but several industries have shown increased interest recently in some county services (for instance, a community college), which the commissioners have resisted. Neither evidence nor inference points clearly to industrial influence, either explicit or implicit, on county policy by means of threats to remove, nor, if such influence exists, would it amount to maintenance of the political organization.

Financial backing—the other possible industrial sanction—is not well reported, but substantial contributions from industry are said by all concerned to have been limited to general elections, except for those from the Pew family, and a decade of opposition from the Pews demonstrated McClure's primary reliance on the courthouse as a resource. Nominations to office are said by all informants to be organization decisions solely, though candidates' acceptability to many interests is doubtless one consideration.[6] Several local industrialists have long backed politicians and sought their protection, but they would probably find it hard to organize for outright electoral action or to justify political adventures in business terms, especially in view of the organization's record of vote control.

On McClure's side, the manufacturers' main attractions seem to have been financial backing, public support or neutrality in factional struggles, and local evidence of successful men's respect. On each side, lack of opposition and consistency of interests were evidently the chief considerations. Overall and a priori the subtle balance of resources has probably favored the political organization.

9. *The character of county government.* Continuity in courthouse careers is striking in Delaware County. Men and women regularly move from top appointive positions (e.g., sealer of weights and measures,

member of the Board of Assessment and Revision of Taxes, warden of the prison, county engineer) to elective office, but people progress in both directions according to opportunity, local pressure, and party discipline. Many jobholders are local party workers, several elective officeholders have held appointive jobs and vice versa, and all the judges have served in appointive office. Delaware's courthouse, like Montgomery's, is a large family.

Its conduct is appropriately informal. Many custodial functions are still performed by hand, such as inscribing of pay checks, recording of deeds, and registering of wills.* Budget methods, central purchasing, stockpiling, and storage are primitive by normal standards. Personnel classification is nonexistent. Overstaffing and incapacity are evident. A consultant's study, ordered by two dissident commissioners in 1962 but never made public, reported that:

> ... the selection process in Delaware County has often resulted in the hiring of typists who cannot type, stenographers who cannot take shorthand, and mechanics who know little about vehicles. In turn, there are an indeterminable number of employees whose attitude, industry, physical condition, or all three do not make them fit employees, but whom the department head must retain because he cannot obtain the permission of the political party in power to release them.[7]

While the direct cost of these practices is reduced by low salaries for top jobs, pay rates for the supernumerous clerical personnel compare favorably with the local average for private employment.

On the other hand, Delaware's management is as honest, on the public record, as that in the other counties. And professional enclaves in public welfare and land planning have been established for more than a decade, though their threat to courthouse custom and morale is carefully regulated by low salaries, limited functions, isolation from policy-making, and retention of patronage for all clerical positions.† Thus the planning commission has been employed far more in local assistance than in comprehensive planning, for which it has not been staffed, and its assistance (e.g., in subdivision review) has been resisted by most municipalities in the lower end of the county, where the county's private consulting engineers are active and well connected politically.[8]

10. *Policy.* In the postwar years of rapid growth Delaware County's officeholders came predominantly from more stable localities, including

* In 1963, when the *Delaware County Daily Times* began publishing an account of courthouse methods, the Recorder of Deeds announced he would recommend to the commissioners purchase of microfilm equipment, which would do the work of nineteen typists.

† When the county incinerator program (described in Chapter 14) was begun it was placed under a professional engineering manager recruited by widespread advertising. After the facilities were in place and the program established the professional manager was fired and all positions became political.

those of lower income and social rank. This distribution can probably be traced to the organization's probationary tests for office, the Democratic threat and the demand for patronage in low-income districts, and the political volatility of more rapidly growing townships. More than in the other counties, Delaware's jobholders and politicians were careerists. Few elected officials were men of more than modest means, and these few were small businessmen and local lawyers.

Both the sectional and the social representation in the courthouse are at least consistent with Delaware's priorities in policy, which differed from the other counties'. Given the lack of electoral competition, personal attributes may, within limits, explain the county's conservatism and resistance to innovation.

Delaware emphasized public welfare and a few utilities to supplement municipal efforts. Services for white-collar residential sections, such as planning, open space, libraries, and mass transit, were relatively neglected, as was industrial development. Delaware County seemed less responsive to new regions than to old, but the new municipalities were more self-sufficient and, *perhaps*, more efficient. Delaware was urbanized earlier than the other counties and its basic infrastructure was already provided in special districts; there was less pressure for county action in fields like sewerage and water supply, except in the unsettled western end of the county.

Thus the pattern of local interests differed in Delaware County. So did fiscal capacity: Delaware's tax rate today is closely approaching the ten-mill legal limit, and institutional district millage is much higher than in Bucks or Montgomery. Pressure from the tax ceiling reflects Delaware's low assessment ratio, but pressure for more services suggests reassessment, which is politically risky. Most elements in Delaware County—organized industry, new homeowners, and perhaps especially lower-income residents in the older sections*—are sensitive to reassessment. The organization's normal resistance to innovation is thereby reinforced.

Ideologies, interests, and institutions are consistent in county policy. Industrial protectivism and the low-tax philosophy of the Manufacturers' Association are rarely challenged in Delaware. Politicians are job-centered, not policy-oriented, emphasizing organizational loyalty. Most business and political interests are complementary, and this bias is fortified by a cumbrous governmental structure.

The organization in the county at large (Chester apart) is far from a monolith. On the evidence in these pages it is alert to potential electoral competition in sensitive areas and always takes elections seriously. Its leader carefully balanced inducements and sanctions among key groups

* In general, older properties are less fully assessed, so that reassessment would especially affect the southern part of the county; in addition, real property taxation is regressive to income, and there is evidence that even proportional or progressive taxation is especially resented at lower income levels. See Angus Campbell, et al., *The American Voter* (New York: John Wiley & Sons, 1960), Ch. 9.

and individuals: business, bench and bar, and local politicos. He heavily relied on formal decentralization and informal centralization, on both co-optation and division of opposition, and on systematic exploitation of county government's political resources. Thus the organization was selectively responsive, while normally it acted to maximize the existing mobilization of bias.

With the growth of population and, perhaps, of social differences in Delaware County the political organization's future was uncertain. In the year after John McClure's death the commissioners and the War Board were more resistant than ever to innovation, professionalism, and fiscal pressure: they held the line on all services and refused to provide the new ones sought by civic groups and even industry (in the case of a community-college proposal). It was possible that, while the habits and attitudes of the organization persisted, its adaptability and responsiveness were impaired by the loss of its leader. Fear of property reassessment was probably of at least equal importance.

PART III. GOVERNMENT

11

Functions and Structure

Local government—especially rural and suburban government—is best understood in its legal setting. Legally speaking, counties and municipalities are creatures of the state, whose constitution, statutes, and courts control local action. Three facets of this formal context are especially important: the limited powers of local governments, their division between counties and municipalities, and the fragmented structure of counties.

Limitations of power reflect two traditions, "judicial" and "custodial." These still shape attitudes today (especially those of bench and bar), despite substantial broadening of county power in recent years. The modern increase in county options justifies comparative study and the analysis of change, but such study best begins with the traditions.

1. *The judicial tradition* is expressed in references to the county government as the "courthouse." Historically, the courts were the most prestigious local offices. Actually, Pennsylvania's county courts are state agencies, and some smaller counties are combined in state judicial districts. Their judges, while locally elected to ten-year terms, are paid by the state. Support of the courts—clerical, coercive, and correctional —is entailed on the counties. Much of county government consists in elective offices that deal in legal instruments and law enforcement— district attorney, sheriff, coroner, clerk of courts, prothonotary, recorder of deeds, registrar of wills—and in correctional institutions.

Judges, for their part, have long performed a number of nonjudicial functions, such as making appointments to vacant elective local office and supervision of public dealings in real property. Courts also make county policy in judicial decisions. Their views of land use (though subject to appeal) shape local zoning and county planning. Assessment decisions can alter the tax base. Correctional and child-welfare actions entail capital facilities. Finally, most public measures may be reviewed in taxpayer suits or by grand juries on judicial initiative.

The judges' involvement in policy puts them in politics. Suburban judges have not lately been political leaders, nor have the political leaders normally been lawyers. The situation was different in the nineteenth century; now the demands of each job encourages a division of labor, and the professional aspects of each favor different paths of advancement. Yet the same factors induce accommodation between the courts and the county politicians.

> One of the eroding influences upon the independence of the judiciary in Pennsylvania is the political pressures to which the local courts are subjected by reason of the vast powers of appointment . . . and the supervision of affairs of local government entrusted to them. . . . The action of the legislature in delegating to the courts power of appointments to or requiring service on various boards and commissions was no doubt originally intended to minimize political considerations and as a mark of confidence in the integrity of the judges. Its ultimate effect, however, was to subject the judiciary to undue pressures from political leaders and other persons.[1]

Complementing the court's appointing power is the political leader's control of nominations. With ten-year terms and no legal retirement age, it turns out that 90 percent of Pennsylvania's nominally elected judges first reach the bench through gubernatorial appointment on political advice from the counties.[2] Elevation by election vests more influence in political leaders, and so does renomination after either interim appointment or a full term. Nomination is often tantamount to election in the typically one-party counties. Since neither political leaders nor local bar associations have favored the sitting-judge rule, few men reach the bench save by political service, and in the politically well-organized counties reliability is sometimes the price of renomination.

There are exceptions to these tendencies. Effective political competition in Bucks County began with the reaction of the county bar to an unpopular court appointment, and the decline of two strong Montgomery County political organizations has, within living memory, been signaled by bitter primary fights for judicial office. The tenure and prestige of the bench place some restraints on its political control, but apparently preponderant influence rests with otherwise strong political organizations.*

For the judges, the line is difficult to draw between political (i.e., partisan or factional) decisions and those of mere governmental supervision. Such acts as making appointments to vacant elective office or delineation of election districts on petition are critical for politicians.

---

* In some counties the bar associations vote on suggested judicial appointments. In 1963 new court positions in Bucks and Delaware Counties went to men who were pointedly passed over in bar association polls: one was county Republican chairman; the other was a township political leader and county coroner.

Contests over substantive acts of government may also have political overtones. In Delaware County, with its robust political structure, some judges are reported to have said that primarily political cases are simply decided on party lines, and members of the county bar who have been interviewed agree that this is so. Inspection of all political cases (appointments, districting, and some others) decided in Delaware County in the last decade reveals no clear instance of decision against the dominant political organization's interest. Yet no lawyer maintained that political ends or the partisan connections of counsel affect ordinary civil and criminal decisions. One may ask what standards exist, other than party interest, by which to decide the most highly political cases; though one must also recognize that some partly or potentially political proceedings involve the civil rights of individuals. One of the most difficult issues in democratic government is that of where to find an impartial umpire for intrinsically partisan questions.

The judicial tradition rests on commingling of local governmental and judicial roles and on judicial review as a constitutional function—paradoxically, on both abridgment and enforcement of the separation of powers idea, and on compromise of local control with state sovereignty. The combination of local roles began with the colonial emulation of English institutions enjoined on William Penn by his charter. Justices of the peace in several county districts held broad powers over commerce and personal conduct. These squires were legal laymen who served long terms (sometimes life terms). In Quarter Sessions or oftener they supervised county administration (especially the construction and maintenance of roads, bridges, and public buildings, care of the poor, and appointment of officials) and rendered justice subject to appeal. The organization of higher courts and regulation of appeals raised hot controversy in the eighteenth century: professionalization of the law was resisted at first by the Friends and later by rural "republicans."

Judicial consolidation grew with the legal profession. In 1759 county common pleas courts, to which lawyers were normally appointed, were established for civil cases. In 1776 the first state Constitution required president judges to be "learned in the law," though laymen served as associates until precluded by the Constitution of 1874. Criminal cases were vested in another county court. The old justices of the peace, appointed by the governor, remained local political powers well into the nineteenth century, when the office became elective.[3] Although elected county commissioners date from 1724, the miscellaneous duties of the courts continued and accrued. Judges were appointed by the provincial (later state) governor until 1850, when a culminating amendment to Pennsylvania's Jacksonian Constitution of 1838 rendered them elective.

Popular election, political obligation, and association with the local bar doubtless orient judges to the counties despite their state salaries.

Exercise of governmental functions involves them in county affairs, while in judicial review they act for the commonwealth. Historical and political forces have produced some compromise of both state sovereignty and the separation of powers in the county courts. One can account for the judicial tradition by the rise of the legal profession and by the close relation of real property to both local government and the common law. One may justify it by the invidious opportunities in local and county policy, the common informality of administration, and the monopolistic structure of politics. Some of its ambiguities might be resolved, however, by eliminating the judges' nonjudicial roles, enlarging judicial districts, and altering methods of selection.

2. *The custodial tradition.* In its legal relation to the state the county is more an administrative agency for essentials than a legislative body responding to wants or relating social purposes. Historically, local government in Pennsylvania has emphasized four nonjudicial functions: roads, poor relief, taxes, and elections. These functions were both shared and shifted between counties and municipalities.

In the Colonial Period roads and bridges were at first the counties' responsibility. This devolved upon the districts and then the townships —except for bridges, which remained with the counties. In the nineteenth century the state, counties, and townships were all involved in laying out roads, but construction and maintenance were municipal functions. Turnpikes were built by private corporations, but counties were allowed to invest in them. Centralization came with the twentieth century: first counties were empowered to build highways; then state and federal aid commenced and was followed by the state highway system, which became one of the nation's most centralized; it even briefly took over township roads in the Depression. Pennsylvania today maintains more state highway mileage than New England, New York, and New Jersey combined; the counties have mostly contented themselves with assisting in the upkeep of bridges and allocating their share of the liquid fuel tax funds to municipalities.

Poor relief also began as a county obligation, but it was transferred in 1705 to local overseers appointed by the justices. Diseconomies of scale evidently set in as indoor relief developed. Early in the nineteenth century most of the older, more populous counties (including Bucks, Montgomery, and Delaware) were authorized to give relief at the county level, and they did so through elected boards of overseers of the counties' almshouses—though local conservatives opposed consolidation.[4] Late in the nineteenth century differentiation began with special treatment of epileptics, the mentally ill, and various kinds of minors, while persons classed as criminal, lewd, or dissolute were removed from the almshouse and lodged in jail. A Juvenile Court was added to the county bench. Outdoor relief was increasingly employed in the counties, and special pension programs were authorized and aided by the state. By the Depression the single, simple function of poor relief was a sprawling public welfare program. Then public assistance—the core of poor relief —was assumed by the state, and it remains entirely centralized; the almshouse became the county old folks' home. Counties were left with care of dependent, neglected, and delinquent children and the indigent aged, thus continuing judicial and custodial traditions. In the past decade the state has sought to consolidate its own programs, professionalize county measures, and relate the two in ways described in Chapter 16.

Administration of taxes was frequently shifted between levels. County courts and then county commissioners were colonial tax assessors; later assessment became a municipal duty, but the county commissioners served as a board of revision after 1842. In 1931 assessment was again vested in third-class counties. Tax *collection* was at first shared by both levels, but after 1845 elected local tax collectors handled both township and county taxes. During most of the nineteenth century state taxes were also collected locally, since the state mainly relied on the real property tax. Finally, election administration has always been a county responsibility, although the inspectors of elections are locally elected.

The functions just reviewed, though not exclusively the counties', were staples in the custodial tradition. Many of the services incidental to courts (such as registry of legal papers) were fee-supported. Each function was substantially unrelated to the others and largely entailed on counties by the state.

A discretionary aspect of the custodial tradition is county aid of private endeavors thought to serve public interests. Thus counties may appropriate up to specified maxima for, e.g., historical societies, agricultural and horticultural societies, and the Society for the Prevention of Cruelty to Animals. There are no limits on appropriations to voluntary charities, which have characterized county action in health and welfare. An example is support of hospitals in Montgomery County, where in 1950 eleven hospitals shared $25,000 in aid; later the assistance was loosely tied to indigent care and by 1962 thirteen hospitals (exclusive of mental health facilities) divided $100,000. County support of the poor by purchase of service or general institutional subsidies is well established, since state and federal programs have until recently left indigent medical care to localities. Today the three counties vary greatly in extent of subsidy versus direct governmental action.

Another public interest supported by counties is military preparedness and remembrance. Counties may appropriate to National Guard units and to veterans' organizations for memorial observances. They must establish a Director of Veterans' Affairs to provide grave markers and burial to deceased service persons and their widows. The counties' martial role began with the local militia in the early nineteenth century and has been sustained by veterans' lobbies. Today the counties are also civil defense authorities.[5]

There was little more to county government than the foregoing in the nineteenth century.* After that began a gradual access of powers that challenged the custodial tradition without extinguishing it. The increase of powers occurred in two phases. In the first, from the turn of the century to the Depression, came the discretionary highway powers and control of assessments already mentioned, together with parks and recreation, libraries, flood control, and hospitals for tuberculosis and other contagious diseases. Most of these were available to municipalities as well as counties. During the Depression and postwar years other optional county powers were congerred, several of which figure in our analysis of county performance. They encompass some provision for the physical environment, economic base, and health and welfare. They include land planning (1937), public housing (1937), urban redevelopment (1945), sewage disposal (1945) and refuse disposal (1955), general public health (1951), industrial development (1955), tourist promotion (1961), airports (1955) and mass transit (1961, 1963), and broader authority in mental health and child welfare.[6]

Together, counties and municipalities are now empowered to provide for most of the public wants of suburban populations. Yet their methods are more ad hoc and service-oriented than integrated and policy-oriented. Tradition is one reason for this: functions are still decidedly finite and discrete. But the judicial and custodial traditions reinforce two structural factors: division of functions between local governments and fragmentation of county government.

3. *Of division of functions*, only the background and implications remain for discussion. Government in the Middle Atlantic colonies was intermediate in form as well as in situation between New England's emphasis on towns and the southern orientation to counties: it was influenced by settlement patterns and economic activity. The dominant elements in Penn's first settlement were the nuclear city and its surrounding large estates. Colonial government began with the counties. After dispersal of settlement, governmental devolution to districts and thence to townships was convenient. As more townships were settled, decentralizing pressures increased—especially with arrival of New En-

---

* In 1884 Montgomery County allocated its taxes as follows: Norristown Insane Asylum, $13,309; elections, $3,478; assessors, $7,693; printing and binding, $3,368; cost of grand jury, $1,195; prisons and penitentiary, $9,041; books and stationery, $487; coroner's offices, $3,900; bridges, $11,033; road damages, $9,567; courthouse and yard, $1,895; court charges, $23,236; miscellaneous, $13,151; county treasurer's salary, $4,500; director of the poor, $30,414. In this year, on expenditures of about $130,000 the county showed a surplus of about $70,000. Theodore Bean, *History of Montgomery County*, p. 330.

glanders accustomed to towns and of the Germans with their emphasis on autonomy and economy.

The shifting of functions between levels reflected urban-rural differences in which farmers sought to avoid support of urban services. Then the problem arose of providing such services in developing, densely settled enclaves. The nineteenth-century solution was the borough, a quasi-incorporated unit detached from its surrounding township when self-determination and higher service levels were desired. At the end of the century townships were classified twofold, essentially suburban and rural.[7] In the twentieth century gradual expansion of first-class townships' powers to parity with boroughs' discouraged further incorporations, but the existing boroughs continued as industrial, commercial, or cultural centers, all of them small in area.

This history and the shifting of functions have not produced a consistent doctrine about local-county relations. Administratively, the counties provide certain framework functions, but legally the two levels are equal and the county courts have superintendence of both. Powers are neither separate nor shared in theory; most county options are also municipal possibilities, and the two jurisdictions are implicitly competitive. Relations are worked out politically. Division of functions limits the distributive aspects of politics, as does restriction of civic interest to municipalities, where the most salient services are rendered. Localities, however, look to the counties for such means as assessments, disbursement of state highway aids, and planning assistance, and local politicians look to the counties for jobs. Thus both levels—but especially the counties—are more narrowly political and administrative than policy-centered.

4. *Fragmented structure.* It follows from legal tradition that counties' legislative and executive powers are negligible.[8] Thus there has been little concern about broadly representative or responsible county institutions. Instead, the law relies on simple suspicion of office holders, evidenced by direct election of many, limitations on the tenure of some, overlapping terms, elaboration of internal checks, and required minority party representation.

The custodial arm of county government consists of three commissioners elected at large, of whom one must belong to the minority party; and of numerous elective row offices including controller, treasurer, and (vestigially) surveyor. All serve four-year terms and are ordained by the state constitution. The county commissioners make policy: they adopt the budget and levy taxes to support it; they initiate new activities and appoint the officials in charge; and as directors of the County Institution District (a separate jurisdiction for welfare services and facilities), they do the same.[9] They also serve as election and registration commissioners. They appoint the county clerk and solicitor; the various commissions, boards, and authorities; and the heads and personnel of several departments.

The commissioners' powers are no more comprehensive of ends than of means. State law prescribes the organizational form of some functions, and it also encourages creation of independent authorities to cope with fiscal limits and local tax consciousness.[10] Most boards and authorities are legally irremovable and appoint their own personnel. Several elective row offices are fee offices; register of wills, recorder of deeds, and prothonotary are largely self-supporting; and there is considerable fee income in the sheriff's office. The spending and appointing power of all officials is checked by a Salary Board, consisting of the commissioners, controller, and relevant row officeholder, which must pass on all new positions. Finally, the controller may in his discretion refuse to allow expenditures and at least precipitate a test in the courts. Although most row-office functions are ministerial, each office, like most boards and authorities, may retain its own solicitor.

The basic form of county government has hardly changed in a century and a half, but extension of county powers has enhanced the commissioners' influence and discretion. In the past they occupied part-time jobs; today some suburban commissioners devote a normal working week to it, taking politics and administration together.* On the present salary ($11,250) many able candidates feel they cannot afford to run. Men in the most flexible, politically relevant professions—law, real estate, and insurance—find the office most convenient, but even they privately complain of the cost.

Public and political attention are increasingly centered on the commissioners. They initiate and finance the new county options, though their administrative powers are limited in ways just discussed. Their chief decisions are fiscal, not administrative. They have every incentive to look to costs and benefits, but less opportunity to choose among means, coordinate activity, or continuously to alter priorities and relate purposes. They may, for example, appoint a park board and a water authority, but in the absence of personal or political influence, they cannot actively direct or connect them. The system of three commissioners acting through isolated initiatives, appointments, and appropriations probably lends itself better to organization politics and specific group responses than to personal leadership and public relations in behalf of general ends. County structure tends to narrow public issues, but it makes political organization important.

In summary, the counties today seem better suited to suburban than to urban problems, to regulations and support of real property than to social and cultural issues. Even planning and taxing of land development

* One of Bucks' present majority commissioners, a dairyman and merchant, promised in his campaign to make the office a full-time job, and Bucks' present minority commissioner resigned his company position as an electrical engineer after his election.

are limited by division of functions and fragmented structure; counties respond to development better than they control it. Finally, counties lack legislative and executive capacity to cope with emergencies, since this, in constitutional theory, belongs to the state.

These points are illustrated in the three chapters that follow. The first two deal with planning and taxing. As extensions of county government's long preoccupation with land, these functions reflect the conservative mobilization of bias affecting county policy, but they also affect political competition and power structure. Chapter 14 compares the governmental characteristics of the three counties and relates them to social and economic attributes. It sets the stage for the study of differences in policy and performance.

12

Planning

Pennsylvania counties are amply authorized by law to plan, but their land-use powers are blocked by municipal zoning and subdivision controls.*

Suburban county planning did not begin until mid-century. James Coke, close student and chronicler of planning in suburban Philadelphia, notes two sources for it that appeared in 1950: one was the projected Pennsylvania Turnpike extension eastward from Harrisburg, traversing three of the four suburban counties and affecting all of them profoundly; the other was United States Steel's decision, in light of available land, rail, and water resources, to locate its large Fairless Works at the elbow of the Delaware in Bucks County. These decisions were made in Harrisburg and New York respectively, but, as Coke argues, ". . . both dramatized the nature of metropolitan area expansion."[1] In the winter of 1950, at state instigation, Fred Peters, then political leader of Montgomery County, asked the surrounding county commissioners to a meeting at the King of Prussia Inn, hard by the projected Turnpike extension. A state planning official spoke to them about the Turnpike and its implications and about county and regional planning. Peters, then at his political zenith, had been trained as a landscape architect, and planning appealed to him. He accepted county planning and sold the other county politicians on it, and that is how suburban planning began. A regional planning commission followed, the story of whose rise and rapid decline in intergovernmental rivalry has been told by Coke.[2]

Despite their common inspiration, the three counties' planning his-

---

* The law provides for an independent county planning commission, which may review private subdivision plans of three or more lots in size but may disapprove these *only* in townships lacking their own subdivision regulations. Counties may zone for second-class townships, but most municipalities zone for themselves, and the suburban counties have not assumed this power.

tories show instructive differences. In particular, they illustrate the relations of politics to planning.

1. *Bucks County.* Oddly, in view of its later prestige, Bucks' planning commission was the last to begin. The county appointed a commission but, suspicious of professionals, withheld appropriations and staff. Pressure mounted from the state and from Philadelphia officials and civic agencies (especially the Housing Association and the Health and Welfare Council), and the Citizens' Council for Bucks County Planning was formed with their support to goad the county. Yielding, the county commissioners sought a planning director; instinctively they sought a local man. They found him in Franklin Wood, who had been trained as a landscape architect and was then employed by the Philadelphia City Planning Commission. By the fall of 1951 a staff was at work and in January 1952 the county adopted subdivision regulations. Bucks' explosive growth qualified it for state aid; and a team of state consultants studied lower Bucks while Philadelphia scholars recorded its progress and proffered advice.[3] In no other county were external pressures so important in the origins of planning. From 1950 to 1955 Bucks grew 60 percent, while lower Bucks doubled; in 1955 the minority Democratic party captured the county and strongly endorsed planning. Thus the shock of growth encouraged planning even as it complicated the job; official attitudes were somewhat altered *before* elections changed county government's complexion.

The lower Bucks consultant studies and Wood's quiet public relations gave planning its start: they developed a fragmentary base for comprehensive planning, while Wood undertook the tutelage of lower Bucks' local governments through meetings, memoranda, and an in-service training program. By 1955 he could work with local planning commissions in most of lower Bucks (There had been only one in 1951.), and federal aid became available for local planning assistance.[4] By then attention was shifting to land and facilities from the county standpoint, beginning with parks and open space, which received heavy emphasis because of Wood's own background in landscaping and the opportunity implicit in Bucks' early stage of development. Both the park board and the industrial development agency began in the planning commission and were later detached with their own personnel. Under political and population pressure consultant studies of airports, sewerage, and water supply were undertaken. On its own motion, the staff by 1957 produced surveys of future county development and, in the same year, a preliminary comprehensive land-use plan. County appropriations doubled in 1952-56 and 1956-58. The county government consulted the planning commission, and limited bipartisanship obtained in two changes in county administration. Planning became an object of civic pride and a source of newspaper copy. It thus progressed from political reluctance to public acceptance; the planning commission moved from troubleshooting for local governments to developing county services and facilities. As both local assistance and specific county studies developed the director kept his eye on overall design. The result was a published county comprehensive plan in 1961—the first in the suburban region—laying out loose configurations for future growth in a modified greenbelts scheme.[5]

2. *In Montgomery County*, as in Bucks, a local man became planning director. David Longmaid, then thirty, was trained at the Massachusetts Institute of Technology, where he wrote a thesis on the projected King of Prussia Turnpike interchange; his socially prominent Main Line family was active in local Republican politics. The new planner began in the county engineer's office—a tacitly competitive but otherwise serene setting. By contrast, Longmaid spoke often at evening meetings to sell planning, patiently negotiated with Harrisburg over Turnpike location in response to local pressures, and single-handedly developed subdivision regulations and began the commission's program—basically one of assistance to municipalities. Behind this emphasis were the canny Fred Peters and the force of county tradition. Peters viewed planning in local and regional foci, with subdivision controls and highways as subjects; his view of county government was dominated by economy. Within this context he strongly backed Longmaid against irate developers and their lawyers in application of subdivision controls. On some occasions the developers' ire stemmed from having already bribed local officials to expedite matters, only to meet new frustrations at the county level; Peters assured them that county planning would save them money and, as he intended, simplify their problems.

The effect of Fred Peters' views and of his characteristic substitution of political for economic support was to direct county planning almost entirely to the local level. The most comprehensive achievements of the first five years were studies of industrial land and of highway planning with the Southeastern Pennsylvania Regional Planning Commission—by then under Longmaid's direction—and a model zoning ordinance widely adopted in Montgomery's municipalities. The Regional Planning Commission fell apart in 1956, however, and the peak of subdivision activity in Montgomery was passed in 1955. Most ominous of all was Fred Peters' departure from the county scene. Political discord ensued in which localism versus county planning became an open issue.

In a sense the issue arose precisely because the county planning commission had not confined itself to the fields of its major achievements: by 1955 it was quietly developing comprehensive planning data (though none were published), including an inventory of community facilities and services. This new emphasis, derived from local planning assistance studies and the planners' desire to transcend research, precipitated the issue late in 1955 after the election of new county commissioners. The county planners publicly suggested that the county perform six new functions: refuse disposal, sewage disposal, water resources development, flood control, recreation, and planning of local roads. When the new commissioners showed a total lack of interest, the planners independently sought public backing.

Also in 1955 the state legislature had amended the county code to deprive county planning commissions of power to disapprove subdivision plans in municipalities with their own regulations. Montgomery's planning commission then tried to enforce its own subdivision review, seeking legal support from the county solicitor and public support in press releases. Soon localism entered the picture as a basic political force. In Pennsylvania, associations of municipalities are active—they were chiefly responsible for the 1955 amendment—and the head of the county Boroughs' Association was the political agent for one of Montgomery's wealthiest, most conservative families. A proposed state highway, on the planning commission's center line, was then threatening his home borough and his principal's property. Editorials about the threat of county planning to local home rule began to appear in the *Montgomery County Boroughs' Reporter*. The Second Class Township Association joined in, while the chairman of the planning commission quarreled publicly with the county commissioners about the role of county planning and shut off all local planning assistance, vowing to fight fire with fire. Both planning and appropriations dwindled; late in the first year of the new administration the planning director resigned, followed by all but one of the staff. Within weeks the commission chairman also resigned in a bitter public letter, followed by several colleagues.

For the rest of the Hammonds administration the planning commission publicly stuck to local assistance studies. It did, however, eventually persuade the commissioners to create a redevelopment authority and an industrial development study committee, both of which were inactive. By the next election, under private pressure, water resources and a county airport were on the agenda.

That election produced the Wetherill administration discussed in Chapter 8. Its sensitivity to public relations led it simultaneously to seek accomplishment and shun controversy; it quickly found in the county planners the only official source of ideas and initiative, and the most respectable means of reserving judgment. In time, therefore, the county planning commission acquired two major emphases: promotion of such county programs as open space, water resources, and regional transportation (described in later chapters), and the traditional local planning assistance, enhanced by closer local relations and regional agreements among municipalities. From the start the new political leadership dealt directly with the staff and ignored the commission, and two planning directors were let out in brief succession before a *modus operandi* was reached.

Certain threads run through the history of planning in Montgomery

County. One is its heavy dependence on political support. Closely allied to this was the weak planning commission and direct staff relations with the county commissioners. A third theme was the nature of planning itself: despite the inclination of some staff men throughout this history, local planning on one hand and county action programs on the other were recurring emphases; planning in its technical and comprehensive sense was deemphasized. There were strong political reasons for the local emphasis and, later, for the concentration on county functions. There were hazards in direct alliance with political leadership and advocacy of action programs without the protection of a strong commission and basic research. In Montgomery's glacially changing balance between organization politics and civic action, between industrial conservatives and developers, the planners had little choice.

3. *In Delaware County*, the region's most stable political environment, planning took a middle course. It began with the largest budget of all, but, while that budget has roughly doubled, both Bucks' and Montgomery's have more than quadrupled, illustrating Delaware's political stability.

A counter-illustration of the same point, however, was early establishment of the principle of the professional staff's freedom from political clearance and assessment. This break with local custom took longer to establish in Montgomery, though it was always followed in Bucks. Delaware's planning staff was wholly professional from the beginning; operating in the most populous and densely settled county of the three, it was also the smallest and most circumscribed in action.

These factors—the dense settlement of half of Delaware County and the slim resources devoted to planning—may help explain the middle course that planning took there: a compromise between county and local planning. Local planning assistance was a major emphasis; but its effectiveness and acceptability were somewhat improved by requiring municipalities to bear half the cost of studies, and by the criterion that requests for assistance would be accepted according to their county-wide significance and their location in relatively undeveloped areas. In these ways, Delaware's planning commission endeavored to maximize its effect on the pattern of future development. It set its local studies within broader areal sketch plans. There is now no county comprehensive plan or comparable statement, but there is a fragmentary tradition of basic data collection with limited staff. The effects of existing densities have not been entirely ignored: early initiatives in urban redevelopment, refuse disposal, and open space preservation are reviewed below. Their political reception and administrative implementation were discouraging, and Delaware's planners have, therefore, stressed technical land use review and eschewed county policy.

Thus the planners have not served as a staff arm of county government (which is not itself a source of initiative). The commission has not been active as a whole, but its membership has been stable. The first chairman served for fifteen years and participated actively; an engineer and transit executive, he was close to both the county political leader and the staff, which, in its turn, has patiently worked within existing political protection and fiscal constraint. The first two executive directors (1951-63) were natives of the county.

4. *County planning appraised.* Planners' professionalism and innovating pressures tend to threaten political careerism and its natural ally, the custodial tradition. The question arises: Why was county planning ever undertaken? Coke, chronicler of the early history, stresses the influence of Fred Peters, based on his state political stature, and Peters' personal background in landscape architecture. He adds that planning seemed cheap, and the early budgets were certainly small.[6] In Delaware and Montgomery, some thought was evidently given to the politically unsettling effects of rapid, disorderly suburbanization, although planning was carefully controlled in those counties by low appropriations. As it turned out, local planning assistance was popular, and served both to support and to limit planning at the county level. Given low county appropriations (except in Bucks), local assistance has itself controlled the comprehensiveness of county planning by rivalry for time and attention.

Three criteria appear to be most relevant to evaluation of county planning: its comprehensiveness, its effects on development through *local* controls, and its role in county policy. From the planners' standpoint the main contrasts among the counties relate to comprehensiveness, yet this, as the technical literature allows, is an elusive concept. When Bucks and Delaware Counties are compared it *may* be that a published document is more appropriate in relatively undeveloped Bucks than in Delaware, where less room is left for broad design and future land use is less malleable. The safest claims for comprehensiveness are two: first, that county-wide emphasis should help avoid incompatible land uses at municipal margins, look to optimal service areas and location of facilities, and offer other economies of scale and perspective, and second, that comprehensiveness implies and entails rationality —searching for data, thinking through goals, reviewing means. Less certainly, there is the symbolic function of providing broad public norms and alternatives for governmental and group action. But such objectives are not necessarily realized in published plans, which may amount only to maps or data collections, or to vague pronouncements about ends unrelated to data or to means.

In achievement of comprehensiveness most regional observers rank Bucks first and Delaware a distant second. The reasons for Bucks' record probably include its relatively late residential development; the related weakness of municipal government, which encouraged county leadership; the head start from state aid in lower Bucks; and its executive director's predilection for design.* Localism, organization politics, and fiscal conservatism have discouraged comprehensive planning in the other counties.

In the absence of comprehensiveness, county planning, especially as expressed in subdivision controls, is frequently said to be defensive, merely capitalizing and accommodating suburban sprawl.[7] Its effects on land use depend heavily upon municipal acceptance of county planners' recommendations and submission of subdivision plans to the county for review. On this criterion success occurs in the same order as comprehensiveness.[8] This is partly a test of public relations, however, and ignores the fact that several *large* jurisdictions (mostly of lower income) in both Delaware and Bucks have neither sought nor accepted county subdivision review, nor are the quality and flexibility of county regulations or the price levels of development considered in this test. Neither planning practices nor economic and esthetic standards are sufficiently general for a fair comparison of the counties, and planners' priorities have differed in emphasis on local land-use regulation versus county programs and priorities. The results in subdivision control are less clearly a function of comprehensiveness than both together are functions of political support.

The effectiveness of county planning also depends on its embodiments in policies about such matters as open space, industrial development, and public utilities. Its infirmities largely stem from county government —limited powers, divided functions, and fragmented structure. But political support evidently helps to overcome formal handicaps and provide common policies. Such backing has been strong in Bucks for both regulation and positive programs; in Montgomery and Delaware it has been weak respecting one or both, with different emphases.†

This suggests that support for planning (and thus its effectiveness and comprehensiveness) has varied with the degree of political competition, though special local conditions obscure the relation between them. All the counties attracted technically capable planners, but some may have been tactically superior, and Bucks offered somewhat more scope for planning than did the other jurisdictions. Still, the restriction of planning in the less competitive counties fits with the old political

---

* As an illustration of formal comprehensiveness, the introduction to Bucks' plan states: "Political boundaries within the county were ignored except for statistical purposes and are shown on the plan only for local orientation." Bucks County Planning Commission, *A Comprehensive Plan for Bucks County, Pennsylvania*, p. 1.

† After the 1955 legislation was passed depriving counties of subdivision-approval authority, wherever local regulations were in effect the Bucks County Homebuilders' Association protested to the legislature, asking reinstatement of county authority (partly for the sake of uniformity). The head of the Homebuilders' Association later became a member of the planning commission.

organizations' avoidance of programs, expenditures, and professionalism. Restraint of planning has recently been strongest in Delaware,
which is most tightly controlled politically. The competition hypothesis
is plausible, but the interests of land developers and local politicians
have also varied among the counties, and they complicate the picture.

13

Taxing

Local government's orientation to land is emphasized by the real property tax, on which it heavily relies. This tax regulates rent, pervasively influencing land uses. It limits the counties' fiscal and administrative capacities. Its fairness may be affected by political and governmental structure. The nature of the tax base may shape voters' attitudes toward local policy. Certain individuals and interests, moreover, are especially sensitive to property taxes and, in tracing out a power structure, the tax system is a logical place to begin, since it conditions all governmental action. For all these reasons taxes warrant a separate chapter.

The property tax's known regressiveness tends to restrict local governments in redistributive functions and to focus attention on presumed property rights, which may be impaired by sectional emphases and the capital impact of taxing. These threats may be hedged against by settlement in small, homogeneous jurisdictions, by legal limits on public functions, or by conservative political organization, all of which reduce what Buchanan and Tullock have termed interdependence costs, or the inconveniences and deprivations of organized society.[1] Such tendencies exist under any tax, but the property tax enhances them by its appeal to the benefit theory of taxation—a change from times past, when property was equated with ability to pay.

Thus, the property tax not only reinforces governmental attributes reviewed in Chapter 11 but, in Pennsylvania especially, confers important resources on politicians. These repose in all three aspects of taxation: assessment, levy, and collection.

1. *Assessment* is a county function, closely connected with politics and policy. Its implications are less broadly apparent than those of the tax *rate;* yet the latter is itself an implication. Others are adequacy of

the tax base, and equity of individual treatment. Politicians say the Board of Assessment and Revision of Taxes is the county's most sensitive office because of its relations with the general public, its opportunities to give individuals special consideration, and its numerous political appointments. It divides the county into taxing districts (municipalities, in practice), appoints an assessor in each district, and hears appeals from their decisions. Ultimate appeal is to the courts.

Despite a wealth of language, state law on assessments in third-class counties leaves much to discretion. Equalization is prescribed, but no methods are provided; assessment's relation to market value is vague. The resulting technical ambiguity and its political aspects are mutually reinforcing.[2] The technical problems affecting adequacy and equity relate to nationwide tendencies to favor older properties, higher priced properties, and commercial properties and to the special characteristics of industrial assessments discussed below.[3] The political implications begin with appointment of assessors, who are often local political leaders and always political loyalists. Favoritism is probably more suspected than practiced, which makes for an economical sanction and is said, without hard evidence, to influence political registration and participation. Some assessors like to estimate residential properties a little on the high side and graciously adjust to complaints; some are under local school board pressure to raise all valuations. Equity, therefore, has two aspects, intra- and intermunicipal.

Electoral competition may tend to reduce favoritism and disparity. This hypothesis is hard to test because market value data are only partial and other valuation methods are laborious. One can observe the assessment *process*, as well as its outcome; but on this point the three county situations are not strictly comparable. In Delaware a management-consulting study recently stated that

> The assessment roll of the county was developed piecemeal as each new subdivision took place or improvement was made. No one-time, comprehensive assessment by professional assessors or in accordance with accepted standards for this work has ever taken place.[4]

It also remarked that, while the Tax Board was overstaffed, it had few trained assessors and no system for discovery of property improvements. Montgomery's methods appear to be only a little more professionalized and systematic. Bucks, most politically competitive, was a fifth-class county until 1962 and thus fell under a special legislative mandate to equalize assessments and establish permanent records. The process was begun in Bucks by a Republican administration and completed by a Democratic one through contracts wtih private mapping and assessing firms, one of which was later retained to keep ratios equal and current. Thus assessment in Bucks was professionalized.

There is tentative support for the competition hypothesis in Bucks' political history; in the occasional adjustments undertaken in Montgomery at local school boards' insistence; and in the dearth of such measures in Delaware despite similar pressures. Equalization efforts seem to have varied with degree of political competition, and some local school board pressures in Delaware have been reversed by intervention from local party organizations. Average municipal ratios of assessed to market value are roughly consistent with the hypothesis except that intermunicipal variations are larger in Montgomery than in Delaware, which appears to be a result of Montgomery's fragmentary reassessment under local pressure, plus greater rural-suburban variety and more rapid growth in Montgomery. Both the methods and the outcomes of assessment in the three counties fit the competition theory, but their force is qualified by Bucks' singular legal situation, which compelled some reform and equalization.*

TABLE 13:1

Municipal Assessment Ratios*: Means and Standard Deviations for the Three Counties, 1950-60

	BUCKS		MONTGOMERY		DELAWARE	
	Mean	Deviation	Mean	Deviation	Mean	Deviation
1950	25.3	3.76	27.7	4.25	29.5	3.42
1955	25.1	3.11	28.7	5.49	26.8	3.14
1960	33.5	1.42	33.7	5.01	25.3	2.49

* The local assessment ratios from which county averages are computed are those between the total assessment and the total market value of each municipality, as compiled and estimated by the Pennsylvania State Tax Equalization Board.

2. *Industrial assessments* raise special problems, both technical and political. Technically, the state constitutional requirements of "uniformity" and market value ("true value") are hard to meet because of the uniqueness of plants and infrequency of sales.[5] Uniformity takes judicial precedence over market value, but as a practical matter, these cannot be distinguished.[6] Both are complicated by pressure on the legislature and judiciary for special exemptions and by the general exemption of machinery and equipment, enacted in 1953, which gives rise to endless, ingenious legal distinctions.[7] Short of litigation, there is ample room for negotiation and tacit understandings in industrial assessment.

The valuation for taxes of industrial plants is thought to mobilize industrialists for political action, or at least to figure implicitly in party

* The logic of the competition theory may need some qualification. Existing ambiguities and disparities in assessment favor established political orders by providing them with sanctions and establishing vested interests. Bucks' Democrats, however, learned that reassessment can mean political disaster. Reassessment may even be especially resented in low-income areas for several hypothetical reasons: its elimination of lags in assessment ratios on older homes, lack of interest in public expenditures, or simply because of the property tax's regressiveness. Thus electoral competition might intensify the political difficulty of reassessment, depending on a county's income distribution. The point has special relevance to Delaware County, discussed in Chapter 10.

finance and county policy. The ambiguity of standards that makes industrial taxation especially important for political structure also makes it difficult to study. But some inferences are possible, especially on the basic issue of extent of entrepreneurial concern.

In interviews industrialists commonly aver that local and county taxes are a small part of the cost of doing business, and they place their evident concern with the subject on philosophical grounds. In general, it can be said that local taxes are relatively low in Pennsylvania; that state and federal taxes are far more consequential; that Pennsylvania state taxes are also low among urban, industrial states; that assessment ratios to market value in the three suburban counties are low by state-wide standards; and finally, that both state and local taxes are deductible from corporate income subject to federal taxation.[8] The importance of the last point is that local taxes now cost industry only fifty-two cents on the dollar. For the individual plant several other factors must affect the salience of tax rates and assessments: degree of dependence on public services; extent of machinery and equipment exemption; success in controlling other costs; and political sensitivity as a function of mobility, profit margin, or prominence. Thus, in Montgomery County it is declining industries and extractive (immobile) industries that exhibit most concern with taxes. And in Bucks, U.S. Steel—which alone pays some 10 percent of county taxes—may have been moved to protracted assessment litigation from a sense of visibility and vulnerability.

Probably most industries are concerned and uncertain about equity—about shouldering burdens that homeowners or competitors have shifted through informal, individual assessment methods. The county Manufacturers' Associations have centrally represented industry, especially in Delaware County, where such representation is vested in the general counsel as a large part of his practice. It was he who argued the 1947 *Gulf Oil Case* on the machinery exemption in Philadelphia, and who drafted the 1953 amendment extending it to all counties. In fact, the amendment altered nothing in Delaware County because of an industrial agreement with the political organization that the next-door Philadelphia exemption would apply in Delaware. While the manufacturers' bargaining position was thought strong enough in terms of industrial location and expansion to maintain the agreement, the legislation was said to have been motivated by fear of a residential taxpayer's suit to undermine it.

Industrial organization seems to have produced a political stand-off, but not uniformity or a "most favored industry" policy. Assessments are rarely changed on existing installations in Delaware and Montgomery, a practice that preserves some original disparities while both creating and correcting others as market values change irregularly. The rigidity seems as likely to result in overassessment as in advantage: in Delaware County some old plants have recently been sold at much lower multiples of assessment than exist in the construction cost of new plants. Montgomery's tax board has a stated policy of temporarily favoring new industries, with equal flexibility for all to encourage development; in Delaware a few new installations are reliably reported to have been distinctly favored. In all three counties industrial assessments are about 10 percent of total county assessments, but these proportions are not valid guides to assessment practice.*

TABLE 13:2

Assessed Valuation by Land Use Percentages, 1952 and 1962

	BUCKS		MONTGOMERY		DELAWARE	
	1952	1962	1952	1962	1952	1962
Residential	53	69	67	70	65	77
Industrial	13	12	7	9	12	8
Commercial	8	9	13	16	15	13
Agricultural	21	7	8	4	4	1
Other	5	3	5	1	4	1

Source: Pennsylvania State Tax Equalization Board.

All this suggests several conclusions about the local tax treatment and tax-consciousness of industry. First, on the view that industries are favored in assessments the verdict is mixed: some are, others are not; though in Delaware County the few known disparities favor local over absentee ownership. Second, this conclusion is valid for plants recently purchased or constructed; no one knows about the rest, even after litigation. Third, despite probable inequities, industrialists in Montgomery and Delaware have not pressed for reassessment—partly because their organizations and attorneys oppose it; partly, no doubt, from inertia and scepticism that it would lower actual taxes in the long run. Fourth, many plants—especially in Delaware County—are located in small "tax colonies" and their actual taxes are therefore low; such industries have more to fear from school district consolidation or a shifting of municipal functions to the county level than from assessment practices. Fifth, the 1953 machinery-and-equipment exemption, which was backed by the PMA, has eased manufacturers' stakes in assessment as compared with those of, say, insurance installations. Finally, counties and localities increasingly look to light industry, commercial centers, and apartment buildings for revenue.

Thus heavy industry is less exposed, has more exemptions, and smaller local taxes in proportion to state and federal than was true before World War II. The limited tax-consciousness of industry in general seems partly to reflect habit and PMA ideology as well as the

* For what little it is worth, the per capita assessed value of industrial property as a percentage of per capita value added by manufacture for 1961 (reported by the Bureau of Statistics, Pennsylvania Department of Internal Affairs) is: Bucks County, 12 percent; Montgomery County, 12 percent; Delaware County, 9 percent. Considered in connection with overall county assessment ratios and industrial development patterns, these figures do not support a charge of systematic underassessment of industry in any particular county.

peculiar interests of a few manufacturers, a prudent concern for an uncertain future in which local taxes might hamper industry, and the fact that local taxes are only a variable or controllable cost if management publicly manifests concern. Protective industrialists oppose expansion of the scope of government in some part from fear of tax increases; development-oriented industrialists, however, often seek new public services. Perhaps the central facts are industry's fixed investment and relative immobility (somewhat lessened by investment credits in recent federal tax law). There is no doubt that politicians credit *some* firms' threats to remove or to redirect expansion elsewhere. Such intimations from other firms, locally owned or relatively immobile, are less credible; yet these firms are understandably the most politically active and (apparently) influential. As political "resources," taxes and assessments have probably declined in importance. The situation varies among industries, but seems, overall, to be at least a standoff between industry and politicians and perhaps to favor the latter, on balance.

3. *The personal property* tax is levied in the more populous Pennsylvania counties, and it is important in the wealthiest of them. It is a four-mill duty on securities (at market value) of corporations exempt from the state franchise tax. In form it violates at least three of Adam Smith's classical canons of equality, certainty, convenience, and economy in collection: it is often evaded, inconvenient to pay, and cumbersome to enforce. In effect it leads to slight shifting out of eligible holdings around the taxable date of December 31 and to minor fiscal fluctuations, reflecting the market, especially in Montgomery County, for which the tax is critical.* There it amounts to two-thirds of the budget, mostly taken from the Main Line and York Road sections; in Bucks it is less than a quarter; and in Delaware only an eighth. Montgomery's situation is exceptional, and its resulting real property tax rate, which alone is alterable and is the lowest in the state, has become a political symbol.

Because of the personal property tax, county programs tend somewhat more to redistribute income, on a social or regional basis, than do municipal expenditures, though the sheer size of counties also entails redistribution. The effect is limited on the taxing side because the four-mill rate is mandatory, but in counties (like Montgomery) comprehending great personal wealth it can drastically affect overall fiscal structure. A paradox results from the fixed rate of the tax and the residual, regressive nature of the effective real property rate: county taxation (expenditure patterns aside) tends to be more progressive as county policy is more economical and thus more dependent on the fixed tax affecting high incomes most heavily. By and large, however, the

* In setting their budget for 1963 the Montgomery County Commissioners estimated a decline in the personal property tax take of $438,000 (about 10 percent) below 1962, because of the 1962 stock market decline. At the county's 1963 assessed real estate valuation this decline was equivalent to a real property tax of one-half mill, in partial consequence of which the real property tax was increased 20 percent.

personal property tax is the concern of accountants and customer's men; it is the traditional and variable real property tax that gets public attention.

4. *County and local tax collections* are performed by locally elected officers for a fee. In this Jacksonian survival of tax-farming collectors are paid by localities, school districts, and counties in percentages of returns that by law may reach 5 percent.[9] They are reimbursed by their several public clients for printing, postage, and bonding, but must meet other expenses from their gross earnings. Collectors' *declared* expenses are heavy in order to reduce net earnings and public criticism. (Some collectors deduct their federal income tax as an expense!) For this strictly part-time activity net incomes range from more than $30,000 in a few large, affluent townships with heavy personal-property accounts through the more usual $5,000 to $10,000 figure in typical boroughs and townships to still less in a few others.

The principal effects of the quaint collection system are two, administrative and political. In the first sense its inefficiency is clear: costs per $1,000 or per assessment parcel are excessive when compared with collection systems elsewhere.[10] The political result of the system is, in each municipality, a position well worth running for: in loosely organized local politics it provokes many-sided primary fights, and in well-organized areas it is either a sinecure for the leader or a source of political contributions or both; in short, it is a source of dissension or discipline, depending on social and political circumstance. Governmental reformers have long pressed for change in the system, often recommending centralization at the county level, but the existing method has vested strong incentives in local home rule. County politicians have sometimes exploited the system, since their ability to set compensation (especially for the personal property tax) gives them some control over the collectors; the most rewarding collectorships are located where the personal property tax take is largest.

Many of these points are illustrated in the case of Albert Swing, political leader and tax collector of Main Line's Radnor Township, one of the region's wealthiest suburbs. The structure of Delaware County's politics has been discussed; here the point is simply how the tax system figured in Swing's downfall. Trouble began when he retained the two jobs of township treasurer and county commissioner after a preelection pledge to forsake the former if elevated to the latter. Swing's opponents in the county organization charged greed, and it is true that the Radnor collectorship paid some three times the county commissionership; yet maintenance of township political control surely figured in Swing's decision, while the example of his covetousness embarrassed a county organization based on job control. Impeached in the county court by his intraparty opponents for two "incompatible" positions (Commissioners set the county fees of tax collectors.), Swing lost in a decision later reversed by the State Supreme Court on the ground that, however undesirable the dual tenancy of office, the evil would have to be corrected by the legislature.

As Swing's appeal to the higher court proceeded, the political bitterness increased. The next issue, less public, involved the chairmanship of the Board of Assessment and Revision of Taxes, then vacant. In Delaware County this sensitive post was traditionally filled by the political leader with someone thoroughly dependable, invariably from Chester, seat of the political organization. Swing's break with the leadership was nearly complete when, in alliance with the minority commissioner, he demurred at appointing to the post the chief of the Chester detective force; it was all but final when, publicly affirming the minority alliance, the two commissioners by majority vote deposed the presiding commissioner and took over the county administration. Then, in a stroke for economy and a blow at organization control, the new majority reduced the county commissions (on real property returns only) of tax collectors, one of whom went to court and had the reduction annulled on a claim of conflict of interest—commissioner Swing had voted to reduce the income of tax-collector Swing.

Although an appeal was taken, Swing was soon through as commissioner. Denied renomination in 1963, he decided to fight in the primary election and sought to encourage support and disable opposition in the courthouse. At one point in the campaign nearly a quarter of the county's local tax assessors were fired by the county commissioners, and fear was reported to rule in the courthouse. The party organization, in defense of its own, threatened suit for violation of the election code, while Swing's lawyers developed a like case against the organization for its promise to rehire the assessors if its nominees were successful. The legal impasse was resolved by restoration of the assessors to office, save for one man who happened also to hold the incompatible position of local inspector of elections. Swing's primary defeat was decisive and did not end with the election. Within less than a month the county organization's state legislative delegation secured enactment of a bar, effective immediately, to the simultaneous tenure of the named positions of county commissioner and tax collector. Finally confronted with this choice and with imminent county retirement, Swing resigned the commissionership and opened a campaign of reconciliation. He could have fought the legislation in the courts and, it was thought, have held out till the end of his term, but organization pressure on Radnor Township was heavy and Swing was discouraged. He sought relief in resignation. On the same day the county court appointed as his successor the organization's victor in the primary. Soon the lone assessor relieved in the primary campaign was back on the job.

5. *Several aspects of taxes* are basic factors in county politics. One is the wealth of political jobs connected with them, and the discipline or

dissensions these contribute to local politics. Another is the opportunity to solicit and sustain political support by subtly adjusting the tax structure; still another is the constraint imposed on government by state millage limits and political reluctance to reassess property. A further refinement is the room for individual favoritism; while a basic element in all factors is the system's legal and administrative ambiguity. Finally, there is the high cost of collection.

Despite their narrow fiscal base the counties are traditionally self-sufficient. State and federal aid have but recently come to bear with new programs in health, welfare, housing, and education and with such promotional and cultural objectives as industrial development, tourism, libraries, and open-space reservation. It will later appear that not all of our counties have entered all of these fields, and their reluctance to do so stems partly from resistance to standards and sanctions accompanying state aid. At present the counties overwhelmingly pay for what they undertake and administer, because of extreme state centralization of functions like highways, health, and welfare. Perhaps the counties' comparative fiscal independence of the state, together with their limited fiscal base, has heightened tax-consciousness and buttressed the custodial tradition, at least among politicians. In the last decade, however, county expenditures per capita have rapidly increased, as described below. A vivid illustration of this fiscal pressure is the fact that in the election year of 1963 two of our three counties were compelled to raise the tax rate, an unheard-of event in past election years.

14

Comparisons and Priorities

Three general factors in county policy and performance have been examined. These may be identified as social, political. and governmental structure, so long it is clear that *structure* need not mean stability or rigidity. The three categories overlap and tend to reinforce each other.

The limited powers and loose framework of county government probably encourage a politics of particular interests rather than of panoramic policy; the division of functions with municipalities reinforces sectionalism. Social segmentation, poor communication, and popular indifference to county government seem to have similar effects; and reliance on the real property tax is congenial to a benefit theory of governmental action that implicitly discourages both income redistribution (social or sectional) and wide-ranging discussion of priorities or abstract purposes. It follows that issues of governmental or political structure, as means to abstract ends, are also discounted, and this may tend to depress some kinds of civic action and facilitate political discipline that rests on specific incentives and contributions among relatively few participants. Where the chief issues concern limited, specific benefits, tax-consciousness is likely to be strong and participation or pressure for public action to be narrow. In this political economy the organization controls most sanctions, especially in the absence of regular electoral competition and a professional public administration. Yet in a context of socioeconomic change, political competition, and modest governmental professionalism Bucks' history indicates that responsiveness and initiative are possible for county government, even as presently organized.

Perhaps the most salient difference among the three counties in the postwar era has been in rates of industrial and residential growth. More rapid growth of both sorts broke down old ideologies and mobilizations of bias and brought political competition. Bucks' population more than doubled in a decade on a small initial base. The increase was concentrated in one section and produced a new society, which is different in its urban origins from the rest of the county. It introduced to business and politics new men who stood to profit from continued development and thus from public response to the critical needs and demands it produced. Bucks has no protective manufacturers' association. Its relatively autonomous past lack of central-city commutation may have led to more county-oriented leaders, tending to offset sectional divisions. Since Bucks' population growth ignored municipal boundaries (especially in Levittown, whose separate incorporation was seriously considered), the county was a logical agency for action, and this was doubtless encouraged by a daily press with more coverage and less metropolitan competition than any other county's making a calculated appeal to its new, youthful readership and hoping to profit from continued growth.

The contrast between Bucks on one hand and Montgomery and Delaware on the other can be seen in census maps of the Philadelphia urbanized area for 1950 and 1960: the greatest expansion was in Bucks, the least in Delaware, with Montgomery intermediate. Delaware began as the most urbanized county: for more than half a century it had experienced steady growth in what became its older, lower-income section, and in the postwar period the most rapid increase was in well-to-do quarters; thus its strong political organization was better able to absorb the expansion around its urban base and to outwait conflicts of political ambition in the new, sociologically Republican sections. Its dominant business and political interests were centered in and closely connected to one city; lower Delaware County was a minor metropolitan area. It experienced little industrial growth. Montgomery County was already dominated by a combination of affluent suburbs and industrial boroughs, and most of its increase was in upper-income sections. Industrial development led to business pressure for new public services from new men with different interests from those of the old manufacturers. Rivalry between sections and generation induced political factionalism, but not interparty competition.

Generally speaking, recent intercounty differences in governmental policy and performance were consistent with differences in political structure. Over the decade Bucks County was most given to innovation, and Montgomery slightly more so than Delaware. One cannot, however, infer cause and effect from this consistency without exploring other variables: growth rates, municipal conditions, fiscal and administrative factors, and inherited or acquired priorities. These are reviewed in the remainder of this chapter.

1. *Rates of growth* and *municipal influences* have already been considered. Because innovation varied with growth rates as well as with

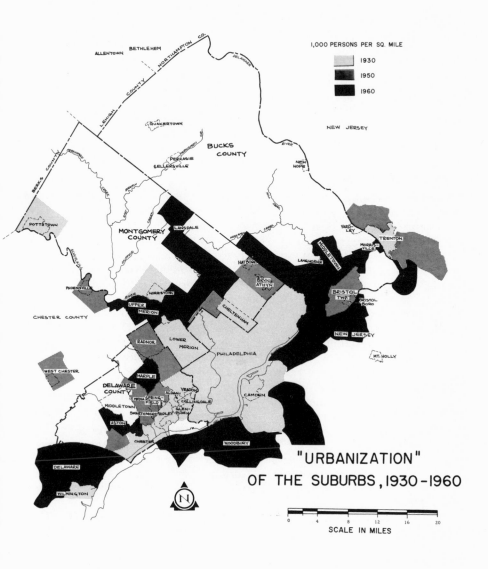

1,000 PERSONS PER SQ. MILE

1930
1950
1960

ALLENTOWN   BETHLEHEM

NORTHAMPTON CO.

DELAWARE

NEW JERSEY

LEHIGH COUNTY

BERKS COUNTY

QUAKERTOWN

BUCKS COUNTY

PERKASIE
SELLERSVILLE

NEW HOPE

POTTSTOWN

MONTGOMERY COUNTY

LANSDALE

YARD-LEY

TRENTON

SCHUYLKILL

MORRIS-VILLE

PHOENIXVILLE

HATBORO

BRYN ATHYN

MIDDLETOWN

LANGHORNE

CHESTER COUNTY

UPPER MERION

NORRISTOWN

CHELTENHAM

BRISTOL TWP.

BRISTOL BORO

WEST CHESTER

RADNOR

LOWER MERION

PHILADELPHIA

NEW JERSEY

MT. HOLLY

MARPLE

DELAWARE COUNTY

MEDIA SPRING-FIELD

YEADON

CAMDEN

MIDDLETOWN

SWARTHMORE RIDLEY

ALDAN
COLLINGDALE

GLEN-OLDEN

ASTON

CHESTER

WOODBURY

DELAWARE

"URBANIZATION"
OF THE SUBURBS, 1930-1960

WILMINGTON

N

0   4   8   12   16   20
SCALE IN MILES

political competition, rapid growth alone is an alternative explanation of it. Where the most explosive growth occurred on the most primitive base there was most encouragement, it might be argued, and least resistance to county innovation. Where growth was slower there were already stronger public programs in consequence of past development. This goes for both counties and municipalities. Undoubtedly it *is* a partial explanation of county innovation, and any assessment of the effects of political competition must take account of it. That it is a sufficient explanation seems doubtful, however, on two grounds: first, that rapid growth rates have encouraged new organized interests and political competition; second, that case histories in the chapters that follow indicate that political competition assisted in governmental response to growth.

2. *Finance.* Fiscal and administrative factors may each be conceived of either as influences on other governmental endeavors or as effects of political organization. Table 14:1 sets out aspects of the counties' fiscal histories. The levels of taxation and expenditure per capita indicate that, while political competition may in most circumstances encourage expenditure, it does not completely explain intercounty differences. Per capita county taxes have consistently been highest in Delaware; in priorities, Delaware is especially high on welfare, corrections, debt service, and salaries. (Most of the debt service is traceable to capital projects in welfare and corrections, plus the county's incinerator program discussed below.) Salaries aside (for the moment), Delaware's profile seems appropriate to its old, urban base; Bucks' pattern has emphasized physical services for industrial and residential development; Montgomery's low county levels reflect its tradition of local self-sufficiency.

The strength of Montgomery's localism is plain when *all* taxes—municipal, school, and county—are considered together: a computed total real property tax bill for a hypothetical average individual in 1960 is highest in Montgomery and lowest in Bucks; the figures are: Montgomery, $250; Delaware, $224; Bucks, $205.* Intercounty differences in the average total tax are impressive, but so are variations in the county share of the total: county ratios were highest in Delaware and lowest in Montgomery; school and municipal proportions combined were highest in Montgomery and lowest in Delaware.[1]

These variations are probably based on three related factors: differences in municipalities' fiscal capacity, population concentrations, and parochial school attendance. In 1960 mean municipal market value per

---

* The computation is made as follows: $\dfrac{\Sigma m[(m-x-v)Pm]}{Pc}$, where m equals total millage in each municipality, x equals ratio of assessed value to market value, v equals market value of residential property per household as computed by the State Tax Equalization Board (which deflates its computed values by 15 percent); Pm equals population of municipality, included to weight the resulting average; and Pc equals population of the county.

TABLE 14:1

Financial Performance of the Counties, 1950–60, Per Capita[1]

	1950			1955			1960		
	Bucks	Mont-gomery	Delaware	Bucks	Mont-gomery	Delaware	Bucks	Mont-gomery	Delaware
Population	144,600	353,100	414,200	231,200	452,600	501,200	308,600	516,700	553,200
Tax receipts	$5.06	$5.43	$7.17	$8.40	$6.53	$9.06	$8.45	$8.86	$13.18
Expenditures[2]	6.90	6.70	8.34	9.00	7.73	10.70	12.17	11.60	15.12
General government[3]	2.16	3.20	2.74	2.49	3.27	3.21	3.47	4.96	4.15
Judicial	1.23	1.14	1.43	1.36	1.32	1.64	1.57	2.06	1.91
Health and welfare	1.33	.86	1.44	1.88	.98	2.21	2.99	1.85	3.99
Corrections	1.51	.67	1.44	1.59	.89	1.67	1.60	.99	2.26
Park & Recreation	....	.39	.15	.04	.62	.13	.25	1.05	.23
Planning	....	.02	....	.26	.12	.10	.28	.18	.11
Private appropriations[4]	.12	.06	.03	.06	.04	.02	.06	.06	.03
Administration[5]	.29	.28	.41	.47	.31	.64	.32	.24	.91
Debt service	.05	....	.65	.54	.01	.97	.94	.04	1.44
Salaries[6]	2.36	3.80	3.60	2.40	4.57	4.96	4.71	5.54	7.23

1. Source: County controllers' annual reports required by law.
2. Difference between expenditures and taxes chiefly reflects intergovernmental aids. To the extent possible, capital expenditures are abstracted and not shown, but this is not always possible—e.g., in Montgomery's park expenditures for 1960.
3. This expenditure breakdown differs somewhat from that in the controllers' reports. General government consists chiefly of the county commissioners' direct expenditures plus those of several custodial offices.
4. Private appropriations are county appropriations to private organizations, such as hospitals, clinics, historical associations, agricultural organizations.
5. Administrative expenses chiefly consist of insurance and pension fund contributions.
6. Salaries are already shown in the categories above and should not be added to them. They are not separately shown in all cases in controllers' reports, thus some arbitrary allocations are involved in these estimates.

155

capita was nearly identical in the three counties, but the variance among municipalities (unweighted by population) was greatest in Delaware and least in Bucks.[2] County population, however, tends to be heavily concentrated in a few municipalities. In Bucks (with one exception) these municipalities are below the county mean—the largest of all especially so—and personal incomes in all of them are relatively low; in Montgomery the populous suburbs, especially the largest, are wealthy and well above mean market value (the industrial boroughs definitely are not); in Delaware the *large* localities show less disparity, but more of the county population lives in small, low- and middle-income municipalities. The Fels Institute study found that per capita local expenditures (exclusive of schools) tend to increase with rising densities and declining wealth (as measured by residential market value), both of which characterized Delaware's small municipalities in the southeastern section of Montgomery's industrial boroughs.[3] Politically, high fiscal effort, like local self-sufficiency, probably exerts a downward pressure on county expenditure and innovation except when county action is an apparent aid to municipalities. Finally, parochial school attendance is much heavier in Delaware County—especially in the lower-income sections—which may explain the high ratio of municipal to school expenditures there.[4]

Thus, in terms of local resources and population proportions it appears that Delaware County may well have responded to its old, low-income region, Bucks to its new low-income region, Montgomery to its affluent, self-sufficient suburbs and to rural areas and small towns with rudimentary wants and parsimonious attitudes. So far as it is sectionally determined or locally effective, county policy *seems to have* an equalizing effect in Bucks and (perhaps especially) Delaware, but not in Montgomery, although the net redistributive effect of county taxes and expenditures is impossible to calculate.

Political traditions probably abet the foregoing tendencies. Bucks County responded to rapid sectional growth at an early stage before local chauvinism and services developed. Montgomery's large size and acknowledged sectionalism, and Delaware's compactness, may also be part of the explanation; and the large personal property tax in Montgomery tended to free real property tax funds for municipal use, thus perhaps fixing a pattern of residual county expenditures, though (a political factor) Fred Peters avowedly preferred this pattern as less controversial.

Table 14:2 contains data relating to county fiscal effort. All measures of this variable are arbitrary, and here the overall figures ignore intermunicipal differences that affect individuals' positions. In 1960 the three counties were closely grouped in tax sacrifice, measured by personal income or property value, but Delaware made the heaviest effort, and its per capita real property tax base showed the slowest rate of increase.[5] Considering all the data, it appears that fiscal pressure could

TABLE 14:2
Indicators of County Fiscal Effort, 1960

	Bucks	Delaware	Montgomery
Market value per capita in county	$3,780	$3,672	$4,595
Personal income per capita	$2,361	$2,725	$3,312
Taxes per $1,000 market value:			
County	$ 2.24	$ 3.59	$ 1.92
Municipal	3.44	5.63	4.84
School	12.84	12.71	13.13
Total	18.52	21.93	19.89
Percent of total taxes collected by:			
County	11%	16%	8%
Municipal	18	25	24
School	69	58	67
Total county tax as percentage of:			
Market value	1.9%	2.2%	2.0%
Family income	3.0	3.0	2.8

Source: Pennsylvania State and Local Welfare Commission, *A Reallocation of Public Welfare Responsibilities*, Harrisburg, Pa., 1963.

have played an independent role in resistance to new county programs in Delaware and (perhaps) Montgomery, where county tax-consciousness is most strongly supported by "localism," and in Delaware political fear of reassessment was an added factor. Data for the year 1960 are used here as most relevant to recent performance; later, Bucks' county taxes increased most rapidly, and by 1963 economizing pressures were evident in survey data, newspaper editorializing, and the 1963 election campaign, as local taxes also rose precipitously in lower Bucks.

Whether spending or retrenching pressures are more favored by political competition probably depends on such details as the objects of expenditure, distribution and palpability of taxes, existing tax levels and marginal sacrifice, and the leverage afforded interests on either side by gerrymandering and governmental structure. The outcome is thus not often predictable in practice (though it may be in principle); one can only note the variations in fiscal context and rationalize about county behavior after the fact. Logically, this weakens explanation.

3. *Administration.* Another effect of political organization and a factor in innovation is the quality (and quantity) of courthouse administration. Overall quality is difficult to judge objectively. One significant datum (Table 14:1) is per capita expenditure on planning (in which Bucks is by far the highest, Delaware by far the lowest), significant because planners are the chief professionals in county government and tend to press for innovation.* Delaware's relatively high per capita salary bill (Table 14:1) suggests the importance of patronage in a well-organized polity: that county has much the highest ratio of county

* Bucks' staff is much larger than Delaware's absolutely, so that internal economies of scale are not in issue here.

employees to county population, and Bucks has much the lowest.[6] Delaware, however, was until recently the only county to accept civil service in child welfare, for which it received state aid. Now all three counties do so.

Differences in the extent and discipline of patronage might affect both integrity and innovation. To judge from public reports, there are no significant effects on integrity: each county has had dramatic cases of corruption in the last decade—fees unaccounted for and expense accounts padded—and in each one favoritism is alleged in, e.g., admissions to the county home or in tax assessments (except in Bucks, where assessments were equalized and largely contracted out). Some of these allegations are disputable because of primitive record-keeping and ambiguous standards, but significant scandals in each county were noted in foregoing chapters. The efficiency of county employees is not characteristically high: many are aged (sometimes retired from other employment) and their working hours are short. Salaries are low. It is unlikely that the dollar costs of patronage are high in either integrity or efficiency, but political employees often see innovation as a threat. Professional workers (at least at the top) would probably foster more innovation and perhaps raise taxes. There are several instances of such tendencies in succeeding chapters.

Pressure for new programs today usually comes from private sources or from the few planners and other professionals. The practice of administration by boards, authorities, or appropriation to private groups often builds in pressures for expansion once a program is started if, as in Bucks, an active citizenry has been involved in its administration. It may also facilitate pursuit of private gain from consulting and capital projects. It seems probable that Delaware County has somewhat reduced the pressure for innovation and expansion by deemphasizing such agencies and appointing to them persons who are politically loyal and conservative.

4. *Priorities.* One indication of county priorities is the fiscal pattern of Table 14:1, already discussed. Another is inauguration of optional programs. In the next section of this volume, county action is reviewed in the fields of recreation and natural resources, health and welfare, industrial development, and transportation. These fields were selected because of the different interests and administrative problems they involve so that, together, they might provide a broad perspective on county action. Other county options, such as libraries, refuse disposal, mosquito control, urban renewal, and surplus-foods distribution are not dealt with in detail despite their potential importance in some counties. They are summarily discussed in the following paragraphs.

Bucks and Montgomery maintain county libraries and bookmobiles: Montgomery's dates from Fred Peters' administration and was primarily designed to serve rural areas; Bucks' system was begun by the Welsh administration, responding to the Federation of Women's Clubs, the Parent-Teachers Association, and the AFL-CIO—primarily to the developing lower section. Delaware County has not entered the field and has recently been resisting pressure from women's organizations to do so. State aid has been available to county libraries since 1931, and a new State Code has increased it, seeking to encourage county libraries within an overall state system.[7] Yet local library committees feel threatened by state and county programs, and "local government officials often consider the library as an activity apart and under private auspices" even when it receives municipal support.[8] By means of bookmobiles all Bucks' and Montgomery's residents have some library service, but more of these residents are rural than in Delaware, where 83 percent are estimated to have access to a local library, however inadequate.[9] Overall, total public (municipal and county) library expenditures per capita in 1961 were slightly higher in Delaware than in Bucks, and in Montgomery were twice those of either of the other counties. This pattern is not altered if private expenditures are added to public.[10] These comparisons ignore the generally low level of service outside the more affluent suburbs in each county. In Delaware the undeveloped western section and the small southeastern municipalities, by and large, lack local libraries, but as the prosperous suburban jurisdictions build libraries by local civic action and taxes, their political leadership tends increasingly to resist a county program.

Turning from culture to utility, county positions are reversed in the field of refuse disposal. Delaware County has built three incinerators that operate at an annual cost close to one dollar per capita (including interest charges). In Bucks and Montgomery such a program would probably appear too sectional in its benefits: lower Bucks' municipalities have been studying cooperative action; Montgomery's planners have proposed county programs in the past without acceptance. The heavier development of Delaware County, with high disposal costs and sanitary problems in its densely settled areas, led to requests for county action by local officials in the early 1950's. At that time Pennsylvania and New Jersey prohibited feeding of raw garbage to hogs, sharply increasing disposal costs in the many municipalities dependent on pigfeeders. The requests led to studies by the county planning commission and Pennsylvania Economy League, and to public debate over sanitary landfill versus incineration and an authority versus a department. The commissioners rejected the study's landfill recommendation and set up an incinerator authority; when this failed financially they created a disposal department and advertised for a sanitary engineer to head it. The county political leader is said to have pressed the program personally, although, as usual, there is only hearsay evidence. Ten years later the program boasted four incinerators and consumed about 6 percent of county taxes. Local collection costs continued to increase, but no doubt at a slower rate than they would have without the county program.

All three counties support redevelopment authorities. Delaware's dates from 1949, Montgomery's from 1958, Bucks' from 1962. Despite the differences in age, Bucks County's authority has in the planning and application stage at least as many projects (with similar projected expenditure) as have been planned or executed by Delaware and Montgomery, though the largest individual projects are in the latter counties. For a decade Delaware's authority pursued one project alone, through persistent delays, with a one-man staff of doubtful competence but sound political connections. Chester, however, has its own redevelopment and housing authorities (as required by state law), and the county's effort outside Chester has recently been increased. Montgomery's program was slow in beginnning because of local sensitivity. All three county agencies now rely on the same regional consulting firm, headed by a Republican former federal urban renewal administrator, who has sold them on more plans and applications. Suburban redevelopment is a difficult program, for the cumbersomeness of federal procedures is compounded by shortage of county administrative resources and protracted negotiations with local officials.[11] Its substance largely consists in minor surgery to enable commercial renewal of outmoded business districts in old boroughs, and in clearance of ancient, ramshackle, insanitary areas, most of which were blighted from birth. In time, especially in the old industrial and residential boroughs, urban renewal may grow in importance. At the moment, its main supporters are local developers and chambers of commerce who want to revive dying business districts, and some borough councils concerned about the tax base. Deconcentration and the suburban shopping center have affected the old boroughs and central-city business districts alike.

Counties have been allowed to kill mosquitoes since 1935.[12] Delaware County immediately established a mosquito extermination commission: until 1942 it was largely reliant on WPA labor for spraying, ditching, and draining; later it became the county's responsibility. Bucks' municipalities began a voluntary program in 1953; in 1956 the county took over with the help of health-board funds, though local contributions are still involved. In 1960 Montgomery began a 40 percent aid program to municipalities for mosquito control, without county administrative involvement. It appears that Bucks' and Delaware's topography and proximity to the river make mosquito control a more logical program for those counties than it is, countywide, for Montgomery, though in both counties some municipalities pursue supplementary programs. The activity is seasonal, as well as sectional, and provides some useful summer patronage.

All three counties now have departments to distribute surplus foods to the needy: the surplus is provided and transported by the federal and state governments, respectively, and the counties distribute it to those eligible under state standards. At state urging all three counties now support tourist promotion, for which state aid is available: Bucks created its Historical and Tourist Commission in 1961; Montgomery recently established a bureau in the county courthouse; and Delaware is inactive, but it is also less attractive for tourism. All three counties maintain police radio systems that transmit state and federal communications and help coordinate local police efforts; Delaware's system now substitutes for (rather than supplementing) many local systems.

Finally, recent legislation has authorized state-aided two-year community colleges in counties, or in combinations of either counties or school districts. As of October 1966 Bucks' college had been in operation for a year after a unanimous action by the commissioners; Montgomery's has just begun, by vote of one majority commissioner with the minority member; and Delaware's commissioners are resisting petitions to establish one, seeking instead to attract a branch campus of the state university despite an active movement, backed by industry, for a local institution.

These programs, and those reviewed in the next four chapters, are not the only county options available besides the old, custodial functions (which may themselves be varied significantly), but they comprise most of those in effect in the three counties. With the foregoing discussion and the cases that follow they permit some comparison of county action.

Bucks has been most innovative of the counties, but some of this is simply catching up with programs already established in counties suburbanized earlier. These programs aside, Bucks still has innovated most. Its priorities have emphasized physical development—economic base and natural amenity—rather than social programs, as is perhaps natural in its early stage of growth. It has responded to heavy sectional development, to the professionals in county government, to the civic and social concerns of old central Bucks, and to the promotional interests of lower Bucks in a broad balance; it will be seen below that initiatives for programs have come from a variety of sources. By 1963 most options had been exercised and tax rates had visibly increased. Under economizing, taxpayer pressures, issues of priority gained in importance.

Montgomery has lately been more innovative than Delaware, but on a smaller base of county programs and expenditures. If local home-rule traditions and self-sufficiency help explain the earlier pattern, the interest of upper-middle-class commuters in the populous, inlying suburbs may help explain recent county initiatives in open space and mass transit.

Delaware County has recently been least innovative of the three, but a decade ago it performed more functions than either Bucks or Montgomery. These functions and Delaware's expenditure pattern suggest that the county has responded to the densely settled, lower-income section of predominantly small municipalities south of the Baltimore

Pike. In that section most municipalities are below the county median in per capita market valuation and above the median in effective tax rates, though a few are favored with high industrial duplicates. Delaware appears to have emphasized functions (such as mosquito control and incineration) that tend to relieve these local fiscal pressures, together with welfare and correctional programs appropriate to a more urban county; it has deemphasized programs (e.g., libraries, open space, mass transit) of potential interest to its larger, more self-sufficient townships. That the lower-income areas are more susceptible to Democratic inroads and therefore are better represented in the Republican organization (see Chapter 10), and their newcomers accustomed to urban services, need not strictly imply that overall priorities are deliberate.

The problem now is to explain the variant behavior of the counties. The attempt at an explanation emphasizes political structure, but it should also contribute to an assessment of the suburban county's governmental role. For both purposes it will be helpful to study policymaking in some detail, and this is done in four fields in Part IV following. All of the counties have felt pressure for action in each of these fields, but action affects different interests in each and has entailed different administrative arrangements.

The following chapters are focused on three possible sources of intercounty variation: (1) organized interests and power structures; (2) electoral competition; and (3) direct, or implicit, response to interests or attitudes, without any organized pressure. These three political explanations are hard to distinguish in practice. Rapid growth and progressive attitudes, pluralism of interests and electoral competition, private elites and political organization may be integrally related. Studying specific decisions (i.e., dynamics) may, however, help to distinguish them. That is attempted in the next chapters, after which the explanations are attacked explicitly.

PART IV. POLICY AND PERFORMANCE

15

Natural Resources and Recreation

The subject matter of this chapter ranges from organized play through natural amenity to public utilities. The whole domain is pervaded by ideology and defined by the special language of lobbies. Narrow definitions of it tend to prejudice the competition and integration of interests in public land and water. What these interests are and how they may be weighed and related in public decisions are best understood in a broad context.

Attempts at integration have lately occurred on the county level. But recreation, amenity, water supply, and sanitation may all be subjects of municipal action. All have regional implications in some degree. The state is primarily responsible for pollution control and is the largest holder of recreational open space in the region. Such federal agencies as the Corps of Army Engineers, Soil Conservation Service, and Department of Housing and Urban Development participate in all these fields.[1] This means that distinct public institutions as well as private interests are involved, and that in considering how the counties have functioned over this subject matter one must think of them as contending with other governments for the leading role—which may never fall to anyone.

The method of this chapter is to summarize (instead of chronicling) the progress of each county on lines that best admit of comparison. But important geographic and demographic differences among the counties must be borne in mind: notably the increase in density of the inner regions, the decrease in open land area from Bucks through Montgomery to Delaware, and the variations in drainage systems and stream valleys, affecting both the logic of public policy and the organization of civic action.

1. *Bucks.* Only 10 percent of Bucks' land area was developed in 1960 (apart from agriculture) and less than half was forecast for development in this century.[2] Thus Bucks set out to contain and bring order to growth in the green-belts policy of its comprehensive plan, but public acquisition of open space was also emphasized, especially in high-density regions. Bucks' land acquisition exceeded that of the other counties, at lower prices. Preservation of existing open acreage partly depends on implementation of the comprehensive plan, which in turn depends on municipal policies. So far, most growth has occurred in low-density, single-family patterns at odds with the plan's philosophy of clustering and green belts. Thus water supply and sanitation became serious problems, and Bucks alone of the counties (starting with a nearly clean slate) approached them on a county-wide basis. The regulations and technical competence of the county health department were important stimuli (and only Bucks had such an agency); others were the Neshaminy Valley Watershed Association (whose basin drained the developing area) and the county-wide outlook of the planning commission. From the collaboration of these agencies (and state aid) came the engineering and administrative studies that led to a county sewer and water authority.

The substantive results in Bucks may be quickly summarized. Expenditures for open land acquisition and improvement, and for park planning and administration, are by far the highest of the three counties, absolutely and per capita. Numerous county parks are in process, an eighteen-year acquisition program is mapped down to parcel numbers, a large state park was laid out through local initiative, existing state reservations and historical sites were successfully held against commercial pressure. (There is, however, some economic support for these efforts because tourism is an important county industry.) The county's major creek system is subject to combined state and federal action for flood prevention, flow augmentation, recreation, and wildlife conservation with local and county financial support and civic coordination (see Chapter 4). A county-wide plan for sewage disposal and water supply into the twenty-first century has been completed, a county agency exists to implement it, and two major projects for water supply and sewerage in areas of poor drainage and rapid growth are now under way with federal aid.

These accomplishments stem from a striking concert of public and private agencies. Bucks County's Park Board was created in 1953 at the urging of an ephemeral, amenity-oriented citizens' group (the Citizens' Council for Bucks County Planning) when the opportunity arose to acquire a farm on the Delaware River: the impoverished octogenarian owner proposed to devise his ninety acres to the county in return for maintenance during his lifetime, and the commissioners began the Park Board with a $10,000 appropriation. In the Welsh administration, appropriations went to $110,000, more purchases were made, some state lands accepted, and the Park Board acquired a professional staff that was housed with the planning commission. With this staff and the compatible framework of county planning, specific projects and vigorous promotion began and bond issues followed. So, predictably, did conflict over properties and the priority of acquisition versus equipment. The aggressiveness of Bucks' professionals (usually backed by the newspapers) was impressive, but by the 1963 election political resistance was building as land values, development pressures, and tax-consciousness increased in lower Bucks County. Open space acquisition, by virtue of location and local tradition, with its main support in old, central Bucks, looked more like a sectional issue than it had earlier.

The close official liaison with civic activists in this field was described in Chapter 4. The county planning commission helped found the Neshaminy Valley Watershed Association. Both NVWA and the Delaware Valley Protective Association receive annual subventions from the county. NVWA, with its own one-man professional staff, now acts as negotiator and coordinator in the intergovernmental Neshaminy basin program. Its president is a member of the water and sewer authority, and DVPA's president serves on the park board. The park board has also created a private Bucks County Park Foundation to receive and hold land contributions from residents and developers until their public acceptance is financially possible. The theory has been to hold small, isolated tracts while the park board emphasizes large areas. Later, municipalities or the county could assume and perhaps extend the small parcels, but the Park Foundation itself began assembling a major reservation in central Bucks.

The Sewer and Water Authority emerged from collaboration by NVWA, the planning commission, and the health board on pollution studies and public education; county support of a consulting study and long-range plan; and a committee on implementation appointed by the commissioners. Because state law did not provide for direct county action in this field the logical alternatives were a county agency to stimulate and coordinate local action (pending enabling legislation), or county creation of an authority.[3] The committee agreed that county leadership promised economies of scale and timing. Those who opposed the authority method as costly and nonaccountable thought the developers and politicians on the action committee especially partial to it, but others also favored the device on the ground of urgency, and it was adopted. Its operating budget was subscribed by the county commissioners; capital costs were met from federal aid (30 percent so far) and from county appropriations to participating communities who then contracted with the authority. In the political division between the majority commissioners this Authority was a major issue, not only as to legality and the sectional distribution of county funds, but as to procedure: Commissioner Boyer's allies dominated the board; instead of hiring a staff they voted themselves salaries; the opportunities for contracts and retainers in the region of Boyer's political strength were obvious.

In these ways the sewer and water program fit into the issues of sectionalism, commerce versus conservation, enterprise versus rectitude that, with personalities, split the county politically. The Authority's critics tended to favor open space and recreation. The commissioners could influence the issue by appointments and appropriations despite the different legal and administrative status of parks and utilities. They supported both, as well as the Neshaminy water resources projects. In time, specific land use and financial priorities would probably conflict, but Bucks was, perhaps by virtue of its rural background and rapid development, in a position to decide those issues primarily at the county level.

2. *Montgomery*. Fred Peters acquired Montgomery's four parks by indirection and donation between 1939 and 1951. He established a politically staffed and frugally administered park board, composed of manufacturers, politicians, and dignitaries. Peters was neither planfully reserving open space nor responding to organized civic pressure; he simply approved of parks. In the next decade there were no more land acquisitions despite the urgent suggestions of planners and civic agencies (which were not supported by the park board). In the 1950's the planning commission mapped the county with an eye to open land and future utilities. It proposed county grants for local land acquisition, county sewer and water development, flood prevention, and parks and recreation. In 1957 a Health and Welfare Council report urged the county to establish a recreation agency and a crash program of land reservation. But for two administrations (Peters' last and Hammonds') nothing happened.

Two private developments took place, however. One was rapid settlement of the Wissahickon watershed, serious flooding in 1955, formation in 1954 of the Wissahickon Valley Watershed Association and its incorporation in 1957. By 1960 the Wissahickon basin held a quarter of the county population in one-tenth the county confines; WVWA had about 500 members, a $12,000 budget, and a professional director. The other development was industrialization in the Lansdale section, severe droughts beginning in 1957, and formation in 1958 of the North Penn Water Resources Association. The Wissahickon group was composed of new suburbanites and old social leaders concerned with natural amenity; the North Penn organization was based on industries and municipalities whose sole interest was water supply. Each group pressed its own studies (stream pollution, water requirements), and the Hammonds administration (1956-60) authorized applications for a federally aided Wissahickon flood control study and a state-supported, county-wide sewer and water study, but it spent no county funds, and only the federal flood-control application succeeded.

Public action began with the Wetherill administration and its encouragement of the planning commission. Under pressure from the North Penn section the administration bought a consultant study of water supply (confined to the North Penn area), while the planners devised a park-and-recreation proposal to accompany it. The combined plan envisioned a large land acquisition program, county construction of a reservoir with related facilities and development of a park, and creation of an authority to equip the area and distribute the water, at a total cost to the county of some $3 million. Part of the plan's novelty lay in the county support it secured for basically sectional benefits, part in its attention to an area long written off in regional planning as chronically dry and costly to supply. Hence its technical boldness: water would be piped across Bucks County from the Delaware River to Perkiomen Creek, thence to flood the county reservoir and sustain the county park. Land acquisition and financial details were developed by consulting engineers and county planners in close consultation with the North Penn Water Resources Association. When, prior to Wetherill's retirement, the county seemed to draw back from the plan, this combination kept working: the planning commission appointed a water supply coordinator and created a North Penn Water Study Committee to promote the merger of all local water systems into one authority for improved water distribution pending completion of the county reservoir. When the Wetherill administration retired, the capital funds, acquisitions, and construction for North Penn were still unscheduled, but the county was proceeding with appraisals and specifications. The next administration began the project.

While the North Penn study was in process the county also contracted with the Corps of Army Engineers and the Soil Conservation Service for flood-control studies on the Wissahickon, negotiated by WVWA. When the North Penn recommendations were revealed in 1962 the county also adopted a long-range open-space program at $200,000 annually. One-third of this program was earmarked for 20 percent grants to municipalities, subject to approval by the planning commission, whose standards favored older, settled suburban areas. A large county park was planned for the York Road section, but no site seemed acceptable to the park board, which favored active recreation over open space.

Thus, in one administration, Montgomery had made substantial commitments to open space, water supply, and flood control. Though retrenchment set in, the first steps were taken in each field; and the county planners were closely allied with interested private agencies. As in Bucks, the problem of detailed priorities among expenditures and pressures would probably follow.

3. *Delaware County's* early park and recreation history was roughly like Montgomery's. A retired scion of an old county family secured establishment of a park board in 1932. During the next twenty years it accepted scattered donations and developed three small picnic sites; for most of this period it was run as one man's enthusiasm. As in Montgomery, the Health and Welfare Council urged public recreation programs, but in Delaware its advocacy began in the 1930's. On two occasions (the early forties and late fifties) the county responded by adding a director of recreation to the park board, but in neither brief instance was a county role in organized recreation defined, fulfilled, or continued. As in Montgomery, creation of the county planning commission led to study of open space reservation, but the Delaware approach was unique in its conception and later rejection.

Delaware's first planners considered the major county creek valleys in terms of flood control, water supply, amenity, and recreation. By 1956 they had evolved the Creek Valley Park and Conservation Plan for purchase of some 4,000 acres at a cost of $5 million, financed by a bond issue and a one-mill tax increase. The county commissioners then directed the planning staff to promote support for the plan and to prepare a brochure for public distribution. In their search for public support the planners approached the Health and Welfare Council, which still emphasized active recreation more than open space, and helped establish a Citizens' Creek Valley Association, which later became the Citizens' Council described in Chapter 4. Planning officials met with John McClure and the War Board and sensed a favorable response. The only objection came from the county park director, a War Board member, who argued that a public plan and bond referendum would drive up land prices. The party organization supplied its publicity man to assist with the public brochure, and all concerned hoped to see the bond issue on the ballot in 1957—until early 1957, when a subtle reaction set in.

The sources of reluctance were obscure. Some thought that old landowning families along the creeks were alarmed, along with the developers, at the open publicity some conservationists gave to condemnation of land. Others credited chronic tax pressure and fiscal conservatism. In any event, the commissioners began to question the estimates, which were pared down. Then they held up publication of the brochure and appointed (without fanfare) a citizens' committee to study the whole proposal, deferring the bond referendum. Considering the membership of the committee, the planners noted several likely opponents and only a few sure supporters; it seemed a tabling rather than a delaying tactic. Whatever the intent, the committee was energetic and inquisitive: early in 1958 it filed a report that clearly favored multipurpose creek-valley conservation, reconciled it with traditional recreation, urgently recommended county action, but also suggested reliance on private generosity and public regulation as well as fee-simple acquisition. It offered no financial advice. The commissioners accepted the report without comment or publication; the planning commission's chairman saw the county political leader but was refused a commitment. The Citizens' Council of Delaware County kept pressing for action, but the planners reluctantly revised their tactics.

Late in 1958 the commissioners began to think about a nonreferendum bond issue to complete the county incinerator program, and the planners hoped to include some creek-valley money in this issue. In 1960 the new commissioners announced a large loan for county buildings, and earmarked part of it for parks and open space. Of this only a little was for creek-valley land (through grants to local governments); the rest was for recreational acres on level terrain. Four years later the county had purchased new acreage adjoining the county home for the aged and had improved an existing park site, but had made no grants for stream-valley acquisition.

The creek-valley program failed completely, despite careful planning and strenuous civic action. Some opponents argued plausibly that the planning was too careful and comprehensive, that it inflated land costs and alarmed taxpayers; some planners later felt that the citizens had been too forthright in their talk of condemnation. It also appeared that a large part of the county population was uninterested in open space, but sympathetic to active recreation, i.e., ball parks and picnic grounds. These attitudes probably reflected social interests associated with incomes and housing densities, and they certainly distinguished agencies like the park board from the planning commission, the Health and Welfare Council from the Citizens' Council. The creek-valley appeal lay in rural amenity, county history, and the Pinchot tradition, but these were minority interests, most accessible and perceptible to those who already lived in low-density regions.

By the 1960's both planners and civic activists were emphasizing other approaches to open space. The Health and Welfare Council had brought municipal officials together in a countywide committee to work on local recreation and land reservation; conceivably it would look to county action in the future. The planning commission had arranged for a federal flood-plain survey of one relatively undeveloped creek valley, local flood-plain zoning was adopted in another, and federal flood-control studies were begun on Darby Creek in the populous eastern section. Thus some exigent, economic objectives were partially met in the creek valleys. Scattered narrow defiles were naturally secure against future growth; piecemeal regulation, enlightened private development, and municipal action might preserve other areas. If the county acquired some more park land and if localities did likewise, and if future densities were suitably varied, then—by the broadest planning standards, and acknowledging the county's economy, demography, and artificial density—the outcome might yet be acceptable. Still later, in 1965, state aid became available. Despite the county commissioners' evident lack of interest the state itself condemned an old family holding and began its conversion to a large park.

4. *Summary.* Standards by which to rate the counties are debatable. In open space and recreation, for instance, one could argue that rapid land acquisition is most appropriate in Bucks (the only county that has actually spent heavily for it) because of lower land costs there. Delaware, at the other extreme in density and fiscal pressure, might more logically emphasize small tracts for local use and narrow creek-valley ribbons; Montgomery would be intermediate, in this view. The converse position is more often argued, but one must then apply open-space standards without regard to development patterns, costs, county boundaries, or probable public wants. Open-space acquisition normally grows more difficult, both economically and politically, as the county fills up; and there is evidence (Chapter 19) that it is most popular in the affluent low-density areas and has low priority for low-income, blue-collar residents. Table 15:1 shows estimated public open-space holdings in the three counties and (for further, surprising comparison) Phila-delphia in 1960, shortly after Bucks' serious land buying began. The estimates are approximate, taken from inventories made between 1958 and 1962; they may be contrasted with a common, if procrustean, standard of 10 acres per 1,000 residents.[4]

TABLE 15:1
Public Open Land in City and Suburbs
(acres per thousand population)

	Bucks	Montgomery	Delaware	Philadelphia
County	3.2	1.9	0.4	3.5
School and municipal	69.2	43.2	45.0	1.0
State and federal parks	4.2	4.5	0.1	...
State forest and game lands	60.3	53.0	...	...
Total: county, state, federal park lands	7.4	6.4	0.5	3.5
Total as percent of all county acreage	0.6%	1.0%	0.3%	8.6%

The arbitrariness of most standards appears in characteristic conflicts of policy and interest in the counties. One is that of commercial develop-ment versus natural amenity, but this normally arises in specific loca-tional proposals rather than in general policy decisions. Only Bucks County has a plan, but its land is so plentiful that industrial promotion has rarely conflicted with open-space interests. A related opposition lies between recreation and scenic amenity on one hand and utilities on the other; this difference occurred in Bucks as tax-consciousness increased and the provision of utilities began to outweigh open space in the last administration. (One of the strengths of action at the county level is the greater likelihood of integrating these interests effectively in land use.)

A third division is between active recreation (with physical equipment) and open, natural land. Planners and upper-income residents tend to favor plain open space, perhaps for aesthetic reasons and a propensity for long-range conservation. But recreational outlets are more readily available where incomes are high and densities are low, and open space may enhance property values there. Politicians have normally favored physical, visible equipment of park lands. In Bucks County the park board (an offshoot of the planning commission) is oriented to open space, though it has equipped its lands in lower Bucks at the county commissioners' dictation; in Montgomery and Delaware the park boards are politically rather than professionally staffed, and they have emphasized playground and picnic facilities.

Finally one should note a regional issue about open space: until recently the counties have refused federal aid for land acquisition because of its condition that the space be open to all comers; better no land at all than invasion and vandalism from the central city. Some homesteaders who have purchased or nurtured their own turf give low priority to tax-supported, regional open space. Selfish as these attitudes may seem, the wide variety of neighborhood effects and benefit-cost ratios implicit in public open land must, from an individualistic standpoint, be acknowledged. The effect of parks on surrounding tranquillity and amenity is difficult to predict, and adjacent residents often resist local park proposals. Nevertheless, when federal aid for land acquisition was increased by the Housing Act of 1962, with a premium for regional cooperation, all five southeastern Pennsylvania counties finally joined in a consultative arrangement.

Open-space reservation and flood control (with heavy federal aid) are common to all three counties. Action in the utilities field depends on local circumstances: most of Delaware County has long been served by one private water company and, after 1947, state clean-streams legislation and enforcement produced district sewer authorities in the densely settled regions defined by the several small watersheds; Bucks and Montgomery had less compact development, less consistency in service patterns, more wells and septic tanks, leaving more scope for county action. Another factor in this field is the awkwardness of state law, which mandates the authority device for county action on sewerage and water supply in separate acts and in uncertain terms. This makes it difficult to combine both functions effectively, as can be seen in Bucks' cumbersome methods, but Montgomery and Bucks have both responded to pressure by action on water supply. In Montgomery the pressure was sectional and industrial, and in Bucks land developers stood to benefit substantially from county action. (In Bucks the president of the county real estate board was head of the sewer and water authority; in Montgomery the head of the North Penn Water Resources Association was chief engineer for a large industrial plant.) Both counties contributed financially to initial studies and capital costs; Bucks also met operating costs. The legal requirement for county action via an authority was probably intended to prevent such sectional redistribution, but without county subscription to initial costs it is doubtful that the critical water supply problem in the North Penn section and in lower Bucks would have been met comprehensively. Direct county action in utilities implicitly raises issues of income distribution and investment allocation, especially when a pattern of services already exists, but in the long run these problems are likely to be minor.

Administratively, some authorities have recommended the counties as units for sewage disposal operations in the Philadelphia region, in terms of topography, existing systems, and logical service areas.[5] Water supply is commonly considered a regional problem, but the logical region is much larger than that proposed for most other functions. Many of the Delaware River's minor, tributary watersheds lie within single counties. Thus, for the distribution of water, disposal of sewage, reservation of open land, and relating of these to future development the counties may be reasonable units, few enough in number to manage the agreements that might be needed in some cases, and capable of integration with the intergovernmental water projects now planned for the Delaware valley.

16

Health and Welfare

Pennsylvania's counties are less active in health and welfare than most American counties. Public assistance is wholly a state program; health regulation is primarily local. Since the Depression the chief county welfare services have been child care (primarily in the juvenile courts) and institutions for the aged infirm—for those most acceptable as social dependents.

The quality and policy of county action in both fields are often criticized. The ancient homes for the aged (which are partly hospitals) are normally administered politically. In Montgomery and Delaware federal Kerr-Mills funds (medical aid for the indigent aged) were at first refused, presumably because of fear of reporting requirements and nonpolitical admissions criteria. Both county homes accept some paying guests instead of authentic indigents; in 1962 half the budget of Montgomery's home was met from fees, a quarter of Delaware's, and an eighth of Bucks'. In Delaware the internal administration, if innocent of civil service, is thought by qualified observers to be adequate; indeed, this is said to encourage political admissions, since the public home is more attractive than many proprietary ones. Bucks' institution appears to be intermediate, while Montgomery's was until recently the most unprofessional and niggardly in its administration, but it is now under qualified management.

Despite increasing state and federal aid for child care several Pennsylvania counties fail to qualify for reimbursement, usually because of judicial and political resistance to state personnel and service standards.[1] Rivalries between juvenile courts and county-child care agencies are thought to hamper programs except where informal liaison is close; child welfare is said to suffer from overemphasis on family separation and institutionalization, and from insufficient "preventive and protective" action, in the social worker's idiom. The shortage of counseling

175

and casework and of medical and psychological services, is partly trace-able to legal traditions and political attitudes in light of which social work often seems officious.[2]

State programs and county options in welfare have been greatly broadened in the last decade. Now federal and state law require qualified public child care in all counties and encourage consolidation of welfare services.[3] Yet there remains no comprehensive community welfare agency. The same is true of health. In both fields consolidation involves a choice among levels of authority: local, county, regional, and state. Although structural and financial compromise are possible (as in most states), three factors have seemed to professionals to favor state cen-tralization: the vast, inverse disparities among counties in needs and resources; the existing centralization of public assistance, with its local unpopularity and lack of integration with county services; and the state's own stringent tradition in public assistance, which, together with the county patronage system, might be countered by combining admin-istrative and political resources at the state level. In public health, the counties' failure to establish the optional departments provided by law in 1951 has led some specialists to a similar view.

A striking aspect of health and welfare at the county level is the mix of public and private. Traditionally, counties have acted through grants and contracts to charitable and sectarian institutions. The changing financial pattern appears in Table 16:1, which understates public con-tributions by excluding capital outlay and services like education, cor-rections, and environmental controls. The outline is clear, however: public money now predominates in welfare but not in health; fees are a large source of income (primarily in health) and voluntary contribu-tions are marginal; local and county expenditures are relatively small except in Bucks; urban and suburban differences are apparent in the distribution of services and the redistribution of income, with Delaware County intermediate in service patterns and close to Philadelphia in financial sources—of which more details are given in Table 16:1.

The pattern of grants and contracts, lack of income-redistributive programs in less-urbanized counties, local charitable traditions, frag-mentation of public agencies, and political suspicion of professional social work all contribute to private initiative in welfare policy despite the dominance of public finance. The principal sources of this initiative are the United Funds and county planning councils. Only in Bucks is the Fund a countywide agency; there it plays an important social role and overshadows the Community Services Council. In Montgomery County and, especially, in Delaware County the planning councils are stronger, allied to a regional office and to the Greater Philadelphia United Fund. Private initiative is tempered by division between funds and councils and by the vested interests of voluntary agencies attached to both. But the councils provide a *county* focus; and it will appear

TABLE 16:1

Health and Welfare Expenditure Patterns in Four Counties, 1959

	Bucks	Delaware	Mont-gomery	Phila-delphia
Total, per capita (dollars)	37.42	54.97	50.84	101.35
Health (primarily hospital)	27.03	37.08	38.12	57.91
Welfare	7.88	14.21	8.81	36.58
Recreation	2.24	3.06	3.40	5.86
Central (federated financing, planning, organization)	.27	.62	.51	1.00
Percentage of expenditures				
Private	67.8	66.8	73.3	51.1
Public	32.2	33.2	26.7	48.9
Percent public in				
Health	21.7	17.3	19.4	34.8
Welfare	67.6	74.6	58.5	72.3
Recreation	39.8	40.4	29.5	48.9
Central	—	—	—	10.1
Income source, percent for all agencies				
Local and county government	16.1	17.5	9.7	18.0
Other government	17.1	27.6	11.9	25.3
Private	66.8	54.9	78.4	56.7
Percentage distribution of public funds among services				
Health	34.8	23.0	32.4	27.9
Welfare	58.3	70.1	57.2	65.3
Recreation	6.9	6.9	10.4	6.6
Percentage distribution of total expenditures				
Health	72.2	67.4	75.0	57.1
Welfare	21.1	25.9	17.3	36.1
Recreation	6.0	5.6	6.7	5.8

Source: Philadelphia Health and Welfare Council, Inc., *Total Expenditures Study*, (Philadelphia: 1959).

below that, together with county medical societies and Tuberculosis and Health Associations, they have sponsored and supported most new public programs.

The three counties can be briefly compared in needs, resources, and programs. All are highly favored among the shires of Pennsylvania. Economic dependency is most serious in urbanized Delaware; Bucks' lower median income is a rural statistical artifact. Poverty and social problems in Delaware County are more concentrated and obvious. Delaware spends most heavily by far for welfare; when state aid is subtracted, the contrast is even sharper. Bucks' chief expense is its heavily state-aided health department; otherwise its expenditure pattern approximates Montgomery's. Over one-third of Bucks' health and hospital outlay was paid by the state (more than half the county health depart-

TABLE 16:2
Some Indicators of Health and Welfare Needs in 1960–61

	Bucks	*Delaware*	*Mont-gomery*
State Department of Public Welfare expenditures per capita	$10.03	$16.21	$13.71
Public assistance recipients as percent of population	0.6%	1.7%	0.7%
Public assistance expenditures per capita	$ 3.97	$ 9.70	$ 5.16
Medical public assistance expenditures per capita	$ .91	$ 1.64	$ 1.10
State and county hospital and mental health expenditures per capita	$ 4.76	$ 6.22	$ 7.30
Dependent, neglected, and delinquent children per 1,000 juveniles receiving service by public or private agency	5.6	13.5	3.8
County child welfare expenditures per capita	$ 3.03	$ 2.77	$ 1.25

ment budget) and, because of fees, only 55 percent was tax-supported; roughly three-quarters of Delaware's expenditures for children and the aged were met from county taxes.

The most striking intercounty differences in policy and performance have occurred in the options of public health and child welfare. These differences and their histories are most relevant to future state and county roles in health and welfare.

1. *Public health.* At midcentury public health administration in Pennsylvania was both centralized in Harrisburg and radically dispersed in municipalities; counties were not involved. In 1947 the state medical society urged a study of health administration, which the governor then commissioned from the American Public Health Association. Among the ensuing recommendations were regional decentralization of state health administration and more reliance on local government (especially counties) with state subsidy and supervision. This report led to legislation authorizing county health departments.[4]

Under the Act of 1951 counties might establish health departments to replace most state functions; with state aid and county tax support these departments were expected, because of financial incentives and superior standards, to supplant municipal administration. State matching grants (up to seventy-five cents per capita) were conditioned on conformity to performance and personnel standards, and the State Health Department was empowered *in extremis* to commandeer county operations at county expense if its regulations were ignored, or if "conditions exist that constitute a menace to health."

Only four counties (including Bucks) have established such departments. When Delaware County's Health and Welfare Council issued its health and hospital study in 1961 it found local programs and organization virtually unchanged since a previous study in 1933, despite the environmental health hazards of higher residential density and industrial technology and the progress of public health administration since federal aid began in 1935. Boroughs and first-class townships had mandatory health boards, while the state department served second-class townships, set rudimentary standards for municipal officials, and shared inspections with the Departments of Agriculture, and of Labor and Industry. Surveys in Montgomery and Delaware made the same point: low administrative standards and local fiscal disparities produced wide variation within each county; in general, communicable disease reporting and chronic disease control were spotty, maternal and child health measures were negligible, vital statistics were primitive, and inspections and sanitary regulation were uneven.[5] Many local officials were part-time plumbers or politicians; almost none were medical doctors. Differences in fiscal and official capacity especially distinguished rich and poor, large and small municipalities. Yet local health officers commonly felt threatened by prospective county action, and this was most evident in the least effective jurisdictions. Actually, the state department functioned throughout Delaware and Montgomery Counties in tuberculosis and chronic disease control, mental and child health, and sanitary inspection.

In the spring of 1952 the state secretary of health addressed a regular meeting of the Bucks County Medical Society on the merits of the recently authorized county health department. A few members of the Society's committee on public health and preventive medicine accepted his suggestion, solicited the help of some laymen, and founded the Citizens' Health Association. When the county commissioners were asked to create a health department they suggested a referendum.[6] This required countywide organization at a time when Bucks was sparsely populated and sparely organized; its United Fund and Community Services Council were just being formed. The movement began with half a dozen doctors, the executive of the county Tuberculosis and Health Association, the president of the Federation of Women's Clubs, and several local Leagues of Women Voters; most of its originators lived in central and upper Bucks. Later a letterhead organization was formed that included a county judge, several clergymen, and organized labor. Petitions were circulated and in August a referendum was scheduled for the November 1953 election. Literature was distributed through the county medical society and the county superintendent of schools. Newspaper support was probably important. The Pennsylvania Economy League endorsed the proposal and its newsletter reached most businessmen; women's organizations were especially active in central Bucks and organized labor in lower Bucks; PTA and neighborhood meetings were emphasized.

Several factors aided the campaign. Party politics was carefully avoided and, save for some endorsements from lower Bucks Democrats, politicians ignored the issue. A typhoid scare in central Bucks and the sanitary problems of rapid growth in lower Bucks coincided with the referendum. Moreover, Bucks County then had only one first-class township and not all its twenty-four boroughs had health boards; there were few vested local interests. Finally, because the campaign was short and one of the first in the state, opposition was slow in forming; it was October before the head of the state Association of Second Class Township Supervisors (the center of resistance to local consolidation proposals in Pennsylvania) joined the issue. He found some support in Upper Bucks, but many local councilmen were ready to relinquish public health. Given the political innocence of the campaigners, this delay was probably crucial, or so they concluded on later analysis. In the election 61 percent of Bucks' registrants voted, 38 percent voted on the health department, and 66 percent of these supported it; in this way the department was established by 25 percent of the electorate.

In a decade the Bucks health department grew from an initial staff of 8 to more than 70 plus 24 part-time physicians in clinics. It began with tuberculosis control and sanitary inspection and proceeded to review and approval of on-lot sewage disposal systems, maternal and child health, well child clinics, and consultation in nutrition and medical social work. It gradually assumed most, though not all, of the medical and sanitary programs of the state district office; the municipal boards closed down, though school health programs (in a different state hierarchy) remained independent. Public health integration was not complete and was unlikely to be, with the competing state agencies and the high unit costs of some specialized medical programs. But in such exigencies as typhoid inoculation after severe floods and the distribution of polio vaccine the county health department took charge. It weathered several political crises successfully: when builders complained of delays in subdivision sewerage approval an advisory committee was established that included builders' representatives; when doctors and hospitals resisted free distribution of polio vaccine the issue was compromised at one dollar a shot; when a willful, erratic director badly antagonized the county commissioners, who were trying to cut the budget, he was ultimately fired and the budget reduction lasted but a year. Despite occasional politicking in board appointments—Eddie Boyer on taking office summarily fired two Democrats and appointed his personal physician—state regulations precluded politics in staff appointments. Appropriations more than tripled in a decade and continued to grow after the per-capita limit on state matching was passed.

The initiative and support for a Montgomery County health department were like those in Bucks; but they encountered more political organization and localistic ideology, and the outcome was different. In the mid-1950's the chairman of the county Medical Society's Preventive

Medicine Committee (also chairman of Lower Merion Township's Board of Health) proposed a county study and asked for the assistance of the Health and Welfare Council and the Tuberculosis and Health Association. These organizations, with the Cancer Society and Heart Association, sponsored a study, staffed by TAHA and served by a large citizen committee and a consultant from the University of Pennsylvania Medical School. Local hospital and public health agencies were examined through the good offices of the county medical society. The study's critical findings were mentioned above; the remedy it proposed was a county health department—which was probably in the sponsors' thoughts from the start.

This recommendation was approved by the medical society and other sponsoring agencies and by several Leagues of Women Voters. The county commissioners were approached, but after some months it was evident they would not approve it, and a referendum was agreed upon. Before this decision was made the county Republican chairman and some local leaders were approached to ascertain the party attitude; they promised neutrality, but refused support.

A well financed campaign began in the spring of 1958, aimed at the fall election. The survey committee became a campaign committee, chaired by the wife of a prominent Republican, herself an experienced civic leader; seven regional chairmen were named; finance and publicity were centrally organized; endorsements were secured from many civic and social organizations (especially women's groups) and from organized labor—but not from business organizations. The state health department supplied a full-time public relations worker and underwrote some printing and distribution costs.

By summer the opposition began to show. At a meeting of wealthy Cheltenham Township's commissioners the local political leader (also township manager) termed the proposal "step one in the collapse of home rule," arguing it would be costly, political (i.e., controlled from then Democratic Harrisburg), and neglectful of the competence of local programs. He was widely quoted in the county press through a release distributed from the county commissioners' office. Further releases were followed by resolutions of the Boroughs' Association, Second Class Townships' Association, County Firemen's Association, and several municipalities. Some quiet opposition even developed among state health department district personnel, perhaps from sensitivity to criticism. The Montgomery Countians For America mobilized to speak at meetings and harass the "Communist" campaign. Other opponents were more concerned with the threat to local home rule, the possible loss of *county* autonomy implied in state standards and sanctions, and the likely increase in county taxes (which was admitted by proponents).

In early September the county Democratic committee endorsed the health department, and was then publicly repudiated by the minority county commissioner. The Republican committee maintained formal

neutrality and distributed a "public service" statement to papers reviewing both sides of the issue in parallel columns: the affirmative lengthily
and technically, the negative briefly and readably. Most daily county
newspapers opposed a department (because they were sensitive to withdrawal of public advertising, proponents said). The commissioners sent
a representative (the Republican Party public relations man) to study
health departments in other counties; after six days in three counties
he filed a report from the courthouse describing them as failures. The
commissioners denied responsibility for the report, but in the closing
weeks of the campaign they finally announced their opposition on fiscal
grounds. In the last week it turned out that opposition literature was
being distributed by the party headquarters, though the chairman
denied knowledge of the source of the unsigned pamphlets, which
argued that the health department could "establish a garbage dump in
your neighborhood" and would "destroy home rule and encourage
Socialism."

The proposal lost by a two-to-one margin. A local scholar who analyzed
the vote and compared it with Bucks' noted a strong correlation between
local turnout and opposition voting and concluded that the factor producing turnout probably induced a negative vote.[7] That factor, he
thought, was party activity. There was ample evidence of it in many
precincts, and the men who staffed the For America campaign were
party and courthouse employees. What mobilized the party is conjectural: counter-arguments noted above weighed heavily with some, and
the local home-rule forces were as active in this issue as they had been
against the county planning commission in 1956. In Montgomery these
forces were stronger than in Bucks, and there were more local health
boards and self-sufficient municipalities. In both Bucks and Montgomery, localities with most rapid growth and high educational levels
tended to be most favorable to the proposal, but this was much more
pronounced in Bucks, where the party factor was not operating and
where growth was more explosive and unsettling of tradition. The
Montgomery referendum came later, when the forces of opposition were
more alert and experienced.

As a result of the campaign a few of Montgomery's communities
appointed doctors as health officers (They usually had little time for
the duty.), and a few more abdicated entirely to the state. Otherwise,
county health administration was unchanged.

In Delaware County the numerous local health boards are formally
organized on a county basis. Their association has long served as a
forum for discussion, but neither uniform local ordinances nor integrated action have resulted from it.[8] Delaware's Health and Welfare
Council began its health and hospital study in 1958 at the county medical
society's request. It was an inventory of all health services and facilities,
public and private, with numerous proposals for expansion, including a
county health administrator to integrate existing state and local pro-

grams. When this compromise was presented to the commissioners in 1961, they were noncommittal, while the intermunicipal association opposed it, sensing correctly that some of its sponsors intended an entering wedge for a full-fledged department. As this is written the Health and Welfare Council is beginning a campaign for a county health department.

2. *Child welfare.* The county histories are reversed in child welfare, the other important optional program. In Bucks and Montgomery Counties in 1963 the function was completely unprofessionalized and thus ineligible for state aid. Bucks' child care was solely provided by the juvenile court. Montgomery maintained a rudimentary child-care agency in the county institution district. The extent of this agency's "protective" service was unknown because it kept few records; in Bucks there was no such service. Citizens' studies in both counties criticized the lack of public staff, professional capacity, continuing responsibility, juvenile institutions, foster-care facilities, or auxiliary services, like day care, homemaker, adoption, and counseling.[9] In Montgomery, relations between the child-welfare office and the juvenile court probation service were vague and sometimes strained; referrals and case determinations were haphazard. Relations between the probation service and private agencies were also unhappy.

The juvenile courts in both counties resented civic and professional criticism and resisted change. The county commissioners respected their judgment. In both counties the distaff constituencies so important in voluntary welfare work took the initiative: in Montgomery the several Leagues of Women Voters and in Bucks the Community Services Council studied child care and prevailed on the county commissioners to appoint citizens' committees which made the findings referred to above. In 1963 Bucks' committee recommended a county child-care agency subject to state aid and standards; the outgoing commissioners, despite judicial reluctance, created it; the next administration staffed it professionally. Montgomery's committee winked at the state aid program, commenting that "there is in Montgomery County considerable resistance to supervision by the Department of Public Welfare. In view of this attitude this committee does not recommend that Montgomery County participate . . . at this time."[10] It did offer broad proposals for reform and expansion of existing child-care and probation agencies, and it requested appointment of a citizens' advisory committee on the subject (which, by statute, is required for state-aided county child-care agencies). The commissioners indifferently appointed the advisory committee and ignored it together with the earlier committee's other proposals. But the advisory committee, backed by fresh state legislation, kept pressing, and the next administration found a politic way to change the agency staff, warily preparing for professionalization and state aid.

In each county, citizen initiative and persistence were important factors that somewhat mitigated the political stigma of social work. Their ultimate influence is, however, uncertain because the state legislation passed in the course of both county campaigns required county child-care agencies by 1968; this was recognized directly in Montgomery and at least remotely in Bucks. The state law, in turn, was required by the federal welfare amendments of 1962.

Delaware County had a different history that, in light (or shadow) of its political structure, merits fuller description. In the Depression, county welfare expenditures were heavy, and after federal and state centralization it was still the habit of Chester politicians to take credit for welfare checks. Professionalization began with the juvenile court in the late 1940's. At that time the president judge was also president of the Media Family Service Agency, which was often consulted by the court. When the judges fought with their probation officer and fired the probation staff, the director of Family Service was retained as a consultant. She sold the judges on a professional, nonpolitical probation service and saw it adopted. Thus the judges' conservatism (or sense of personal responsibility for both children and incumbent staff), so important in other counties, worked differently in Delaware, and a base was laid for change in child welfare (legally, care of dependent and neglected, but not delinquent, children). Private agencies acted as contractors to the court in arranging institutional and foster care, and the county handled the clerical work; "preventive and protective" services were entirely lacking. By 1949 the program was under fire in some private-welfare circles, and the court was conscientiously discontented with it. Influenced and supported by the president judge, the chairman of the commissioners developed misgivings about the system's cost and quality. A letter campaign sponsored by the Health and Welfare Council surprised and impressed the commissioners, though the public involved was narrow and newspaper coverage was negligible. At this point John McClure accepted the idea of a nonpolitical county agency, despite its departure from courthouse tradition, and through intermediaries, he circumspectly backed its establishment. The director of the Family Service was retained as consultant on procedure and personnel; the commissioners publicly pledged to create a qualified county agency "even if it means raising taxes"—though they seem to have hoped for savings. Within three months the case load was reorganized and a professional director was hired.

The origins of Delaware's Child Care Service were remarkable in several respects. One was the personality of the social worker upon whom the court and commissioners relied: she had worked in Media for more than a decade and had taken her graduate degree *after* arrival there. In her previous jobs she had worked closely with politicians. Through her counseling work, she became the close confidant of two successive president judges. The attitudes of these judges, who were sincerely and sensitively affected by juvenile decisions, and their influence on the political leadership was a second striking aspect. A third was the commissioners' sensitivity to mild public criticism. A fourth was acceptance of professionalism and financial support in these circumstances by the county political leader. Finally, it should be noted that the program was undertaken five years before state aid was available, though state grants and standards later made professional salaries and social workers easier for the commissioners to accept.

Subsequent commissioners were alert to political sensitivity about professionals, and at times the program was threatened by political appointments or low appropriations. On one occasion the president judge appeared before the commissioners and vowed to resign if they carried out a budget reduction. Tax-supported appropriations increased in every year, two institutions were built in a decade, the professional staff became the state's largest outside of Allegheny (Pittsburgh) and Philadelphia Counties, exceeding state training standards, and the program was distinguished by steady growth in the proportion of "preventive and protective" cases. As this account is written, however, the Child Care Service is receiving criticism from other agencies for low service levels, and the County Commissioners are resisting requests for larger appropriation increases.

The explanation of Delaware County's welfare program—its professionalized sectors and its relatively high service levels—is conjectural. In this conservative, highly politicized county the attitudes so plain in the other counties existed but did not prevail. Some observers put this down to a happy conjuncture of personalities, especially the president judges'; and to the longer existence and greater acceptance of the county's welfare constituency, especially the Health and Welfare Council. Given the indication of McClure's intervention, a political interpretation of this success seems logical. This would begin with population characteristics in the area where the political organization, qua organization, was most heavily based (cf. Chapter 10), noting the threat of Democratic voting there. To this should be added the estimate of the child-care agency's director that some two-thirds of the cases came from the same region of the county (south of Baltimore Pike) and a plurality from Chester. The agency's strongest official supporters have occasionally said that it is a means of keeping the county Republican. The political factor cannot be isolated as an explanation, for there is more dependency in Delaware than in the other counties, and it is more highly concentrated. This alone may explain Delaware's welfare history, but it also supports the other explanations: the political account depends on it, and the welfare constituency and personalities involved may thus have met political response.

3. *Summary.* County health and welfare in Pennsylvania are national anomalies, and are matters of private initiative primarily. The pattern fits political tradition and organization: it favors particular benefits,

appropriations, and patronage rather than programs and professionalism. Yet rising costs and broader concepts of health and welfare are, with federal aid, producing change: professional county child care is now required, and since 1963 both Bucks and Montgomery have established professional agencies. County action in health is harder because vested local positions must be displaced. In both fields some state centralization accompanies consolidation at the county level, through finance and standards. Full centralization, however, would tend to separate public responsibility from private concern; for health and welfare is one of the best organized, most socially acceptable county constituencies. The redistributive role of state and federal financial aid, often adjusted to local fiscal effort, is well established elsewhere; if all decision and administration were also centralized in Pennsylvania, this might circumvent both the favorable and unfavorable elements in county politics.

17

Industrial Development

Industrial development became an optional county function in 1956. State legislation vaguely empowered counties to establish agencies for this purpose, authorized state grants to public or nonprofit bodies for research and promotion, and created a state authority to help finance industrial relocation in critical areas, for which only Bucks, of the three counties, was qualified.[1]

At the same time (1954-56) the Southeastern Pennsylvania Regional Planning Commission made a major study of industrial land and facilities requirements in the suburban counties.[2] It found the region's manufacturing growth lagging behind the nation's. It nevertheless concluded that prime industrial land would probably fall short of local demand by 1980; that most industrial growth would occur in clusters close to the city; and that available land varied greatly among the counties with Bucks high, Montgomery medium, and Delaware low. Also in the midfifties industrial employment declined in all the region's five counties except Montgomery, falling off most sharply in Philadelphia, which began heavily to emphasize industrial redevelopment. Over the whole decade five-county industrial employment declined more than 10 percent—the nation's slowest rate of major metropolitan area growth.[3]

As rapid residential expansion occurred suburban county planners emphasized industrial development, primarily for taxes but also—in Bucks and Delaware, where employment declined sharply in 1955—for payrolls.[4] Bucks undertook an energetic promotional program; Delaware and Montgomery followed with substantially lesser efforts. These will shortly be reviewed for their political and administrative lessons, but the question may first be considered: Is the county a proper level for such activity? (The actual effect of such activity is problematical; its productivity will be assumed for now and briefly considered later.)

Three jurisdictional levels contend in industrial development: local, county, and regional. Municipalities vary in their attitudes: many are active in promotion, some are uninterested, others are highly resistant or divided; almost all are at least selective, seeking clean industries that are low in employment but high in tax yield. Compared with localities, counties have several advantages: county planners can appreciate that industrialization will almost inevitably cluster instead of dispersing, and they have the perspective to encourage reservations of prime land and preparation of facilities, and to relate industry to the pace and pattern of local growth. Clearly, not all the localities that desire industry are destined to have it, but county action can be helpful (as it has been in Bucks and Montgomery) in working with communities to soften resistance to industry, while preserving planning standards.

Since transportation is a critical factor in industrial location and is usually considered appropriate for regional planning, one can argue that industrial development is also properly a regional concern (at least incidentally affecting welfare and income distribution), but their logical connection need not lead to regional consolidation. A more persuasive argument for the regional approach is that of intercounty competition: more than half the plants in Montgomery's two largest industrial parks migrated from Philadelphia; Bucks County's biggest catches so far have also been central city fish. One of the leading suburban industrial developers has argued, on the other hand, that "You can't do industrial development in midair"; you've got to "know the territory." If this bespeaks a frankly competitive attitude, others have argued that the central city move-outs were bound to occur—the industries took the initiative—and the only question was where. If central city–suburban competition is the main concern, it is doubtful, on this view, that regional activity will moderate it much. The issue depends in part on the proper blend of planning and promotion in industrial development, but if promotion is of doubtful effectiveness, the county seems an acceptable place for planning. In fact, promotion occurs at all three levels, since the Greater Philadelphia Chamber of Commerce has long had a regional program, as has the state Commerce Department, and a private regional corporation was recently formed by banks and utilities to finance promotion and relocation.

Formal industrial development in the counties is a new activity, still feeling its way. If its promotional effectiveness is doubtful, its importance for county planning is clear. Under state law, three organizational alternatives have emerged: the wholly private organization, with state and county grants; the wholly public agency, an arm of county government; and the quasi-public corporation. Each of the three counties has followed a different approach.

1. *Bucks* was the first suburban county to enter industrial development, and it makes the heaviest effort today. In this it is aided by

qualification as a critical area and eligibility for state-aided financial inducements to relocation.[5] The program's origins may illuminate the effects of political structure when contrasted with the other counties. By the 1955 election unemployment was serious in lower Bucks; the county began surplus-food distribution and requested state aid. (Later the planning commission commented that Bucks' residential growth after 1954 looked like the normal suburban pattern; it was not linked to large industrial projects as the first spurt had been, and manufacturing employment actually fell off.)[6] The Lower Bucks County Chamber of Commerce surveyed industrial prospects and urged a public effort; early in 1955 state officials (from a Democratic administration) began consultations aimed at local and private endeavor pending state development legislation.

In the fall election campaign John Welsh promised an industrial development program; once in office he ordered the county solicitor to explore available methods. Welsh evidently hoped for a private organization with county appropriations, but the solicitor ruled this out under the pending state legislation. Accordingly, the planning commission was named the county agency to receive state aid; its budget and personnel were substantially enlarged for this purpose, and the executive director was placed on leave to give full time to industrial research and promotion. An industrial development committee of ten carefully selected bankers, industrialists, newspapermen, and developers (all registered Republicans) was appointed to oversee the program. With this committee the county went as far as it then could to involve the business community. A later alteration in state law allowed county appropriations to private development agencies; then the committee itself recommended a private corporation, which was created in 1958. The new Industrial Development Corporation hired its own executive director, who was paid from county appropriations and state aid, which later (in the Boyer administration) went to IDC directly instead of through the planning commission.

Changing the original committee of ten men to a corporation of more than thirty created the closest thing to a power structure in Bucks: most of the large absentee firms and local businesses were represented, though some old industries remained outside. The best test of the corporation's effectiveness is probably its ability to finance expansion; with state support its financial resources could provide substantial inducement with more tangible effects than simple advertising. IDC began with a drive to raise a $1¼-million fund, which failed utterly. In five years, so far as can be discovered, private contributions totaled less than $100,000, of which slightly more than half came from United States Steel. Six relocations were secured with state financing; in the largest of these IDC failed to raise the required 10 percent local participation even with Big Steel's contribution. (The prospect, Strick Trailer, settled near the Fairless Works and purchased steel in small quantities.)

Save for U.S. Steel the county's large absentee-owned plants had only public relations as an incentive to contribute; the county banks were conservative and too small for large-scale industrial finance, while the metropolitan branch banks were wary of intraregional competition. In the five years, 1956-63, county support of IDC substantially outran both state aid and private contributions and averaged over $50,000 annually.

IDC's private direction with reliance on county funds gave rise to subtle issues, though not to overt problems. During the Boyer administration the county's shift of emphasis to industrialization and infrastructure was chiefly expressed in IDC. By 1959 the planning commission had come to doubt the possibility of large-scale industrial development in Bucks, and its draft comprehensive plan reflected this doubt: an all-out development effort *might* have conflicted with the nucleated, green-belts emphasis in the plan had it succeeded and had land not been plentiful; but as it was, wrangles over land use were rare. Competition between economic development and residential amenity remained implicit, and IDC became something of an institutional rival to the planning commission, assuming the planners' old role of spinning off new organizations. The county Airport Authority and Water and Sewer Authority had earlier been backed by the planning commission; the Redevelopment Authority was created almost entirely on IDC's initiative after cursory study. In the last year of the Boyer administration this urban redevelopment agency commanded the largest appropriation ($104,000) of any county authority; it had seven projects in process, most of which were aimed at commercial and industrial facilities.* Still later the Boyer administration appointed a committee to study the feasibility of a Delaware River port; the study was generated and carried out by members of the Lower Bucks County Chamber of Commerce and IDC, and its favorable report nearly resulted· in another county authority. Boyer's most serious intraparty opponents then raised the issue of patronage, and the newspapers strongly criticized the proposal on grounds of economy and county capacity; the county's congressman was persuaded to sponsor legislation empowering the Delaware River Joint Toll Bridge Commission to construct a bi-state port on both sides of the river, and commissioner Boyer and other sponsors reluctantly abandoned the authority.

While land and tax resources were relatively slack and growth was rapid, the corporate approach to industrial development did not forcefully pose issues of coordination and county planning. For similar reasons the issue of public versus private benefit was diminished, except as it entered Republican party factionalism. There was an implicit issue in the ambiguous position of IDC's executive: Was he working for his board or for the county government? Since board participation in the

* Of the $104,000 appropriation for 1963, $76,000 was earmarked for a prominent Philadelphia consulting firm in the redevelopment field, whose partners had close business connections with one of commissioner Boyer's close political allies.

financing and specific projects was narrow and since the majority county commissioners were badly divided, questions arose on both the private and the public sides of the issue. Politically, commissioner Boyer was charged with favoring IDC's governmental proposals for the patronage they conferred. Privately, IDC's major proposals and projects were of potential direct benefit to those few board members who pressed them hardest: this was true of the Redevelopment Authority, the port, the leading industrial park, and the few state-financed relocations. The board member who probably was the most active was a land developer, while the other principal participants included representatives of three service industries, a banker, the largest daily paper, and U.S. Steel.

In Bucks' financial and administrative pattern, political and pecuniary interests were evidently harnessed together in industrial development and its adjuncts, but it could not be cogently argued that no public purpose was served or even that county progress was only apparent. What could be argued, however problematically, was that priorities were wrong. This was the view of the county planners, who favored appropriations for open-space reservation and residential water and sewerage over industrial development and allied physical facilities. And it was reasonably clear that the planners' priorities would—in the first instance, if not ultimately—have spread the benefits of county appropriations more broadly. The effects of the industrial development effort itself may be left to later consideration.

2. *Montgomery's* industrial promotion took the form of a small office in the county courthouse, a wholly public operation. It began with the Hammonds administration in 1958, at the instance of the planning commission staff, which was probably responding to state pressure (though this cannot be firmly established). It is clear that the county commissioners had little enthusiasm for it: after the planning commission convened a meeting of businessmen for discussion they appointed a ten-member study committee, and the study lasted for more than three years. Late in 1961 the county office was organized by the Wetherill administration, and the committee continued in an advisory capacity. Courthouse support was always lukewarm, and appropriations ran less than $35,000 annually.

There were reasons for reluctance apart from Montgomery's normal courthouse tradition. One was the Manufacturers' Association's evident lack of enthusiasm; Association members still acknowledge concern about industrial development's effect on local labor markets and transportation capacity and about help for declining, older industries. Another reason was scepticism about the need: in the 1950's the Pennsylvania Turnpike extensions brought a rush of industry into central Montgomery County (the Norristown and Lansdale sections), so that Montgomery as a whole never showed the decline in manufacturing employment that affected other counties in the midfifties, and its payrolls have risen most consistently of any in the region. For these reasons the public intent of the county development office has differed from those in other counties: it has emphasized high selectivity, protection of existing industries (without being able to do much about it), and liaison with municipalities to try to interest them in industrial development. Apart from these emphases its work has been entirely promotional; there has been no local financing of location, and Montgomery is not eligible for state financial aid.

This approach suits the few parties who favor county action—the local banks that are large enough to participate in industrial loans, who are represented on the development committee, and an industrial park developer, who pressed for the committee and has since been a member of it. For these interests, advertising and advice, without location assistance, are adequate. But the pattern has certain general disadvantages: there has been relatively little research on and planning for countywide industrial development, and despite some effort by the county office, little has been done for the county's less-favored sections. A minor effect has been scepticism about the county program by two of the three major industrial parks in central Montgomery County: they see it as too close to the third park's developer, who helped initiate it; and they have tended to go their own way with the aid of their site advantages.

3. *Delaware County* began the last decade with the most serious tax and employment situation of the three counties, and it has done least about it at the county level. As in Bucks County, it has a history of employment decline combined with residential increase, but in Delaware these occurred in different parts of the county. Unemployment was centered in Chester and complicated by unskilled labor, automation in large plants, and lack of transportation and available land.

The Chester problem was chronic: with its dense population, residential clearance was prerequisite to industrial development but threatened political organization; relocation would intensify race prejudice; most existing factories were old and outmoded; some large employers (e.g., shipbuilders) were unstable and dependent on government contracts; must labor was unskilled (even illiterate) and socially disorganized; automation was a serious problem, for value added by manufacture has increased as employment has declined. Considering these facts and the pattern of Chester industry, the consultant of the Chester City Planning Commission concluded in 1959 that further large-scale employment declines were unlikely, "but stagnation or a further slow decline may well continue."[7] Yet its reversal was necessary to relieve the city's social and fiscal problems, which might well spread through lower Delaware County.

Still, in Delaware, industrial development is less visibly a *county* problem. Those professionally concerned remark that business leadership lives in sections of the county that are unaffected by unemployment and tax erosion, and there is vigorous civic opposition to industrial zoning in some residential sections. Since Chester is the center of depression, its jurisdictional separation from the county may hamper action despite the city's political power in the courthouse. In Chester, political inertia, fiscal and administrative incapacity, and fear of the politically unsettling effects of the urban redevelopment that is necessary there to industrial development have delayed action. A large-scale county program might appear partial to Chester and to the county's unpopulated western end, where land is available. More plausibly, new industry might upset the old mobilization of bias as it has in other counties, though there is no evidence of such a calculation by the political leadership. Development is the kind of issue that the leadership leaves to private interests; because it is sectional, short on benefits at once widespread and direct, administratively complex and professional, it is foreign to the courthouse tradition.

The industrial community and the Manufacturers' Association have been virtually inactive, perhaps deferring in their turn to politicians. Privately, some industrialists say prevailing wage rates and labor's troublous reputation are deterrents to growth; some express concern that county action would raise taxes. The tax issue seems problematical: continued deterioration in Chester might also raise taxes there, though assessment increases attempted so far have fallen mainly on commercial and residential property.[8] Outside of Chester most large plants are located in small tax colonies. General conservatism, acceptance of political initiative, and scepticism about the prospects for development are probably factors in business inaction, but lack of industrial self-interest, at the least, is important. The national orientation of the county's large firms, despite the native leadership of some, may damp locally oriented altruism. As in Montgomery, most of Delaware's large firms are not in consumer products and are thus not public relations conscious; the leading exception, Scott Paper, sponsored an industrial development study in the late 1940's and has urged action on other occasions without arousing enthusiasm. Competition for skilled labor would inevitably be increased by industrial development.

In action on industrial development the Chamber of Commerce, centered in Chester, has been the only group to show an interest. Sparked by the Philadelphia Electric Company, it surveyed land and facilities with the city planning commission in the midfifties. In 1957 it was designated by the county commissioners to receive the state grants for promotional work. County appropriations came later at the rate of $12,000–$13,000 a year, and in 1960 the Chamber hired a development expert, who had retired from the Greater Philadelphia Chamber. In 1962 it organized a nonprofit corporation as the basis of a land-bank operation (modeled on Philadelphia's method), but the corporation existed only on paper, without the funds to acquire land.

Few new firms have located in Delaware County, though there have

been important expansions of existing industries. Industrial development has been a private affair, with the least public support of the three
counties. Manufacturing employment has declined absolutely in the last
decade. Yet one can argue, and some conservatives have, that the only
realistic alternatives are a crash program on a grand scale or the present
holding operation and that the former is highly speculative and necessarily dependent on private capital for land development. Since the
business community has not sought public aid, it would require, by
Delaware standards, exceptional political initiative for the county to
do more.

4. *Evaluation* of the counties' programs is difficult not only because
of their disparate problems, but because no one knows just how specific
industrial locations are determined. The priority of transportation is
clear, and Montgomery, Bucks, and Delaware rank in that order in
transportation advantages. Transportation is largely a function of the
state highway department, which is notoriously poor at regional planning and action.[9] Bucks and Montgomery are presently blessed with
available sites; Delaware County is not unless its transportation network
expands. Other factors, such as residential amenity, political reputation,
and public images of growth or decline are widely thought to disadvantage Delaware. Most developers argue that location heavily depends on
executives' residential preferences and that Bucks and Montgomery
offer a better choice within closer range of the plant; at the least their
assets are better advertised. Professionals at the regional level say that
when a prospect arrives in the region he often has a county at least
tentatively in mind, and it is usually Montgomery or Bucks.

TABLE 17:1
Industrial Employment by County

	1919	1930	1940	1951	1954	1956	1960	1962
Bucks	15,834	11,594	15,143	24,403	35,756	30,948	32,324	34,307
Delaware	68,718	37,703	37,231	55,413	53,166	48,881	48,488	48,209
Montgomery	27,087	33,118	43,912	64,677	60,524	65,012	74,231	81,390
Philadelphia	264,933	273,431	277,547	348,882	n.a.*	306,331	288,301	275,000

Source: Pennsylvania Department of Internal Affairs, Bureau of Statistics.
* Not available.

Against this background and the employment trends in Table 17:1, it
can be said that Philadelphia and Delaware have made the heaviest and
weakest public efforts respectively and have done least well; Montgomery has substantially outdistanced Bucks (via the Pennsylvania Turnpike) with much less public effort, though a large number of small
plants have located in Bucks. Perhaps something like value added is a
better measure of success than is employment in an age of automation,
and this may be so for the long run, but Philadelphia, Delaware, and
Bucks have all been equally concerned with payrolls and taxes, though
Montgomery, ironically, has not.

The variations in county success seem most dependent on basic factors such as decentralization, space, and highway transportation, though financial inducements have been marginally helpful in Philadelphia and even in Bucks, despite Bucks' failure at fund-raising. (Developers disagree on the effectiveness of financial inducements; they are probably most effective in the more labor-intensive industries, and thus most appropriate to the counties where employment is a problem. Plants relying on automation or highly skilled labor are likely to give more weight to residential amenity and community services.) For financial purposes the nonprofit corporation has advantages over direct governmental action: it may reduce the public-purpose issue intrinsic to tax-supported inducements (depending on the level of county appropriations), and it can rely instead on commercial self-interest supplemented by governmental planning and local liaison.

Where private involvement in presumptively nonprofit operations is desirable the county experiences, especially Bucks', afford some relevant lessons. (1) In private hands, industrial promotion depends heavily on specific or demonstrable benefits to participants. (2) If substantial public funds are involved, as in Bucks, the problem of public purpose and private advantage may become acute; *strong* governmental control and integration with planning will be needed to minimize it. (3) Most existing industries are more clearly threatened than benefited by industrial development, especially where the main taxing authorities are small municipalities. (United States Steel in Bucks is one exception: it is so large that it now pays some 10 percent of county taxes and is alert to public relations needs, and it may supply steel to some incoming industries.) School-district consolidation, now under way, may alter this picture, since the school tax dominates local finance. (4) Most commercial firms and utilities that are interested in industrial development and large enough to help finance it operate on a regional basis; they may be persuaded to subscribe to county efforts, but they are more likely to favor a regional approach as more efficient and controllable. Significantly, a regional organization has recently been formed by these interests. (5) The counties' role would thus seem basically limited to planning, promotion, and local liaison, but these are nonetheless important aspects of industrial development, likely to be neglected in private endeavors at the regional level. Conceivably a pattern of county planning and promotion with regional financing will evolve.

18

Transportation

Planners and academic critics agree that metropolitan transportation requires regional management. Growing acceptance of this view in federal policy has stimulated some institutional beginnings in greater Philadelphia, first through financial incentives and later by requirements attached to federal grants-in-aid.[1]

Suburban development depends largely on state highway construction, and counties are consulted in state highway planning. Industrial location, especially, has been a function of highway planning: Montgomery's prosperity is based on it, and Bucks' position would surely improve if long-projected regional arteries were built. Indeed, the remoteness and rural orientation of state operations has led some to suggest that state and regional highways be distinguished and that responsibility for all the others be redistributed to the counties and localities.[2]

Water, air, and (recently) rail transportation, on the other hand, are subjects of direct local action. Port construction is under discussion in Bucks County, and port improvements are mooted in the city of Chester. This chapter deals primarily with airports and mass transit. Both raise distinctive issues besides that of their regional impact. One concerns the sectional distribution of public subsidies within the counties—a matter of the radius of use, the extent of indirect benefits, and the external costs of location (especially of airports). Another issue is the more general public-purpose issue raised by public ownership or subsidy.

1. *Airports.* The airport problem in the counties concerns small feeder facilities for private traffic, not common carriers. The question of public participation arises because private fliers want a field or an existing airport seeks public assistance. In the three counties, according

to surveys, roughly half the private fliers are pleasure fliers, but all are enthusiasts: civil aviation enlists strenuous dedication. Public ownership of local airports permits federal and state aid, elimination of taxes, relief from zoning difficulties, and possible reduction of condemnation costs.[3] More than a score of private airfields in the three counties have been sold since World War II for a "higher and better use," raising the question whether the small public airport is economic. Even Philadelphia's International Airport is far from self-supporting, and the city has unsuccessfully sought suburban help in defraying its deficits. Indirectly, the economic value of an airport probably depends most heavily on its contribution to industrial development, and developers disagree about the short-run relevance, though all profess its importance for the long-run future. Directly, the success of the county airport may well depend on the number of other small airports and thus on the overall state of civil aviation. The interests involved in this problem include the producing industries and related groups, like the Aircraft Owners and Pilots Association (organized by Montgomery County residents), which calls itself the "Triple A of flying."[4] The federal government, under the Federal Airport Act of 1946, has been an important factor through matching grants for airport development, but during much of the period covered here the Eisenhower administration was attempting to shift air terminal support to states and localities while increasing federal outlays for safety research and equipment. Pennsylvania also matches local contributions, so that the latter are only 25 percent of most basic public airport costs, though some appurtenances are not covered by federal aid.

All three counties have faced similar decisions about airports, with different results. As usual, contextual differences make evaluation difficult, but comparison in broad terms will help illuminate county decision-making processes. For this purpose a brief history of airports in each county should serve, though more detailed case studies could have been written from the information at hand.

Only in Bucks did a county airport "get off the ground." There several small facilities existed, but only one (in lower Bucks) had a paved, all-weather runway. The pressure for county action came from a salesman and small manufacturer who, like many pilots, had learned flying in the war and bet on its postwar future. He bought sixty-seven acres near Quakertown in upper Bucks, declared fifty acres an airport, formed a local corporation in which he received stock for his land, deeded the acreage to the municipality, and leased it back. This arrangement was designed to provide municipal support, which, save for occasional rolling and mowing, was not forthcoming; the corporation was a steady loser and its founder sought county aid, i.e., county ownership and improvement (paving and purchase of navigation equipment) and a lease to a private operator. The corporation proposed to locate an industrial park on the remaining acreage. Its approaches were unavailing until the Welsh administration; then the planning commission was directed to study the proposition, and a consultant's study was ordered. These studies favored public airports in upper, middle, and lower Bucks, but the commissioners deferred action on the ground that public concern was not yet sufficient. During the Boyer administration the Quakertown approach was repeated and reinforced by a Doylestown operator in similar straits. Another consulting study resulted, this one from Louis R. Inwood Associates, who, probably more than most specialist consultants, were partial to public airports. Inwood himself had been head of Denver's municipal airport and later of Philadelphia's. As will appear, he did consulting studies for each of the three counties and for each recommended airport acquisition by county authority. This was his recommendation to Bucks. State and federal officials informally approved the sites. The authority was created, though without any definite instructions; it read the earlier reports, heard the proposals from Quakertown and Doylestown, applied for federal aid, and negotiated on price. The commissioners backed a $500,000 bond issue without referendum for acquisition and improvement of both facilities, and Bucks County moved into the air age.

Bucks' planning commission had early favored the airport idea as an aid to industrial development, especially in Upper Bucks. The Industrial Development Corporation was also favorably inclined, though it was less interested in Upper Bucks and did not press the issue. Commissioners Boyer and Bodley were both sympathetic to airport development, and both had allies on the authority; Boyer regularly favored county facilities, and Bodley had been counsel for the Doylestown airport in question. Yet the airport authority was given no public instructions, and when criticized in the press for favoring Upper Bucks, its chairman simply said that no one from Lower Bucks had yet made a proposal. The combination of official sensitivity to all prospects for development and specific entrepreneurial pressures evidently put the airports across; significantly, both sites were already on the Federal Aviation Agency's National Airport Plan and were not substantially opposed by local residents.[5]

The *Montgomery County* story is focused on one facility, Wings Field, which was established in 1930. Beginning in 1950 its management sought county aid (i.e., county ownership and a leaseback) for paving the main runway. Fred Peters considered the proposition, consulted the Manufacturers' Association, found no enthusiasm, and decided, he said, that he could make more friends paving roads with the money. Wings Field paved its own runway through loans from stockholders and flyers and the willingness of a nearby materials company to do the job cheaply on a demonstration basis. In 1957 the management went back to the county again. Their problem was that the field needed modern facilities and a longer runway; it was losing industrial traffic because it could not handle most twin-engine planes; nor could it afford the facilities or the land for expansion, which the county could condemn. The controlling owner was probably approaching financial distress: he could have sold out to developers for a profit, but, with the dedication of most airmen, he hoped to preserve the field.

The approach to the county was well organized. A businessmen's committee for a Montgomery County Airport was founded, which formally enlisted hundreds of businessmen (including most of the manufacturers), prepared a prospectus, and stimulated a letter campaign. The county commissioners purchased a feasibility study from Inwood Associates (suggested by the businessmen's committee), received a recommendation for county support that implicitly approved the Wings Field site, were urged by the State Aviation Agency to proceed, filed a preliminary application with the federal government for assistance, and nearly closed the deal. Why they finally did not is unclear: Commissioner Hammonds appeared to be interested, but managed to delay until the end of his term; his colleagues disliked the sites more as local opposition developed. When the Wetherill administration felt the same pressures it appointed a citizens' committee to reconsider the question, received a report similar to the previous one—based on it, indeed, but more specific —and then ignored it. By this time local residential opposition to expansion of the airport was serious, and the commissioners privately decided to shelve the project. This proved difficult for, when they ignored it, another letter campaign began and a new organization was formed called the Montgomery County Airport Association. This group picked up the citizens' committee's proposal for purchase of Wings Field by a county authority, which would hire an operator, and engaged a prominent financial consultant to refine it. They argued that the venture would be virtually self-sustaining and pressed the commissioners to a public hearing. The hearing revealed a highly organized local opposition based on the estates of several notables. The Pennsylvania Economy League then questioned the financial figures (as they had earlier, in 1959), counseling delay and further study. The county solicitor advised against the venture on the ground that surrounding zoning would be hard to change, and the condemnation costs for air space would be high under recent judicial decisions; he doubted the public purpose of an airport, since the beneficiaries were so few. The planning commission passed a resolution favoring a county airport in the future but not at present; a month later it resolved more explicitly that the county was then "adequately served" and that the subject be dropped for two years (i.e., until the next administration). The county commissioners then unanimously adopted this position, without providing for further study.

This brief synopsis of a restricted but bitter conflict necessarily ignores the more subtle maneuvering of the campaigners and commissioners—e.g., the early understanding that the first consultant's report would favor Wings Field or the commissioners' use of the planning commission in disposing of the issue. Wetherill early made clear to the planners that the project was not politically feasible, and the planners stated it as an issue of priorities in which other administration projects came first. Yet, if the project would really cost the county little or nothing, the priority question was academic (or at least political, not economic); this question was not squarely faced because the county never spent the funds for a serious professional study. The problem was that the airport sought to expand, not merely to remain, and that the area had developed residentially. Those who cared deeply about the project were the owners and pilots on one hand and the residents on the other. There were socially and politically prominent persons on both sides, but seemingly large numbers on the negative. Though the Manufacturers' Association, Chamber of Commerce, and industrial park owners formally endorsed the project, not all were solidly behind it, and for the Manufacturers it posed a conflict with traditions of private ownership and public parsimony. Politically, it appeared that the commissioners made the right decision, so far as numbers and intensity of preferences were concerned. Wetherill's decision was made while he was still a long shot for the gubernatorial nomination, and several local airport opponents were his social peers and political supporters. On the merits, there was insufficient information about costs and benefits to weigh in the commissioners' decision, but this insufficiency and the postponement to the next administration without providing for further study make the political factors appear paramount.

By 1957 there were no airports left in *Delaware County*, except that Philadelphia International Airport's runways extended into the county's southeast corner. Although this major facility was convenient to many county industries, it was extremely busy and the future of private aircraft there was in doubt; already there were lengthy take-off delays. Thus a campaign by local pilots began for an independent county site. In 1959 the Delaware County Aviation Association (not normally an active organization) sold the Chamber of Commerce and county commissioners on a study by Inwood Associates, which was formally requested by the commissioners and paid for by the two private groups. Inwood recommended a county authority and a specific site for an airport with a capital cost in excess of $600,000. The site was in the county's sparsely settled western end.

The Inwood recommendations were not submitted until after the election of new commissioners late in 1959. Then, at a meeting of the old and new commissioners, they were accepted, a resolution was adopted, and a federal application begun. The speed of these steps seems to confirm what one Republican commissioner has stated: that the project was approved by John McClure. Yet the county resolution met a vigorous reaction in the western townships; they had not been consulted, and they opposed the airport. The new chairman of the commissioners lived in one of these townships, and after a few local demonstrations, the commissioners reversed themselves, referring the project to the planning commission for study; Commissioner Watkins shrewdly emphasized the question of need, which would surely be hard to demonstrate. On the other side, the county's flying enthusiasts formed an Airpark Council to provide business backing for an airport with an industrial park attached, and the county Manufacturers' Association also appointed a committee to support the project.

Late in 1960 the planning commission reported: it favored an airport in principle and emphasized the need for preemptive speed in land acquisition, but it proposed no specific site and suggested a joint venture with neighboring Chester County. Its statement of need was extremely tentative. The commissioners accepted the report without releasing it and, characteristically, appointed a citizens' advisory committee whose membership included amateur pilots and industrialists; its minutes showed it to be a serious, hard-working committee. Its function, as defined by Commissioner Watkins, was to reconsider the question of need, to settle the issue of location and local acceptance, and to decide about financing. Within six months the committee had a draft report endorsing the need, suggesting several sites for an airport combined with recreational and industrial parks, and requesting federal aid for engineering and financial studies; federal aid was anticipated because the county was on the Federal Aviation Agency's National Plan. The commissioners accepted the proposal but failed to procure federal funds; they agreed to appropriate the money themselves after the 1961 election, but they never did. Commissioner Watkins thought better of it and Albert Swing, whose defection was then in its early stages, refused to break with him on the issue. The amount estimated for the study was $5,000.

The problem of local opposition was difficult in Delaware because a new facility, not merely an extension, was proposed, but it arose in a relatively unsettled section without many votes. If John McClure had already agreed to an airport (and not merely to a study) then the local political sensitivity of the organization would seem to have been extreme. Probably this episode does evince high sensitivity, but the county's usual conservatism and tax-consciousness seem to have favored it. The county lawyer who was attorney to McClure and counsel to the Manufacturers' Association strongly believed the project to be unwarranted and wasteful; he was originally appointed to the Citizens' Advisory Committee, but resigned immediately. Despite their early participation, neither the Manufacturers' Association nor the Chamber of Commerce strongly supported the airport once the commissioners began to retreat. The lawyer put his case to McClure, arguing that Commissioner Watkins was being placed in political jeopardy. Since McClure's views on the airport were not a matter of record, a retreat was feasible once it was clear that the county's pilots were the project's chief backers. (By count of the planning commission these numbered about 140 and nearly half of them were inactive.) The airport decision was rather like the creek-valley decision studied earlier in that the political leader was

ambiguously involved, the commissioners used a citizens' committee
for protection and gradually backed off despite the committee's advice,
and no one could say for certain where the decision, or nondecision,
was made.

The economic aspects of the airports were never clear. Except for
Bucks' consultant study of 1958 no one seriously examined the benefits
and costs in any form and most findings seem to have been prede-
termined. In each county the planners privately favored airports, but
not with high priority. It could be argued that this very uncertainty,
other things being equal, made airports a good test of the progressive-
ness or conservatism of the county governments. But other things were
not equal: Bucks' government and industry were especially air-minded
(perhaps because of their highway problems) and were farthest from
a major airport. In Delaware County, Philadelphia International was
close if not wholly convenient. Bucks began with existing facilities and
relatively spacious surroundings; in Delaware and (especially) Montgomery the local opposition was stronger. Conceivably factors like these
entirely account for the different policies, but, in view of the serious
official consideration given airport development in Montgomery and
Delaware, the histories suggest that county government is highly sensitive to sectional issues, since only a few hundred petitioners were involved in the opposition. This sectional sensitivity is the negative aspect
of the airport's public purpose, which is so hard to demonstrate affirmatively and of which tax-conscious interests in Delaware and Montgomery
were sceptical.

2. *Mass Transit.* Another problem in the spending of county funds for
sectional benefit was raised by the Southeastern Pennsylvania Transportation Compact (SEPACT). This was a stop-gap regional program
of county aid for rail commutation, based on the immediate availability
of federal funds. Two of the three counties participated; Delaware
County did not.

SEPACT's history is exceedingly complex and can only be sketched
here; detailed accounts exist elsewhere.[6] After Philadelphia's home-rule
charter was adopted in 1951 Lennox Moak, its leading draftsman and
head of the Pennsylvania Economy League, proposed that the next city
administration consider a comprehensive approach to its inherited traffic problems. Two years later Mayor Joseph Clark appointed the Urban
Traffic and Transportation Board to study these problems: its members
included railroad, petroleum, taxi, and automobile-club executives and
civic leaders; its mission was to save the center city from traffic con-
gestion and economic decay. In another two years UTTB's report was
ready. It proposed a regional approach to transportation, including a
regional transportation agency, and a balanced reliance on rails and
rubber in which highway tolls and mutual financial support were suggested to equalize advantages over the total system. The report was thus

a victory for the view that preservation of the central business district depended on regional control of transportation and restoration of rail transit to a prominent role. Two of Philadelphia's distinguishing characteristics were the inability of the eighteenth-century business district to accommodate automobiles, and the continued existence of a serviceable, radial rail and trolley system. Postwar highway development had brought the suburban railroad lines to financial distress, and they were threatening to cease commuter service. Thus the most direct beneficiaries of the plan would have been the railroads and commuters, but investors in the center city had high stakes in it ultimately.

When UTTB's proposals were submitted in 1956 Richardson Dilworth had become mayor of Philadelphia. The city's early phase of governmental reform was over and wholesale urban redevelopment was beginning. Salvation and enhancement of the center city became Dilworth's ruling purpose, and transportation—especially mass transportation—his regnant interest. Thus Dilworth enthusiastically accepted UTTB's premises, but its methods were for the time being undermined by stubborn suburban and city-council opposition, and by passage of the federal highway act of 1956 with its 9:1 matching formula and prohibition of tolls. Dilworth followed one recommendation in appointing a second UTTB, composed of both city officials and business leaders, to supervise transportation policy—an outgrowth of Moak's original proposal. This body sought to allay suburban concern by proposing a state-financed regional transportation study. Late in 1958 the Penn-Jersey Transportation Study was created to produce in three years a regional transportation plan that, as this is written, remains incomplete. Concurrently, PENJERDEL came into being with Ford Foundation money and moral support in the universities and civic agencies. Soon Penn-Jersey and PENJERDEL had engendered a Regional Council of Elected Officials (RCEO), a forum of local and county officers for discussion and study of intergovernmental problems.

Within the city the administration began the mass transit improvements recommended by the first UTTB and opened negotiations with the railroads for subsidized improvement of intracity commutation through a nonprofit corporation. These negotiations were complicated by the railways' attempts to reduce interstate passenger trains through Philadelphia and by the city's legal endeavors to enjoin the abandonments; when, in 1958, the State Supreme Court upheld the city, its solicitor was able to bargain from greater strength on local transit, which the railways also wished to reduce and subject to higher charges. The sticky issue of costs allocable to the commuter lines was resolved by resort to mutually acceptable accountants. Later that year Operation Northwest was launched to test the effects of improved commuter transportation at subsidized rates. The city paid for heavier service at reduced fares and established cut-rate transfers to feeder bus lines. By 1960 the railways were convinced, and the Passenger Service Improvement Corporation (PSIC) replaced UTTB as a nonprofit corporation subsidizing six commuter lines within the city. At the end of 1961 passenger traffic on subsidized lines was up 43 percent over 1958. By then direct subsidies ran $1⁹⁄₁₀ million annually and the city had committed $14 million to long-run capital improvements, but, in the city's view, it was justifiably underwriting the central business district, not the railways or commuters. Meantime the Pennsylvania Economy League concluded a major study of regional transportation by recommending a regional agency to extend the work of PSIC.[7]

The logical next step was to bring in the suburbs. Negotiations began late in 1959 between the city solicitor and the suburban county solicitors (instead of elected officials). Elkins Wetherill of Montgomery was also approached, which was natural because of his Philadelphia social connections. Wetherill found his own county planners sympathetic to the idea and interested in a specific operation; the problem was to participate on the county's own terms and avoid the stigma of being taken in by the city. This was a difficult political problem: enlightened regionalism could be a good horse for a gubernatorial aspirant to ride, but city-suburban party divisions and Montgomery's traditional localism were difficult hurdles. The county planners arranged a consulting study, while Wetherill assumed formal leadership of the newly founded RCEO. Publicly, Mayor Dilworth pressed for action, concentrating on Montgomery (the most logical extension of the city's own operation), but Wetherill refused to buy a "pig in a poke" until the county's own transportation study was completed and the county's own interests clarified.

Montgomery's consultant study was published in March 1961 and provided a basic planning justification for county action.[8] Its central argument was that rising densities along the old commuter lines raised local problems akin to Philadelphia's of declining property values and increasing need for remedial public services. Because highways require low densities for efficiency, continued reliance on highways would spread uneconomic low densities and erode values in older areas. The county, therefore, needed an overall transportation policy geared to its own interest and to that of its localities, and an important aspect of the policy would be to save the existing railway net and emphasize supplementary rather than competitive relations with other transportation methods. The argument that rails had suffered through public subsidy of other methods was fully accepted, and public subsidy of all public transit—railways, trolleys, and buses—was recommended. Philadelphia's method of direct payments to railways was rejected as not providing incentives for efficient operation, and the alternative proposed was supporting the purchase and maintenance of equipment, thus encouraging improvement and placing railways on a subsidy basis similar to competing forms of transportation. It was urged that the railways' suburban commuter operations ultimately be placed under separate management and accounting, and county action was suggested:

These problems have reached their present severity because of the way they spread across political boundaries. They are now too big for exclusively local and municipal action—even for a city the size of Philadelphia. At the same time they are both too small and too local for effective state action. Although the problems are bigger than a single county, the county remains the only existing locally based unit of government of adequate size to handle the matter. Effective action will require cooperative and joint county efforts on behalf of the region as a whole. This presents admitted political difficulties, but it is considered superior to the only two alternatives: allowing it to be handled by the state, or creating a new regional layer of government.

It is recommended that Montgomery County take the initiative and leadership in developing and building a practical, effective means for instituting and sustaining joint county efforts and action.[9]

With their report in hand the county planners were eager to proceed. During the summer of 1961 Elkins Wetherill, in a television debate about mass transit with Philadelphia's city solicitor, stated that he favored public action in principle and expected to act in the future, but that he would not be taken in by the city. The city solicitor proposed a regional agency as an alternative and pressed Wetherill to verbal agreement to initiate it soon. The agreement was confirmed in press releases after the program, and informally Wetherill also agreed to begin an operation on the Reading Railway's North Penn line to Lansdale—an extension of the scheme already favored by county planners. The long negotiations culminated in Norristown in September when Philadelphia and Bucks, Chester, and Montgomery Counties formed the Southeastern Pennsylvania Transportation Compact. SEPACT was a vehicle for intercounty action, though it committed no county to action; it made clear that individual counties could run operations on their own and that no county would be involved in any operation without its consent. Although Philadelphia's solicitor argued that counties had the power to act alone or in concert it was decided to seek enabling legislation, and the city's large delegation was pledged to a bill introduced by Montgomery's state senator; within weeks it was law. Within the next year two operations were begun: North Penn in Montgomery and Levittown in Bucks. Neither of these served more than one suburban county, but three- and four-county operations were projected.

Five aspects of SEPACT were especially important. One was that initiative for regional organization came from the city. The counties had cause for action, but the institutional and operational beginnings were all inspired in Philadelphia, whose solicitor pursued the negotiations for two years, though the formalities were carefully arranged in the counties. Second, SEPACT stemmed from the advent of federal aid: two-thirds of the operation and planning costs were met from demonstration grants available under the Housing Act of 1961. Third, the demonstrations achieved provisional success: despite a debilitating transit strike in Philadelphia there were estimated passenger increases of 20 percent and 50 percent in Montgomery and Bucks respectively in the first six months; new rolling stock, station and parking facilities were provided, though the railroads still ran in the red.* Fourth, SEPACT's regional framework was a necessary condition for access to federal grants. Finally, however, SEPACT was conceived by all concerned as a temporary arrangement: in Montgomery especially the burden on the county's operating budget was unwelcome, and the federal demonstration grant was terminal. Though further operations were planned, a permanent program with state or federal aid was hoped for from pending legislation in Congress and perhaps the Penn-Jersey plan.

There was a political basis for Montgomery's suburban leadership in SEPACT: it brought Elkins Wetherill publicity—especially in the metropolitan press—as a regional statesman, it appealed to the cosmopolitan attitudes and commuting interests of his most logical constituency, and it potentially served the county's most populous sections. There was criticism from outlying areas and a few manufacturers and merchants about sectionally oriented expenditures and unwarranted subsidies, but this was not serious. As to the economic warrant for subsidies, the planning commission had done its homework. Like Philadelphia's administration, they saw the project as supporting proper land uses rather than as subsidizing individuals or businesses, they noted that eastern and central Montgomery could not expect rapid access to the center city by expressway, and they pointed to the prospects of reverse commutation for industrial development; in fact, Fort Washington Industrial Park had a distinct interest in SEPACT because many of its workers still traveled from Philadelphia to their new plants.

Bucks County simply joined, with virtually no study or discussion. Most county interests were sensitive to the transportation issue (cf. the airports), and two commissioners represented lower Bucks, site of the Levittown operation. (One distinct possibility, which cannot be documented, is that the residence in Doylestown of the president of one of Philadelphia's major banks who was also a board member of PSIC helped motivate acceptance of SEPACT by Bucks' other county commissioner.) There the project received strong newspaper endorsement, and the operation produced notable passenger increases. Montgomery's "Operation North Penn" was also used by neighboring Bucks Countians, and the Reading Railway lines to Newtown, Doylestown, and Quakertown, where many trains had been discontinued, were expected to become operations soon.

In SEPACT's brief history each major railway had one operation. The

---

* This is only a partial measure of success. It does not include effects on the Philadelphia central business district, which are not recorded, nor on the railroad's finances: the railroads claimed still to be below the break-even point on the specific lines involved.

Pennsylvania Railway, however, badly wanted to add the Main Line—
its largest suburban carrier by far, with the best chance to break even
at higher volume. The Main Line, however, passed through Delaware
County and even served Delaware commuters over much of its Montgomery run. Montgomery would not agree to an operation that stopped
short of Delaware because, it said, this would still subsidize Delaware
commuters. And Delaware would not join SEPACT.

Early in 1960 a Philadelphia *Bulletin* reporter asked three county
commissioners whether their counties would join with Philadelphia in
PSIC. Bodley of Bucks said he had no information on which to comment;
Wetherill said he would be glad to explore it but didn't yet have the
facts; Watkins of Delaware said, "No," categorically—the county could
handle its own problems.[10] Nevertheless, Delaware was in on the negotiations and, at Montgomery's conference in July 1961, was close to
participation, but it refused to sign in September. By then the War
Board was said to have turned down the plan, and municipalities began
to adopt inspired resolutions of opposition.

Several factors evidently helped keep Delaware County out. One was
political; the organization's riposte to John F. Kennedy's electoral gains
was aimed at the city and all its works; SEPACT's signing and the War
Board decision came at the start of the 1961 county and local election
campaigns. Another factor was Delaware's pattern of economic interests: the Pews' petroleum industry and commissioner Watkins' trucking
business *may* have been predisposing factors against the railways, but
most important was the role of the Red Arrow Bus and Trolley lines
in the county's transportation system. Delaware County was historically
more dependent on trolleys and buses than were the other counties,
and Red Arrow was based in Upper Darby.* Aid to railways also threatened Red Arrow, which was a profitable system. These two elements
were combined in a sectional factor: workers in the southern part of
the county were more dependent on the Red Arrow system than on the
railways, while north of Baltimore Pike the position was reversed; the
Pennsy's priorities for SEPACT operations began with the Main Line
and declined from north to south. Merchants in Chester and Upper
Darby resisted subsidies for central-city commutation; the county
Chamber of Commerce opposed it, as did Chester's daily paper. Finally,
there was the tax-consciousness of some county leaders and their fear
of pressure toward reassessment.

These factors were well represented in the county's political structure
despite the then division between the Republican commissioners. The
sectional balance of the organization has been described, as has commissioner Watkins' remote, noncommuting constituency. Red Arrow's
legal counsel also served John McClure and the Manufacturers' Asso-

---

* "Red Arrow" was originally one of several traction systems which became divisions of the Philadelphia Suburban Transit Corporation, but the name was usually
applied to most of PSTC's lines.

ciation; he intervened with McClure (arguing that SEPACT was uncon-
stitutional) and threatened a taxpayer's suit if the county adopted the
plan. The chairman of the county planning commission was a Red
Arrow vice-president. The planning commission staff came to oppose
not only the Main Line operation but SEPACT as a framework, ques-
tioning its limitation to railways and the equity of the proposed county
operations. It argued that railway lines in lower Delaware County should
have higher priority, and that municipal tax contributions should be
levied in proportion to the commuter service received. It suggested that
because most commuters rode in automobiles the plan was unlikely
to succeed. Actually, Delaware County led the other counties in proportion of railway commutation, but the land use and transportation
considerations of the other counties were perhaps not quite so cogently
for mass transit in Delaware. Moreover, nothing in the SEPACT agreement itself was specifically limited to railways, and each county was
entirely free to devise its own financing, but for political and strategic
reasons it was probably best to resist the proposal *in limine*.

TABLE 18:1

Employment and Transportation by County

	Bucks	Mont-gomery	Delaware
Percent employed outside county	43.4	35.5	45.0
Percent employed in Philadelphia	19.3	26.5	34.3
Percent of total using railways	3.5	8.1	11.4
Percent of total using railways, buses, or streetcars	5.5	12.3	19.2
Percent employed outside using railways	8.2	22.9	25.5
Percent employed outside using railways, buses, or streetcars	12.7	34.7	42.7

Source: 1960 U.S. Census.

Most of the opposing arguments were developed gradually after Red
Arrow's attorney and the War Board had taken their early positions.
Commissioner Watkins criticized SEPACT, Welsh (Democrat) favored
it (if Red Arrow were included), Swing sat on the fence. The Pennsy
continued to press for action, while the political organization continued
to stir up opposition. In Philadelphia, the railroad and the city solicitor
reasoned that if a truncated Main Line operation could be started the
county would be forced into SEPACT by commuter pressure, though
they agreed that Red Arrow should be taken care of too. In Delaware
a partial Main Line operation was considered infeasible.

This impasse and SEPACT were jarred by events late in 1962. Philadelphia's bus and subway system suffered a strike that severely damaged
the central-city Christmas trade and disrupted SEPACT's commuting
traffic. After settlement of the strike the transit system was granted a
fare increase by the state Public Utilities Commission.

Meantime, Red Arrow was seeking a fare increase, opposed by the Delaware County commissioners. Early in 1963 its labor contract expired and a thirty-four-day walkout ensued. Business in Upper Darby and Chester was crippled and traffic on the Pennsylvania Railroad rose precipitously; state mediators and the county commissioners labored to settle the strike. Ultimately the majority commissioners withdrew their opposition to a fare increase, which was granted. The union reduced its demand, and the strike was terminated. But Red Arrow reported heavy losses for the first quarter and management viewed the future pessimistically. During the strike the line's president said that he was ready to sell the system to a regional transit authority, the governor endorsed public ownership of mass transit, and the city started work on a proposal. Elkins Wetherill once again hosted county officials at a series of conferences; the city solicitor and Lennox Moak guided the drafting. Legislation was introduced in the spring and passed in the fall, with Delaware County's participation. The Southeastern Pennsylvania Transportation Authority (SEPTA) was created, without taxing power, in which each county had two votes and three votes sufficed to veto; SEPTA would sell revenue bonds and hope for federal aid; it was to lease the railways' commuter lines and purchase the region's main transit systems to provide an integrated network. The city and counties appropriated operating funds to get it going, but the future would depend on federal legislation and the reception of its debentures.

The nature of SEPTA and the basis for Delaware County's acceptance of it remained conditional for some time. One of Delaware's principal objections was met when Red Arrow and intracounty commutation were covered; legal and sectional doubts about subsidy were removed, at least temporarily, by the authority device. Moreover, the Pennsy was seriously planning Main Line and Media operations at least to the city line, which might have embarrassed the county. The political climate had also changed in two years: neither the city nor the Democrats appeared as immediately threatening as they had, and survey data for the present study showed widespread if latent acceptance of tax-supported regional transit.

Delaware's representatives to SEPTA were vigilant and resistant to central-city interests: they initially vetoed appointment of PSIC's executive to a similar position on SEPTA, and the county refused to appropriate its pro-rata share of SEPTA's budget. For a time it considered the purchase and operation of Red Arrow by Delaware County alone—to drive the system's price up, some critics said, or to provide more political jobs, others said. Although nothing came of this uncharacteristic proposal for public action, Delaware's commitment to SEPTA remained the most conditional of any of the counties'.

SEPTA was the result of steady pressure, patient negotiation, waiting, and exploitation of opportunity by a few individuals primarily identified with Philadelphia; it was not planned, and it emerged (in Pennsylvania alone) before the Penn-Jersey Transportation Plan. It would have to grow piecemeal by hard bargaining, just as it originated. Its staffing and financing began in this fashion. But it could become the nucleus of a regional transportation agency, just as the Penn-Jersey later became a regional planning agency.

19

Power, Politics, and Policy

The time has come to try to connect the foregoing descriptions of political structure and governmental action, and to test some explanations of intercounty differences. The situation is complex: there are the county policies and estimates of performance, varying in priorities, responsiveness, and competence; the suggested explanations by way of organized private interests and influence, electoral competition and organization, and implicit response to public attitudes and demands; and the several environmental elements that condition policy and tend to invalidate single-factor comparisons.

The central problem is to explain innovations, that is, the adoption or rejection of new programs. These are usually the clearest instances of change, the most explicit decisions, and involve the most evident pressures pro and con. By broadening the scope or role of government, innovations often alter the distribution of influence even as they reflect it. But innovations occur in the context of existing policy, and so intercounty differences in priorities or emphases should also be explained, if possible. The evidence bearing on each of the suggested explanations— private power structures, electoral competition, and immediate response to various publics—may now be reviewed. Later in this chapter the possibility is also considered that prevailing ideologies or rates of growth alone afford still more basic explanations of policy.

1. *Private interests and influence.* The polar alternatives may be stated as pluralism versus a restricted power structure.[1] Distributions of influence may be studied in many dimensions: the reputation for power of certain individuals or interests, the formal organization or

informal cohesion of such interests, the resources they appear to command and employ, their actual participation in decisions, and their profit from the outcome of decisions or nondecisions. It appeared in Chapter 5 that, if there *is* a restricted, private power structure in any of the counties, its most likely locus is business and, especially, heavy industry. The foregoing dimensions of influence are, therefore, reviewed below with special reference to local industry.

As to reputation, interviewing in the counties reveals thoroughgoing agreement on the fragmentation of private power in Bucks; a tendency to credit Montgomery's small circle of wealthy, established manufacturers with high (negative) influence over county policy; and the view that Delaware's large industrialists wield influence through the political organization—though perceptions of relative private and political power there are most conflicting and ambiguous. In Bucks, respondents generally agree that the county commissioners make policy and that direct private influence stems from several groups of individuals involved in discrete fields of policy, an interpretation that is supported by the case histories. In Montgomery and, especially, Delaware private influence is said to operate through the dominant party organizations and to rest on financial contributions (discussed below).

The unity and specificity of business interests were described in Chapters 4 and 5. The counties differ strikingly: Bucks' business community shows no systematic resistance to county innovation; it is organized to promote industrial development and supporting functions. Montgomery's manufacturers have not favored innovation and acknowledge their lack of interest in industrial development, but, as development has nonetheless occurred and failure has overtaken a few old firms, a latent conflict of interests has grown between developers' commercial and distribution interests versus long established industries. In Delaware, which lacks development, the potential unity of industrial interests is greatest; it consists in limited concern about the cost and scope of government, together with indifference, rather than active resistance, to economic growth.

The formal organization of business has been described. The Manufacturers' Associations in Montgomery and Delaware are characterized by protectiveness, tax-consciousness, and limited political participation, all of which amount to an ideology. In McClure's Delaware the PMA's liaison with county government was largely maintained by its attorney, who evidently served his own legal and political interests at least as much as industry's. In Montgomery the manufacturers' relations with politicians are more commonly direct and financial. Commerce and industry are not well coordinated in Montgomery; they are closer in Delaware through a common center (shared with the political organization) in Chester. Bucks' leading business organization, the Industrial Development Corporation, was formed by the county government: its outlook differs radically from that of the PMA, but most of the steadiest members have been local merchants and developers, who have more to gain from development than manufacturers have.

The chief political resources of industry would appear to be wealth (for contributions), and control of the jobs and profits of others. Today, political contributions from industrialists are largest and most highly leveraged in Montgomery, where the county organization— indeed, the state Republican Party—has long leaned heavily on a few extremely wealthy men.[2] In Bucks, party finance is broadly based today; a few individuals and small enterprises are said to contribute generously (some to both parties), but they are neither an organization nor a group. Delaware's organization welcomes business and industrial contributions, but it is not highly reliant on them.

With the decline of direct job control, industry's other potential resource is the threat of removal or slowdown. This threat, however, would appear to be most effective in the most pluralistic, competitive, developing environments. Significantly, in Delaware and Montgomery Counties the least mobile and most local industries are, with some exceptions, the most active politically. In Bucks, other kinds of resources, such as newspapers and communications, are especially important because of electoral competition and a stronger sense of county identification, at least among elites.

Business participation in specific county decisions has been most overt in Bucks, where IDC and the Lower Bucks County Chamber of Commerce have behaved as pressure groups in several projects: port development, urban redevelopment, and continued county appropriations for industrial promotion, but the chief participants have been individual beneficiaries. Representatives of business and industry commonly serve on committees and advisory boards in Delaware and Montgomery—e.g., Delaware's citizens' advisory committees on creek-valley acquisition and airport development; Montgomery's park board and Industrial Development Committee—but the case histories of both reveal that they clearly failed to establish county policy. Both county Manufacturers' Associations endorsed airport development, but in each case the endorsements were merely formal. In both counties leading industrialists frequently confer with the political leadership, but (with the exception of the Pew family in both Montgomery and Delaware) they have rarely participated in local slate-making or primary elections. The politically active industrialists in these counties are chiefly interested in state affairs. In Bucks' recent, bitter Republican primaries those businessmen most closely concerned with county projects remained on the sidelines, at least publicly.

Finally, in specific policy outcomes there is little evidence of business or industrial success achieved behind the scenes. The record of political sponsorship of policy in Bucks County is reasonably clear. In the one-party counties, test cases—confrontations of narrow power structures with public opposition on specific issues—were rare. Most victories were nondecisions, not vetoes, and when issues were explicit local industry was often divided. In Montgomery, modest political competition and professional initiative brought about programs in water resources, open space, and mass transit that were not favored by the manufacturers. In Delaware there were no confrontations until after McClure's death. It is in these two counties that the case for a negative mobilization of bias is most plausible on the ground that both industrialists and politicians favor a low-tax policy and a low-pressure politics. Still, Montgomery's Wetherill administration outflanked this interest, and in Delaware the absence of explicit political competition plus heavy fiscal pressure on the county may equally account for lack of innovation.

Initiatives for innovation have normally come from private interest groups and the professionals of county government, which is hardly surprising. These have been most effective in Bucks County (except, perhaps, in public welfare); there, interest groups for land and water conservation and industrial development have been financially supported—indeed, created—by county government. Professionals in planning, recreation, conservation, and industrial development have worked closely with constituencies and elected officials. These statements hold true relative to the other counties, though it must be recognized that organizational participation is narrow and that identifiable individuals or enterprises are the initial, direct beneficiaries of some initiatives in county projects. During two innovative administrations most initiatives met with quick responses from the commissioners. Moreover, several initiatives were those of politicians—most notably the industrial-development, open-space, and health proposals in the 1955 Democratic platform. In the period of expansion after 1956 a plurality of interests rapidly developed; later as fiscal pressure increased priorities became important, and it looked as if Bucks had arrived at a pluralism of specific and sectional interests, mass communications, tax-consciousness, governmental professionals, and electoral competition.

In Montgomery the governmental response to private initiatives (water resources, public welfare) was slower and more reluctant than in Bucks and change occurred partly from physical and legal necessity. The Wetherill administration's main innovations—SEPACT and open space—were urged by the professional planners in county government. They found their principal support in the Citizens' Council of Montgomery County, which was, however, at least as much regenerated and supported by these issues as it was a generating and supporting force. The same interests in innovations exist in Montgomery as in Bucks, but they have been less successful. One reason would seem to be the more heavily vested interests in localism, fiscal conservatism, and political careerism.

The same observations apply to Delaware in greater degree, with the reservation that fiscal limits and pressure on assessment are more apparent there than in Montgomery. The initiatives of the county planners and civic action groups were least effective in Delaware, but refuse disposal and child welfare were important advances. In summary, there is clearly most and closest interaction among commissioners, professionals, and a plurality of interest groups in Bucks, and probably least in Delaware. Conversely, the reference of policy questions to the party organization for decision was most pronounced in Delaware and least in Bucks.

The strongest case for the influence of a cohesive private elite would be that equivalent constituencies for most programs exist in all three counties, except that the interests and positions of organized business differ among them. In this view, policy variations among the counties would depend primarily on alignments of social and economic interests, not on electoral organization. The principal intercounty differences could then be said to take two forms: (1) the relative agreement among Bucks' elites on county action in principle (though not in detail) and the disagreement between business and civic interests (or even within business interests) in the other counties, and (2) the greater vitality and diversity of civic interests in Bucks as compared with Montgomery and Delaware. In the latter counties restrictive business interests could, therefore, more easily veto innovations and discourage public expenditures.

There are difficulties in this theory, however. One is the lack of evidence for elite interest, activity, or influence in some decisions. Another is the likelihood that, at least in certain circumstances, the relative absence of organized pluralism benefits politicians more than private elites. More fundamentally, in referring policy differences directly to variations in the same social base, no matter how situations vary, the theory is proof against disproof by the comparative method, though case histories suggest that it is inadequate. It also presents a paradox in combining organized pluralism with agreement on policy, and a well-defined elite with division among interests. There are two points in this paradox: that some measure of agreement is necessary for positive action, and that in conditions of disagreement a mere veto can sometimes preserve a negative policy. But the less innovative counties also display less organized pluralism and electoral competition—i.e., less overt disagreement, less explicit issues—and the mobilization-of-bias conception, which takes in a wider range of variables, therefore seems preferable to the power structure theory. The variables that seem most relevant to government are reviewed in the remainder of this chapter.

2. *Electoral organization.* Evidence for the generative role of electoral competition in Bucks includes the Welsh initiatives based on his campaign platform of 1955, though it is qualified by changes already begun under the old regime. The response of Boyer and other lower Bucks Republicans to competition in their area by endorsement of existing county programs and adoption of still more is further evidence.

Their emphasis on employment and welfare rather than planning and amenities seems—besides serving their own interests in jobs and contracts—to have reflected public preferences, according to survey data. State legislators from both parties in lower Bucks were liberals. Bucks' commissioners always acted on proposals directly, though in several cases they had the option of a referendum.

In Montgomery, there was more resistance to group importunities for innovation, and more sensitivity to opposition, which was also more evident. In that county, electoral competition was intraparty only, which was less effective than party competition because a smaller electorate was involved in it. Primary elections in Pennsylvania are in no sense open, and organization resources and loyalties had to be carefully balanced against civic and presumptively public interests. Most initiatives in Montgomery were as much governmental as they were reactions to pressures or expressed public demands, and it seems reasonable to attribute them in some degree to Elkins Wetherill's political aspirations.

Delaware displayed the least political initiative. Decisions were highly centralized there. On two occasions—the incinerators and child-care service—the political leader quickly opted for action, but his characteristic pattern was to explore proposals and then back off from them as the balance of interests became clear. Lacking electoral competition or much public communication, the overt interests reflected in decisions were apt to be narrow or sectional, and the covert counsel of individuals (such as McClure's attorney) seems to have influenced several decisions heavily. The political system was one of high sensitivity but also of high selectivity.

One can argue that a strong, substantially unchallenged political organization could most freely take initiatives in county policy, as did occasionally happen in Delaware when the balance of interests and apathy was plain. Such an argument, however, tends to ignore the competition for power implicit in a polity, much as one might tend to take for granted the scarcity of resources intrinsic to an economy. The normal resistance to innovation and programmed expenditures of the old organizations seems logical, a priori: it lessened attention to county policy and thus damped controversy and electoral competition; it minimized the risks of adverse public reaction and the prospects of interest group organizations that might back opponents; it avoided competing, programmatic demands on the loyalty of courthouse personnel and the threat to patronage of professionalism and state-imposed standards; it preserved the decentralization of issues to municipalities (and, where possible, to the precincts) that the organization encouraged, leaving the organization alone in control of county political perquisites. Programs, controversy, professional loyalties, electoral competition are all threats to the organizational economy because they tend to bring new values and new players into the game. Decentralization, within the existing division of governmental powers, would seem to be especially effective in preventing controversies from cumulating, separating policy issues from county political organization, and keeping politics on a stable, face-to-face basis in which personal relations, loyalties, and sanctions are emphasized. In such a system political leadership was more likely to respond to what Robert Dahl calls the direct influence of people in the organization who could deliver loyalty and precincts or of others who offered specific contributions for specific inducements, rather than to indirect influence from an electorate that was rarely concerned with policy and whose threat of action was remote.[3]

One possible effect of electoral competition, then, would be to reduce corruption, or excessive response to direct influence, but there is no persuasive evidence that it has. In the old organizations the extent of corruption probably depended on the leader's character and the social foundations of his party. Recently, good government, at least in the limited sense of honesty, has been considered good politics, and there have not been observable differences among the counties in this respect. Ironically, in Bucks the two commissioners most responsible for prog- ress stood trial for their political (not governmental) methods, but juries found neither indictment legally sufficient. It is possible that political competition (both within and between parties) spurred illicit financial methods, and also that competition helped uncover them. The systematic assessment of employees in the better organized counties is no more lawful, however, than the fund-raising methods of Boyer and Welsh. As to governmental methods, Bucks' recent innovations amply demonstrated the opportunities for personal gain in capital planning and spending, but intraparty competition did offer a corrective, which, on the theory of electoral competition, was likely though surely not inevitable.[4]

Perhaps more significant is the apparent fact that degrees of profes- sionalism and of legal and administrative standards vary among the counties consistently with extent of electoral competition. The less competitive the county, the more ambiguous and informal are policy and administration; though the differences between Montgomery and Delaware would seem to be minimal. Bucks' court has been less one- sided in political cases than have the other county courts; tax assessing and planning in Delaware and Montgomery are less professionalized and comprehensive than in Bucks; intercounty differences in welfare administration are diminishing. In each case there are extenuating cir- cumstances and satisfactory, nonelectoral explanations—but each func- tion *could* be reformed in the less competitive counties. Party competi- tion began in Bucks with the election of a (temporarily) Democratic judge, after which another Democrat was appointed to the bench by a Democratic governor, and professional planning and property assess- ment were backed by factions in both parties. Organized pressure groups asked for professionalism and programmatic standards. In elections, politicians could take credit (and did) for professionalization or standardization of the most general and pervasive services, and there is testimony that some of them sought to avoid blame for favoritism.

The discussion thus far indicates that electoral competition affects governmental policy primarily by altering political organization; outright electoral competition *is* a change in organization. In view of the governmental resources available to county politicians it appears that strong organizations are well advantaged versus private elites and may themselves (especially in Delaware) be the principal power structure. Such political resources as regulation, taxation, procurement, and intervention in state action are enhanced by ambiguity in the absence of publicity and of some insistence on standards. Perhaps more important, resources on the political side are both enlarged and better employed by centralized leadership, as in Delaware (cf. that organization's reliance on private financial contributions with that of the Montgomery Republican Party). Primary competition undermined organization in Montgomery enough to give more initiative in policy to other interests, though the organization was already in decline. In Bucks a concern for broader publics in elections was most evident and least at odds with organization concerns; private interests seemed to be most leveraged, but more evenly so than in the other counties.

Perhaps the most important effect of electoral competition is this evening of group advantage, rather than an equalizing of distributions among all individuals. Competition diminishes the potential organization sanctions that can inhibit group formation or participation. This may help to explain the lack of industrial action on some policies in Delaware, or the expedition of public action in Bucks and the tendency to delay or to rely on referenda in the other counties, where group pressures for action were weaker and public tax-consciousness was probably stronger. Presumably, competition's effects depend, *inter alia*, on electoral organization, on extent of public interest and participation, and on what a mobilized group can contribute to a politician's election either directly by influencing votes or indirectly through other resources. In the suburbs, public interest and cleavages are weak respecting county government, so that organized interests are advantaged. Neither party loyalties nor county government itself are widely regarded as relevant to local policy or the good life. But, at the least, electoral competition seems to make politicians more public-relations conscious; and turnout in county elections is consistent with the degree of *party* competition: it is largest in Bucks, intermediate in Delaware, and least in Montgomery.*

* In 1959, turnout in the county-commissioner elections, as a percentage of 1960 presidential election turnout, was 67 percent in Bucks, 62 percent in Delaware, and 55 percent in Montgomery, and similar relations held between the 1963 and 1964 elections.

There is thus a plausible, a priori case for the role of electoral competition in redistributing political resources, altering the mobilization of bias, and influencing governmental policy and performance, and there is some empirical evidence for this. But the case is qualified by comparative and conceptual issues. For one, Bucks, with its explicit party competition and sharp primary-election rivalry, is easily the most competitive county, but *implicit* general election competition in Delaware— the threat of sociologically potential Democratic voters—may have been as effective in public policy as was primary election competition in Montgomery. In these terms, Delaware may even be the more competitive county, for in either county primary-election turnout has not recently exceeded 25 percent of registration. There is testimony to awareness of this factor in Delaware's political leadership and circumstantial evidence of its selective, anticipatory reactions. The meaning of electoral competition is both a *ceteris paribus* and a conceptual problem. The possible effects of implicit competition, in this sense, are further discussed in the following section.

Secondly, there are other *ceteris paribus* factors, some of which may be reciprocally related to electoral competition. These include different fiscal pressures, state-county-local relations, and the superior media of public communication in Bucks County.

Third, indices or outcomes of competition in governmental policy and performance are arbitrary, and here the principal test may be biased. The competition hypothesis has been made to work by distinguishing between innovations and priorities; but the usual case for competition has rested on its distributive or inclusive tendencies in policy, which are less demonstrable here. It does appear from Montgomery's parsimony that it is the least egalitarian of the counties (failing to redress municipal disparities, perhaps because of the balance of local political leverage), that Delaware's cast of county policy has favored the old, low-income areas, and that Bucks' priorities are probably the most inclusive at the county level, but the evidence for this is impressionistic, and socioeconomic differences among the counties and their municipalities are important, uncontrolled variables. Delaware's cast of policy has itself combined with fiscal limitations to discourage innovations favored in other counties. Thus innovation is not strictly separable from distribution: Delaware's innovations (child welfare, refuse disposal, a pass at recreation) have favored its blue-collar constituency; Montgomery's (SEPACT, open space) probably hold more appeal for white-collar commuters. Extent of innovation has been consistent with degrees of explicit electoral competition in the counties, and case histories help document the role of competition in policy and performance, though they do not prove it.

Finally, allied to these problems is the possibility that all three counties have been equally responsive but that the interests of residents or constituencies have differed from one county to another. Some of these alternative explanations of policy in terms of both situational pressures and direct response are considered in the following sections.

3. *Response and constraint.* Among the other factors are Bucks' more rapid growth on a smaller base, its relative lack of entrenched local interests averse to county services or consolidation, the greater prominence of county newspapers favoring county action, and the lesser influence of Philadelphia connections on potential county elites. State aid was a little easier to come by in Bucks when both it and the state were Democratically controlled. Overall, fiscal pressures were heavier in Montgomery and Delaware through the last decade. Sectional differences were relevant: Bucks' political competition was centered in the county's newly preponderant region, where a young population may have favored public services; Montgomery's dominant municipalities were well-to-do and self-sufficient. In Delaware's implicit social-cum-sectional distinctions the older, southern region was probably leveraged in county policy by electoral sanctions as well as through representation in the political party structure.

In looking at specific initiatives and innovations, the case for political competition as cause (i.e., as the principal facilitating factor) seems strong, viewed in the light of overall county priorities, it needs qualification. These priorities were reviewed in Chapter 14, and they seem thoroughly consistent with the later case histories. They are consistent, too, with the stage of development and socioeconomic makeup of each county. *Ex post*, Bucks' emphasis on physical development, Delaware's contrasting stress on social programs and utilities in other areas, and Montgomery's minor supplements to local and private self-sufficiency seem logical, though not ineluctable.

State law entails on the counties a modicum of response to social needs, but it does not mandate a certain level of service. County welfare and correctional expenditures are forced in some degree, but administrative alternatives with different fiscal implications are available in each, so there is scope for political decision.* The difference between Delaware and Montgomery Counties' per capita public welfare expenditures is probably no more than a partial function of socioeconomic differences. Delaware's expenditure levels in welfare and corrections satisfy political logic but have not been strictly forced by socioeconomic circumstances. Once undertaken, they imposed fiscal pressures against other innovations—yet the incinerator program (as expensive as any other county physical program considered here) was accepted at a time

---

* For instance, counties may economize on correctional facilities by sending long-term (greater than one year) prisoners to state prisons, they may contract with private agencies for welfare services, and they need not (historically) maintain qualified juvenile-court probation services. With minimum county administration and niggardliness in appropriations to private agencies, welfare expenditures can be controlled— cf. Montgomery County.

when open-space acquisition, for example, was a live alternative. Given the incinerator project, the fiscal pressure against more county programs was further intensified, especially because tax reassessment became a political threat—but the pressure and the programs that produced it resulted in some part from political choice. In Bucks and Montgomery the major choices all involved optional rather than mandated programs, except for child welfare.

TABLE 19:1

Attitudes Toward Industrial Development, Open Space, Mass Transit

Township	Approve Ind. Dev.[1]	Approve Open Space[2]	Favor Ind. Dev. Over Open Space[3]	Favor Open Space Over Ind. Dev.[3]	Favor Public Mass Transit[4]
Radnor	71.1	77.7	37.7	44.4	60.0
Marple	86.0	84.0	40.0	38.0	44.0
Springfield	82.3	82.3	27.4	52.9	54.9
Ridley	86.6	82.2	46.6	31.1	53.3
Bristol	90.0	48.0	76.0	14.0	48.0
Middletown	97.2	78.3	78.3	16.2	59.4

[1] "Do you think it is desirable for the county to try to get industry to locate in _____ County for jobs and taxes, even if it has to spend some public funds in this effort?

[2] "Would you favor a county program of buying open land for parks and recreational areas while the land is still undeveloped and available if this program meant an increase in county taxes?

[3] "Quite a few people think it's desirable to attract industry to _____ County for employment and taxes, and a number of people think it's important to provide more open land for beauty and recreation. If these two policies were to compete for the same land or public funds, which would you tend to favor?

[4] "Some people think that a public regional organization, using tax money, is needed to help mass transportation (railroads, buses, trolleys) in this area. How do you feel about this?"

The apparent priorities of the counties have thus stemmed from choice. But choice was affected by factors besides overt political competition and can at least be conceived of as direct anticipation or satisfaction of demands, unaffected by political structure. The limited survey data available shed some faint light on this point. These data come from four townships in Delaware County and two in lower Bucks; thus the extremes in political structure are represented, though Montgomery County is not. Questions were asked about support for possible county programs. One set dealt with industrial development, open space, and mass transit, with the results recorded in Table 19:1. There is substantial support for both industrial development and open space,* but presenting them as alternatives provokes interesting differences: Bucks County's open-space program then gets low priority in lower Bucks (consistent with the Boyer administration's emphasis over most of its

* An exception is lukewarm support for open space in Bristol Township, where municipal officials were then battling the county park board over proposals to (in effect) take more land off the local tax rolls.

tenure), and there are pronounced local differences in Delaware, where the relative emphasis on open space increases with the income and social rank of municipality and, within municipalities, by income and social rank of respondents.* In general, industrial developments gets stronger support in lower Bucks than anywhere in Delaware—perhaps because a county program existed, perhaps because of the job insecurity that originally gave rise to the program. Mass transit, on the other hand, gets equal support (a small absolute majority) in both counties, with intermunicipal differences in both. (The question asked was not specifically about SEPACT.) The samples in intramunicipal breakdowns are too small for firm conclusions, but the following tendencies uniformly exist: support for mass transit increases with educational level and with employment in Philadelphia; it is associated with occupational level in Bucks County, but not, in either county, with income.† The dominant explanation seems to be place of employment, which is associated with education and, perhaps, with cosmopolitan attitudes; Dye's work, referred to in Chapter 3, found that respondents' approval of public support of mass transit significantly increased with cosmopolitanism on an attitude scale.[5]

Table 19:2 sets out reactions to a miscellany of other programs. Briefly, these indicate a widespread interest in parks and recreation (potentially a municipal activity and not necessarily equivalent to open space). Dissatisfaction with library service seems primarily a matter of the extent of existing service and only secondarily of education or social rank of community.‡ There is high satisfaction with refuse disposal in Delaware compared with Bucks (except in Marple Township, where a county incinerator is unpopularly located). The significant interest in mosquito control seems to be a function of proximity to the river, and thus to the mosquitoes! It also appears in the last column that satisfaction with services increases with the income and social rank of the municipality, a point discussed in Part V.

Only limited inferences from these data are valid. Acknowledged

---

* The intermunicipal differences and aggregate Delaware County differences in income, education, and occupation are statistically significant; the latter differences are not statistically significant *within* municipality—probably because of sample size. It is also possible that, in Delaware County, interest in industrial development is a function of lack of industry in the municipality; this would explain the difference between Marple and Springfield, but not that between Radnor and Marple (unless wealth and fiscal effort were added).

† According to the 1960 census the percentages driving cars to work rather than relying on public transportation were: Radnor, 53.0; Marple, 76.2; Springfield, 70.2; Ridley, 73.8; Bristol, 86.5; Middletown (Bucks), 83.5.

‡ Summing mention of libraries either first or second, the communities in Delaware County vary inversely with quality of library service as evaluated in surveys cited in Chapter 14. Incidentally, this seems to indicate more concern about library service in low-social-rank communities (It is greatest in Ridley Township.) than is sometimes hypothesized, though the selective response rate in the Ridley sample may account for this.

TABLE 19:2
Attitudes Toward Public Programs*

Percentage mentioning	Radnor	Marple	Springfield	Ridley	Bristol	Middletown	Delaware Co.	Bucks Co.	Total
Mosquito control	0.0	7.0	10.7	13.3	11.0	9.5	7.9	10.3	8.6
Libraries	6.7	10.0	2.9	16.6	9.0	14.9	8.9	11.5	9.7
Health and sanitation regulation	11.1	12.0	2.9	7.7	11.0	10.8	8.4	10.4	8.7
Police protection	2.2	2.0	3.9	7.8	18.0	5.5	3.9	12.6	6.6
Traffic control and parking	24.4	15.0	16.6	11.2	3.0	8.1	16.8	5.1	13.1
Fire protection	3.3	5.0	2.9	2.2	4.0	10.8	3.4	6.9	4.5
Aid for needy and neglected children	6.6	7.0	15.6	16.6	13.0	14.9	11.5	13.8	12.2
Recreation and parks	15.5	18.0	14.7	14.4	17.0	10.8	15.7	14.4	15.3
Trash and garbage removal	1.1	11.0	1.0	4.4	12.0	8.1	4.4	10.3	6.3
None	28.8	13.0	28.4	5.5	2.0	6.7	19.0	4.0	14.8

* "I have here a list of several possible functions or activities of local and county governments, and I'd like you to tell me which two you think are most in need of improvement or enlargement."

interest in several county options varies with the self-interest *and* social rank of residents, which tend to be unevenly distributed sectionally as well as intermunicipally. Bucks County's priorities seem roughly consistent with the expressed preferences of lower Bucks' residents. In Delaware there is some confirmation of the conjecture that county decisions have responded to lower-income, lower-social-rank concerns of residents located farther south. Ridley's interests seem a little better served than Radnor's, but Radnor, we know, is more self-sufficient and safely Republican than Ridley, with Springfield and Marple intervening in rank order.

One other survey datum bears ambiguously on the question of electoral competition versus direct response to publics. Respondents were asked how they thought the two major parties differed nationally and in the counties and municipalities. Overwhelmingly (more than 80 percent in each county), registered voters perceived no significant interparty differences at the county level, and this indiscriminate view was about as prevalent in Bucks as in Delaware.* The meaning of these responses is unclear, however, for in Delaware many of those not remarking any difference did state that the Democrats were simply too weak to present any, and of Bucks one could argue either that interparty competition *should* reduce policy differences to the vanishing point, or that intra-party divisions were a distraction.

These survey data, with those mentioned in Chapter 3, suggest a county political system in which people accept partisanship and party competition as desirable, do not (no doubt for good reason) perceive differences between the parties, but also are relatively innocent of interest in the county and ignorant of innovations that have occurred in the county. Given concrete suggestions, voters can express or invent dissatisfactions and preferences. Such results, and residents' evident tax-consciousness, suggest that there is ample room for political leadership and maneuvering, including resistance to group importunities. Close party registration in lower Bucks and the sectional direction of policy in Delaware suggest a response—purely and selectively anticipatory in Delaware—to electoral sanctions. In Montgomery there was little evidence of response to overt local demand in the open-space and mass transit programs, but there was plenty in the case of water resources.

4. *Interests and ideologies.* So far, the analysis has focused on socioeconomic pluralism and electoral competition as factors in governmental action. More broadly, population differences among the counties have been considered as giving rise to different interests to which politicians and officials may respond. Finally, the structure and functions

---

* National party differences were much more generally perceived (more than half the total sample); perceptions of local differences were like those for the counties except in Marple Township, where party competition was developing.

of local government itself, including its legal traditions, have—it has been argued—influenced both the forms and the ends of political action, since local government is more relevant to some interests than to others.

These aspects of political structure, broadly construed, have for the most part been discussed in terms of competition, pressure, and response among relatively concrete, discrete interests. It is possible, however, that the behavior of local government is more largely determined by the beliefs and attitudes—the ideologies—of either leaders or plain citizens than by specific interests in projects or programs. The hypothesis of direct political response to constituencies seems most consistent with this possibility, since widely shared ideologies might then account for policies. Prevailing ideologies have a high potential for conservative mobilization of bias, and it has been argued by some scholars that electoral competition is most securely established in conditions of ideological cleavage. Thus, to state the matter more broadly still, the present study may emphasize structure at the expense of culture.*

The distinction between interests and ideologies is not sharp at the margin; witness the civic concern with conservation of resources. It might also be argued that organized pluralism and electoral competition produce similar effects whether differences of interest or of ideology are primarily involved. But the two may not always be consistent; that is, an analysis that imputes certain interests to a group may ignore beliefs or attitudes with different implications for policy that may be appealed to or relied upon by politicians. One would expect this inconsistency to be least sharp in pluralistic, competitive conditions simply because issues are likely to be more explicit. Thus, the role of ideology in change and comparison among the counties must be considered.

This study provides no survey or interview data that can be scaled into ideologies, either of leaders or of the population at large. If such data were available then the problem would arise of defining ideologies. Studies of the political subcultures of America have focused on a few contrasting attitude patterns: community interests versus individual or group benefits as bases for policy, convention versus innovation, personal versus rational relations as bases for politics, and ideal versus material motivations. Liberal versus conservative now seems much too simple a dichotomy of attitudes. The view taken in this study is that, while something like innovative and conventional, conservationist and protective, communal and individual, orientations evidently vary among the counties, logical socioeconomic bases for all of them are present and that probably political competition and public communication have altered the balance among them in the counties where one or more of these exist in significant degree. True, new populations in Bucks and Montgomery may have brought new orientations toward politics and

* Some of the conceptual and methodological issues raised by this possibility are discussed in Appendix A.

policy, but such orientations also exist in Delaware County, where, however, they lack outlets. Neither observation, interviewing, nor the limited survey material suggest that ideologies of the populations at large, the civic activists, or the rank-and-file politicians are characteristically much different among the three counties; though there are some contrasts among strategically placed elites, to be discussed below.

Most of suburban politics, moreover, appears to be interest politics, centered on specific measures. Such a politics may itself amount to an ideology or culture, but plausible sources of it may be found in political and governmental structures common to all the counties. For instance, the nonpartisan elections and one-party cultures of Western and Southern cities, respectively, may leave more room for local ideological cleavage than Pennsylvania's party alignments are likely to do. Class cultures and national party positions tend to be incongruent with respect to such local issues as health and welfare, education and culture, amenity and (re)development, or the general level of public expenditures. Local *party* competition is rarely ideological anywhere in America. Moreover, the counties and localities are less complete governmental units than, say, cities; they present less scope for ideological differences. Most of the policy issues studied above (the principal issues explicitly raised in the last fifteen years) were low pressure, interest issues, and, in particular, questions of race and poverty were not salient. Perhaps the most ideological issue was that of conservation, and it also prominently involved economic interests in two counties.

Perhaps, however, the beliefs of political leaders and other influential persons are more relevant to policy and more likely to vary by chance or circumstance than public attitudes. Most of the leading politicians and industrialists of Delaware and, especially, Montgomery Counties were intensely conservative in their attitudes toward expenditure of public funds and centralization of public functions, but these ideologies also appear to have served material interests. Some of the political leaders were inflexible with respect to policy, and others were not: for instance, Fred Peters was, and John McClure was not, but their political contexts were different, as has been emphasized. The writer has discovered no instance in which these leaders allowed doctrine to prevail over profit, and there were some occasions discussed above in which the reverse occurred. In Montgomery County the split between modern and orthodox Republicans was *partly* a matter of basic attitudes, but it was neither a clean nor an enduring division, and personal ambition figured prominently in it. Certainly new business groups in lower Bucks County espoused growth, progress, and county programs; however, these appeals reflected business interests, and some of their authors—for instance, the principal newspaper publishers—were men of very conservative outlook on state and national policy. There is ample evidence that ideological differences among Bucks' politicians were frequently inconsistent with the positions they took on county measures.

Sometimes when the Montgomery or Delaware political organizations became involved in a public issue—for instance, public health, child care, or community colleges—ideology would be invoked after a position was established, perhaps to help mobilize the courthouse and the precincts, but it does not appear that the leadership was constrained by ideology to adopt one position or another. It seems more plausible, because more consistent, to explain these positions in terms of specific organizational interests served by low taxes or local autonomy.

In the suburban counties the effects of competition on consolidation among specific interests have probably outweighed those of rival or prevailing ideologies, although both interests and ideologies have been involved in policy. In general, confinement of political issues to specific interests seems to fit best with a conservative mobilization of bias, and ideological divisions would seem most likely to arise in an open political system. Such issues may, as some scholars have argued, contribute to the maintenance of electoral competition by redefining interests, aligning citizens, and enlarging the attentive electorate, but such issues have not been typical in suburban Philadelphia. If in the future county government expands, society diversifies, civic action increases, and social or esthetic issues compete with questions of utility, ideological divisions may become more general and intense and more directly relevant to policy. These are likely developments, but their discussion may be deferred until the conclusion of this volume.

In summary, the counties are similar in governmental framework and somewhat less so in social makeup. They have evidently varied most decisively in political structure and rate of economic growth. Thus it appears that change in social, economic, and political structures and interests has so far played the larger role in them. Historically, say up to 1950, the political cultures of the three counties were much the same. After that changes began that altered specific interests, which, in turn, produced new attitudes among some participants, and new participants with different attitudes. The role of economic structure as an alternative to political structure in explaining policies is discussed in the next section.

5. *The effects of development.* Closely connected with the question of structural and cultural change is the view that organized pluralism, electoral competition, and policy innovation are all common responses to residential, commercial, and industrial development in the counties. Development generates a wider range of interests, facilitates change in political affiliations, creates competition for office, and leads to pressures for public policies to accommodate development. It involves in politics people who were put off or untouched by the old organizations.

In this view probably differences in rates of development contribute most to policy changes. During the decade, 1950 to 1960, the three counties grew by nearly equal numbers (Delaware slightly less than Bucks and Montgomery), but Bucks' *rate* of population growth was by far the greatest. Similar intercounty comparisons hold for economic growth, which may have deeper implications because of the specific and substantial interests it entails. Finally, the conditions existing before the 1950's can be described as primarily rural in Bucks, rural and suburban in Montgomery, and suburban and urban in Delaware.

TABLE 19:3
County Growth Indicators
(absolute and percentage increase)

	Bucks		Montgomery		Delaware	
Population (1950–60)	163,947	113%	163,614	46%	138,920	34%
Manufacturing employment (1951–63)	12,158	51%	15,604	24%	−4,408	−8%
Value added by manufacture (1947–63)	$426,500	577%	$685,797,000	242%	$269,247,000	106%
Value of retail sales (1948–58)	$197,087,000	193%	$308,392,000	99%	$260,714,000	89%

Source: U.S. Census and Bureau of Statistics, Pennsylvania Department of Internal Affairs.

From all this one can argue that the relative shock of development accounts for differences among the counties in policy, in organized pluralism and electoral competition, and in the interests and ideologies discussed above as proximate causes of innovation. Clearly the shock was most severe in Bucks and least so in Delaware, with Montgomery intermediate. The question, however, is whether the effects of development on policy are direct and ineluctable, or whether they work by altering political structure and culture (perhaps especially the former) and generating competition that makes policy outcomes uncertain. The first hypothesis is not far from the power-elite theory in supposing that politicians transmit influences instead of mediating them, nor in its assumption that the factors influencing policy are simply categorical in every sense of the word. There do seem to be good grounds for expecting a specific pattern of development to create strong pressures toward a general type of political system, and even toward certain policies, but this is much less than predicting a pattern of specific public decisions. To sustain the theory that rates of development directly account for policies one would have to show that all the outcomes discussed in the four preceding chapters were predictable. This seems unlikely, and increasingly so as development continues and interests proliferate. There is also a possibility that decisions (or nondecisions) *not* to foster growth, especially industrial growth, in the more conservative, fully developed polities stemmed from recognition of its probable consequences and from a desire to forestall or control them. The economies of these counties, it will be recalled from Chapter 2, long emphasized manufacture of intermediate products by family firms in declining industries with relatively unskilled labor. No doubt these structural factors influenced political cultures, which could later be altered by new patterns of development also.[7]

The most sensible conclusion seems to be that development has recently altered the mobilization of bias in those counties where it has occurred most rapidly. It has created pressure, both implicit and explicit, for measures (1) that confer what Dahl has termed collective instead of divisible benefits for sections instead of individuals, and (2) that tend to entail governmental action, to involve broader publics in politics, and to foster professionalization and formal standards. For instance, development may have made the pressure of private-watershed and conservation groups most effective in Bucks County, less so in Montgomery, and least so in Delaware simply because of the different county needs for infrastructure, and the same possibility exists for industrial promotion. However, the balance between these interests and policies could not have been predicted in advance. Development has favored innovation, but it has probably made many policy outcomes less certain, not more so. It is continuing in different ways in all the counties, but electoral competition itself creates an opportunity for growth-oriented groups (which exist in all the counties) to influence policy, which in turn contributes something to cumulative pluralism.

6. *In summary.* Political structure, broadly construed, may be said to vary in several dimensions, including (1) variety of interests, (2) degree and intensity of differences among interests, (3) the generality or specificity of interests (or attitudes and ideologies), and (4) both the forms and extent of organization and competition of interests. These variables characterize factions, parties, pressure groups, and publics. The relations among the variables, and among electoral politics, pressure politics, and governmental action may take many forms, apparently. Or, in the terms with which this study began, the relations among social, electoral, and governmental patterns are reciprocal and cumulative; change in one is likely to lead to change in the others.

Electoral organization relies on sanctions and incentives in both the private and public sectors, and relates these two sectors. Private elites, politicians, or public officials may consolidate resources and dominate policy or the kinds of resources available may favor pluralism. Many patterns are possible. In Delaware County the combination of governmental sanctions and incentives, specific private interests, and a mobilizable vote advantaged politicians, who employed these resources intensively. Montgomery County, during the Peters era, seems to have had a less tractable vote in primary elections together with more persistent, highly motivated private elites, and thus to have developed a slightly different balance of influence. The *possibility* of electoral competition, however, means that widespread indifference, illicit sanctions, lack of organized pluralism, or anticipatory response to opposition are likely to be required for continued consolidation of power.* Where a diversity of strongly motivated private interests exists, a monopolistic political organization might have to respond (in anticipation of primary challenges, for instance) to the point where governmental innovations themselves would result in broader publics and some explicit electoral competition, or the organization might successfully resist by inaction and appealing to public tax-consciousness. The combination of interest and resource characteristics that determine this (apart from sheer political talent) amount to a mobilization of bias, and the problem in each case is to spell these out.

Explicit electoral competition probably alters both the nature and the distribution of political resources, forcing politicians to offer governmental measures that may restrict their flexibility of action, and placing voters and diverse private groups at greater advantage. Electoral competition seems to encourage more diversity among organized interests, since politicians will listen or appeal to those who feel intensely if they are likely to influence others. Diversity of interests is also likely to encourage electoral competition by providing support for political opposition. The distribution of influence between rank-and-file voters and organized interests is likely to depend on the specificity and intensity of interests, including party loyalties.

Strong electoral organization provides an independent set of interests that are not simply derivative from private or governmental resources, but that combine some of these. It seems likely that it would challenge and dilute the self-fulfilling effects of a reputation for power on the part of private elites by mobilizing voters and governmental resources. Where such electoral organization is lacking, the potential for private power structures would seem to be greater. The same probably holds where the scope of government is narrowly limited. In the Philadelphia area, even when the programmatic scope of government has been narrow, governmental benefits and regulations with respect to individuals have been plentiful. Variations in the nature of public functions tend to alter the resources for influence available to officials, politicians, and private interests and to alter interests themselves in terms of their specificity or generality, among other dimensions.

Thus, some general statements are possible about the kinds of relations that obtain among private, electoral, and governmental variables, but the specifics depend in high degree on the precise nature of the variables, on the interests and resources at stake. It does appear that electoral organization and competition are especially influential in the Philadelphia area because of the bases of control available to politicians and the loyalties of voters, but they are only the *most* influential in some

---

* Another possibility is that a cultural (ideological) mobilization of bias may render a minority "discrete and insular," in the words of the United States Supreme Court, thus blocking its possibilities for effective coalition in the electoral process.

circumstances. If the three basic variables are implicitly related, then change in the system at large might be induced by altering any of them—for instance, the functions and structure of government. This possibility is considered in the concluding section, after a study of the same elements in the municipalities.

PART V. MUNICIPAL GOVERNMENT

20

Political Theory and Local Variety

Suburban municipalities—townships and boroughs—in the Philadelphia region vary widely in area, population, tax base, and social characteristics, including their homogeneity or diversity, recency and density of settlement. Municipalities also vary in the extent to which they comprehend an effective community. Some large townships take in several distinct neighborhoods with their own place names, post offices, and social organization; some small boroughs now seem to lack all but legal identity and are submerged in larger areas despite their earlier incorporation as separate communities. But many municipalities, perhaps most, seem to be loosely congruent with local social identifications and loyalties.

Municipal differences are most interesting in combination. They probably work their effects on politics and policy together instead of individually. In this section fifteen municipalities, selected to exemplify such differences, are studied from the standpoint of politics and policy, of political democracy and governmental adequacy. Two of these municipalities are located in (lower) Bucks County, four in Montgomery County, and nine in Delaware County.

In this inquiry one should recognize that the relevant standards of democracy and adequacy may vary among levels of government. Size, diversity, and authority apart, municipalities differ from government at higher levels primarily in their relative lack of formal bureaucracy and organized pluralism. What, then, might be the relevant tests of political democracy and governmental adequacy?

1. *Local democracy.* Some people feel that organized electoral competition is out of place in the relatively small, homogeneous community.

235

The more appropriate conception of democracy is said to be one emphasizing broad agreement on community values and, ideally, broad participation in their appreciation, implementation, and change. This might be termed a communal as distinct from a competitive model of politics. Broad participation may be highly valued (though it need not be) in both conceptions, but, at the least, it takes a different form in each.

The advantages of organized competition doubtless vary among communities. In some circumstances it might be expected to undermine old local oligarchies (There have evidently been some in the Philadelphia suburbs.), encourage innovation in policy and redirection of priorities, protect small minorities from discrimination, and check public corruption or even incompetence. These possible advantages are even harder to evaluate at the local than at the county level. This is so for several reasons: the narrow range of variation in local powers and policies, the lack of agreed criteria for administrative service levels, the hypothetical direct responsiveness of municipalities to popular demand and—at the other extreme—absence of viable alternatives. Moreover, most Philadelphia suburbs exhibit neither regular party competition nor autocratic party structures, neither governance by private elites nor by nonpartisan groups. Instead they display changing patterns of bifactionalism, multifactionalism, irregular primary challenges, and unbalanced party competition, combined with varying degrees of civic activity, so that the effects of electoral competition and civic participation are hard to distinguish.

A few summary observations are relevant, however. One is that partisanship is pervasive in greater Philadelphia and tends strongly to control selection for local public office. This may even be observed in school-board politics, which determine the largest local expenditures. In many communities the party leadership avoids school-board policy and even abstains from nominations, except to see that all are loyal to the majority party. In contexts when party competition is lacking this practice has the effect of reducing factionalism, while the minimal partisanship automatically disqualifies minority-party members. This is not a Machiavellian strategy: several party leaders have learned the hard way—from public rebuffs and primary defeats—to keep politics out of the schools, except, perhaps, for custodial appointments.

Other local offices are far more partisan. Also, as already indicated in Part I, local politics is heavily influenced by competition for, or control of, two vestigial offices: justice of the peace and tax collector. Reformers have long sought their abolition. As fee-producing positions, they promote either party factionalism or discipline, depending on circumstances, and they are often used for party finance. However, the officeholders make no municipal policy. The biggest local consequences and political bounties flow from control of development, which belongs to the local council.

Local political leadership is not without sanctions and incentives.

There is room for discrimination in patronage (county and local), permits and inspections (business advertising, home improvements), assessments, and services. Local politicians vary in the intensiveness with which they use these tools and—paradoxically—their usefulness depends on the extent of local expenditures, services, personnel, and regulations; the more a municipality does the more sanctions and incentives it has. For the most part, however, these affect individuals only; they do not work well on *issues*, which, in a municipality, tend to affect whole sections alike, and to occur singly rather than cumulatively, and which often lack organizational embodiment. In a plurality of organized interest groups politicians might be forced into minimal-issue positions; as it is, they have every reason to conciliate and co-opt opposition and to avoid issues. The result is a system potentially responsive on broad issues but with ample room for individual discrimination. The first characteristic tends to keep political organization out of policy; the second helps maintain political organization. The common exceptions to this pattern occur where party competition or factionalism or both are vigorous, or in small, homogeneous communities where both political organization and governmental programs are minimal. Competition most commonly occurs in larger townships of lower social rank where Democratic voting is most likely and politics is most job-oriented.

Rank-and-file residents exhibit far more partisanship than the literary view of suburbia attributes to them.[1] A majority of those interviewed in the sample survey disagreed with the statement that "local issues are not political, and political parties should stay out of local government." (Since nonpartisanship is often thought to be a middle-class attitude, it is interesting that responses were unrelated to the education, occupation, or income of the individuals.) Overwhelming majorities in all six townships surveyed agreed that "it would be a good idea to have close competition between the two parties in local government," and in most communities majorities accepted the statement that "having a strong political party organization is the best way to have sound and efficient local government." The distribution of responses set out in Table 20:1 probably reflects different local experiences to be discussed in this and the following chapter. But it does appear that in the Philadelphia region the communal image of local democracy is shaped, if not overshadowed, by party organization for elections and by public acceptance of this pattern of government.

2. *Governmental adequacy* is no easier to define than political democracy. Tests of it might include strict administrative efficiency within agreed standards; the absence of corruption not only in procurement and ordinance enforcement but, more subtly, respecting the community's future development; innovation in the present and planning for the future; and even such distributive concerns as measures of social integration in diversified communities and substantial equality in serv-

TABLE 20:1
Partisanship in Public Attitudes Toward Local Government

1. "Local issues are not political, and political parties should stay out of local government."

	Strongly Agree	Inclined To Agree	No Opinion	Inclined To Disagree	Disagree Strongly
Radnor	8.8	20.0	13.3	20.0	35.5
Marple	6.0	14.0	22.0	34.0	24.0
Springfield	7.8	21.5	13.7	23.5	33.3
Ridley	17.7	20.0	13.7	24.4	20.0
Bristol	22.0	14.0	12.0	36.0	16.0
Middletown	16.2	21.6	2.7	40.5	18.9

2. "It would be a good idea to have close competition in elections between the two parties in local government."

Radnor	53.3	40.0	0.0	2.2	2.2
Marple	72.0	24.0	0.0	2.0	2.0
Springfield	47.0	41.1	3.0	7.8	0.0
Ridley	66.6	26.6	2.2	2.2	2.2
Bristol	38.0	42.0	8.0	10.0	2.0
Middletown	67.5	24.3	2.7	2.7	2.7

3. "Having a strong party organization is the best way to have sound and efficient local government."

Radnor	20.0	26.6	8.8	20.0	24.4
Marple	12.0	18.0	10.0	36.0	24.0
Springfield	21.5	33.3	3.9	35.2	5.8
Ridley	24.4	31.1	4.4	17.7	22.2
Bristol	20.0	34.0	12.0	22.0	12.0
Middletown	40.5	27.0	5.4	18.9	8.1

ices and facilities. None of these tests is politically neutral; all are hard to define and apply, and increasingly so throughout the list.

Three related criticisms of municipal government recur in the literature. First, most local governments are said to be too small to provide administrative proficiency and efficiency. Second, they are said not to be self-sufficient because problems and economic resources are rarely well matched among municipalities and because pressures from the external environment tend to override their capabilities. Third, municipalities are said to lack policy options; their actions are thought to be forced by circumstances instead of following from conscious choice.

The first issue—that of internal economies of scale—is extremely complex, and scholars are more skeptical of this argument now than they used to be.[2] The larger townships may be most economic and in the future a majority of suburbanites may live in such low-unit-cost townships, though this is uncertain. Such a development, with school district consolidation and, perhaps, commercial and industrial dispersion, would diminish external diseconomies and fiscal inequities among many suburbs, except for those afflicting the smaller, less well-to-do municipalities. At the moment, however, these issues of internal and external economies are still open, together with the question of the reality and range of local policy alternatives. Several attempts to explain local expenditure patterns by statistical correlation with geographic, demographic, and economic factors leave enough unexplained variation to sustain a political process.[3] The capacity for political choice will vary among municipalities according to factors just discussed. Even in favorably situated communities it requires administrative ability to perceive alternatives, to make and maintain decisions, and political ability to manage the community's divisions. In studying the subject one can usefully distinguish between *development* and *expenditure* decisions, i.e., policies about future settlement patterns and policies about current services.

Two recent studies of the Philadelphia region bear on the question of effective local choice. One is the Fels Institute inquiry referred to in Chapter 3 above. Focusing on social differences among suburban communities, it finds, statistically, that expenditure levels and patterns are functions not alone of physical needs and fiscal resources, but also of some kind of political decision.[4] The authors' political variables are basically social (social rank), and their method tells us most about homogeneous communities. They suggest that individuals tend to locate in communities with compatible tastes and that, in this economic model of democracy, moving may be the basic political act—voting with one's feet, albeit in a positive sense. The question remains what effect, if any, political structure and process have within communities.

The Pennsylvania Economy League's *Adaptability* study is less statistical, more judgmatical.[5] As that study's full title implies, PEL dealt with development policy, as well as with services and expenditures, in selected municipalities over a decade of generally rapid suburban growth, 1950 to 1960. It reviewed communities' experiences in the decade, and sought to judge their success in solving some conventional administrative problems without evaluating basic policies—a difficult line to walk, but one enabling some inferences about the range of local alternatives.

The present study supplements these recent inquiries by asking how political structure affects municipal decisions and administration. Nine of the fifteen communities studied were also in PEL's sample. As in the case of the counties, political structure is difficult to isolate as an explanation, but some inferences about its effects will be possible.

3. *A comparison of two communities.* The difficulties in identifying both causes and effects of political structure may be illustrated by comparison of two adjoining, upper-middle-class municipalities in Delaware County. These communities show significant political differences. Their populations are similar in central tendencies, but they differ in diversity and in rate of development.

Marple and Springfield Townships were both founded in 1684. Modern, "dormitory" growth began in Springfield in the 1920's (extending from Upper Darby), virtually ceased in the thirties, and burst out again after World War II; Marple's still more explosive growth began about 1950 on a smaller base and on a more primitive public infrastructure. By 1940 both communities had zoning ordinances and building regulations. But Springfield had long since become a first-class township with a larger governing body elected by wards and the power to enact subdivision regulations: its first sewers were laid in the 1920's, and an industrial and commercial tax base had developed from its location on state highways; these factors were lacking in Marple in 1950. By 1960 the townships were similar on conventional census indicators of social class and status, but there were subtle cultural divisions in Marple that were lacking in Springfield, an exceptionally homogeneous community. By the time of this writing Springfield was fully and uniformly developed at single-family, quarter-acre density while Marple remained half empty; Springfield had settled down to housekeeping and holding the line, while Marple had future land-use to argue about.

TABLE 20:2
Springfield and Marple Townships, 1960

	Springfield	Marple
Occupational distribution (percent):		
Professional and managerial	45.2	44.1
Clerical and sales	21.7	21.2
Skilled blue collar	18.5	18.6
Unskilled blue collar	14.6	16.1
Educational distribution:		
Median years of schooling	12.4	12.4
Percent with some college education	34.0	31.2
Economic Distribution:		
Median family income	$9,236	$8,663
Percent families over $10,000	42.4	36.0
Percent families under $4,000	4.9	7.1
Population	26,733	19,722
Area (square miles)	6.3	10.4
Density (population per square mile)	4,243	1,896
Percent population increase 1950–60	145	313
Percent of population in 25–34 age group	19.3	24.7
Percent of 1960 housing built before 1940	21.3	9.9
Per capita market value	$4,340	$4,759
Percent of assessed value in residential use	85.1	91.3
Total local property taxes per capita	$83.77	$92.24

Source: U.S. Census and Pennsylvania Economy League, *Exploration of the Adaptability of Local Governments in the Penjerdel Region*, 1950-1962 (Philadelphia: 1963).

There were not, then, dramatic, apparent differences between the townships except in dynamics and social diversity. By small margins Springfield had gradual growth and social homogeneity going for it; it grew with less acrimony and more settled policy—though the results may yet be roughly similar in Marple. This will depend on political decisions and administrative capacity—variables now to be explored in each community on the hunch that political structure itself plays a minor role in development.

The evidence for this conjecture in Springfield includes a mixture of old-fashioned reform and implicit political responsiveness. Springfield's Republican leaders were normally allied with the county organization, and in 1951 the local leader was county prothonotary as well as president of the township commission. In that year, however, the independents won a local majority. The first of them had been elected in 1938; others were added with rapid postwar growth and new election districts. Some of their victories in the late forties were assisted by the countywide antiorganization fights of the time, but the Springfield independents were locally inclined, and the county relation was a weak one. Even before they were in the majority the independent commissioners sponsored more sanitary sewering and a planning commission; after 1951 they tightened zoning, building, and subdivision controls, appointed full-time inspectors and a new solicitor, replaced the county's consulting engineer with a regular engineering department, and reduced the tax collector's personal return. For these practical signs of independence the township paid a small price in county highway aid and other minor forms of cooperation; some independents felt that their position affected a few zoning decisions in the county courts, but there is no solid evidence for this.

The reforms were marginal, for the independents inherited a firm base to build on. The policy that emerged has been described by some officials as made in a business image, while others liken Springfield to a large civic association: it has stressed both planning and public relations. The new planning commission relied on university consultants, who produced a public development plan and revised it periodically. Despite the usual piecemeal amendments of the zoning code (35 in the 1950's), there were general standards and an evident concern for balance in the fiscal base. The commissioners used their essentially negative powers effectively: zoning changes had to wait for the right developer with the right use; those requesting individual variances had to pay the cost of a public hearing; developers dedicated parks as the price of cooperation. In 1950 Springfield had three parks on fourteen acres, in 1960 there were fourteen parks on 131 acres plus a municipal country club and golf course; several of the parks were developed with the aid of neighborhood civic associations. Capital improvements were informally scheduled. Nor were services slighted in development: residents paid higher per capita taxes than in most municipalities and received a wider range of services at higher levels than most; Springfield's highway and police departments were extremely strong by prevailing standards. PEL paraphrased the local officials it interviewed in 1961:

> The old residents . . . were pretty set in their ways, but the new peo-
> ple were different. They had been used to living in apartment houses
> in Philadelphia and having everything done for them. They wanted
> us to do much more for them than we had been doing. This forced
> us to enlarge our municipal force to meet the demands. No town
> "pampers" its people the way we do.[6]

The principal public issue in Springfield during this period was that
of the cumulative effect of zoning changes—especially in balancing the
fiscal base against residential amenity. According to newspaper accounts
and survey data this issue aroused steady popular interest and private
pressure, but it did not reach serious political proportions.

The other development of the fifties was the gradual emergence of
strong local party leadership, its eventual close alliance with the county
organization, and its displacement of the old independents. Most of the
independents were chiefly interested in Springfield, but one, a business
executive who became party chairman, later joined the county War
Board and in 1961 became president of the township commission. He
rose by hard work, steady attention to detail, evident ambition, and the
obvious advantage of county courthouse ties: both township and county
patronage increased with growth and both were fully employed. The
old independents feared that the local regulatory powers and capital
projects would also be used for political ends rather than long run
amenity and efficiency, but these values were kept in balance—at least
by prevailing standards.

In Marple, Harry Eastburn became constable in 1924 and, despite
chronic factionalism, was de facto Republican leader there in 1950 while
his formal party chairman served the township organization in the
county courthouse. Eastburn ran a rural township: the first subdivision
came in 1938, also the first zoning ordinance and building regulations,
and by 1939 a two-man police force operated from Eastburn's gas
station. In 1943 the zoning ordinance was rewritten, largely by a few
estate owners, in order to restrict growth. Marple remained a second-
class township, governed by three supervisors elected at large. Its population doubled in the forties, but on an insignificant base; there were
only 1,000 voters in 1940, and Eastburn knew most of them. Eastburn
may have fitted the literary image of a suburban political boss quietly
assimilating the new suburbanites, but it was not to continue. During
the fifties Marple grew more than twice as fast as Springfield with two
concomitants: political division and overt developmental issues. These
were closely linked, but each was so intricate that they must be separately described.

Fred Dunkerly, professor of metallurgy at University of Pennsylvania,
bought his gas at Eastburn's station and thereby became involved in
politics; Eastburn made him Republican committeeman in 1948, township supervisor in 1949. With Eastburn, Dunkerly tried to bridge the
political and governmental gaps between the old and new: he wrote

party by-laws to encourage rank-and-file participation, he appointed a township manager from the Fels Institute, he required developers to provide playgrounds, lower densities, and capped sewers (and fought them through the U.S. Supreme Court, which upheld him on capped sewers), and he amended the old-timers' zoning ordinance to permit more commercial land use for tax purposes. His development policy and indifference to patronage raised opposition. The first independents elected were congenial, but by the end of his term a rival Republican taxpayers' faction was formed with support from several local developers of large subdivisions whose county political connections were solid.

Fred Dunkerly met defeat in 1955, and factionalism spread. In 1957 Eastburn's regulars turned back two rival groups of independents and taxpayers who then merged and captured the township committee in 1958. To unravel the factions would be pointless. The most important aspects of political change were the co-optation of newcomers by old local rivals, the corporate spirit of the new Republican organization in its general membership meetings, the gradual centralization and ascendency of the elected party committee over the membership, the emergence of one man—a newcomer to Marple (though a county native)—as party leader, and the establishment of stable patronage relations with the county organization. The last three developments were closely connected. In time the party was reunited and some use was made of the talents of all who remained in politics. The man who emerged as leader was a Media lawyer who, unlike Springfield's party chairman, held no public office. Since much of his legal practice lay in service to builders and developers, old residents and new Democrats began to sense a gray eminence behind the township supervisors. Development policy—downzoning and spot variances—met bitter criticism, and the rising Democratic minority implied corruption.

In this Democratic threat Marple differed from Springfield. It evidently stemmed from the fact that one of Marple's early subdivisions was of slightly lower income and of more direct city derivation than any concentration in Springfield, and that another was predominantly Jewish. In 1959, when a county incinerator was located in the first (Lawrence Park) section, the Democrats cashed in: they blasted the township and county Republicans for down-zoning and residential desecration and demanded an outside audit of the municipal books. They elected one school-board member and a justice of the peace and nearly carried a supervisor. With their strength concentrated in a few neighborhoods, the Democrats then began a movement for first-class-township status, which would permit election by districts. When they won a referendum on the issue, the county court appointed five Republicans at large; the Democrats petitioned the Election Board for a division into wards and won; and in 1963 they elected two of seven supervisors and closely contested some others. In the meantime, court-appointed

(Republican) auditors, who retained a private accounting firm, had cleared the administration of error while criticizing its methods. Subsequent Democratic demands for audits and access to municipal records were refused by local officials and the county court.

The township administration was unstable, a victim of managerial personalities and political factions. In 1950 Marple was the state's first second-class township to hire a manager; in 1952 he resigned when the supervisors refused to accept his personnel recommendations. (He briefly entered business, was made a supervisor by the taxpayers faction when a vacancy occurred, earned a law degree, entered partnership with the new political leader, and ultimately became tax collector!) There were four more managers in the next decade, the last a local man earlier a member of the controversial Board of Auditors. As PEL delicately expressed it: "His lack of formal training for the position was also considered by some to be an advantage . . . as it was believed that he would be able to adjust better to conflicting pressures and political feuds in the township."[7] Cooperation and policy improved. Accounting was reformed with first-class-township status. Regulatory administration was weak:

> In 1954 it was decided that a full-time building and·plumbing inspec-
> tor would be necessary. The political sensitivity of the position was
> apparent from the manner in which appointments to the position,
> at various times during the period, changed with changes in the polit-
> ical composition of the governing body.
>   Enforcement of plumbing and subdivision regulations were cited
> by a number of knowledgeable persons contacted by the staff of the
> study as a major problem during the fifties and at the present time.
> There appeared to be clear opinion that the regulatory ordinances
> were good but that enforcement was inadequate and influenced by
> political considerations.[8]

In expenditure policy the township rapidly matured, and by 1963 it was spending (per capita) roughly as much as Springfield on recreation, library, and police. Development policy was the major political issue, and it was intensified by the resentments of old residents at new residents and of new residents at developers. The zoning ordinance, an act of the the old residents, was in fact amended two dozen times in the decade, mainly to broaden the tax base.* Newcomers put heavy pressure

* PEL paraphrased municipal officials on this point: "We've been criticized for this, but we thought rather than go through a survey and try to change the whole ordinance—which would have disrupted things and might tie us up in court—it would be better to adjust the existing ordinance as we went along. The township was growing so fast that we believed that whatever attempts we made, as far as overall planning was concerned, wouldn't work out. As we saw things developing, we stepped in and amended the ordinance here and there to meet the changing situation, and in that way we have expanded our tax base considerably—but not without a lot of public opposition." Pennsylvania Economy League, *Exploration of the Adaptability of Local Governments in the Penjerdel Region*, 1950-1962 (Philadelphia: 1963), p. 273.

on the schools, indirectly straitening the township, and as mortgagors, they were anxious for amenities and services, and irritated by builders and tax collectors. Most of Marple was built by a few developers, still active there, and embattled by active civic associations. Marple's Republican leader, with the developers, privately took the position that full densities, single and multiple family, were democratic and economic; the Democrats took the civic associations' part in opposing downzoning. Old residents sought to reserve more open space and resented taxation of estates as residential property. Strip commercial growth proceeded (in accordance with the zoning ordinance), while industrial development lagged for lack of transportation. Apparently Marple Township had feasible alternatives—varied densities with amenity or rapid growth with uniformity—but party competition never clearly posed the issue, and there was no local planning commission (save for an informal citizens' committee) until 1962.

4. *Politics, administration, and the community.* The comparison of Marple and Springfield Townships illustrates the intricate relations that obtain among social characteristics, political structure, and local governmental action. It also illustrates the difficulty of isolating politics as an independent force. Several suggestions emerge from it: (1) that local political competition is largely derivative from social composition, (2) that local government is highly sensitive to both, (3) that social and political divisions may affect planning and management adversely, (4) that county organization (in Delaware County) can be a stabilizing factor in local politics, and (5) that skillful political leadership also makes a big difference in governmental adequacy. In particular, the case for competition versus communalism seems to need qualification.

Party competition came to Marple and not to Springfield. It probably stemmed from Marple's slightly more diverse population and more rapid development. Marple's new homeowners included more young families with lower incomes than did those who lived in Springfield, and more Jews with Democratic political sympathies. These factors, evident in the census and survey data, meant more economic insecurity and pressure for public education.* New Democrats were less readily absorbed in their rapid arrival in Marple, and differences became more visible between old and new—between rural lanes and estates, strip zoning

* The possibilities of tension implicit in rapid growth may be seen in two aspects of new suburbs peopled by city emigrants. One is the high ratio of Roman Catholic population, many of whom find themselves paying heavy school taxes without direct benefit; the other is the expectation of high public-service levels derived from city living, fulfillment of which is incidentally checked by school taxes. Finally, both these factors clash with the expectations and habits of older community residents. Another cultural variation, according to some elected officials, is that new Jewish residents place especially high priority on educational expenditures. These points have rather general applicability: in most of the rapidly growing communities surveyed in the next chapter the proportion of the elementary school population in private schools was at least one-third in 1960.

and pastel subdivisions. Several large developers in Marple were salient antagonists of both old and new, while the political leader befriended them.

The *effects* of party competition in Marple are hard to assess. The rows over down-zoning, also common in Springfield, were more the result of civic than of political action. Democratic and factional election-eering emphasized corruption and incompetence more than the pattern of development, and it may have brought about some record-keeping reforms together with first-class-township status. Did competition raise and clarify issues? Interviews with community leaders suggested that issues existed and that competition influenced policy; yet there was little agreement in identifying specific election issues (other than occa-sional notice of corruption and the accomplishment of first-class-town-ship status). In the sample survey of residents those in Marple were only a little more apt to perceive local differences between the two parties than were Springfield respondents, though they also showed slightly more agreement in defining the issues. Most of those remarking a difference expressed it in terms of inclination toward activity or com-placency; a very few mentioned the regulation of development. Several registered Republicans spoke favorably of the Democrats' role in local controversy. Competition seems to have raised issues about govern-mental conduct rather than developmental policy, and to have soft-pedaled social divisions. The minority party was available to residents as a means of venting dissatisfactions, but it was not a vehicle for leadership in local policy.

In Marple, social and sectional divisions, political competition, and dissatisfaction with government are found together; in Springfield, none of these is significant. Local civic associations are more active in Marple, compared with functional groups for schools, libraries, and recreation (at official initiative) in Springfield. Survey data from the two commu-nities indicate that Marple residents are less inclined to regard their government as broadly representative and responsive, more disposed to the view that, although decisions are made in the open, a small group controls them.* This small group is usually identified as the political leadership. A substantial majority of Marple respondents acknowledged such minority control, while a like majority in Springfield denied it— although Springfield's political leadership is at least as tight as Marple's, and some civic leaders in Springfield privately express concern about dictation of policy by the political leader (after the ground has been carefully prepared) and discouragement of political dissidence through use of the township's regulatory powers. Two factors seem to be at work in this contrast: one is superior management in Springfield, where, in surveys, residents and civic leaders far more commonly express satis-faction with governmental action than is the case in Marple. The second factor, contributing to better management in Springfield, is relative

* These survey data appear in Table 23:5 in Chapter 23.

TABLE 20:3
Satisfaction with Local Governmental Action

PERCENT WHO SAY
THAT LOCAL GOVERNMENT IS DOING:

	Not Enough	Too Much	The Right Amount
Marple			
Residents (N=50)	36.0	0	56.0
Leaders (N=20)	65.0	0	35.0
Springfield			
Residents (N=50)	8.0	2.0	88.0
Leaders (N=14)	0	14.0	86.0

social homogeneity. Governmental responsiveness is easier in Springfield because there is more agreement; policy, indeed, is far more a matter of leadership than of responsiveness.

Public management may have been hampered in Marple by political competition, as PEL concluded.[9] The comparison suggests that in small jurisdictions relations between the two sides of government (politics and administration) are especially close and sometimes cumulative. The same may be said of relations between governmental adequacy and popular satisfaction: dissatisfaction, division, and factionalism may inspire *more* political (partial, unprofessional) administration rather than less, and so on. Another point in the comparison concerns the character of political leadership. Springfield's management—governmental and political—was evidently in capable hands; moreover, the same man held formal public responsibility for both. His leadership was decisive, even dictatorial, with colleagues, but anticipatory and explanatory with the public. In Marple, governmental policy was perceived by many civic activists to derive from wire-pulling by a party leader privately allied to developers—an apparent ground for popular dissatisfaction.

In administration, Marple was also handicapped by transportation disadvantages relative to Springfield that complicated its fiscal balance, and by rapid growth with high capital and carrying costs; thus Marple's combined taxes were higher than Springfield's though its municipal service levels were lower, partly because of school expenditures.[10] Marple's administration was more primitive, with more apparent politics and less actual planning than Springfield's, reflecting in part the social, physical, and fiscal differences between the two communities. Marple has alternatives today, and its tribulations may be only temporary, while disagreements may emerge in Springfield, especially if the present leadership retires. Still, early situations and decisions tend to cumulate and to influence later public action through their effects on social and political patterns as well as by their inner logic.

The comparison of Marple and Springfield suggests that social and political factors may work differently at the local and county levels.

Perhaps local politics is so close to administration on one hand, and to intimate or invidious issues on the other that political competition simply lowers administrative capacity and residential morale reciprocally without compensating advantages. Perhaps this occurs because municipalities lack the organized pluralism and formalized institutions that help keep competition stable and impersonal. If so, competition may have less to offer locally than has communalism. Yet, where the social similarities and the agreement on policy presupposed in communalism do not exist, competition may provide protection for minorities and more responsiveness in administration. And Springfield's social homogeneity has *not* led to widespread civic activity; there is less than in Marple, though political leadership is stronger in Springfield. These municipalities may be too large (at about 25,000) for the communal approach to local government, in which case the relevance of that approach is severely limited. These possibilities are further pursued in the following chapters.

21

Competition

Competition and communalism are two crude models of local politics. One emphasizes electoral organization, the other direct participation. The Marple-Springfield comparison suggests that the more specific forms these take depend especially on rates of social change and degrees of social rank and diversity. Variations in political organization and civic action, respectively, are examined in this chapter and the next. The division between them parallels that between parties and elections on one hand and pressure and influence on the other that was described in the discussion of county politics.

1. *Townships and boroughs.* The analyses in this chapter and the next are based on comparisons among fifteen communities that differ in many respects. The discussion of political structure is focused on nine large townships: two in Bucks County, three in Montgomery, and four in Delaware. In Table 21:1 these townships are grouped according to social rank, the variable that seems most closely related to political competition. Cheltenham, Lower Merion, and Radnor are all extremely high in social rank and income, though Radnor exhibits more diversity than the other two, with less development and lower density. The two Middletowns and Upper Merion are intermediate in class and status: all are about half white-collar, half blue-collar; all are in different stages of rapid growth; and all are second-class townships. Aston, Bristol, and Ridley are of lower wealth and social rank, but they vary in density and stage of development. While the nine do not provide all combinations of the main variables, they cover a broad range, with enough overlap to provide some checks on one's inferences.

For some purposes six small boroughs are compared with the nine townships. The boroughs are compact, quasi-incorporated, relatively densely settled, and less populous than the townships, but they cover an

TABLE 21:1

Social Profiles in 1960 of Townships Considered in Chapter 22

| | I | | | II | | | III | | |
	Cheltenham	Lower Merion	Radnor	Middletown (Bucks)	Upper Merion	Middletown (Delaware)	Bristol	Aston	Ridley
Occupational distribution (%):									
Professional and managerial	52.0	56.0	43.0	38.9	36.5	38.7	19.8	20.1	20.5
Clerical and sales	23.0	18.0	19.8	16.8	15.8	13.8	15.4	10.2	16.0
Skilled blue-collar	11.1	7.2	10.7	21.9	20.8	26.5	27.6	34.9	30.0
Unskilled	12.6	14.0	26.6	22.4	24.5	21.0	37.2	34.8	33.5
Educational distribution:									
Median years of schooling	12.4	12.6	12.5	12.3	12.3	12.2	9.4	11.6	11.8
Percent with some college	37.0	44.0	40.9	27.6	28.9	29.5	7.7	12.7	12.2
Economic distribution:									
Median family income	$9,985	$12,204	$9,894	$7,656	$8,300	$8,500	$6,692	$6,926	$6,992
Percent over $10,000	49.9	58.7	49.3	28.0	28.5	34.9	12.8	17.0	17.7
Percent under $4,000	9.6	9.9	10.9	8.2	8.1	7.6	10.7	9.3	10.2
Population:									
Total	35,990	59,420	21,697	26,894	20,000	11,256	59,298	10,595	35,738
Density per square mile	4,090	2,550	1,572	1,393	1,066	840	3,616	1,892	6,873
Increase in decade (%)	57.5	21.9	47.5	439.3	167.0	86.9	386.7	90.0	107.6
Percent of population in 25-34 age group	19.2	9.2	17.9	36.9	33.7	22.0	35.4	32.9	30.1
Percent housing built before 1940	45.5	58.4	50.4	13.4	25.7	33.3	12.6	20.7	22.2
Per capita market value of housing	$5,540	$7,612	$5,767	$3,372	$5,891	$3,024	$2,654	$2,691	$3,051
Percent of assessed value of property in residential use	77.5	75.5	73.9	86.0	59.7	93.2	81.0	86.8	81.1
Total local property taxes per capita	$125.65	$130.65	$110.27	$62.94	$117.63	$57.75	$70.55	$55.58	$57.90

Source: U.S. Census and Pennsylvania Economy League, Exploration of the Adaptability of Local Governments in the Penjerdel Region, 1950-1962 (Philadelphia: 1963).

TABLE 21:2
Social Profiles of Six Boroughs

	Conshohocken	Aldan	Glenolden	Collingdale	Yeadon	Swarthmore
Occupational distribution (%):						
Professional and managerial	11.5	26.6	18.5	16.6	28.8	63.7
Clerical and sales	12.1	20.9	15.0	19.3	22.5	17.3
Skilled blue-collar	21.5	29.7	32.1	29.7	21.7	7.0
Unskilled blue-collar	51.0	22.8	34.4	34.4	27.0	12.0
Educational distribution:						
Median years of schooling	9.8	12.1	11.4	10.6	11.6	16.0
Percent with some college	6.3	22.0	11.7	9.1	17.6	70.8
Economic distribution:						
Median family income	$6,205	$7,761	$6,828	$6,559	$7,856	$10,000
Percent over $10,000	16.5	32.1	17.7	14.5	29.3	58.2
Percent under $4,000	18.6	8.6	16.4	14.6	12.3	6.0
Population	10,259	4,324	7,249	10,268	11,610	5,753
Density per square mile	10,259	7,207	8,054	11,409	7,256	4,109
Increase in decade (%)	−6.1	26.1	12.4	21.6	4.9	19.2
Percentage of population between ages 25 and 34	7.8	14.9	19.2	21.3	14.1	12.6
Percent of 1960 housing built before 1940	84.7	53.8	63.6	72.8	69.9	66.4
Per capita market value of property	$2,641	$3,873	$2,792	$2,617	$3,557	$4,925
Percent of assessed value of property in residential use	60.8	89.1	87.0	85.5	82.7	90.1
Total local property taxes per capita	$41.92	$64.62	$52.05	$49.62	$62.20	$114.15

Source: U.S. Census and Pennsylvania Economy League, *Exploration of the Adaptability of Local Governments in the Penjerdel Region*, 1950-1962 (Philadelphia: 1963).

equal range of social rank and economic resources. They were commercial and residential centers half a century ago, when the townships were rural, but their recent rate of growth has been slow, and none exceeded 12,000 persons in 1960. Five of the six are in Delaware County. Conshohocken, in Montgomery, is an old industrial center—that is, a center for industrial workers and, originally, for entrepreneurs, but the employing industries lie outside the borough line, a fact of dire fiscal significance. The five boroughs selected from Delaware County are residential concentrations, in some cases combined with commercial development.

In terms of political competition the boroughs vary, as do the townships soon to be described. Most boroughs are too compact for much sectionalism and lack many social divisions. Their public issues concern services and (especially) expenditures more often than they do development, but there are few public issues. Organized interests vary with local social rank, but include merchants and service clubs, volunteer fire departments, recreation groups, PTA's, and taxpayers' organizations. Party organization is least apparent and patronage is least important in the smaller boroughs and especially in those of most social prestige.

2. *Patterns of political organization.* The following discussion of local political structure is confined to the townships because of their greater size in area and population. Divisions of interest and policy issues are normally more acute in the townships today because of their rapid development and potential sectionalism. Many of the townships are more populous than any of the boroughs, and they are now the dominant political units in the counties. For all these reasons competition for control of some townships is serious, while small boroughs and sparsely settled townships offer fewer sanctions to and incentives for leadership, and they stimulate less serious factionalism.

Each county has always had a few critical jurisdictions in which patronage and local stability were especially important and closely related. With population growth there are more such localities, but population changes have also weakened the old bases of local control. In these larger townships political leadership has come to reply more on organization and less on personal acquaintance. In the political tendency of the counties and localities to centralize control of perquisites and decentralize competition there are now more levels of control and competition; in large townships the districts and precincts are increasingly important.

Still, local political systems vary widely in tightness of organization and electoral competition, as well as in styles and tactics of leadership. Nine township political systems are described in the order of their listing in Table 21:1 because of the seeming importance of social rank in political style and structure.

The three communities of high social rank differ significantly in political organization, but partisanship goes deep in all of them. Cheltenham has long been one of Montgomery County's most tightly organized localities, crucial to the county leadership. A long settled township with several distinct communities, it has nonetheless grown over 50 percent in the last decade, largely through apartment construction. Party organization is under heavy pressure for recognition of newcomers, and the Democrats are mildly threatening in state and national elections.[1] Cheltenham's high status population is more cosmopolitan than most, heavily Jewish and Catholic, with an old Negro enclave dating from the Civil War: more than 35 percent of the township population falls in the census' foreign-stock category; 57 percent of its public school children in 1960 were Jewish. These political pressures have emerged only in the last decade, and Cheltenham shows exceptional continuity in public office-holding. For most of this century one man has been the Republican leader; and the dominant township commissioner, his political backer and conservative ally, was a New York banker who served thirty-eight years before retiring in 1962.

Cheltenham's Republican leader became township secretary about 1912; he came to control the party committee through acquaintance, appointments, and through the backing of those who wanted a strong township organization for more county aid. In 1937 Cheltenham (a first-class township since 1900) adopted the manager plan, and the political leader became manager. In the pattern that prevailed until recently most township appointees (e.g., engineer, chief of police, county tax assessor, etc.) were part-time political workers, and the formal party chairman was township treasurer—yet, save for some complaints in interviews about individual favoritism (said to be linked to party fund-raising), Cheltenham got extensive services at seemingly reasonable rates; it was a wealthy, well-run township. Party decisions were centralized in half a dozen persons, and nearly half the local committee people held township or county jobs and were below the community average in social rank. Party finances were said to be similarly centralized in local businessmen and entirely independent of the county (though hard evidence is lacking on this point). The political leader's influence on the township commissioners was based on friendship and respect in some cases, business and political sanctions in a few others, and more generally on control of nominations and elections. Political sanctions and incentives were freely used: several respondents felt that the loose zoning ordinance and the political background of inspectors left room for pressure on local businessmen, and that committeemen were generally expected to fix traffic tickets. This was still the pattern in the 1950's despite primary and general election competition, cleavage over school expenditures and zoning decisions, and a growing liberal-conservative division in the commissioners over commercial and apartment zoning, redevelopment, planning and overall land-use standards, and expenditure levels.

Lower Merion, larger and even wealthier, with more distinct neighborhoods than Cheltenham, is a thoroughly one-party township. As in Cheltenham, the Democrats criticize expenditures and service levels as too low (Lower Merion is about the region's highest on both counts.), but in recent years the commissioners have been retrenching, presumably in fear of primary competition in their districts. The difference in Lower Merion is the undisciplined Republican organization, whose postwar wrangling has also weakened the Montgomery County organization. Two hypotheses are commonly offered for Lower Merion's factionalism: one, the affluence and indifference to patronage of most elected officials and committeemen; another, the township's sheer size and sectionalism. Except in blue-collar areas, local patronage has little appeal, and those eminent residents who want state positions often secure them on their own. The chief administrative jobs—manager, engineer, solicitor—are not considered patronage, and the manager has the conventional personnel powers of his position except that blue-collar jobs are increasingly used for politics and that employees are expected to register Republican. There have been sharp primary contests for state and county office and for several township commissioner positions, far more in response to ambition than to policy issues. Lower Merion has more residents with political interests than can easily be accommodated, and the township Republican Committee has resorted to open primaries for local office. The board of commissioners covers the spectrum from conservative to modern Republican, which has more relevance to local affairs as pressure on the high tax rate increases. There are not, however, firm factional lines among the commissioners, and the ward system may discourage them by encouraging responsiveness to constituents. Most commissioners now hope to reunite the local party for more influence in county decisions, and to redress what is generally believed to be the county's collusive underassessment of new apartment buildings.

Radnor Township, in Delaware County, shows lower density and wider social diversity than Cheltenham, but less Democratic voting. Its broad distribution of occupations and incomes is striking; it results from a few old settlements with numerous blue-collar residents amid areas of large estates, expensive apartments, and low density single-family residences. The seven wards, however, are drawn to include this diversity (rather than separate communities) in each, which protects the majority party and tends to prevent sectionalism among the commissioners. There has been substantial continuity on the board of commissioners, a majority of whom hold county political jobs. (The others are well-to-do businessmen.) Radnor is the political seat and tax-collectordom of Albert Swing, whose county political vicissitudes were recounted above. These shook his twenty-year leadership by depriving him of county patronage temporarily and nearly overturning the township committee; yet one year after his county defeat Swing regained committee control in the local primary, forcing a truce with

McClure. His tight organization was heavily based on patronage—some two dozen white-collar county jobs were held by committee people, retired and distaff residents, and an equal number of township blue-collar jobs were said to be influential in the lower income areas. Yet Radnor's government has generally produced high satisfaction with high service and expenditure levels. The political leadership has normally avoided involvement in school decisions and land planning, leaving these to independent boards and civic associations. As in all the upper-income communities surveyed here, membership of boards and commissions is highly valued by some residents, and civic associations are lively. As one commissioner put it in an interview, the civic associations are important in his ward (There are twenty in the township.), but he has "pinned their ears back by meeting all their demands."

In these three communities, where half the working population is professional or managerial and three-quarters are white-collar (Radnor is of slightly lower social rank.), the nonpartisan ideal might be expected to operate. In a sense it has in policy (though not in personnel), since all may be classed as one-party communities despite Cheltenham's cosmopolitan traditions and recent Democratic increase. A striking characteristic of these communities is the strength of party activity and patronage (growing in Lower Merion, as low-income areas are gradually recognized and defended against Democrats) and the traditional absence of regular alignments on issues. The latter may, however, be emerging in Lower Merion and Cheltenham with resistance to high expenditure levels and pressure for more apartment and commercial development; the fiscal base and community way of life are marginally at issue.

The next group of municipalities are almost equally the homes of white- and blue-collar residents. They are all rapidly growing communities and, in each, an effect of growth has been a large increase in social rank and average family income over the last decade on an old rural or industrial base. Each presents overlapping regional and social divisions, but all are second-class townships without formal district representation. Each township displays a different (perhaps transitory) political structure, which may be briefly described.

In 1953 Middletown (Bucks) had an implicit Republican tradition and almost no party organization; it also had a zoning ordinance drawn up by the Fels Institute in 1948. At this point William Levitt appeared on the scene; having quietly purchased 1,500 Middletown acres, he sought code changes to permit extension of Levittown over the line from Bristol. There were persuasive arguments for accepting Levitt: that the area would soon come under pressure anyway and might better all be developed at one time with proper utilities (There were no sewers in Middletown.), and that Levitt had an appropriate interest in his land investment as against his opponents, some of whom had sold land to him. Middletown's sewerage and subdivision ordinances were passed *after* Levitt's purchase. In the bitter political division that followed, Levitt's supporters ran in the next election as pro tem Democrats, after losing the Republican primary. The full financial extent of Levitt's campaign activity is unknown, but his local managers were busy in the election, along with a full-time publicity man from New York, and the temporary Democrats triumphed 2:1. Although they returned to Republicanism, and although Middletown got Levittown's highest-priced homes, party competition came later. By then the township had made several basic decisions: to zone for industry, to adopt the manager plan, and to remain a second-class township. None of these decisions were made on party lines. Divisions based on section and length of residence were more important than party affiliation. Both parties were based in the newly populated south and bid for the disgruntled north. By the end of the decade party registration was almost evenly divided, though the commissioners (elected at large) remained at 4:1 Republican. Each party was divided into the county factions described in Chapter 7. Party competition consisted in maneuvering on minor issues, with the Democratic commissioner a constant watchdog over expenditures, services, and regulations. This led to petty sniping and aventitious issues, since both sides operated before an extremely tax-conscious, regionally sensitive public, but it may also have provided checks and incentives. Both parties (in their majority factions) supported the manager-plan principle; there were continuity in managers and virtual freedom from patronage (unique in lower Bucks County). In a decade Middletown's population climbed from 5,000 to 27,000, with evident political tension: some 40 percent of the respondents surveyed there for this study thought taxes were the township's major issue; yet similar percentages felt the township did less than it should and neglected major problems. To an outside observer aware of its growth rate Middletown looked like a success: it had planned and zoned for a balanced tax base, and it had achieved a competent, nonpolitical administration; policy-oriented elected leadership; and party competition without sharp party cleavage on issues. Its political patterns were rather like Marple's, but its administration was more effective.*

Rising expenditures and densities evidently raise civic tensions; and dissatisfaction seems to increase with the rate of growth. Upper Merion, which grew 167 percent during the decade, 1950 to 1960, also developed party competition, if only temporarily. This resulted from registration changes in one old, low-income section and the advent of new Democrats

---

* Despite the lack of clear performance standards for administration, a direct comparison is possible in this crucial case. The same man was successively township manager of Marple and of Middletown (Bucks), in each case for a period of at least two years. He left each position voluntarily. He told the author that intervention by the supervisors in administration was much more common in Marple, and public support of the manager's decisions much less common there than in Middletown, despite, the hot political competition in each township. Indeed, Middletown's *party* competition was tighter than Marple's.

in modestly priced homes—yet the Democrats' registration had not reached 25 percent when, in 1957, they obtained a majority on the Board of Supervisors. Civic and sectional discontent provided the majority, which was lost five years later. The Democratic Party was a vehicle for protest and political advancement rather than a stable opposition. Both parties developed factions, or personal followings, and the governmental coalitions crossed party lines. Upper Merion faced virtually the same issues as Middletown (Bucks): down-zoning, industrial development, sewerage, first-class-township status and the manager plan. All of them were settled by interparty coalitions. Substantively, the issues were decided as they were in Middletown, but the results worked out differently: Upper Merion, with its strategic location by the Pennsylvania Turnpike, more easily attracted industry, and its manager plan was more politicized in operation.

Middletown (Delaware) represents a tentative decision to retain low-density, residential and institutional land-uses with minimal services: i.e., not to join suburbia. Unlike neighboring Aston (described on p. 258) it had no sewers, police, or trash collection; yet its school millage (in a consolidated district) is almost the county's highest because of heavy capital costs on an entirely residential tax base. Its politics is one-party; but when growth began, an "independent" Republican faction organized to improve the schools and stimulate local planning; it maintained its own local committeemen and elected a few school and municipal officials. In time it declined, and the county organization co-opted some of its winners; one of them became township party leader. Middletown's big developmental issues—installation of utilities, balancing the tax base, resisting commercial-strip zoning—all have been deferred or defaulted because of heavy tax pressures and serious sectional differences separating old from new, high income from low. The independent faction, while it lasted, favored more expenditures and regulation to met these issues.

Political competition in the three middle-rank municipalities has been less about broad policies than about specifics in zoning and expenditures or preferences in political style—patronage and personal business advancement versus planning and management. Possibly norms affecting political conduct are most divided in these townships, reflecting their close balance in social class. Party lines have not been directly relevant to local policies. Middletown (Delaware's) brief factional competition was, however, an encounter over both development and expenditure policy.

Invidious as it may seem, the group of municipalities with substantially more than half the population in blue-collar occupations shows more unanimity in the matter of political style: politics is more job-oriented. Party competition is also more probable in these jurisdictions, and is often acrimonious, perhaps because of the personal stakes. The political organization of three such municipalities may be briefly compared: Bristol in Bucks County, Aston and Ridley in Delaware County.

Bristol grew 386 percent in the 1950's to a population of 60,000; it and Lower Merion are the largest townships surveyed. The two parties in Bristol were tightly competitive; yet each party was badly factionalized. Coalitions often crossed party lines on the ten-member board of commissioners. After the 1961 election the board was evenly divided, and it took three attempts to pass the budget as Democrats pressed heavy economies and personnel reductions in the previous (Republican) board's appointments; such have been the usual grounds of party division. Sectional rivalry (especially between two centers) was strong in Bristol, but generally adequate services were provided despite administrative and fiscal strain.[2] Political differences complicated administration. The manager plan was adopted in 1956 (at which time there were two resignations over personnel authority and frequent intervention in administration by committees of the township commission before the president of the board of commissioners took the job of manager in 1961).*

Aston Township, in Delaware County, has aspects of several municipalities studied so far: pronounced sectionalism with steady postwar growth in the south; old, low-income mill towns and rural areas in the north; and a net rise in social rank and incomes over the decade. The older region shows much less need or concern for utilities and services, for which it will nevertheless be taxed (except for sewers, which are specially assessed). It is more subject to Republican organization control and is heavily overrepresented on the board of commissioners and on party committees; Democratic court fights have failed to change what the county court has termed the historical integrity of the upper wards. In 1962 15 percent of the township's voters were in the upper wards, electing three of the seven commissioners. Aston's fiscal and administrative experiences are similar to Bristol's.[3] Its distinguishing characteristic is two-party competition with less factionalism than is usual—probably because county patronage and the Democratic threat have held the Republicans together with a like, feedback effect on the Democrats. The local Democratic party is, however, an outgrowth of postwar sectional division of the township's Republican leadership; as the split deepened, the northern Republican leader backed Democrats

* A typical wrangle occurred over this move: Democrats termed the (Republican) president a furniture salesman; Republicans rejoined that he was a kitchen planner. (He was then employed as kitchen-planning specialist for Sears, Roebuck). Philadelphia *Inquirer*, October 6, 1961. Police administration was especially sensitive: in 1957 a Democratic justice of the peace and party chairman, to whom Democratic commissioners directed the police to take cases, fought with the police chief, who pressed a criminal libel charge on the justice of peace, who then revived a two-year-old perjury suit brought by a critic against the chief. Three years later the police chief was fired, and successfully appealed for maintenance of his civil-service status to the county court. He was the second chief fired in that decade; discipline on the force was difficult because of the individual policemen's contacts with commissioners.

in the south. Later, with more population growth, the party became independent, with the Democratic independence movement in the county. Both parties have held the township government. There has been no explicit competition over developmental issues, but competition has probably brought about administrative reform and raised service levels by giving an electoral weapon to independent civic critics and southern residents generally against the old-line organization politicians and overrepresented north. The first Democratic administration activated a planning commission and health board, appointed a full-time, Democratic building inspector (The part-time Republican incumbent, a party committeeman, was fired.), expanded the police department, and increased trash collection. The manager plan was also adopted, but it did not survive later political turnover. In lower Aston the Democratic registration is about 30 percent, but the vote is close; acknowledging normal Democratic underregistration, especially in Delaware County, this may still indicate a tendency to use the party for local protest instead of affiliating with it.

Finally, Ridley Township in Delaware County is rather like Radnor in its strong leadership; the leader for the last decade was a War Board member, who was county coroner and is now a county judge. Over the decade Ridley's party registration changed only marginally around its 4:1 ratio despite growing closeness in state and national elections. (Kennedy and Johnson both carried Ridley.) The solid Republican hold on local offices probably resulted from relatively gradual growth: population doubled in the 1940's and again in the fifties, but it did so on a larger base, with more middle-class residents and well settled communities than in Aston and Bristol. There are often serious primaries in Ridley, but the Republican organization tends to keep them decentralized in the wards and to co-opt the winners; the township's distinct sectionalism abets this policy. The political leadership is also said not to intervene in municipal and school-board policy except when jobs are at stake, but it has the reputation (evident in interviews) of using regulatory sanctions hard, especially on local businessmen. The township's planning commission was dissolved soon after the county commission was established: informants report that this was because the planning commission objected to zoning variances and changes that were widely said to be related to party finance. Controversies over spot zoning have been especially common in Ridley, and township administration has never contained any specialist or professional in planning or management.

3. *The effects of political competition.* One must begin with the fact that *implicit* electoral competition—the law of anticipated reactions—is significant in most localities. This may be inferred from the turnover of officials in developing communities, from the record of primary competition and organizational co-optation in most one-party jurisdictions,

and from the fact that close implicit competition is probably enhanced
by district (rather than at-large) representation in first-class townships.
Electoral competition between the two parties occurred in three townships just discussed where the minority (Democratic) party had less
than 30 percent of the registration.

The form and extent of organized competition seem largely to depend
on local growth rates and social bases. Rapid growth stimulates electoral
competition. *Party* competition most often occurs in communities of
low social rank or of pronounced cultural diversity.* There is also a
close local relation to county political systems. In Delaware, a strong
county organization encouraged strong local leaders (with county aid
and sanctions); in Bucks and Montgomery, county competition came
with local competition in key districts, and it occurred together with
faster growth and social change than in Delaware.

Local electoral competition is less a matter of general issues than of
specific measures and pursuit of perquisites. Factions emerging in one-
party areas sometimes focus on broad issues, perhaps reflecting the life
styles of upper-middle-class residents of those areas. Party competition
rarely occurs over basic developmental alternatives or community goals,
but it sometimes seems to improve the honesty or responsiveness of
government. (In more homogeneous communities government is usually
responsive anyway.) The most bitter and often immobilizing competition occurs when party and factional rivalries are combined. This
happens when rapid growth (and consequent factionalism) are mixed
with cultural diversity or a blue-collar population to produce a substantial Democratic vote. From these observations it appears that the
subjects of political competition in small communities basically depend
on the social conditions that produce competition in the first place.[4]

Does competition make a difference in the kinds of people who are
elected to office, that is, in the social representativeness of local government? There is little evidence that it does. Instead, officeholders tend
to represent the numerically preponderant elements of the population
in all communities, in terms of education and occupation as well as
ethnic and religious minorities, where these are important. In the high-
social-rank townships local offices are largely occupied by professional
and managerial people, including some of extremely high standing both
economically and socially. In the middle-ranking townships officeholders come almost entirely from white-collar callings, but these cover
a wider range than in the high-ranked municipalities. Finally, in the
low-social-rank communities *skilled* blue-collar occupations are almost
as well represented in office as are white-collar, but there does seem to
be a tendency for their representation to vary with the degree of party

* Technically, party competition seems most likely where the central tendency
of social rank is low *or* where it is quite high and the dispersion is large. In the
Philadelphia suburbs there are no low-social-rank, homogeneous jurisdictions that
are as solidly Democratic as the high-social-rank units are Republican.

competition, except in the lowest ranked communities, where they are normally in the majority in any event. In general, the working class (especially the unskilled) are somewhat underrepresented numerically in low-social rank jurisdictions and more so in those of middle rank. Local merchants are the white-collar element that is usually most prominent in the politics of such communities. Party affiliation is not systematically related to the cultural or occupational backgrounds of officeholders. In the middle- and, especially, low-social-rank communities, however, local officials are likely to hold low-level white-collar state or county jobs, when they belong to the right party. Strong political organization seems as likely to produce some local officeholders below the prestigious community's social norm (cf. Radnor) as to favor white-collar politicians in blue-collar communities. Both primary and inter-party competition evidently have some effect on the social composition of local government, but the effect is marginal. More important is the tendency of party politics to attract participants to whom nonpartisan, policy-oriented, civic endeavor is not attractive; this is a fact of social relevance discussed in the next chapter.

The social and growth determinants of political competition do mean that normally competition is least organized in communities of the highest average income and status. Large communities of this type contain substantial low-income minorities. Thus the possibility of discrimination in policy should be considered. No systematic study of this subject has been made. Tax rates (not per capita revenues) tend to be lower in affluent communities, but assessment ratios are frequently higher on low-priced homes; and these two factors may roughly balance out. Most local public functions are relatively uniform and nonredistributive. There are certainly instances of failure to provide adequate services, such as paving or lighting, police or fire protection in some low-income areas, but these do not appear to be general or systematic. School policy offers a better illustration in the shortage of vocational education in rich districts, although some of the low-income residents of those districts would benefit from it (as might wealthier adolescents, whose families, however, can afford to send them to college). In most well-to-do communities the social, or low-income, minority is a relatively small one; if it is sensitive to such issues, it is also probably distinctive. In such circumstances it is not clear that electoral competition would significantly alter policy in the minority's interest. In general, municipal options in development and expenditure policies probably leave less room for discrimination within than among municipalities, and it appears that neglect of low-income groups or social discrimination in policy is at least as serious in communities of lower rank with more electoral competition. Social or cultural bias in policy may seem especially invidious *within* communities, but this study provides no evidence on this point because small minorities were not adequately sampled in its survey of attitudes toward local government.

There remains the question of whether narrow, private power structures dominate the municipalities. In most, the answer seems to be a nearly categorical "No." Electoral competition (explicit or implicit) and partisan attitudes are too strong: neither community leaders nor random samples from interviews perceive any power structure other than party leadership and the possibility that builders exert control in development policy. (They are often not residents of the community.) Local businessmen—the township Main Streets—are not considered influential except in Upper Merion, where the businessmen (including realtors) have become factional political leaders, or in some older boroughs, where they are highly influential and commonly hold office. As individuals, local politicians and officeholders often have positions of natural business advantage or even positions that constitute a conflict of interest, but they are not cohesive elites. For the most part, the balance of sanctions seems to favor politicians over local businessmen, and the financial and developmental groups most interested in municipal policy are not usually local. As with socioeconomic discrimination, private power seems most likely to be exerted *across* municipal lines by utilities and developers.

If there is a group, organization, or individual that "runs things," respondents most likely to be informed think it is political leaders or governmental officials (often they are the same). When asked about specific subjects, civic associations are also perceived as influential in decisions about education and services; civic associations *and* builders are often thought to figure in development policy. These perceptions differ somewhat by community among the six large townships where community leaders were interviewed extensively.* Only in Cheltenham and Lower Merion is there a suggestion that a socioeconomic elite may wield especial influence: in Lower Merion several members of the possible elite are township commissioners and others are important Republican party contributors, but those informants (a small minority) who think the elite exists add that it disagrees on specific policy issues. In Cheltenham the possibility is suggested that the few businessmen, party contributors, and commissioners who are close to the Republican leader constitute a ruling elite of sorts. As in Lower Merion, most of their business or professional work is outside the municipality, and they are not thought to be promoting personal business interests.

Only in Lower Merion do histories of major issues over the last decade

---

* Cheltenham, Lower Merion, Marple, Middletown (Del.), Springfield, Upper Merion. Several interview questions were relevant: whether any special person, group, or organization was especially important or influential in decisions in various areas of policy; which three groups or interests (from a list) were most important or influential in getting things done; whether private organizations and individuals, elected officials, appointed officials, or political leaders and parties had most influence on local policies and actions in each of a list of functions and fields of policy; plus other questions on the representativeness and responsiveness of local government (including school boards).

(as compared with community leaders' opinions) indicate an elite capable of employing social and economic sanctions to win against organized opposition. This has evidently happened at least three times in the last decade over development proposals that threatened the character of Lower Merion's estate areas. In each case a large but identifiable group was able to swing several civic associations and township commissioners into line (in one case the party organization itself opposed the position of a majority of the commissioners), and there was common testimony in interviews that social and business sanctions as well as party finance were used.* Similar issues in Cheltenham did not give rise to similar alignments; the elite hypothesis seems less plausible there, where cultural divisions are sharper. In both communities, despite rising taxes in the 1950's, there was no clear civic cleavage over expenditures.

Does local politics contribute to the good life? In part, this depends on its administrative effects, discussed in a later chapter. Anticipating, these may be rated indifferent to negative, except for occasional checks on corruption. Political competition and administrative capacity tend to vary inversely in municipalities because of their inverse relations both to social differences and fiscal capacity. There are, however, instances above of innovation and redirection of policy through political competition.

The following tentative generalizations emerge from this study of political structure. (1) Of the forms of local electoral competition, *party* competition least often focuses on specific issues. Among more general concerns it deals most successfully with governmental *methods*, less so with expenditure levels, and least well with development policy. (2) One reason for this seems to lie in the relation of party competition to community social rank. Lower-social-rank communities are most likely to exhibit party cleavage but least apt to be interested in broad development policy. In those communities the tax issue, though salient, is intractable, but either corruption or mistrust of officials is most common. (3) Factional competition sometimes directs more attention to policy issues than does party competition; this occurs when factions are formed for this purpose, as they sometimes are, in upper-middle-class places. (4) Electoral competition seems least effective in dealing with issues under conditions of extremely rapid growth and social change, or in situations where professional management, to define and follow through on issues, is lacking. (5) What has earlier been termed *implicit* competition is significant; most local governments are highly

---

* The issues were school construction in an elite area, apartment zoning in the township, a redevelopment project (with federal funds) to create an open park along the Schuylkill. The last project was also opposed by liberals since it would displace some low-income residents. Negroes and lower-income groups in Ardmore did not appear to be effectively represented in township and county discussion of a current major urban renewal there.

responsive (some critics think too much so) unless trapped between conflicting demands. (6) Electoral competition is probably better at inducing response to social interests—such as neighborhoods, cultures, or new residential groups—than to either abstract or specific issues. (7) One reason for this seems to be that such general policies as expenditure levels or development patterns are hard to debate effectively in the abstract, while the concrete actions of which they are composed have limited salience or narrow effects considered singly. (8) Direct civic action, backed by implicit electoral competition, is most likely to focus on concrete policies because civic associations are typically based in neighborhoods where the effects of governmental actions—especially developmental actions—are most visible. (9) As would probably be expected, voter participation increases with the closeness of local elections, ranging from 65 to 80 percent of that in national presidential contests. It also tends to be high in those small boroughs with strong political organizations. Voter turnout does *not* vary systematically with either the size or social rank of the municipalities studied here, admittedly a small sample. (10) There is no evidence that electoral competition has any effect on the generality or intensity of the civic participation discussed in the next chapter.

In the foregoing discussion the effects of electoral organization were judged in terms of intangibles. Governmental performance was not categorized or statistically linked to political structure. The same statement holds for relations between political and social structure. The analysis was qualitative, and its conclusions refer to tendencies, not necessities. Local political structure and governmental performance are not entirely derived from a few social forces, and significant departures from tendency can sometimes be traced to individuals. The same points apply to the following discussion of civic participation.

22

Participation

Widespread participation in local affairs might, hypothetically, occur under conditions of either electoral competition or communalism. If, however, the communal mode of policy-making implies a homogeneous citizenry, then the question arises whether many suburban municipalities qualify. And while widespread, direct participation without either electoral competition or social homogeneity is conceivable, it seems unlikely to occur. Thus a review of the extent of diversity of interests—especially in the larger townships—seems advisable before turning to the study of participation.

Two divisions of interest are common in township politics: social, involving rank and wealth, differing tastes and tax capacities; and sectional, having to do with tax-expenditure ratios and land-use or locational decisions. Often these vertical and horizontal divisions overlap, as in conflicts between old and new residents, and these differences are usually sharpest in rapidly developing jurisdictions, where they include the burden of support and the level of service in education, recreation, and utilities. An example is Middletown (Bucks), where the large Levittown development in the south aroused resistance from old residents in the north to heavy expenditures on education and recreation for the new, young families—though highway expenditures were said to be heavier in the north, where the roads were older. Township records do not reveal the actual sectional balance of expenditures.

The social homogeneity of suburbs was discussed in Chapter 3. There it was noted, that, at least in terms of census data, variation from community modes or norms is sometimes considerable. Similarly, some municipalities exhibit sectional differences. Among Delaware County's large townships, moving from north to south, Radnor consists of several distinct communities with separate identities and dates of settlement; Marple is less variant in these respects; Springfield still less so; while

265

Ridley contains the most numerous and distinct communities. These characteristics are acknowledged by many residents when they are asked about community differences. Thus Radnor's broad income-range is recognized in Table 22:1, as are Springfield's exceptional homogeneity and the sectionalism of Middletown (Bucks). Citizens of Middletown, Bristol, and Marple are most conscious of the cleavage between old and new residents that is evidently the result (at least temporary) of their rapid growth. In interviews community *leaders* were still more likely to perceive such divisions.

TABLE 22:1

Perceptions of Community Diversity

1. "Do you think of _____ Township as being made up of different neighborhoods or regions—or is it all pretty much the same?"

	Different	Same	No Opinion
Radnor	57.7	42.2	0.0
Marple	52.0	44.0	2.0
Springfield	41.1	58.8	0.0
Ridley	60.0	40.0	0.0
Bristol	58.0	40.0	2.0
Middletown	81.0	16.2	2.7

2. "Are there other important differences or variations within _____ Township, such as social or economic differences in the population?" Interviewers were instructed to probe respecting income or wealth, old versus new residents.

	None or No Opinion	Income or Wealth	Old-New	Both 2 and 3	Other (including Religion Nationality)
Radnor	26.6	53.3	6.6	8.8	4.4
Marple	42.0	26.0	18.0	6.0	8.0
Springfield	58.8	15.6	13.7	7.8	3.9
Ridley	62.2	13.3	13.3	8.8	2.2
Bristol	48.0	24.0	26.0	2.0	0.0
Middletown	43.2	18.9	29.7	8.0	0.0

The communal approach to policy-making would seem to have least to offer under conditions of social and sectional diversity, though it did appear above that electoral competition often responds to such diversity and at least indirectly reflects it in governmental policy and performance. According to the survey, neither social, sectional, nor proprietary differences (including length of residence of the community) affect the extent of participation, either in voting or in civic associations.

1. *Patterns of participation.* Civic participation can be variously defined. In the small jurisdiction an individual expression of views may

alter public policy, and public opinion may be formed or take effect through organizations devoted to normally private ends. That is one common justification of the small jurisdiction: that it affords a level on which public and private, government and individual, politics and society are closely linked. Thus, civic participation is sometimes extremely informal. In this study, however, more overt participation is emphasized, if only because it is more observable. The focus is on organized activity and individual membership of organizations, especially those most directly concerned with public policy, but the effects of more subtle factors such as people's satisfaction and identification with the community are also explored.

Participation in local associations has been much studied by sociologists. It is well established that membership and leadership vary with income and, especially, education, though the latter variables probably function more like thresholds than like escalators. Moreover, when such life chances are controlled in sample surveys, there is some evidence that people of similar life styles tend to cluster together in neighborhoods, and that some neighborhoods have richer civic participation than others of like wealth, culture, or status. It is less well established that civic participation is richer in the suburbs than in the central cities of large metropolitan areas, other things being equal, but this seems to be the tendency.[1] In general we know most about the demographic factors in local participation, somewhat less about the personal needs participation serves, and least of all about its effects on policy, political systems, and individuals.

The present inquiry is focused on how participation relates to community size and social rank. It rests on interviews with community leaders, both civic and political, on the sample survey of six townships, and on a second survey undertaken in two large townships and two small boroughs specifically to compare community size and social rank as factors in participation.*

A logical place to begin the inquiry is with the states of citizen interest in local affairs, information about local affairs, and access to local officialdom that obtain in suburban communities. These conditions may be regarded as forms of participation in themselves and as bases for further participation. Scattered survey data from other metropolitan areas indicate that residents have relatively little interest in local affairs, and less interest in local than in national affairs.[2] The present study tends to qualify these findings. In no community surveyed did a majority declare a greater interest in national than in local affairs, nor were there consistent differences among communities in this respect,

---

* The two townships were Radnor and Ridley, which were also included in the first survey. (Thus, the second survey served in some part as a check on the first, since several identical questions were asked in both.) The boroughs were Swarthmore and Glenolden. The social and demographic characteristics of these four municipalities appear in Tables 21:1 and 21:2 (p. 250 and p. 251).

although individuals of higher social rank were most inclined to favor national over local affairs. In the second survey respondents were asked how closely they followed the activities of their local governments (closely, occasionally, seldom, or never), and attention was found to vary inversely with size of community, especially in the two municipalities of lower social rank. When people were asked about the principal problems or issues in their community and, later, about the sufficiency of their information for making decisions about local issues and elections, there were no significant differences among three communities. However, residents of the community that was both small in area and high in social rank were far better informed (though it is clearly an exceptional, intellectual community). In each township more than half of the respondents said they had access to sufficient information about local affairs (though standards of sufficiency must be diverse), and more than half named local issues or problems that they thought important. Municipal size and social rank together affect people's interest and information regarding local government, but in none of the communities studied do these seem to be either alarmingly low or surprisingly high.

Local newspapers are important sources of information. In the survey of six large townships heavy majorities in the high-social-rank jurisdictions said they regularly read a weekly community paper, and most of those who did felt it was informative. The lower-social-rank communities are less well served by weeklies, perhaps because they are closer to the urban centers served by daily papers, but most survey respondents in these communities reported reading local news frequently.

For most residents the printed page is the principal source of local information; yet many know one or more local officials, however casual the acquaintance. Table 22:2 presents some measures of direct access to municipal and school authorities. In the second survey the same questions were asked about *both* officials and political leaders, which resulted in even higher proportions (substantial majorities, in each community) who knew someone in a representative position and more people who had conversation or contact with officials and politicians about local affairs—especially in the smaller communities, as would probably be expected. Direct and even informal access to local government seems readily available, though it is somewhat related to size of jurisdiction.

Table 23:3 provides data on rates of participation in such local groups as civic associations, PTA's, and charitable organizations.* The rate varies little among communities, though the lower survey response rates

---

* Respondents were handed a list of types of organizations from which they picked the types to which they belonged and then specified their degree of activity in them, if any. The organizations dealt with in Table 22:1 are local (confined to the municipality) and are neither professional, religious, nor social; they have to do with public policy, except for charitable organizations (of which there are few at the municipal level).

TABLE 22:2
*Access to Local Government Through Either Elected
or Appointed Officials*

PERCENT OF RESPONDENTS WHO:

	Know personally one or more local officials	*Frequently discuss local affairs with officials*	*Occasionally discuss local affairs with officials*	*Never discuss local affairs with officials*	*Have contacted an official on some occasion*
Radnor	40.0	6.6	15.5	37.7	40.0
Marple	40.0	2.0	12.0	46.0	40.0
Springfield	37.2	3.9	11.7	47.0	39.2
Ridley	37.7	2.2	6.6	53.3	51.1
Bristol	20.0	0.0	20.0	60.0	28.0
Middletown	37.8	2.7	13.5	45.9	40.5
Swarthmore	72	—	40	60	68
Glenolden	70	—	44	56	62

in the lower-social-rank communities probably mean that their participation rates are overstated in this table. Membership is not significantly
related to length of residence, nor does it vary with place of employment
except for the tendency of the *most* active participants to work in the
same county instead of commuting. Nevertheless, these more active
members are (on their own testimony) as apt to be regional as local
in their orientations and they are more concerned about both the region
and their municipality, less concerned with the county and their im-

TABLE 22:3
Participation in Local Civic Organizations[1]

Percent who:	Radnor	Marple	Spring-field	Ridley	Bristol	Middle-town
Belong to one or more	26.6	18.0	25.4	33.3	16.0	32.4
Say they are active or an officer in one or more[2]	22.0	30.0	13.6	8.8	22.0	13.5
Total of first two rows	48.6	48.0	39.0	42.1	38.0	45.9
Say they belong to no organization at all, local or national	2.2	16.0	13.7	15.5	24.0	21.6

[1] The organizations include neighborhood improvement or civic associations,
charitable and welfare organizations, parent-teacher associations or other school
groups.
[2] Does not include respondents in the first row.

mediate neighborhood, than are those who belong to no local civic organization at all.*

In all six communities civic memberships—and, especially, active memberships—varied with residents' age, reaching a peak in the forties. People under thirty and over sixty are seldom involved. Since middle age dominates in civic endeavor it seems unlikely that the most specialized community in terms of age levels—the young and the old—will be hotbeds of voluntary action.

The socioeconomic factor most closely associated with extent of civic participation is education, and this holds in all the communities surveyed. Occupation is somewhat less closely related to activity, and income shows no independent effect in most municipalities. In all these relations of individual social rank to civic endeavor the social rank of the *community* makes no difference; respondents at relatively low educational levels were no more likely to participate in low-social-rank than in high-social-rank communities, nor were the effects of other socioeconomic factors altered by the local setting.

The foregoing findings have to do with avowedly civic activities, including those oriented to the public schools, but not with other organized interests that may affect local politics or policy. When membership of other local organizations—service, fraternal, social, recreational, religious—is in question neither individual nor community social rank matters as much for the extent or patterns of activity revealed in the survey. But observation indicates that formally civic associations are least persistent and pervasive in lower-social-rank communities, while voluntary fire departments and recreational associations are more prominent in them, together with nationality and fraternal groups. The less steady, widespread civic activity in the blue-collar communities no doubt leaves the field of policy more completely to party politics, and other kinds of local organization—e.g., volunteer fire departments—often function as political clubs. In those predominantly blue-collar boroughs that are also old commercial centers, local businessmens' associations are sometimes political nuclei as well as watchdogs over government.[3]

It thus appears that middle-class civic associations, concentrating on policy, bear a different relation to electoral politics than do other, less policy-oriented local organizations. Politicians have more civic interest to contend with in the higher-social-rank municipalities; patronage and favoritism are somewhat less influential in those communities, and civic activity is more independent of politics.

---

* For the distribution of these orientations by community, see Table 3:1 p. 30. In the second survey people were asked to react to the statement: "The most rewarding organizations one can belong to are those that are basically concerned with local affairs rather than those whose interests are beyond the local community." Active local participants were no more apt to agree with this statement than were less-participative residents.

Civic and political activity are often unrelated. People are less likely to pursue both than they are one alone, or so the survey data indicate. Some 30 percent of the total sample had been active in local election campaigns, civic associations, or both, but three-quarters of these were active in only one of the two areas. The social rank of respondents or communities was not related to extent or kind of specialization, although it was, of course, to the extent of activity in general. Since local civic and political activity are both more intense in the more highly educated, professionalized communities, this should tend to make their governments more responsive in policy even though they are less electorally competitive than most communities of lower social rank. Again, organization politics seems dominant in the low-social-rank municipalities, where civic participation is less common and less policy oriented; though the relatively organized nature of Pennsylvania local politics probably accounts for some of the specialization of public activity in all communities—perhaps especially in Delaware County, where the bulk of the sample was taken.[4]

TABLE 22:4

Political Participation

(PERCENT WHO HAVE WORKED ACTIVELY IN A
POLITICAL CAMPAIGN WITHIN PAST FIVE YEARS)

	Radnor	Marple	Spring-field	Ridley	Bristol	Middle-town
No activity	46.6	68.0	78.4	82.2	66.0	75.6
Local only	13.3	10.0	7.8	6.6	28.0	10.8
State and national	17.7	10.0	1.9	2.2	2.0	5.4
Both	22.2	12.0	11.7	11.7	8.8	8.1

Finally, there is the question of effects of community size on organized participation. The second survey disclosed no significant differences in the distribution of organizational membership between large and small jurisdictions with social rank controlled. It did, however, turn up one suggestion about extent of activity: in three of the four communities about 70 percent of local organization members claimed to be active, regularly attending members of at least one group, but in the large municipality of low social rank only 50 percent made this claim. Statistically, this difference is one of the more significant ones in the survey. The consistency of self-attributions in three communities, and the fact that most associations exist within municipal boundaries, provide some support for the view that small jurisdictions facilitate participation for residents of lower social rank. Though tentative, this evidence fits with testimony about interest, information, and access reviewed above, and thus merits consideration, though certainly not implicit acceptance.

2. *Citizens' perceptions of municipal government.* Most suburban residents feel that their local governments are broadly accountable and

responsive. Some do not, however; and both community size and social rank seem to influence their opinions. Residents of the six townships were asked four questions about governmental representativeness, which are set out in Table 22:5. Majorities in all six municipalities say that their government is generally representative rather than that it

TABLE 22:5

Percent of Respondents Who See Local Government as
Open, Representative, and Responsive

Question:

1. "Some people think that local governments are sometimes a bit unrepresentative—that is, that they tend to favor some groups of people or one group over others. Do you think that is true in _____ Township?

2. "Some people think that, no matter who is elected to the local government, there is a rather small group of people in the community who are still able to influence or actually make most of the important decisions or policies. Do you think that is true in _____ Township?

3. "In your judgment, are important community issues here usually settled quietly without the public knowing what they are, or are they usually brought out into the open?

4. "In general, if a group of people want something done in this community, is the local government likely to do it?

5. "Suppose a group of people object to something the local government is doing or proposed to do—is the local government likely to change what it is doing or stop what it is doing?"

			QUESTION 3.		
Percent with "favorable" perception[1]	1. *No*	2. *No*	*Brought into Open*	4. *Yes*	5. *Yes*
Radnor	55.5	28.8	53.3	60.0	51.1
Marple	46.0	32.0	76.0	64.0	52.0
Springfield	64.7	49.0	68.6	80.3	60.7
Ridley	42.2	33.3	55.5	73.3	46.6
Bristol	56.0	48.0	62.0	40.0	30.0
Middletown	48.6	40.5	59.4	54.0	37.8

[1] Does not include "Don't know" or "No opinion" answers.

favors certain groups, and most of those who believe that a particular interest is favored identify it as the political party or its leadership. Two questions were asked about private, minority influence on policy: whether public decisions were normally closed or open, and whether a small group tended to determine them. In most townships small majorities thought a small group made policy and overwhelmingly identified it as the local party leadership, and the higher an individual respondent's income, occupation, or education the more likely he was to acknowledge the role of a small group in policy-making. Many respondends added, however, that they saw nothing sinister about this, or that active minorities are to be expected. Majorities of those who believed that a small group made policy also thought that local decisions were public and that local government was representative, but they were somewhat less likely to endorse the openness and representativeness of local government than were those who did not preceive a local elite. Finally, most residents believe that their local governments are responsive to civic pressure for action, and the lowest sense of governmental responsiveness occurs in the two communities with the sharpest sectional divisions and party competition.

TABLE 22:6

Satisfaction with Local Governmental Action

PERCENT WHO SAY THAT
LOCAL GOVERNMENT IS DOING:

Township	Too Little	Too Much	Right Amount	Don't Know
Radnor	17.7	4.4	73.3	4.4
Marple	36.0	0.0	56.0	8.0
Springfield	7.8	2.0	86.2	4.0
Ridley	24.4	2.2	64.4	8.8
Bristol	46.0	0.0	50.0	4.0
Middletown	35.1	2.7	45.9	16.2

Thus, most residents evidently find their municipal stewards sufficiently representative and responsive. Negative evaluations vary with several factors. The differences resulting from cross-tabulations within municipalities are usually too small for statistical significance because the samples are too small. They do suggest, however, that confidence in local democracy varies with civic morale and satisfaction—i.e., with reluctance to move from the community and with approval of township management.* These sentiments are, in turn, most evident in the wealthier, more prestigious municipalities, and in those whose growth is relatively slow. These are typically communities without much electoral competition but with relatively widespread civic participation. There is most criticism of governmental performance, both politically and administratively, in municipalities of rapid growth and lower social rank.†

*Respondents were asked whether they would be sorry to move from their township if they moved to a similar home in a place just as convenient to work; whether there were any local public services that they considered inadequate; and whether their local government was currently doing less than it should, enough, or too much. The generalizations above depend on responses to these questions.

† It should be clear that the statements above describe responses in terms of the communities in which they occur, not in terms of characteristics of the individual respondents. It is *not* the case, for instance, that individuals of low social rank living in high-social-rank communities are especially inclined to think their governments unrepresentative, nor are high-social-rank respondents more critical in low-social-rank communities. Overall, the tendency to be unhappy with one's local government on democratic grounds increases with respondents' social rank (that is, with education, occupation, and income separately considered). Thus, the sense of representativeness seems to derive from community, not individual, characteristics primarily.

Democratic evaluations of local government are associated with municipal size as well as with the social rank of individuals and communities. In the second survey, with community social rank controlled, residents of the two boroughs more commonly considered their governments representative and less frequently thought them ruled by small groups than did residents of the townships. The effect of size is less substantial, however, than that of social rank (and especially of educational level). Only the difference of opinion about small-group dominance of policy was statistically significant (that about general representativeness was not); and, since the group usually identified is the political party, which is more organized and visible in the townships, the perceptions are probably accurate. Perhaps they do not lead to significantly different evaluations of municipal democracy because other aspects of morale and satisfaction do not vary with size of jurisdiction.

TABLE 22:7

Mistrust of Local Governmental Action

PERCENT OF AGREEMENT WITH STATEMENT THAT FAIR
TREATMENT DEPENDS ON PERSONAL ACQUAINTANCE

	Strongly Agree	*Inclined to Agree*	*No Opinion*	*Inclined to Disagree*	*Strongly Disagree*
Radnor	4.4	20.0	17.7	44.4	13.3
Marple	16.0	38.0	10.0	26.0	10.0
Springfield	13.7	17.6	7.8	35.2	25.4
Ridley	33.3	22.2	13.3	20.0	11.1
Bristol	14.0	50.0	18.0	10.0	8.0
Middletown	18.9	27.0	27.0	27.0	0.0

In a battery of general-attitude questions residents were also asked to react to the statement that: "With local governments around here, if you want to get fair treatment you should know someone in government or politics." Their reactions appear in Table 22:7. There are significant differences among communities, varying with social rank and growth rates and with recent political history. There was a slight tendency, within each municipality, for respondents of higher social rank to express more confidence in official impartiality, but the differences among communities were more significant than those among individuals within them—cf. Marple and Springfield, Bristol and Ridley. Indeed, the intermunicipal differences are among the most significant in this study. They indicate that *both* social rank and local experience, which are themselves in some degree related, affect people's trust in government's treatment of them as individuals, and this would seem to be a critical aspect of local government.

Most respondents, however, were confident of their ability to influence local governmental action, as Table 22:8 shows. In this respect it is individual, not community, differences that count. A low sense of

TABLE 22:8
Civic Self-Confidence

Percent who agree:	Radnor	Marple	Spring-field	Ridley	Bristol	Middle-town
1. "People like me can't really hope to have any effect on what local government does.	2.2	12.0	7.8	17.7	18.0	10.8
2. "Although it takes time and energy, to make your views count in local government, it's possible for me to have some effect if I work at it.	86.6	74.0	84.3	64.4	74.0	86.4
3. "I feel I can easily affect the actions of local government if I try to."	11.1	12.0	5.8	17.7	8.0	2.7

civic efficacy is overwhelmingly associated with low education. In the second survey, however, with education a controlled variable, there was significantly less sense of inefficacy in the smaller of the two low-social-rank municipalities. Putting the last two tables together, it appears that most residents think they can reach local government at least on policy (though one should allow for the low response rate among those probably least confident), but that many (a majority of those surveyed) are uncertain of its impartial administration, at least unless they can reach it for their private ends. One may interpret these two attitudes as either optimistic or cynical. The evidence gathered in this study suggests that together they reflect reality as it has varied with the social composition and the political history of communities, but they also condition reality to some extent, insofar as politicians respond to expectations.

3. *The effects of participation.* Some of these findings about participation and satisfaction confirm common knowledge: that direct access to most local governments is easy; that residents generally feel they can affect local policy; that civic organization is a matter of active minorities, although the minorities are sometimes substantial; that some kinds of participation vary inversely with size of jurisdiction; and that all of these characteristics are affected by social attributes of both individuals and communities. A few of the findings, in combination, are either more surprising or more significant.

First, the functions of participation, for both individuals and political systems, evidently vary with social rank, perhaps especially in the large municipalities. The findings of this chapter afford some support for the common hypothesis of different class political cultures.[5] It draws a broad distinction between middle-class and working-class cultures, suggesting narrower variations within each that reflect educational, occupational, and residential circumstances, especially the first two. In local participation the principal difference appears to be that people of higher rank assert broader values or interests in civic action; their voluntary associations are more policy-oriented, less ad hoc, more purposive, less purely gregarious or utilitarian than those in blue-collar communities—perhaps because there are fewer private amenities to protect in the latter communities and less fiscal capacity for public action.[6] The same kinds of class differences have frequently been remarked in electoral politics and were evident in the preceding chapter. In this way, participation functions differently according to social rank for both individuals and political systems. In the latter, it seems to serve more effectively as a check on electoral politics in the middle-class setting (especially the upper-middle-class setting), and more nearly as an auxiliary of political organization in the working-class context. In terms of organization theory this says that working-class participation provides politicians with somewhat more in the way of sanctions and incentives; the policy focus of middle-class involvement provides an independent civic sanction.

Second, recognition and acceptance of small group or party "rule" are more general among middle and, especially, upper-middle-class residents. Quotation marks quality *rule* because respondents who acknowledge this are also apt to be confident of the responsiveness of local government to civic and electoral pressure. They are evidently most sophisticated in the use of this pressure and least suspicious of official favoritism. In general, people who feel this way are most likely to be found in the least competitive but most professionally managed communities. Most respondents, however, seem to think of municipal policy-making more in terms of political leadership and electoral control than in a town-meeting or voluntary-action framework. The communal model does not appear to be in most residents' minds.

Third, there is the question of whether civic participation contributes to higher morale or satisfaction, whether participation demonstrably affects individuals and communities in ways that it is often claimed to. Evidently this question cannot be answered in general; much depends on the social composition of the community, which affects attitudes toward government and ends of participation independently. Several elements—participation, satisfaction, homogeneity, and social rank—figure in constellations. For instance, Springfield Township exhibits exceptional homogeneity and its residents express exceptional satisfaction with governmental policy and process, yet there is no more widespread civic or political participation in Springfield than in other communities; in fact there is probably somewhat less (within the limits of sampling accuracy). Satisfaction there seems a function of homogeneity, high social rank, and—perhaps—a stable growth rate. In Marple, civic and political activity are more general and intense, but satisfaction with policy and process is less than in Springfield. These are the most striking contrasts between communities. As for individuals, those in the total sample who belong to civic associations are somewhat less likely than others to perceive their local governments as unrepresentative, and this is especially so in the case of the most active, but the differences between participants and nonparticipants are not substantial. Civic and political participants are only a little more reluctant to move from their communities than are nonparticipants, though the difference increases with degree of activity, but social rank is far more controlling of attitude on this point than is participation. These are the only indicators of satisfaction or morale for which participation makes much difference, and even here the differences are not large. Participants' views of their community vary with its social and economic *and* with its political circumstances.

Finally, there are the relations of municipal size and social rank. Of the two influences on participation the latter is probably dominant. Still, one finding, though tentative, is suggestive. This is that the small jurisdiction most facilitates participation in regions of lower social rank. This finding entails a paradox, however, because, as the next chapter indicates, the small, low-income municipalities commonly have the greatest administrative disadvantages and the narrowest options in policy, especially at low social rank. It may be, therefore, that participation is least significant for local government in the regions where it has most to contribute to political socialization.

In the preceding chapter it appeared that local electoral competition does not commonly focus on broad policy issues, although it often deals with specifics and reflects social differences. Many critics of the small jurisdiction maintain that civic participation is also irrelevant to most specific issues. Thus Robert Wood has argued that, as governmental complexity, professionalism, and centralization increase, civic action is unlikely to be informed or effective with respect to most local services, facilities, and controls.[7] He therefore rejects the town-meeting conception of local government—a conception that is not prevalent in the Philadelphia suburbs, however, where civic action takes the form of pressure on politicians.

The question, then, is whether small elective jurisdiction makes sense in terms of their facilitation of effective participation on one hand and, perhaps, frustration of effective administration on the other. It is not clear from the present study that participation is generally more intense or effective in small jurisdictions, that these contribute relevantly to political socialization, or that on balance they tend to protect individual choice and social autonomy or to spread participation more than they reinforce invidious social distinctions and economic advantages. I hope the discussion has opened up these issues, though certainly it has not settled them. Some implications for policy will nevertheless be suggested in the concluding chapters, after a review of municipal administration.

23

Administration

Standards of governmental adequacy are no more self-evident than those of political democracy. Nor, realistically speaking, are the two sets of standards entirely distinct. This chapter, however, is organized around a few discrete concerns: the relations between politics and administration; the problem of corruption; and local capacity for planning, deciding, financing, and managing.

1. *Politics and administration* are closely interwoven in local governments. In most of the suburbs patronage outweighs professionalism, but neither is significant in policy. Most local patronage consists of blue-collar positions in the highway and police departments. Manual labor positions afford some party or factional influence in low-income districts, but control of the local police is more important because of the constabulary's functions in public relations and enforcement of minor sanctions. Policemen are formally protected from dismissal by civil service, but the law also provides for their direction and promotion by elected officials and thus allows their political use.*

A more difficult balance between politics and administration is to be found in the role of township managers in the region. Local managers potentially dispose important development privileges and determine expenditures and amenities. Traditionally, the manager plan is supposed

* In second-class townships the only safeguard is a public hearing on dismissal. In first-class townships a three-member civil service commission with six-year staggered terms must be appointed if there are more than three policemen. Competitive examinations are required for appointment (under the "rule of three") and promotion; the tests are administered by the civil service commission, whose rules, however, must be approved by the township commissioners. The latter also appoint the chief of police (with civil service commission approval) and determine salaries. The same first-class township provisions apply to firemen, but most townships have volunteer fire departments.

to distinguish policy from administration, professionalize the latter, and connect the two at arm's length. The ideal has been approximated in Lower Merion and Middletown (Bucks), but not in the other municipalities studied here. In Upper Merion a single manager lasted for six years, including a change of party control, before leaving under fire from factions in both parties and from civic leaders who found him aloof and "hard to work with." In Radnor, Marple, Aston, and Bristol the manager's power to hire and fire employees and his nonpolitical status broke down in other ways. In Cheltenham the manager was the local political leader. The plan has succeeded only in relatively high social-rank communities, and not in all of them.

Two factors have evidently strained the manager plan in suburban communities. One is politics and the quest for control of patronage and permits. The other is policy and the fact that, especially in fast-growing townships, most tax and land-use decisions are more legislative than administrative in effect. Thus managers have found their sphere hard to define and defend and, as the literature has it, the line between politics (policy) and administration tends to disappear.

De facto, the municipalities display a broad spectrum of political-administrative devices. Springfield's township secretary is roughly equivalent to Marple's politically domesticated manager, and in both communities—as in most—the elected officials or political leaders decide particulars of development and expenditure. In some communities they decide almost everything. On the other hand, there are a few borough clerks or secretaries who dominate their local councils in varying degree by virtue of seniority, experience, respect, and the common belief that no policy issues exist.

2. *Personal gain and corruption.* The writer has no certain knowledge of corruption in the municipalities under review, except for three cases proved in court during the last decade.* The incidence of official dishonesty is unknown, though in some communities permits and zoning variances are widely thought to be sold at least occasionally, and the interviewing for this study produced some first-hand testimony to it. Concern about improbity is widespread among civic and political leadership: among nine possible goals of municipal action, prevention of corruption ranked first or second in priority in all nine communities where leaders were interviewed, except for Lower Merion, where it ranked third. (The question that was asked is noted on p. 283.) This concern parallels the one with favoritism displayed by rank and file residents (Table 22:7), though its relation to community social rank is less pronounced. Many local regulations affect individuals singly, not collectively, in the first instance. The individual involved may be a resi-

* Two of these involved schools: one, the sale of promotions by school-board members; the other, embezzlement by a school superintendent. A different selection of communities, aimed at this issue, could have produced more examples.

dent or a developer; in either case, political ends may be served with discretion. Personal or political financing from regulatory or development policy are both more feasible and more consequential for the community than they are in expenditure policy (e.g., contracting); development especially vests local officials with disposal of valuable privileges and remote consequences.

In suburban municipalities the question seems to be whether the closeness and directness of electoral controls outweigh the absence of formal administrative hierarchy and procedure as a check on malversation; electoral pressure is often effective where neighborhood values are palpably threatened but not, typically, against administrative nibbling at ordinances. To be sure, big-city legislators and administrators can be reached, and Philadelphia has recently provided published examples. However, small jurisdictions, though long on legislative responsiveness in policy and judicial restraints on power, are short on internal administrative safeguards. Some observers have argued to the writer that strong local solicitors, engineers, and inspectors provide internal checks on chicanery superior to external, competitive, political checks; others have remarked the danger of conniving advisors and administrators. One should note that the communities most commonly suspected of official venality have part-time engineers and inspectors and in most cases no local planning commission with even advisory review powers. There is no sure cure for corruption, but experience suggests that encouragement of political competition offers no more hope than legal safeguards, administrative professionalism, and organized civic concern.

3. *Planning and acting capacity.* To most scholars, the capacity of municipal governments for effective planning and action together is the ultimate test of municipal value, though to many residents of reasonably well-developed communities this evidently seems irrelevant. This capacity varies significantly among municipalities and is divisible into several aspects. One basic distinction is that between the *internal* capacity of municipalities and the strength and adversity of *external* factors; another is that between developmental and expenditure policy. The elements of internal capacity may be defined as fiscal, political, and administrative. The external factors include private market forces, population movements, and the public actions of other jurisdictions— neighboring municipalities, the county, and especially (in this region) the state highway department, on whose behavior industrial and commercial prospects and rezoning pressures largely turn.

Fiscal capacity was examined in the studies of the Pennsylvania Economy League and Fels Institute.[1] In the thirteen municipalities PEL surveyed (nine of which appear in the present study) it found that quantity and quality of service varied directly with fiscal resources, and it also found convincing internal evidence of the limiting effect of fiscal incapacity. The Fels study indicated that *expenditure* policy is determined by "needs, preferences, and resources" in that order—i.e., by land-use patterns (especially the extent of nonresidential development), social rank, and residential wealth. The Fels scholars also concluded that in *development* policy "choices exist only under limited circumstances," primarily in "high class residential communities" in early stages of development. Fels' priority for *needs* in expenditure policy may seem at odds with PEL's emphasis on resources, but this is only because Fels' data included *all* communities in the region. Needs, Fels discovered, tend to distinguish *types* of communities (industrial and commercial, high- and low-density residential, old towns), but among residential suburbs, such as those that PEL studied, fiscal resources were the most important variable in explaining expenditures.

Four conclusions are in order. First, there is little question that both needs and resources, as derived from patterns of development, are serious contraints on expenditure levels and patterns; this is statistically demonstrable and intrinsically probable. Second, despite the statistical demonstration, there remains a modicum of municipal free will to vary levels and patterns of expenditure according to preferences; there is room for a political process. Third, local volition is easier to exercise at higher income levels; both the Fels and the PEL study point to greater fiscal strains in lower income jurisdictions.[2] Finally, constraints tighten as development proceeds, but development never ends, and both early and late, there seems to be broader choice for communities that are large in area (so that land uses may be segregated) and high in income (able to attract and select the right developer).

Administrative capacity is hard to distinguish clearly from either fiscal or political capacity. But when one sets aside the makeup of the tax base and matters of political structure—together with fortuitous external effects—there remains the element of community size in both area and population. Population relates to internal economies, and so, in all probability, does physical size for certain municipal services.[3] Area also affects external economies, the relative ability of communities to segregate, insulate, or control the effects of surrounding land-use changes and population pressures. These questions have not been closely examined in the Philadelphia suburbs. PEL's *Adaptability* study did find that most of Delaware County's small, low-income boroughs ranked badly in market value per capita but relatively well in market value per square mile. It found heavier fiscal burdens and lower service levels in these communities than in most others, but it did not precisely measure these or directly connect them to municipal scale. In development policy it appeared that land-use controls were least effective in the small boroughs, both because controls were more primitive and (perhaps) because pressures toward high density were heaviest in these

TABLE 23:1

Fiscal Data for Selected Municipalities, 1961*

Per capita expenditures ($)	LARGE AREA (10 or more sq. mi.)			MEDIUM AREA (5 to 9.9 sq. mi.)			SMALL AREA (less than 5 sq. mi.)		
	Bristol	Lower Merion	Upper Merion	Marple	Aston	Springfield	Collingdale	Glenolden	Swarthmore
Operating expense:									
Municipal	16.04	51.80	28.59	21.49	15.29	32.22	17.22	21.75	29.66
School district	76.05	86.69	102.68	81.97	70.15	75.41	52.22	58.42	115.39
Total	92.09	138.49	131.27	103.46	85.44	107.60	69.44	80.17	145.05
Debt service:									
Municipal	1.37	4.53	8.58	3.49	1.36	3.35	.96	.86	3.01
School district	19.96	12.18	32.46	25.94	18.39	18.52	3.94	10.09	16.77
Total	21.33	16.71	41.04	29.43	19.75	21.87	4.90	10.95	19.78
Capital improvements:									
Municipal	10.04	7.05	7.64	9.71	11.81	13.86	2.45	.85	3.94
School district	.77	4.06	2.31	1.84	1.55	1.47	10.44	.14	2.58
Total	10.81	11.11	9.95	11.55	13.36	15.34	12.90	.99	6.52
Total governmental expenditures:									
Municipal	27.46	63.38	44.81	34.70	28.47	49.43	20.63	23.45	36.60
School district	96.78	102.93	137.45	109.75	90.10	95.41	66.60	68.66	134.74
Total	124.24	166.31	182.26	144.45	118.57	144.84	87.23	92.11	171.34
Per capita market value of real property	2,654	7,612	5,891	4,579	2,691	4,340	2,617	2,792	4,925
Ratio of assessed to market value	34.4	34.3	34.4	23.5	21.7	26.2	24.8	25.1	28.3

* Adapted from Pennsylvania Economy League, *Exploration of the Adaptability of Local Government in the Penjerdel Region, 1950-1961,* (Philadelphia: 1963).

older areas. (Lack of cooperation among the small municipalities contributed to problems of land-use and sanitation control.) The suggestion emerges that size affects development policy at least as seriously as it does expenditure policy because most types of "neighborhood effect" are more pervasive in the small community. Such communities are less adaptable and in time intense development may impair their fiscal capacity.

Political capacity is usually thought to be outweighed by local fiscal and administrative abilities. The Fels study provides some evidence that opportunity exists for local choice among policies—though its basic political variable (social rank) implies that residents' locational preferences *among* communities are more important than political processes *within* municipalities. Political capability seems to be at its maximum in early stages of municipal growth, and it is greatest in wealthy communities. The question is whether local politics tends to enlarge and illuminate public decisions or only to hamper planning and harass administration. In several jurisdictions—e.g., Aston, Bristol, Collingdale, and Marple—the PEL study concluded that political divisions were simply distracting administration. The present inquiry has suggested that electoral competition rarely contributes much to policy.

Some further perspectives on local policy decisions come from interviews with elected officials and civic activists in nine municipalities. Among other topics, the interviews sought to discover extent of awareness of and alertness to local policy alternatives, and extent of agreement about the ends of policy. On the first point leaders were asked whether, in their opinion, local action was forced or real alternatives existed, and this admittedly general question was followed by inquiry about specific fields of policy.* Two reactions to these questions are suggestive. One was the common acceptance of constraints and discounting of alternatives in the only two low-income communities (both high-density boroughs) studied; the other was broad division of opinion in most other municipalities (among both officials and civic leaders), except that in Springfield there was overwhelming rejection of the view that decisions were coerced, with frequent references to the township's fiscal balance, park and recreation program, and high level of services. Once again, the contrast between Springfield and Marple was striking— especially because it was officials in Marple who were most doubtful about the existence of alternatives, even though land use in Marple ap-

* The first question read: "Some people think that there aren't many alternative policies open to most local governments, that decisions are simply forced by patterns of development or by fiscal necessities, that local governments just do what they have to do, so that there's not much point in discussing alternatives. Do you think that's so here?" Following this interviewers asked: "Can you think of real alternatives—and has there been discussion of alternative policies—in some of these areas: zoning, schools, parks and recreation, public safety, roads and traffic, health and sanitation, services like trash and garbage disposal, the tax rate?," recording answers separately for each.

pears more malleable today than in Springfield and there is more political competition. When asked about community experience in specific fields, leaders more often perceived real alternatives in zoning and development than they did in taxes and expenditures. It was apparent that many—probably most—community leaders had not thought explicitly before about the range of alternatives available, though a few certainly had.

As to *goals,* the same selected leaders were shown a list of nine possible goals and asked which three they considered most important.* Here the most impressive result was the broad scatter of opinions in all communities. (There was also some difference *among* communities, which seemed realistically to reflect community situations, but this is less significant because it may depend heavily on the selection of leaders.) From this pattern one should not infer that local consensus is impossible, for the most compatible sets of goals were predominant in most communities, and there is often ample room for compromise among members of the sets. But the scatter suggests that broad agreement among community leaders on abstract goals is unlikely to occur spontaneously.

The range of alternatives open to localities varies with conditions reviewed above. Few municipalities achieve a focus on goals that would maximize their range of alternatives, though agreement on goals *might* be possible in a different governmental process, less directly responsive or less politically controlled (depending on size and social rank). Most communities could use more professional aid than they get in the posing of alternatives and imposing of regulations to keep alternatives open, and in the informing of civic and political action. In small communities a balance—almost any balance—of politics and administration, leadership and responsiveness, is difficult to sustain. The reasons for this seem to be more political than economic, less what the community can afford than what politicians or civic leaders will allow. In this sense local political structure tends to limit political capacity for decision.

4. *Local democracy and adequacy: some suggestions.* A summary judgment on the municipalities is difficult. The more values one thinks relevant the more variables are important and the more impressive is local variety. Thus generalization is also difficult.

It does seem clear that political democracy and governmental ade-

---

* The goals were: maintaining the same quality of residents in the community; improving public services; obtaining more commercial and retail business; obtaining more industry; beautifying the community; providing open space, parks, recreation; keeping the tax rate down; protecting property values; keeping government free of corruption. A residual "Other" was available but rarely used. The procedure in four Montgomery County municipalities differed slightly in that respondents were asked to rate all the goals as most important, fairly important, or unimportant. I have, perhaps arbitrarily, adjusted the two methods in comparing responses.

quacy must be closely related in most judgments. The small jurisdictional size that encourages responsiveness and involvement may impair ability to deal with meaningful issues, though both factors also depend on socioeconomic composition. Thus local politics and administration, jurisdiction and population are complexly related.

Some common tendencies obtain, with common exceptions. Size and wealth are critical factors in administrative performance. Social rank and cultural diversity are crucial variables in political competition and civic participation. Local politics is often most responsive where overt electoral competition is lacking, for competition tends to create or (especially) to reflect intractable differences. Political cleavage most frequently affects administrative performance adversely (in terms of effectiveness), but evidently it sometimes broadens accountability, alters policy, or frustrates corruption. Conversely, local administration is commonly of most assistance to policy decisions in noncompetitive political situations. From most standpoints local government seems to work better with social homogeneity than with diversity, with communalism rather than with political competition. But homogeneity is never complete and discrimination is always a possibility, against which limitation of local powers is the main safeguard.

Local government displays paradoxes and cumulative processes reflecting wealth and stage of development. Those communities most able to control growth are least apt to exhibit political competition. This seems partly the result of early success, which in turn relieves exigency and generates fiscal and administrative capacity as well as political satisfaction and consensus; partly it is because the most self-sufficient municipalities exist at socioeconomic levels that tend to preclude party competition. Political alignments are often most confused in the initial, critical stages of rapid growth, and planning and administrative capacity are crippled then, when they are most needed and potentially most influential. PEL concluded of its thirteen communities that "only Lower Merion and Springfield show evidence of development guided by a formal process of planning."[4] Both communities are wealthy and advanced in development, with moderate political competition at most.

Thus the elements of political, administrative, and fiscal performance seem not to be well related. Large municipalities can normally best control development and afford expenditures, while small jurisdictions seem to favor participation, especially in lower-income communities. Wealthy communities best control growth and provide amenities; they have the most choice but, typically, the least political competition.

The foregoing strictures most apply to what has been termed *development* policy, in which a few decisions or nondecisions can drastically affect the future character of a community, particularly of a small community. As compared with expenditure policy, development policy decisions are especially technical and recondite, heavily influenced by external pressures. It is important to note, therefore, that development policy continues implicitly; it is not alone a matter of initial subdivision and improvement (most of which took place in the eighteenth century). Thus, in plain English, most municipalities are bad planners, though many large ones are capable of holding an established line, perhaps indefinitely.

The factors mentioned above, especially wealth, seem to operate most strongly in the small boroughs (where diseconomies of scale may occur despite higher densities), affecting both needs and services. In the vast majority of boroughs per capita market values are well below the county averages discussed in Chapter 14. Both Fels and PEL found more strenuous fiscal effort in the low-income boroughs. PEL found their services least sufficient in police, public health, streets, parks and recreation, and added that their developmental alternatives were extremely narrow. It discovered scant local concern: . .

> They [the boroughs] are no longer the cultural centers, the shopping centers, the school centers, nor the social centers. . . . Neither do they appear to be the jurisdictions where the best performance of local government is found. . . . Yet, in the boroughs there appears to be little dissatisfaction on the part of the citizens with their community services, and the dominant sentiment is to be "left alone." On balance, we believe that the boroughs face the greatest problems of the municipalities in our study; but they are not obvious problems of the moment. For that reason, theirs will probably be the hardest problems to solve.[5]

This seems a harsh judgment, but one should note that in all three counties the old, low-income boroughs most often provide areas for urban redevelopment (residential and commercial) and for social services. Their health and safety functions are often strained, typically part-time and unprofessional; they have little open land or public recreation. That is one reason for including the boroughs in this account: except at high incomes their fiscal and administrative difficulties may slowly become serious. The *may* should be emphasized in view of the lack of firm evidence about need and economies of scale, but the possibility should be considered because up to this point their control of development has been weak for a variety of reasons: lack of technical skill in ordinances and of administrative will in enforcement, inability to diversify physically and economically within narrow boundaries so as to modify the consequences of early decisions or external development, and progressive urbanizing of some suburban regions with the need for more public services in consequence.

Municipal capacity is a matter of degree; no local government is omnipotent or impotent. It is a matter of opinion, too, depending on how one defines *problems*, which in turn depends on breadth of social and geographical perspective, and even on beliefs about collective free will versus social determinism. Over the whole range of municipalities (in area, wealth, and phase of development) there are large variations in fiscal and administrative capacity. These may provide a new logic for certain county functions now optional—perhaps especially redevelopment, health and welfare in old sections, planning in new areas, and utilities in all districts. This point is further considered in the concluding chapter.

PART VI. CONCLUSIONS

24

Political Democracy

Democratic institutions may be conceived of as either confining governmental power or directing governmental action, or as both in some
balance. Several mechanisms serve these ends, including (1) social
consensus and voluntary, ad hoc participation; (2) socioeconomic diversity and organized, pluralistic pressures; (3) electoral competition; and
(4) formal orders and controls, such as checks and balances or legal
norms.

The relevance and the operation of these democratic elements will be
different in local, state, and national settings, and among levels of local
government. Probably one cannot learn much about modern democracy
in general from the study of nonsovereign polities with limited powers
and primitive institutions. Historically, local government, at least in the
Philadelphia region, has heavily emphasized the first of the foregoing
mechanisms and the fourth, especially at the municipal level.

There seem to be good reasons for reliance on negative, legal controls
over local government. One of these reasons is the closeness of local
politics: the visibility and directness of individual costs and benefits,
the invidious discriminations open to local policy and administration.
Another is the fine line between official and voluntary behavior. Still
another is the common weakness of organized pluralism and electoral
competition together with the scope for personal favoritism in local
government. These may tend to justify the pervasiveness of judicial review of municipal action. Dillon's Rule seems more relevant at this level
than do models of majoritarian or pluralistic democracy.[1] The situation
might be altered by enlargement of local boundaries to enhance diversity, formality, and publicity, but the sovereignty of the state, including
state courts, will doubtless remain a vital supplement to distinctively
local governmental values.

This study has, however, emphasized the first three mechanisms suggested above: loosely, communalism, pluralism, and electoral competition. These will be identified more fully in the review and evaluation that follow. Because electoral competition, implicit or explicit, is to some not precisely definable extent a condition of effective communalism and pluralism, and because it is most heavily emphasized in this study, the summary discussion begins with that central democratic element.

1. *Electoral competition.* The specific effects of local electoral competition remain problematical, though some of the theoretical expectations outlined in the Introduction and Appendix find limited confirmation in this study. It also appears, however, that, while electoral competition is a condition of communalism and pluralism, it is reciprocally conditioned by them in ways discussed below. Electoral *organization* is another important influence. These conditions vary, *inter alia*, with the size and scope (or the level) of local government.

The evidence in this study leads one to suspect that generally the degree of explicit electoral competition required to achieve governmental responsiveness or accountability is less in local government than it is in national politics. Opposition is probably easier to organize at the local level, or the relative homogeneity of population may mean that the close bidding for the marginal vote contributes less to equality or inclusiveness of treatment. On the other hand, in some situations opposition may be *harder* to organize locally because of a prevailing ideology or other mobilization of bias, or social distinctions may be so pervasive and invidious as to create a permanent minority. Thus, the effects of electoral competition depend on social and governmental contexts.

These effects are also dependent on electoral organization itself: on the ability of politicians to consolidate the resources they find in government and society. Again, these vary in some degree with the size and scope, or level, of local government. In Pennsylvania the governmental benefits are sufficient at the county level to discourage opposition when they are effectively centralized, or to encourage it once a monopoly of control has been broken. The principal advantages of county political leaders seem to have been the low visibility and vast patronage of county government, and the combination of centralized perquisitites and decentralized issues that stemmed from the structure of local and county government combined. These advantages are lacking at the municipal level, where social change is also more pervasive; thus electoral organization is much less stable in the municipalities. Indeed, in Bucks County the instability of a few large communities was an important source of *county* political competition.

In general, then, electoral competition makes more difference for official policy and performance at the county level than it does in the municipalities; it varies more and its effects, by most standards, are more beneficent. Enough was said above about the municipalities in this respect: they may be better served by *implicit* competition than are the counties; but *explicit* competition in them is often debilitating. At the county level what has been termed implicit competition is more limiting because government is more remote and interests require more organization. Implicit competition permits selective responsiveness, forestalls the organization of interests by anticipatory concessions, and sometimes allows the use of illegitimate sanctions against potentially explicit competition. Similarly, competition in primary elections, as in Montgomery County, is likely to be more selectively responsive than interparty competition, at least of the explicit sort.

The principal way of evaluating the effects of competition in the counties was in terms of innovation in policy. Innovation then seems to have the effect of extending the scope of government, heightening its visibility and the interest of individuals, promoting broader interests (civic groups, growth-oriented businessmen) in what Dahl has termed collective instead of divisible, individual benefits, thus favoring further governmental action and altering the mobilization of bias. It seems likely in time to produce a little more ideological cleavage, though it has not so far involved broad publics intensely, not even in Bucks County. Perhaps the chief effects of competition in Bucks were to open government to group access, and encourage group action; whereas in Delaware County, at the opposite extreme, politics largely consisted in anticipatory appeal and response to public tax-consciousness and in managing incentives and sanctions against limited interests. Without explicit competition group importunities carried little weight. Where it existed, electoral competition also led to some governmental initiatives, but in such cases it also helped provide group support for them.

The distributive—as distinct from the innovative—effects of electoral competition are more difficult to assess because of the fiscal and functional limitations of local government, both county and municipal. It is not strictly demonstrable that policies in Bucks County are now more broadly responsive to wants, or prospectively more general in their effects, than those in Delaware, nor is it clear in theory that one should expect them to be more redistributive or nondiscriminatory. As was suggested in Chapter 19, however, there do seem to be differences among the three counties, consistent with degree of competition, in *administrative* performance, which is likely to affect *individuals*. This has probably come about through some extension of the scope of government, restriction of the scope of political organization, and the greater sensitivity of political leadership to publicity and opinion—to what Robert Dahl terms "indirect influence."[2] More competition appears to have meant more professionalism in government, less parochial loyalties in judicial appointments, and a more even balance of sanctions between private individuals and public administrators. These are subtle, qualitative, debatable differences, and the matter of sanctions is to some extent one of subjective evaluations by those directly involved. To the extent that these differences exist they *may* reflect courthouse traditions that antedate the political change in Bucks County, though most observers do not think so. To the extent that they are attributable to electoral competition these administrative differences are important because, while *policy* changes in Bucks and Montgomery seem largely to reflect group influence (regardless of their distributive effects), the performance differences affect all individuals who have business with government, i.e., nearly everyone.

Thus, one way to state the effects of electoral competition is to say that it has encouraged pluralism and altered governmental performance, and that these two effects are more evident than initiative or leadership in policy, which tend to be politically risky. This is to say that it has broadened responsiveness in policy while narrowing it (i.e., broadening the application of standards) in administration. Still another statement of the outcome of competition can be made in Dahl's terms: it has multiplied the sources of direct influence (group pressures on government) by changing the distribution of sanctions and incentives: for instance, Bucks County's newspapers are less sensitive to the withdrawal of public advertising and are more influential, because of close elections, than are Delaware's, so that the bearing of communications has been altered by competition, and the same effect holds for other resources. By altering the content of politics and broadening policy alternatives, competition has probably also enlarged the role of indirect influences, i.e., anticipatory response by government to the electoral reactions of publics. To the extent that the distinction between direct and indirect influence holds, however, the former may well have been more enhanced than the latter by electoral competition; at least, it is the more apparent influence on policy. One reason for this is probably the limited relevance of party alignments and identifications to local policies, but there are other reasons as well, which are closely related to the distributive effects of competition in the counties.

The distributive effects of electoral competition are unclear. The broadening of direct influence evidently leads to more group inclusiveness but need not lead to more equality for the unorganized. Indeed, the contrary may be true, especially where, as in Delaware and Bucks respectively, the contrast lies between implicit and explicit competition. In some sense, electoral competition is always implicit or contingent, but in Delaware the party balance in national elections makes close local elections a possibility if government does not appear responsive to those who form a social potential for the (Democratic) opposition.

The issue then is what one means by responsiveness. Conclusions on this issue entail questions about *what* benefits and deprivations are relevant, and *how* individuals should be grouped in considering distributions. Many distributions are necessarily *imputed*: tax-benefit ratios alone do not reflect peoples' attitudes toward public expenditures or services. Usually, distributions are discussed in terms of social classes, which involves some assumptions or conclusions about class interests and attitudes. To the extent that class groupings are appropriate respecting local governmental actions, it may well be that the limited effects of electoral competition on policy innovation and administrative performance have largely served middle-class interests, or, more accurately, reflected upper-middle-class values: i.e., the concerns of highly educated professional and executive people. The encouragement of pluralism, group inclusiveness, and direct influence has probably favored those most apt to be active participants, while the indirect influence of larger publics may be limited by the low salience of local issues; primarily, it seems to work through tax sensitivity.

There is, then, a normative issue in the analysis: that of the values or standards by which the effects of electoral competition are to be assessed. If the democratic or distributive test is one of responsiveness to expressed wants over the population as a whole (or in terms of proportions of the population), and if nonexpression of wants or high sensitivity to taxes is construed as satisfaction with existing management, then Delaware County may be as broadly responsive as Bucks. The innovative and administrative criteria may serve upper-middle-class values; or, to relate them to this study in another way, they may be more relevant to governmental adequacy, defined as leadership in meeting needs, than to political democracy understood as responsiveness to wants.

2. *Partisanship.* In considering the effects of electoral competition it is important to note that partisan, not nonpartisan, elections are in question here. Moreover, partisanship is intense in the two senses that people generally identify with parties and expect partisan, organizational behavior from public officials; and that the resources (sanctions and incentives) for electoral organization are plentiful. Of these two aspects —so to speak, the ideological and the organizational—the latter appears to be paramount in the counties, and especially in the less competitive counties, since competition alters the characteristics and distribution of political resources. Thus, a special *kind* of partisanship is in question. In the three counties the closest thing to nonpartisan competition was that in Montgomery, which occurred in primary elections along vaguely ideological (or partially class-cultural) lines, but it was drastically modified in operation by common party loyalties and organizational concerns. This study has, therefore, but limited relevance to the question of whether partisan or nonpartisan elections are preferable either generally or in certain circumstances. On the other hand, the fact of partisanship, in its Pennsylvania form, is distinctly relevant to judgments about local governmental organization in the Philadelphia region because political and governmental structure are so closely connected.

Two conclusions about local partisanship in general do appear to be plausible. One is that, in terms of a distinction stressed in Chapter 19, the patronage-laden Pennsylvania brand of partisanship favors a politics of interests over one of ideologies, or, in Dahl's terms, of "individual" over "collective" benefits.[3] The other is a suggestion that partisanship is of doubtful democratic value in municipal (as distinct from county) elections, since it rarely provides any focus on policy and sometimes suppresses competition because of its dependence on local social composition. Even this suggestion is extremely tentative, however, for it may be, too, that party organization and loyalty moderate the possible bitterness of social divisions in local elections.

At the county level, especially, the organization politics of Pennsylvania probably has several effects, though none of them is wholly demonstrable. It may tend to distribute participation in governing more broadly among social strata, since party involvement seems more attractive than civic endeavor to people of lower social rank; thus it may lead to broader representation and help to balance the middle-class bias of interest group politics and local ideologies. To be sure of this, one would need to demonstrate that rank and file party work is directly influential in official decisions, and that its effects on administration (at least in noncompetitive circumstances) really tend to broaden advantage. These conditions seem much less likely in *implicit* than in *explicit* electoral competition, though the effects of lower-social-rank participation in politics are apparently felt in Delaware County.

Second, as suggested above, partisanship may mitigate cultural or ideological cleavage. No doubt, as the scope of government expands, such cleavage will increase. However, partisanship is still likely to moderate it, not simply because of the job-oriented cast of Pennsylvania politics, but because popular party alignments are often inconsistent with cultural and ideological divisions. Bucks County today is a good example of this, with its conflicting cultural tendencies in both parties, and similar divisions exist in Montgomery and Delaware. Partisanship may also produce in political leaders something like avoidance of issues: a tendency to caution and careerism in face of the electoral uncertainties posed by forthright positions. (Local politicians are assisted in this tendency by the option of putting some decisions to public referenda.) Partisanship creates a more definite career line than nonpartisanship: one has to bear a party label, to become a politician and not simply an officeholder. These conditions no doubt exclude from politics some persons primarily interested in policy, and they tend to give to those who enter politics a concern with organization, and with their position and advancement in it. Partisan politicians may also avoid issues more successfully than nonpartisan officials because they are able to concentrate their public tactics on party loyalty as a substitute for policy and to discredit the opposition by discussing methods instead of ends. This is not always the case, of course, but the convergence of both parties in competitive Bucks County on common policies with but marginal issues between them seems at least to illustrate it. Similarly, the Democratic minorities in Montgomery and Delaware were much less critical of county policy than they were of bossism, corruption and inefficiency —perhaps in part from concern about public tax-consciousness, which was cultivated by the incumbent Republican Party, but in some degree from personal indifference to policy. The survey data for Bucks and Delaware Counties show no significant differences in popular attitudes toward policy issues between rank and file Republicans and Democrats in Bucks, but in Delaware there was a tendency for partisans to disagree about the proper governmental role in industrial development, open-space preservation, and mass transit, and to disagree in ways at variance with the normal effects of socioeconomic position.* Bucks' politicians *could* converge on common positions, though they may have led the general public to them in response to specific group pressures; Delaware's politicians did not divide as much over policy as did the rank and file, though common tax-consciousness may have been a factor.

Finally, partisanship has evidently affected the conduct of government in ways detailed above, which probably vary with electoral competition. Programmatic interests, professionalism, and administrative methods must compete with maintenance of the political organizations. This point suggests once again, however, that partisanship works differently under competitive and relatively noncompetitive conditions, and that the effects of partisanship per se are overlaid with those of the kind of partisanship peculiar to the region—effects that might be altered by legal changes in the conduct and structure of government, if these were thought desirable.

The desirability of such changes may depend in some part on the prospects for intensive two-party competition in the counties. If one valued the (somewhat speculative) effect of organized partisanship in mitigating cultural cleavage and social bitterness in local government and the role that patronage may play in broadening the social and cultural bases of participation, then one might not favor tight restrictions of patronage if party competition were in prospect. Or, one might favor retention of patronage for blue-collar and "ministerial" duties, extending professionalism in discretionary and technical positions.

The electoral future of the suburban counties is, however, quite unpredictable, primarily because so much depends on the course of national party alignments. What can be said from the survey data in this study is that younger voters are more likely to be Democrats no matter what their socioeconomic positions; that about one-third of the total sample identified themselves as independents—significantly more in Delaware than in Bucks (with social rank constant), and more in both

* It should be noted that the survey data covered only a few townships in the two counties. See Appendix B.

counties than in national samples (though the national samples are more accurate); that, in Delaware County, the incidence of independent registration is greatest in the most electorally competitive township surveyed; that only about a quarter of respondents identify themselves as strong Republicans; that weak Republicans outnumber strong Republicans among lower-social-rank respondents and in lower-social-rank townships; and that about one quarter of the respondents say they have changed their party identification at some time in the past.[4] In these changes, defections from the two parties were almost exactly equal, but the largest proportion of changes occurred among residents of the least competitive local environments. The numbers involved are not large enough for a reliable estimate, but they suggest, when matched with length of residence in the community, that newcomers to Delaware's lower-social-rank communities tended to turn Republican, while long-time residents of low social rank have been more apt to change to the Democratic party. The fact that population growth in the low social rank (Republican) townships sampled in Delaware was far slower than that in similar townships sampled in Bucks that were Democratic or competitive suggests that the conversion theory of suburban Republicanism may apply in conditions of gradual growth and help explain the continued Republican hold on lower Delaware County.[5]

These data, taken with the stabilization of party registration in Bucks, the slow trend toward close party balance in Montgomery and Delaware (which still has a long way to go), and national tendencies toward more Democratic presidential voting in the suburbs, indicate that party competition is a possibility in all three counties.[6] It could be, too, that the intensity of partisanship in terms of national issues will continue to decline, or that local parties will be used more often by social or sectional groups to influence policy, or that both developments will take place. In Delaware and, especially, in Montgomery party competition is unlikely to be close (say, within a range of 10 percent of the vote), but it was suggested above that competition of this order is probably not essential to most benefits attributable to electoral tension. There is also the distinct possibility that intraparty rivalry will develop in Delaware as it has in Montgomery.

I have argued that the prospects for electoral competition are relevant to proposals for reform of local government, but surely the prudent reformer will hedge his bets on this particular future. On the other hand, alterations in the functions, structures, and staffing of local government are likely to affect electoral competition. Broadening county powers, consolidating county structure (perhaps especially by providing a more broadly responsible executive and a more broadly representative legislative body and, less clearly, by mandating professional personnel) would probably enliven electoral competition in general or primary elections, though one cannot be certain of it.

The theory on which this projection rests is that changes in the scope or focus of government and in the intensity of electoral competition go together. The more usual view is that an increase in competition will lead to an increase in scope, that more public benefits will be offered as political bidding quickens—though this may be limited by a tax-conscious electorate. The reverse progression, from extension of scope to intensification of competition, seems less likely to occur, but either more electoral competition or more governmental activity should encourage more group interests and pressures. There is also some prospect that interest-group action will encourage electoral competition in at least one of the forms mentioned just above. This study suggests, without clearly demonstrating, that a reciprocal, cumulative relation obtains between socioeconomic pluralism and electoral competition. It also suggests that pluralism (both of interests and of ideologies), electoral competition, and governmental scope and focus are among the most important elements in any mobilization of bias. The strategy, then, would be to intervene in these relations by statute: perhaps to mandate some powers on the counties. This strategy would seem most valid when the emphasis is on the innovative, instead of the distributive, aspects of government, though it assumes that pluralism and electoral competition together produce some balance between these two. All this will depend in part on the prospects for pluralism versus a consolidated power structure.

3. *Pluralism.* A common view of politics is that its outcomes depend more upon social, economic, and cultural forces than upon governmental and electoral organization. In recent years this view has been especially influential respecting *local* government. Both power-structure and pluralist theories tend to focus attention on the role of private groups in public policy, pluralist theories somewhat less so. If these theories are correct, then governmental and electoral reorganization should make little difference to policy except, perhaps, for consolidation and devolution between levels of government that provide the administrative means to effectuate private decisions.

At the county level, I have argued, the degree and organization of electoral competition, together with the scope and organization of government, have been important factors in the establishment and influence of private groups. The argument rests at least as heavily on historical narrative as on formal comparison, but a schematic comparison alone is unlikely to give an accurate measure of the effectiveness of several forces because the definitions of *forces* or *factors* and the indices of their activity are so arbitrary. Politics in the counties seems to have been more a matter of governmental and electoral conduct than either an incidental or a deliberate effect of social and economic action. True, politicians have exploited resources in both public and private sectors; but they have heavily relied upon public resources to produce the organization through which they have dealt with private groups.

The large role of professional politicians in the counties rests on material perquisities and intergovernmental leverage available to them under Pennsylvania law, and on popular expectations to which the law has probably given rise.

Political organization has been most centralized and disciplined where electoral competition and socioeconomic pluralism are both weak. In this situation, as in Delaware County today, the possibility exists that private interests are dominating politics. When this putative power structure is studied in terms of the reputations and positions of individuals, the histories of decisions, and the broader context of all these, the conclusion of this study is that two factors are more important in county policy. One is the conservative mobilization of bias produced by the structure, divisions, traditions, limited functions, and fiscal system of local government. The other is the strength of party organization, based in public perquisites. In the absence of electoral competition political leaders have dominated policy; in the presence of explicit competition these leaders have been responsive to more interests. Political leaders play important roles in both electoral monopoly and competition, but are probably more important in the former.

Electoral competition has led to a high degree of voluntarism in the governments of Bucks and (if less so) Montgomery. The initiative and support of private groups—sometimes even of individuals—have evidently been critical determinants of governmental direction. This being so, it is important to note that the membership of civic or public-interest organizations is an infinitesimal portion of each county's population; and there is no satisfactory way to assess its representativeness. This is not because these groups are exclusive, even implicitly in most cases, but simply because most residents are indifferent. Private interests (i.e., pecuniary interests) are also most active (though not necessarily more influential) in public policy in the more competitive counties, giving rise to an interplay, with some overlap in membership, between the two kinds of groups. No single interest or circle has dominated policy.

Despite the narrowness of participation, where some pluralism and electoral competition coexist individuals have ready access to county government through group membership. No doubt expansion of the scope of government would further widen the range of participation. Even with increases in county bureaucracies and county populations this group avenue of individual participation is likely to be effective in the foreseeable future, and the private groups are hardly bureaucratized at all. This pattern of participation does, however, have social, economic, and cultural limitations in terms of the interests, attitudes, and aptitudes of citizens. In particular, it is limited by and large to the white-collar population, and primarily to the upper middle class. Thus it can be argued that electoral competition and electoral organization provide important alternative avenues of participation, and that professionalization of some county functions—especially health, welfare, and education

—provides another way of taking account of the interests of those who lack associative or political skills. If neither group action, political competition, nor administrative responsibility can be counted on alone for thoroughgoing inclusiveness in policy and performance—as seems to be the case—then county government may still be capable of providing these in a balance that facilitates both participation and inclusiveness.

4. *Communalism*. Municipalities, this study finds, differ from counties in the incidence and effects of organized pluralism, electoral competition, and professional administration, and in the ways in which these interact. There is a qualitative difference between the two governmental levels, though municipalities themselves vary over a wide range.

In municipalities political competition is sometimes debilitating, by most standards, even when necessary to reflect diversity and protect minorities or individuals. There is little evidence that electoral competition broadens civic participation, but it sometimes undermines morale and administration. In terms of current political sociology, some municipalities are more like voluntary associations than polities. Their success seems to depend on consensus. Many of their functions are wholly or partially voluntary; and the distinction between official and voluntary activity (as in recreational and cultural fields, as well as several other services) is often unclear. When these activities are considered altogether the participative side of municipal life seems extremely important. Again, it has most effect on policy in predominantly upper-middle-class communities.

One literary, participative ideal about local government (not widely shared in the Philadelphia area) may be termed communalism. It implies small enough jurisdictions to contain homogeneous populations, and it need not entail *overt* participation. With a diverse population, however—or even in a large jurisdiction—participation must presumably be overt if oligarchy or inequity are to be avoided. Communalism, then, consists in direct response, which is often anticipatory, of government to community attitudes and in the minimization of distinctions between public and private. Such responsiveness is equitable only if attitudes are relatively homogeneous. Finally, communalism probably implies (at least as a literary theory) something like community-regarding attitudes in the population at large, and to this extent it *may* be an ideal that fits only upper-middle-class communities.

One can picture the community on two dimensions having to do with the extent to which decision and administration are governmental or voluntary (i.e., the actual scope of government) and with the degree of homogeneity-diversity in the population (i.e., of its wants and attitudes). Following the dichotomizing bent of the sociologist, we have the patterns of community activity in the accompanying diagram. It should be noted, however, that an important aspect of the communal ideal is the *absence* of clear distinctions between public and private, explicit

	Homogeneous	Diverse
Voluntary	Individual _____	Associational
Governmental	Communal ‑‑‑‑‑‑‑‑‑ Official	Electoral

and implicit decisions, and of clear differences among individual inter‑
ests or attitudes. In a sense, communalism rests on informality and
ambiguity.

It should also be noted that this diagram and its arbitrary labels re‑
flect some other dimensions of the small community: the amount of
active participation, the degree to which such participation is formally
organized, and the extent to which such organization is centralized.
Where the community is small in area and homogeneous in population
these three dimensions do not seem to matter much, but otherwise all
of them are probably important. In a diverse population, participation
must usually be overt to be effective. This is likely to require some
organization. Then the question is whether organization (civic or elec‑
toral) is centralized, that is, how the sanctions and incentives are dis‑
tributed. It is in this connection that the governmental‑voluntary
distinction is important: in conditions of social diversity a high concen‑
tration of power in either sphere is likely to spell oligarchy. Further‑
more, some balance or plurality among social interests seems desirable
to preclude a permanent majority and minority.

Communalism, viewed as direct governmental response to voluntary
action or community attitudes, is something like direct democracy, as
distinguished from representative democracy. It is not precisely that,
however, for its effectiveness rests ultimately on the electoral sanction.
Given free elections, the problem of oligarchy is unlikely in the munic‑
ipalities studied here, though there may occasionally be a problem of
majority domination. The ideal of communalism fits only a few of the
smallest municipalities. Others approximate it by reliance on *implicit*
electoral competition, where social differences are not intransigent or
where party lines are not salient. Where the latter conditions do not
exist, *explicit* competition is often debilitating.

In this situation, if one places high value on deliberate political action
and response, one can conclude that municipalities are too small to
handle diversity well, even though they are seldom highly homogeneous.
Implicit competition may disadvantage those people who do not get
mobilized, while explicit competition may lead to permanent minorities
or to immobilization of government. Excessive responsiveness, not
oligarchy, is in the opinion of most professional planners and managers
the problem of municipalities. In this view, it is the lack of stable organ‑
izational elements commonly found in larger, higher‑level government

and of *sufficient* diversity—of bureaucracy and pluralism—that hampers municipal effectiveness without facilitating an inclusive responsiveness.

In general, where the communal ideal is not relevant, municipalities commonly lack the means by which more comprehensive jurisdictions handle diversity; they are neither homogeneous enough nor diverse enough. Moreover, the communal ideal is seldom relevant. Yet the material in Part V above suggests the perils of generalization on this subject. In some communities something like organized pluralism, electoral competition, and a modicum of professional administration do provide seeming satisfaction and effectiveness. In others, something like communalism functions to avert differences or resolve them by a combination of firm leadership and anticipatory responsiveness. In some communities diversity is shifting and limited, and communalism is nearly realized.

What can be said is that the operation of political democracy is more intimately linked to both social class and governmental adequacy (by almost any standard) at the municipal level than it is elsewhere, though there are some regional criteria by which the municipalities are inadequate no matter what their political structure.

5. *The problem of participation.* Most American norms for democracy have looked beyond formal, arm's length, representative arrangements to the incorporation of social forces in government, or the pervasion of the state by society. Decentralization has been favored because local government has been thought especially susceptible to informal influence, directly responsive to interests without having to settle the issues raised by significant diversity, and often serving a community instead of a society. Modern studies of local politics have tended to stress similar characteristics: the responsiveness of local government to existing social forces, whether to diversity of interests, community of interests, or concentration of advantage.

Paradoxically, perhaps, the prevailing tradition has also emphasized the negative checks on governmental power that intimate knowledge and direct involvement might afford to citizens. Today, as local jurisdictions seem less well related to physical, social, fiscal, and administrative issues, the negative, exclusive, tax-conscious effects of local control are commonly held by scholars to outweigh the positive, community-regarding aspects of local responsibility.

Traditional theories emphasized individual participation as a means of limiting central despotism and stimulating civic responsibility, and linked it to local government. In the nineteenth century Tocqueville, Mill, and Bryce all wrote of local participation, ultimately based in elections, as a mode of civic education, or political socialization. Recently a transnational survey, in much the same tradition, found that most respondents felt more competent to deal with local than with national public matters, and that feelings of both technical and political competence and of civic obligation varied with the autonomy of local government in the nations surveyed. These feelings also varied with other factors (such as formal education), but it did appear that the role of local government itself was a significant influence.[7] American respondents scored highest in all the above respects, and American local government was most autonomous; yet few Americans actually participated in local affairs beyond voting in elections. This suggests that the *opportunity* for participation may be more important to a sense of obligation, competence, and effectiveness than is overt participation itself. (It is also possible that local autonomy was important in the past in creating a tradition but is no longer a vital source of these virtues, which might mean that decline in local government would be followed by civic deterioration.) In any event, the characteristics mentioned are said to be elements of a civic culture that balances civic activity and passivity, participation and obedience, obligation and disengagement, providing sufficient emphasis on the first member of each pair (even in the same individual) to produce self-reliant citizens with a sense of community.[8] Thus they may contribute to stable democracy.

To contribute most in this way local participation, or the opportunity for it, should probably be direct; that is, the individual should be close to and able to compass the ultimate result of his involvement. Second, participation should probably be made effective with some frequency; that is, the voluntary and governmental spheres of action should have the power, in whatever sense is necessary, to alter circumstances or events. Finally, to consist with democratic criteria and contribute most to the democratic mold, the opportunity, at least, if not the habit of participation should probably be well distributed without rank inequality. One cannot say that these conditions should certainly obtain because the sociology and psychology of democratic governments and cultures are not well enough known for that, but these seem to be the most plausible conditions. In an equally tentative way one may say that they imply *local* governmental participation in jurisdictions loosely coterminous with communities, in inclusive rather than exclusive associations, to adopt Scott Greer's term for the governmental-voluntary distinction.[9] Functional decentralization is unlikely to involve enough interests or provide enough autonomy to serve the same purposes.

The conditions just mentioned of directness, effectiveness, and inclusiveness or equality are, in fact, those noted by the nineteenth-century writers who extolled the virtues of local government—except that they took inclusiveness or equality more for granted than we do today. Then, by those who cared, it could be argued that the average municipality provided these virtues in a satisfactory balance. Today that argument is less persuasive; the balance is harder to maintain. Thus, the role of local participation may be most important in political socialization at lower socioeconomic levels, where cosmopolitanism—skill in formal organization and interest in abstract policy—is least to be expected.

Small, relatively homogeneous jurisdictions may, at this socioeconomic level, promote equality of opportunity to participate. On the other hand, these are the communities that are weak in fiscal and administrative capacity and least effective in controlling their own destinies, so that participation means least in them objectively or effectively. Civic participation in such municipalities tends to center on quasi-voluntary activities, such as social recreation, that might equally be financed and then decentralized by larger governmental units, and political participation is more job-oriented than policy-oriented. The practical advantages of civic participation in suburban communities seem to be chiefly middle-class advantages. They may be important for political understanding and stability in a nation of dominantly middle-class political traditions, or they may serve to perpetuate these traditions without broadening participation in them. The sense of opportunity for direct involvement in local policy and performance may also contribute to citizenship, and it seems to be generally felt at most suburban social levels, though least so at lower levels. On the other hand, people also need the opportunity to master less direct modes of participation for effective citizenship in a modern, "great society," and larger local governments might provide this. Inescapably, local participation and jurisdiction are closely linked to social rank.

Three modes of participation were reviewed above: electoral and partisan activity; relatively large-scale voluntary organization; and local participation that is communal, associative, and electoral in some balance. In a larger sense of *local*, these processes could take place in regional, county, or municipal governments, so far as greater Philadelphia is concerned. The existing system of county and municipal government (with a very few regional functions) provides a mixture of all three methods of participation, but this may not be the right mixture in terms of either political democracy or governmental adequacy. At least, it is clear that political democracy and governmental adequacy cannot be cleanly separated in considering local organization, and it is fairly clear that standards of both are related to social position. When these aspects are considered together it also appears that no optimum organization is probable if one feels strongly about all the complex fiscal, administrative, distributive, and participative elements involved in it.

The following chapter does not offer anything like a complete discussion of these elements, but it suggests some of the ways they interact in the principal options available. It may provide materials for the reader's own critique of local organization.

25

Governmental
Adequacy

The question about local democracy and governmental adequacy that were posed in the Introduction have now been pressed at least as far as the evidence allows. It turns out that political structure probably does affect governmental policy and performance. It also appears that there is more than one model of local democracy, that conceptions of governmental adequacy are closely associated with models of democracy, and that alteration of governmental forms and powers is a likely way of changing local politics.

The point about governmental reform should not, however, be allowed to obscure the severe limitations of any political-governmental model for predicting or controlling the outcome of change. A study such as this contributes more to understanding than it does to manipulation.

Still, the study's implications for local organization should be explored, at least briefly. This involves balancing considerations common to all large American metropolitan areas with attention to special, local conditions. The balance itself amounts to a philosophical position, and some scholars are more platonic about it than are others.

1. *Alternative approaches to local organization.* The principal alternatives for greater Philadelphia today appear to be three. One is regional: creation of a regional government or increased emphasis on regional agencies (perhaps in Pennsylvania alone.) A second is consolidation of more local powers in counties. Finally, institutional change might be minimized by increasing reliance on state and national finance and administration, perhaps encouraged by state legislative reapportionment and constitutional reform. These are not mutually exclusive

alternatives. All are likely to occur together, and the third is likely to entail the first two, perhaps with federal emphasis on the region and state reliance on the counties. Thus the discussion in this chapter is focused on the region and the counties as alternative emphases.

Municipal government is often too small to comprehend or control many problems that affect individuals and communities. Regional government—at the other extreme—would be competent to identify and deal with most potential local concerns, but by virtue of its remoteness and formality, it is likely to provide less of the voluntary, participative side of community life. In particular, it might tend to disadvantage persons of lower social rank and "locals" (versus "cosmopolitans") in terms of direct participation even while redressing fiscal and income inequalities among communities and populations. Its policy would depend on organized political action in parties and pressure groups and on professional bureaucracy.

Thus, two models of local democracy are involved. One is that of the polity at higher levels, emphasizing formal administrative arrangements and organized political competition. It rests on socioeconomic diversity. The other model stresses voluntary activity—informality and direct participation. It rests on socioeconomic homogeneity. Most political scientists probably value the first model more highly for its greater effectiveness in coping with metropolitan problems and, perhaps, because of its consistency with democratic theory and methods of other governmental levels.[1] Sociologists, however, have long valued direct participation and the sense of community, though many are critical of suburbia on these grounds.[2]

The two models of democracy might be combined in a regional-local federation. Alternatively, the counties are a possible compromise: large enough for a modicum of administrative effectiveness, professionalism, and formality; diverse and distant enough to sustain organized pluralism and political competition; small enough to permit direct access by individuals and local interests and to combine governmental with voluntary action; few enough to negotiate about properly regional problems. On this view the suburban county—like the central city—would serve as a bridge between voluntary and bureaucratic, private and public action, linking communities to the "great society" and the federal system.

On the other hand, there will be those who think the counties offer the worst of both worlds: cumbersome bargaining over regional issues; possible immobilization by local pressures; insufficient administrative formality and political competition; too deeply rooted political organization; not enough voluntary action; inadequate redistributive capacity with an overbalance of suburban to urban interests; weaker civic and cultural loyalties than either the metropolis or the municipality. On this view the county is neither a community nor a modern polity; it is a red herring.

Municipal governments are unlikely to approach closely either the pluralistic ideal, as they grow larger, or the communal ideal, if they ever did. Both ideals imply more widespread participation than is common in them. Yet the *opportunity* of participation—either directly or through elections—may nevertheless be important for individuals' civic development. Among alternative forms of regional organization, more consolidation in counties seems about as likely to foster both types of involvement as would a regional-local federation. Probably the two approaches would distribute each kind of participation differently among socioeconomic interests, and it is not clear which would be more egalitarian.

Politically, the balance of values in these two systems seems a close one. The *administrative* issues include the number of governmental levels thought desirable within the region, the measure of regional problems (as distinct from problems within the region), the extent to which these require regional government (as distinct from mere regional management), the degree to which income redistribution should be a regional as well as a higher-level concern, the appropriateness of regional administration for many functions with but indirect regional implications, the necessity of connecting all policy implications at one governmental level, the proper delimitation of a region for various public functions, the right balance of public and private sectors, the correct proportion of administrative formality and professionalism, the feasibility of regional government in a tristate area, and the possibility of reforms in local and county government. Some of these are discussed in the next section.

Local prospects should probably be viewed in light of at least four *general* issues that are not unique to the Philadelphia region. The first of these is that of the effect of alternative organizations on the distribution of active citizenship and passive satisfactions among the social classes. If the present fragmented system provides service levels that reflect local abilities to pay, it also seems to respond to local tastes and utilities, as they are linked to class cultures. While a larger political system might shift fiscal and electoral advantages in the direction of lower-income voters (perhaps altering tastes and utilities in the process), initiatives in decision would almost certainly gravitate toward professional public administrators and those other professional and managerial residents for whom direct metropolitan participation comes naturally, and to whom public services are attractive. Of all the issues in local government we probably know least about how to involve all social levels actively, and how equitably to respond to the tacit expectations of all levels. Indeed, the principal issue is whether structure or culture is primarily involved, whether tastes and utilities would be significantly changed by the fiscal and political implications of larger local governments, or whether diminution of the middle-class bias of local government is (if desirable) more a matter for voluntary action and education. (Before attempting to eliminate this bias one should probably consider the extent to which our principal democratic institutions are based on it.)

Closely related to the social issue is one of physical planning: that of metropolitanism versus regionalism, of the existing trends in location of activities, and of the extent to which governmental reorganization itself will tend to settle the issue. Of the constituent issues in regionalism versus metropolitanism two are of special significance. One of these is the thesis that growth in local scale and social variation have rendered city limits and municipal democracy irrelevant, but one must then ask whether regions can be felicitously or even satisfactorily defined for a wide range of functions.[3] The other issue is whether vesting many functions in counties is likely to worsen central city–suburban distributions, perhaps especially with respect to race; yet further centralization might strengthen political rivalry without significantly affecting private discrimination.

Allied to this issue in turn are considerations of trends in the federal system and of the kind of federal system one wants. To those who favor the conventional federal-state-local pattern of grants-in-aid the counties should be acceptable, but they will not be to those who wish to by-pass the states with direct federal-local subsidies and conditions and to mix public and private institutions (such as universities) in regional programs. These two approaches to federalism increasingly compete in health, welfare, housing, transportation, and other urban services at both federal and local levels. Local organization affects federal programs, and conversely, though lately the balance has shifted toward more federal initiative. The point is that deliberate choice about local organization implies decisions about federalism generally, in both its form and its performance.

Finally, allied to all of the foregoing issues, is the fiscal issue of whether metropolitan consolidation would provide for significantly more fiscal capacity, "progressivity," and responsibility than would a county emphasis. Since so little hard information is now available on this issue, in the writer's opinion, it must be viewed as open, so long as other tax devices are available to the central city for linking the wealth it engenders to the services it renders.

2. Functions and structure. Clearly, the foregoing issues—social, physical, organizational, and fiscal—are closely related. One's conclusions about them overall may serve as predispositions toward one or another approach to local organization. There remains, however, the issue of where specific functions are best administered, which may now be summarily considered.

There has long been a scholarly sympathy for regional administration of many, perhaps most, local functions. This study's concentration on counties and municipalities probably leads to an opposite bias. The following brief review of major functions is partly an attempt to salvage some traditional local governmental values by exploring the counties' prospects for coping with metropolitan problems. In the end, the balance of virtue between regional and county arrangements seems a close one to the writer.

The problems most commonly mentioned as requiring regional management (and, perhaps, decision) are air and water pollution, sewage disposal and water supply, transportation, and the larger aspects of land planning. Some would add social functions in welfare, health, housing, and police protection. It can be argued that some of these problems are less urgently regional in greater Philadelphia than they are in some other areas. Much of the basic transportation net has been either planned or constructed by state and interstate agencies or by private carriers, and the railway system has not been abandoned as it has been in some regions. Industrial development and residential densities are already well advanced on this basis. Water and sewerage are probably not uniquely regional, for reasons advanced in Chapter 15. Pollution control could be defined as a separate regional, state, or federal activity. Mass transit is suitable for administration by an authority, even if a general tax subsidy is involved in it. Most social programs need a broader tax base than the metropolitan area is likely to provide, and the case for regional police administration is probably not a basic one, save for a few activities.

Any or all of these functions (and others) might, however, be performed by a regional government, with four general effects. One would be the relating of them to one another more centrally and deliberately. A regional government might also generate broader civic loyalties and cultural concerns than now exist. It might respond more sensitively to the social and economic problems of the central city than does the present system, though the possibility of bitter urban-suburban conflict should not be ignored. Finally, regional government would probably enlarge the public sector and strengthen control of private market forces, prompting their more open involvement in politics. Political and economic boundaries would more closely coincide than they do now. Local voluntary action would be less effective, but social and market areas may never coincide.

Scholars have emphasized the potential for social, economic, and political integration of metropolitan government together with its performance of specific functions. Although speculative, these integrative effects are important because most prospectively regional functions can be administered individually. Moreover, the financing and administration of most functions are separable, and for several functions the fiscal and administrative criteria that are most often applied point to different governmental levels.[4] Thus, consideration of more general effects is relevant to one's ultimate judgment about the location of public functions even if the interests at stake are less palpable and predictable.

The same issues are involved in the partial alternative of county consolidation. The first question that arises concerns the county's capacity for specific functions, which must be briefly discussed.

Water and sewerage can logically be provided at the county level, as argued in Chapter 15. The existing legal requirements for management by an authority could be changed to separate finance and administration and to promote integration with land planning and recreation. Reservation of open space has not, by most standards, been a success in the counties except for Bucks. But federal and state aid has recently led to a five-county regional open-space compact and has increased acquisitions. It has lowered the cost of action in a situation where widespread local demand was lacking and political resistance was natural.

Land planning is frequently said to require a regional framework. Regional planning might consist of research or regulation or both. While regional land-use regulation might provide a framework of "circulation" system, nonresidential zones, basic public facilities, and general density controls, comprehensive planning in more detail (including zoning, subdivision control, and public services) would probably be cumbersome and insensitive to local situations.[5] As argued above, many of the regional basics already exist in greater Philadelphia, but regional data collection, projection, and posing of issues could be useful functions. County planning is potentially important for both newly developing areas and old, renewable districts for reasons suggested in Part V (see pp. 285–87). Comprehensive planning (in the city tradition) *is* a county possibility, including zoning, subdivision control, and integration with public services. County capital programming, while less important for comparison and rationality than in large cities, would assist publicity and accountability. Actually, county planners have lost statutory power in the last decade, but the functions here suggested would, legally speaking, be easy to confer.

Transportation has three aspects: highways, mass transit, and terminals. The case for regional planning and management of some aspects, and the integration of all, is a strong one, though it need not entail a regional polity. The most salient regional aspects of road and rail transportation are interstate in nature and could be handled by user charges and fiscal agreements. Thus the present mass-transit authority could in time be extended to other states and combined with a regional planning agency. Terminal facilities might ultimately come under regional management or remain with the counties. Pennsylvania could return to the old system of county roads, leaving regional arteries at the state level, as some have urged.[6] In view of suburban residents' concern about transportation (evident in the survey data), this combination of regional and county action might significantly enlarge the public for county activities as well as county planning capacity.

Health and welfare administration are traditional parts of the federal-state-county pattern. This pattern provides them at once with a broad, redistributive tax base and a combination of uniformity and local responsiveness in administration. In Pennsylvania today the immediate issue in both fields lies between degrees of state and county responsibility, as suggested in Chapter 16. Federal pressure for regionalism is growing, however. A regional framework might most effectively tie health and welfare into existing private institutions (e.g., university medical centers), while a county emphasis would bring them closer to most voluntary organizations and constituencies. Health and welfare, like some other functions, pose the problem of relating regional provision of a few basic services to state standards and local participation; perhaps some balance is possible between these approaches to local organization.

Finally, besides the large complexes in natural resources, public utilities, land planning, transportation, social services, and the old custodial and judicial duties, there are individual functions worth considering at the county level. These include such cultural services as libraries and recreation, utilities such as refuse disposal, extension of police functions in law enforcement and arterial traffic control, and vocational education and community colleges. Most of these are presently authorized.*

Not that the counties lack disadvantages (by the writer's biases). Socially, they fail as city states, though geographically they qualify, especially if better roads and local mass media are in sight. Their personnel, structure, and customs are more oriented to government on the squeaky-wheel principle than to deliberate policy and initiative—to ambiguity instead of to standards. Compared with regional government, they might be more susceptible of control by small combinations of large municipalities, and organization politics might undermine both policy-making and administration. Yet this study indicates that with social change, as in Bucks, the county can range rather broadly along the democratic spectrum of leadership-responsiveness and provide modest administrative competence and inclusiveness in policy. Perhaps the chief problem is the creation of county publics. Assumption or conferral of more powers would help, especially in more interesting fields like planning, highways, and public safety. The constituency for public goods seems to be growing in the counties; the old mobilization of bias is breaking down both ideologically and institutionally. Political cleavage may well develop further, broadening the potential for direct civic influence on policy.

In terms of both political democracy and governmental adequacy the

---

* Some of these functions, especially the cultural, meet what economists call merit wants: activities are socialized because they are considered good for those who do not have them. If municipal tastes could be assumed to be homogeneous, then local administration (perhaps with county financial aid) might well be preferable for such functions. On the other hand, administration by the county might well provide a wider range of services in each field and more combinations among fields, thus catering to variety in local tastes and favoring local minorities.

best step might be home rule, in its admittedly limited, legal sense, for third-class counties. On the political side, this would permit experiments with new representative institutions: large and small councils chosen by districts or at large, elected or appointed executives. It would allow abolition of most independent row offices, and an increase in the salaries of responsible officials. It might produce more positive and more broadly responsive government. Not everyone wants this, however, and constitutional change will not be easy.

If county politics has been parochial, so has county administration. Like the municipalities, if in lesser degree, most counties lack the formal, hierarchical, internal checks, which, if inadequate by themselves, are a flexible supplement to negative, external, judicial controls. Largely absent, too, are the standards and procedures, coordination and specialization, that collectively serve as bases for something called policy, to distinguish it from administrative routine, and to insulate the latter from direct pressures. It appears in this study that professional initiative has sometimes been critical in county progress, and that *municipal* administrative shortcomings limit political capacity. Local administrative competence is increasingly a condition of political effectiveness, and conversely. This suggests that consolidation of some powers in counties should be accompanied by some professionalization.

Closely allied to the issue of professional competence is the ambiguity characteristic of both local and county action, especially in the regulation of land. Enhancement of county planning powers would help in this respect. So would state standards of tax administration and larger judicial districts more remote from political control.

Consolidation of powers in counties would reduce municipal functions. Presently, as school district consolidation occurs in Pennsylvania, the municipal role as an organized social area is declining.[7] Moreover, most municipalities large enough to minimize internal or external diseconomies contain several distinct neighborhoods; they are not congruent with the most intimate social areas.

The future of the localities, therefore, presents some dilemmas. The political and administrative attributes of municipal government indicate that its most appropriate functions are probably those most closely bordering on voluntary action: those in which social homogeneity can enhance the benefits of direct participation. The same reasoning supports centralization of regulatory and expenditure functions that reinforce or increase maldistribution among communities or in which political competition and administrative distance are important checks on individual discrimination. This argues for devolution to localities of cultural and recreational functions and centralization of most others. Yet the most viable municipalities, financially and administratively, tend to be the largest ones, which are socially most diverse. The most capable governments are also those of the wealthiest communities, least in need of public support of recreational and cultural activity or of local avenues for individual participation in policy. One justification of county consolidation is the variety of local fiscal and administrative conditions, but this may also provoke resistance to county action by the richest communities with most potential influence. Gradual centralization might be achieved through county grant-in-aid programs, administration by contract, and review powers over local regulations (such as zoning) with substantial "neighborhood effects" on other communities.

Thus the counties compete with both the region and the localities. They threaten the latter more directly than do regional arrangements. Nevertheless, the writer suggests that counties can provide a satisfactory balance of competition and competence, civic participation and professional administration, private and governmental action. Emphasis on counties also fits the logic of conventional federalism while providing larger building blocks for regional institutions.

3. *Striking the balance.* The discussion began with three alternative emphases: regional, county, and federal. Recent developments in southeastern Pennsylvania have combined them all. Both Montgomery and Bucks have recently expanded and professionalized their child-care programs, and the state welfare department has opened a regional office for coordination of services. All the counties, including Delaware, have entered a regional open-space compact and have worked with the state in land acquisition. All now support a state and federally aided regional mass-transit agency. All have expanded their planning commissions, while participating in a new, regional commission. In these fields two factors have led to change. One, emphasized throughout the volume, has been the opening of county political systems, the advent of new men in office, and (perhaps) of a new middle-class interest in public amenity and welfare. The other has been federal subsidy with conditions—professional requirements applied through the state, and regional stipulations attached to direct grants. Both factors have combined to alter the local balance of interests, and it is not clear that either alone could have done so. The old county leaders resisted regional and professional administration from interest and ideology. The new politicians accept innovation but fear tax increases; thus state and federal aid have made change feasible.

Now the question is whether recent developments will ultimately favor regional-local federation, county consolidation, or state and federal action. In the counties that have changed least the political leadership is likely to resist a new role and support localism, but change is probably cumulating in all the counties. Cosmopolitans in well-to-do communities may prefer a regional-local combination; metropolitan transportation and abstract planning would enhance convenience and amenity without threatening to redistribute citizenship or income directly. Federal preference for regional planning and financial disbursements may be balanced by state ties to the counties, and county expansion will doubtless occur in some fields discussed above where no other agencies are available. Perhaps the safest prediction is that vested interests and conflicting values will produce compromise among the three alternatives and no broadly responsible local government.

It is often observed that cosmopolitan and local, progressive and conservative forces compete within the separation of powers and the federal system. Similar forces compete in the Philadelphia region. One supports a trend toward encouragement of regionalism and direct liaison with it by some federal agencies. The other backs the traditional federal-state-local hierarchy. One presently emphasizes professionalism, the other political control. Professional administrators and local politicians are the most specific competing interests. The issue between them can be posed as one of professional versus elective local government, but neither interest is consistently concerned or unconcerned about public accountability.

To the writer, counties stand the best chance of combining professionalism, control by elected officials, and civic participation with sufficient opportunity for political and voluntary action. If this implies acceptance of the conventional federal system it also involves acceptance of many criticisms of it. Reform of county government would probably help create the recommended balance of values, but the weakest link in the federal chain is the state (which alone can reform local government). County political systems cannot be wholly depended on for the diversity, formality, and publicity that sustain broadly responsible government. Thus the state's sovereignty structure, including legislative revision, administrative supervision, and judicial review of county functions is a desirable framework for county politics. The same holds for administration, where the state can help identify regional needs and provide instrumentalities to deal with them. Counties have always acted in part as state agencies, and most of the policy innovations studied above involved facilitation and sometimes pressure by state law and administration. States have been notably unresponsive to metropolitan needs, but legislative reapportionment is expected to help, and constitutional revision is a possibility in Pennsylvania. The county can best become a general purpose government within a strengthened state framework. The conventional federal system with its contrasting values of formality and cooperation, hierarchy and local control can be adapted to the metropolitan area problem, and conversely.

Perhaps this study's emphasis on institutions instead of on social forces or functional problems accounts for its seemingly conservative conclusion. On the other hand, neither administrative, political, nor social analysis necessarily leads one to thoroughgoing regional consolidation. No one can clearly foresee the shape of the metropolitan area a generation from now. It may be that new techniques of forecasting, communications, and physical control will make local variety and participation more possible and important, not less so. In its outline, though not in detail, the existing system may provide more flexibility than would something fundamentally different. But the balance of values between alternatives is close, and the choice is not obvious.

APPENDICES

NOTES

INDEX

APPENDIX A. THEORY

As the first chapter states, this study deals with the two broad subjects of political democracy and governmental adequacy at the local level. The emphasis stems partly from a sense of obligation, under the PENJERDEL grant, to address myself to practical problems, as well as from doubt that the two sides of local government are sharply distinguishable. There are interesting theoretical and methodological issues about governmental adequacy, such as how to conceive of both internal and external economies, or the relative applicability of rationalistic and pragmatic models of policy-making at the local level. All of these ultimately have to do with political values, I think; they are not purely administrative. This study does not deal with such issues in depth, and it draws heavily on other studies for its evaluations of local governmental adequacy.

With respect to political democracy, the principal issues considered are whether political structure matters for local government, and, if so, how. These issues require one to identify first the critical elements of political structure, and, second, the effects that might be expected from it. The principal aspects of political structure dealt with are (1) electoral structure (competition and organization), and (2) power structure, so called, or the extent to which social, cultural, and economic resources for mobilizing people or otherwise influencing policy are consolidated among a few holders or are dispersed and pluralized. Electoral organization and the distribution of influence more generally regarded are hard to distinguish conceptually, and they are closely related empirically. Most of the American studies that report consolidated private power structures have occurred in communities with nonpartisan elections or one-party political systems, while most of those that find influence to be more broadly distributed have been made where elections were more organized or more competitive or both. These relations and those between political structure and the other major variables of this study—social structure and governmental structure—are further discussed below.[1]

319

Electoral competition and socioeconomic pluralism—rather than monopolistic political organizations or dominant power structures—may be desired as ends in themselves, and some inquiries seem to start from this premise. Or they may be desired from a concern with certain qualities of representation, participation, and protection as aspects of democratic liberty and equality: breadth and accountability, responsiveness of leadership, facilitation of popular involvement, or avoidance of arbitrary deprivations, to the extent that these can be distinguished from political structure as an independent variable. Some of these points verge on what is presumably a more directly observable concern: the effects of political structure, broadly construed, on policy in its distributive effects or on degrees of innovation, including its collective aspects. Finally, political structure (and especially, electoral organization and competition) has been held to affect governmental performance, or the regularity, competence, and creativity of administration, its balance of leadership, neutrality, and responsiveness, and other attributes that may have either distributive or collective effects.

In general, investigations of community power structure have centered on who participates in decisions and administration; studies of electoral politics have focused more explicitly on policy and governmental conduct as political outcomes. There are, however, plenty of exceptions to these generalizations. Moreover, all the outcomes of political structure appear to be closely connected (to vary together), just as obligarchy and electoral consolidation, pluralism and electoral competition are closely connected, and most of the connections seem to be reciprocal. The following review of theory and research in this area emphasizes the effects of electoral competition.

Two questions arise with respect to electoral competition: first, what effects would be expected from it, and second, whether they are demonstrable. The empirical problems of demonstrating effects are such that the theory still largely rests on logic, but even the logic is uncertain without some assumptions about the structural and cultural context of competition. An example of this is the question of whether two-party competition tends to produce similarities or differences in party programs, continuity or discontinuity in governmental action. Probably the effect depends on the existing distribution of opinion (including intensities of opinion), which is itself in some degree affected by electoral competition.

The most general proposition about electoral competition seems to be that it promotes equality of treatment in terms of both concrete benefits and personal respect.[2] It may well be that, compared with noncompetitive national systems, organized electoral competition has this result. Yet reflection on American national policies with respect, say, to social security or agricultural subsidies suggests that the income-equalizing effects of close party competition are limited, and the history of race relations suggests that "discrete and insular minorities" may long suffer discrimination despite party competition. Some of this experience may be put down to federalism and other governmental forms that—both alone and by influencing party organization and alignments—affect the scope of electoral competition and the directness of its translation into policies. This interpretation seems most plausible (although not inevitable) with respect to racial discrimination.

It is possible that most Americans believe in tolerance, or inclusiveness of consideration in policy-making, but not in material equality. *If* competition leads to more (or most) people getting what they want or believe in, then inclusiveness of consideration is a more likely outcome of it than equality of condition. Still, inclusiveness is a form of equality, less thoroughgoing and more subjective than that respecting the distribution of material benefits and deprivations. The tendency of the vote-seeking process in competition is no doubt to promote inclusiveness, though there may also be distributions of opinion that limit this, at least temporarily, unless or until they are altered by the process of competition. While the proposition that electoral competition tends to limit oligarchy seems to make sense in terms of political processes (and not simply to be true by definition), there seem also to be limits on the tendency of competition to promote equality in the distribution of whatever ends one has in mind.

Several problems thus complicate analysis of the mechanics and effects of electoral competition. First, the wants to which competition is responsive include both values and interests, opinions and positions, tastes and utilities. One effect of competition may be to cause a citizen's ideology and interest to coincide more closely than they otherwise might by promoting individual involvement, responsibility, and appreciation of policies' consequences. Still, the wants to which competition responds are so complex as to invalidate any simple index rating them to policy outcomes.

Second, there are limits on the inclusive and equalizing tendencies of competition set by existing dispositions and distributions. For instance, reflection on public welfare policy suggests that a strong income-redistributive effect of competition would probably hold only when politics was explicitly about income shares and where the existing distribution was a type (à la Pareto) in which redistribution could run from the affluent minority to an indigent majority instead of the reverse. Otherwise the hypothetical tendency of parties to move toward the medians of opinion distributions would make income redistribution to minorities unlikely except in the event of an altruistic public opinion. Inclusiveness or recognition seems a more likely result of competition than does more material equalization because of the desire of politicians to broaden appeals without offending majority opinion (or to alienate neither minorities nor majorities), but even inclusiveness might not result where a small insular minority confronted an intolerant majority.

Third, electoral competition probably operates to broaden both "direct" and "indirect" influence, in Robert Dahl's terms: i.e., the immediate pressures of active and interested persons on political leaders and officials, and the anticipated, uncertain sanction that the rest of the electorate wields periodically. The distinction between the two is not sharp and, presumably, the direct influence of some persons rests ultimately on their ability to influence others' electoral behavior. The balance between direct and indirect influence, given close electoral competition, seems likely to depend, *inter alia*, on electoral organization, electoral cleavages, the degree of public attention to elections, and the structure and extent of socioeconomic pluralism.

Finally, it follows that the distributive effects of electoral competition depend on several variables: electoral organization and alignments; the structure of the public, including patterns of communication and participation; the prevailing political culture(s); socioeconomic structure; and existing governmental structure and functions as they shape interests and facilitate accountability and responsiveness. Electoral competition would seem in general to broaden governmental responsibility and undermine private oligarchies, but even this tendency is subject to limitations and exceptions, or to preconditions. Moreover, definite indices of distributive outcomes in policy are extremely difficult to construct, as will be seen below.

All of the outcomes of competition in which theorists are interested have, at least incidentally, effects on the distribution of benefits and deprivations in the society. In two of these presumed effects, however, the distributive aspects are not necessarily paramount. The first of these effects is innovation in public policy. This would be expected because of the tendency of competition (especially party competition) to undermine private oligarchies and respond to group demands: both equality and inclusiveness imply continuing policy innovation in a world of changing wants. One survey of national policy-making in the twentieth century has suggested that the periods of most innovation were those of least intense electoral competition, following decisive political realignments.[3] A plausible argument is that very close bidding for votes may discourage innovation because of the political risks or the unforeseeable consequences it entails, or the even balance of pressures favoring innovation and opposing it, so that moderate or secular (instead of intense or continuous) party competition might be most innovative. This also suggests that, since some policy changes are necessarily discontinuous or highly visible (especially in governments performing few functions, such as suburban counties), intense party competition may discourage innovations until majority sentiment or the balance of intensities is clear, although competition may also increase the search for compromise or integration of wants and thus tend toward creative resolutions or conflicting pressures. The most general statement, once again, of the effects of electoral competition is thus that it tends to give more people what they want and that this tendency increases with intensity of competition, but it does not necessarily give everyone what he wants or anyone all of what he wants. The precise effects of competition still depend on political structure and culture, social structure and culture.

Innovation suggests characteristics of governmental performance as well as of policy. Electoral competition may enhance the honesty, accountability, competence, and creativity of administration, given approval of these virtues in the prevailing culture or by those groups with most direct influence on government.[4] A priori, honesty and accountability go with extending the inclusiveness of government and reducing privilege or favoritism. Competence, of a professional sort, is often associated in our culture with these qualities, but it also may make possible more effective response to wants (not to mention needs) without the kind of undue responsiveness that verges on favoritism, and creativity accompanies the integration and innovation discussed above. Usually it has been argued in part that electoral competition both tightens and broadens party organizations, and that the organizations' interests in their own reputations tend to produce these performance attributes in government, whereas competition between unallied, unlabeled politicians would not.[5]

The foregoing observations apply primarily to the putative outcomes of electoral competition, not to the extent of electoral competition itself. One implication of some of them, however, is that the relation between degree of electoral competition and some policy desiderata may not always be linear; it may even be the case that an increase in electoral competition sometimes results in less of some valued policy outcomes. For instance, innovation in policy may be better promoted by a modicum of competition than by close competition, since the latter may induce extreme caution, or risk-minimizing behavior, in politicians. Or it could equally be argued that stability in policy, or long-range planning, is favored by an electoral situation that provides a challenge to the majority party without actually dislodging it from office. Some kinds of egalitarianism in policy (other than those that by definition are associated with close competition) may be advanced by allowing a tolerant and reforming leadership sufficient latitude, or it may be that substantial electoral margins sometimes help professional administrators resist group importunities that tend to undermine general standards.

The problem is that theorists often have several potential benefits in mind when they write of electoral competition. Not only is the competitive optimum not known for any particular benefit in a given social context, but it is even more difficult to state the proper degree of competition for producing an optimal mix of benefits. There are probably state and local situations in which some democrats would favor a degree of competition that makes it possible to turn the incumbents out of power in case of a major scandal or of widespread dissatisfaction, but that also gives incumbents enough security to plan, innovate, and to resist demands from small minorities. Thus, if one conceives of a "goodness of government" function of electoral competition, it is possible that diminishing returns to competition would set in at some point (say, a sixty to forty percent balance in the vote, or alternation in office no oftener than every fourth election), or that the function would be otherwise nonlinear. The same comment probably applies to degree of cohesion of party organization. In their theorizing political scientists have not completely related electoral competition to its social context, to party organization, to the specific governmental attributes that exist, and to those that are desired.

Demonstrating the effects of electoral competition and organization— as distinct from direct governmental response to population diversity —has been extremely difficult. V. O. Key's classic *Southern Politics* suggested ways in which one-party systems affect the responsibility (i.e., the breadth of responsiveness and accountability) of state governments with presumptive effects on inclusiveness or equality in policy and integrity in administration, but this study did not draw expliict comparisons between competitive and one-party states or exclude the possible effect of local political culture.[6] Duane Lockard took the next step in his *New England Politics*, wherein six state polities (three one-party, three competitive) were contrasted with respect to certain policies (welfare expenditures, progressive taxation, and legislative apportionment).[7] While policies in the one-party states more clearly favored the haves over the have-nots and were less even in legislative representation than those in the two-party states, some of the differences were ambiguous, and Lockard was not able to separate cleanly the effects of party competition and organization from the effects of socioeconomic diversity alone. To do so he needed some states that were high in diversity and low in competition, and conversely, as well as clear standards for comparing policies.

Recently, two scholars took another tack: they analyzed statistically all states outside the South to see whether variations in policy (mainly tax structures and welfare expenditures) were more closely associated with variations in socioeconomic or in political structures.[8] They found that policy variations were more closely associated with economic variables, especially per capita personal income, than with degree of electoral competition. Their method was to compare rank-order correlations of the policy variables with economic and election data, respectively, a method less sensitive than, say, multiple regression. Indeed, their study is subject to several reservations that illustrate the problems of clarifying policy variables and explaining their variation. The policy outcomes analyzed included state tax patterns (the elements of which were not closely associated with one another), educational expenditures (which are partly a matter of traditional state-local fiscal relations), and public assistance (on which the federal categorical grants are likely to work a distorting effect because they do not well reflect per capita income in the states).[9] Intergovernmental relations complicate almost all state and local studies of this sort.

Welfare policy is especially difficult to work with for both empirical and theoretical reasons. First, urban, industrial, high-income states in this open-ended federal program tend to have high case loads, which are not solely due to state eligibility policies. (The other area of high incidence is the South.) Indeed, some scholars have argued that variation among state per capita incomes is poorly related to variation among state welfare expenditures, though it is a better explanation of inter-state policy differences in many other fields.[10] Second, despite the close relation of welfare policy to equality and thus, by implication, to some notions of democracy, one may wonder whether party competition is likely to help small, heavily disadvantaged minorities in our society if its tendency is to move both parties toward the middle of opinion distributions and if prevailing opinion is critical of welfare benefits and beneficiaries.

Federal grants and standards complicate the comparison of state policies. So, however, do local, contextual factors that might be mitigated by federal grants and standards if the latter were less responsive than they are to local factors. It may be that state policies are affected by regional cultures or outlooks whose relation to state economic interests remains unclear. That state policies are more highly related to fiscal capacity than to political structure is hardly surprising, but electoral competition may still influence policy within the context of state culture, economy, ecology, and government organization; it may even tend to alter some elements of the context. All of these contextual points suggest that the effects of electoral competition may be most pronounced at the national level—yet other factors may invalidate the comparison of nations in this respect.

The question of the effects of political structure on public policy in the states remains open, then, for both theoretical and methodological reasons. In yet another approach, V. O. Key proposed that political structure makes more difference for administration than it does for policy in the states:

> Doubtless within the states the element of new, broad policy bulks less large within the total government task than it does in the federal sphere. The work of state government consists in higher degree of the unglamorous chores of administration. State political processes have their role, to be sure, in the compromise of differences within the social order and in the performance of the grand functions of politics. Yet a major problem of the politics of the states is to provide administrative direction, powerful enough, honest enough, and stable enough to manage competently the very considerable services of the states. In the accomplishment of these ends the party system has no less a potentiality than it does in the solution of the greater ... issues of policy.[11]

Key's suggestion may help explain why state policies have been found to vary so little with electoral organization, but it has not led to much comparative study of the relations of governmental conduct to political structure.

At the local level, as the text suggests, the theory of electoral competition may be least applicable of all. There may be less policy variation than in the states, and the problem of isolating electoral variables may be more acute. One possible test concerns the effect of nonpartisan local elections, which, by tending to undercut electoral organization and by obscuring party labels, are supposed to produce effects like those that V. O. Key suspected in the one-party South, further disadvantaging the have-nots because the haves tend already to be organized and to control communications.[12] Attempts to study this proposition empirically and comparatively have suggested (1) that a different pattern of social and economic representation occurs in small nonpartisan cities (but without direct comparison of these with partisan cities), and (2) that lack of party labels and organization seems to affect the stability of office-holding in large cities.[13] The attempt to relate electoral organization to actual policies, or indices of policies, has not so far disclosed systematic differences between partisan and nonpartisan cities.[14]

As for different degrees of party competition, Edwin H. Rhyne examined three North Carolina counties ranging from two-party competitive through one-party bifactional to one-party multifactional (none was a monolithic one-party county).[15] Focusing on the characteristics of policy-making, rather than on policy outcomes, Rhyne argued that party competition should increase the proportion of effective decision-makers who depend on elections for their positions, and that, to improve accountability, the more competitive elections (organized around two parties) should more overtly turn on the merits of governmental policy. He found no evidence for either proposition, and suggested that a close party balance may have increased officeholders' incentives to keep concrete issues out of politics, in which they may have been assisted by the rigid, traditional party balance of the competitive county, which seemed largely determined by sectional orientation to national issues. Significantly, none of Rhyne's three counties displayed much organized socioeconomic pluralism, and the formally competitive county contained the most highly concentrated, heavily invested potential for economic (industrial) power. Rhyne therefore recommended agnosticism on the "organizational theory of democracy" at the local level, suggesting that "power-structure" explanations of policy, despite their blind eye to formal political structure, are about as likely to be valid.

The counties in the present study are more urbanized than Rhyne's. Moreover, the county with the greatest division of incomes and occupations is the most strongly organized one-party county. It is also an industrialized county with high potential for a private power structure. Thus the three suburban counties provide at least a limited test of the effects of interparty competition, intraparty competition, and solid organization, all in the presence of considerable socioeconomic diversity. But they raise the problem of disentangling power structure from party political structure.

The literature about power structures, or the distribution of influence in communities, now defies summary.[16] What Polsby has called the "stratification theory" can be traced through the community-study tradition in American sociology.[17] The modern controversy may be said to have begun with Floyd Hunter's *Community Power Structure*.[18] Hunter's conceptualization of power has been generally held to be unclear, especially in its confusion of actual and potential power; and his reliance on the "reputational" method has been much criticized both in theory and in application.

A few points about Hunter's study are relevant to the present volume, but I shall not review in any detail the controversy to which it gave rise. Hunter examined a community (Atlanta) that lacked party competition; that partook of the Southern culture and race consciousness, compelling some white unanimity and tending to suppress some social issues; that lacked other ethnic diversity; that contained a number of large, established, local businesses; and that had a tradition (no doubt related to its political structure) of private instead of governmental action in such fields as health and welfare and economic development, which were those that Hunter principally studied. In all these respects Atlanta differed strikingly from, say, Robert Dahl's New Haven, and this may account for some of the differences in Dahl's and Hunter's conclusions about their communities. The point about private endeavor is also suggestive with respect to Hunter's method. As a community-organization professional, Hunter was specifically interested in potential power as well as actual power: he wanted to know who could be mobilized to get something accomplished—especially in the health and welfare fields, which were then traditionally voluntary and heavily dependent on private charity. Not surprisingly, he found that potential donors held potential power. Furthermore, he had a special understanding of local democracy, as primarily a matter of voluntary association and direct participation, with which the distribution of influence that he found was substantially at variance, and his expectations, or model, of democracy doubtless directed his interest to its perversion in the voluntary sector and heightened the sense of social criticism that pervades his work.

The question of the relation between the extent of socioeconomic pluralism and that of electoral competition is explicitly raised in Robert Dahl's study of New Haven.[19] As Dahl describes the community, resources that might be used for political influence are not concentrated in a few hands, official positions are not typically held by members of social or economic elites, and the participation of such notables is usually confined to specific fields of policy. It thus appears that political and governmental roles in policy are not outweighed by private power structures, and the question then arises of political and governmental responsiveness. On this topic Dahl's argument proceeds by a series of distinctions: between the active "political stratum" and the indifferent remainder of the population; between leaders and subleaders in the political stratum; between overt and covert policies adopted by leaders, for the population at large and for subleaders respectively; and between direct and indirect influence. Dahl argues that the "indirect" influence of the population at large on the overt policies of leaders, exercised through popular elections, is considerable—sufficient to hold them broadly accountable and to help counter the potential power (or direct influence) of private resources and political actives. This is partly because private-resource concentrations are "dispersed" rather than "cumulative" and are rarely used to the hilt, and partly because of the influence of the democratic myth or "mold," but it is also attributed to New Haven's intense, well-organized two-party competition, a local peculiarity.[20] *Who Governs?* does leave open the questions of how important New Haven's exceptional electoral competition was in the overall distribution of influence in that city, of how electoral competition and socioeconomic pluralism are related, and of what specific difference the combination of them made for public policy and governmental performance. Dahl's analysis does lead to the suggestion that electoral competition operates as much by broadening sources of "direct" influence as by facilitating indirect influence; therefore it tends toward group inclusiveness instead of overall equality, but in either case to weaken local oligarchies or cohesive elites.

Another, minor issue in the New Haven study seems to me to concern the role of what structuralists call the economic dominants in the community. The main power bases (or resources) examined by Dahl are social status, wealth, political popularity (primarily ethnicity), and strategic position with respect to certain kinds of programs or policies (those that confer collective benefits), though Dahl notes that the range of potential political resources is infinite and continuous. The emphasis on wealth may not adequately answer the structuralist claim that *control* by some economic interests is implicit in their positions. For instance, the size and potential mobility of some large industrial employers might tacitly bring about tax concessions (implicitly affecting other policies) simply in order to keep payrolls and tax bases in the community. This kind of possibility is explored in the present study, since local industry's political involvement has long been close in the suburban counties, and its power potential is generally rated high.

The mobilization-of-bias notion suggests, in this connection and some others, that concrete demonstrations of outcomes in discrete decisions are not enough to settle the question of elite influence.[21] Case studies almost always make the world appear especially pluralistic and contingent because they take the institutional background for granted. They are not more empirical than the study of institutions and ideologies, but, as narrative instead of schematic description, they may be easier to keep free of values. Still, without the broader context, they are partial in another sense.

Much, perhaps all, mobilization of bias can be spelled out in terms of resources that are convertible into influence, but there are difficulties with the concept of a resource. The resources sustaining influence must vary indefinitely with tastes, utilities, and expectations. Categories like wealth, organization, formal position, reputation, legitimacy, skill, and job control (proposed by Dahl) are neither definitive nor exhaustive, and the resources in question cannot be independently valued with any precision. The observer has to impute value to resources—and even to impute the use of resources to participants—in a *post hoc* explanation. Often, in the present study, I have likened political systems to economies of incentives and contributions (resources), but sometimes the counters are necessarily hypothetical, resting on inferences or assumptions about mens' values and motives. This seems to me unsatisfactory, just as the structuralist's assumption about the influence inhering in basic social relations is unsatisfactory: it is not a demonstration of influence or of the lack of it, but in proper context it should lead to a more specific, painstaking analysis and test the plausibility of a theory. Sometimes the explanations or theses that are cast in these terms in this study seem to me too neat, but I have thought it awkward to qualify them, and I have hoped to provide enough context so that qualifications would occur to readers.

The relation of resources to institutions and expectations gives rise to the issue whether interests or ideologies are more important in explaining actions and decisions. To some considerable extent this must depend on local circumstances, and the bearing of this on the issue in this study is discussed in Chapter 19, Section 4, page 224. To some extent, too, structure and culture, interests and ideologies refer to the same phenomena in different perspective; but beyond this overlap they refer to different facts (social and psychological facts) that are reciprocally related. In the circumstances of this study, priority in sequences of change seems to have been structural rather than cultural. Moreover, insofar as explanation of change is aimed at practical utility, it is structure that seems most promising.

One apparent problem in emphasizing interests is that they must often be imputed to individuals, whereas ideologies are expressed verbally. Yet ideologies may reflect an individual's rationalization of his own motivation or an observer's rationalization of expression. Usually, students have inferred both ideologies and interests from the overt behavior of groups or individuals. Recently, Agger, Goldrich, and Swanson went further, deriving several distinct ideologies about local government from interviews and survey data, and making these the defining elements in types of power structures.[22] They also made citizen beliefs about the operation of power structures a defining element in types of electoral regime. In four cities of the South and West they found that ideological cleavage made electoral competition more effective, and that it was a critical factor in most public policies and issues. My reasons for deemphasizing ideological determinants of policy are given in Chapter 19, but this study contributes little to the questions of whether in general surveys or observation, attitudinal or behavioral data are more relevant and reliable in the study of political influence; whether structure or culture takes priority in explanations of policy. Peoples' definitions of the situation are always important, but in the suburban counties studied governmental, electoral, social, and economic organization so far seems to have encouraged a politics of relatively specific interests. The situation might be different, for instance, in nonpartisan election systems, primarily residential communities, or jurisdictions more directly relevant to social diversity. In comparing the counties some differences appear in the mix of political subcultures contained in them, but in explaining change or innovation, structural factors or specific interests seem to be more significant in contextual analysis and in case studies.

My approach to this study has been more qualitative than quantitative. In particular, I have not relied primarily on objective indices of governmental policy and performance, though I have taken account of fiscal and personnel data. I have used some survey data to try to get a line on wants, felt by elements of the population, but I have also relied heavily on statements by politicians and active participants about their views of popular attitudes and demands. From observation and interviewing I have tried to reason about the relations that obtain among some basic variables, which are broadly identified as socioeconomic, political, and governmental structures. Within the category of political structure I have focused on the relations between electoral competition and organization on one hand and factors in the informal distribution of influence on the other. For context, I have endeavored to provide sufficient social history and description of local institutions, and within this context to follow the course of some policy decisions in detail. I hope that the foregoing discussion indicates why I feel that this approach, less highly formal and focused than some others, was appropriate to the several ends I had in view. The specific things that were done are described in the Appendix B.

APPENDIX B. METHOD

The published chronicle of local and county affairs is not extensive. For this study metropolitan and local newspaper coverage was reviewed for the last decade. The three county planning commissions generously made their resources available. At nearly every point, however, the study heavily depends on interviews. More than fifty informants were interviewed (several more than once) in each county about county affairs, and some in each municipality on either general or specific points. These were unstandardized interviews. The writer did the interviewing in Bucks and Montgomery Counties and some of it in Delaware County. Because of his participation in Delaware County politics and civic affairs, however, it seemed desirable to provide an independent check and perspective and a less-suspect scholar; thus, within the broad topical outline for all the counties, Cyril Roseman took initial responsibility for, so to speak, evidentiary findings and a number of judgments about Delaware County. His influence is most pronounced in that aspect of the study, though I am sure it is generally pervasive.

As to the municipalities, three Swarthmore College undergraduates made an exploratory study of five of them (Radnor, Ridley, Aldan, Glenolden, Yeadon) under a Ford Foundation Public Affairs grant administered by Swarthmore College in the summer of 1962. All the work on the four Montgomery County municipalities was done by Stephen Decter, then a graduate student in political science at the University of Pennsylvania; he reviewed the newspapers and documents in detail, held standardized interviews with an agreed selection (largely his own) of about thirty informants in each municipality, and wrote in-depth reports upon which I have drawn in Part V. In five Delaware County municipalities—Marple, Springfield, Middletown, Glenolden, and Yeadon—standardized interviews were held from ten to twenty-five community leaders (both civic and political) in each municipality. As in Montgomery, the persons interviewed were selected primarily as informants rather than as representatives on the basis of a record of participation and responsibility or on the recommendation of other informants as to their knowledge of local affairs, but an effort was made

331

to balance various sectors or types of leadership and participation. The number of persons interviewed varied with size of community and apparent dispersal of leadership, and because we stopped interviewing in some communities when virtual unanimity persisted in answers to questions deemed most important. In all municipalities there were a few unstandardized interviews with persons thought to be especially influential or well informed.

The sample survey was decided on rather late in the study when it appeared that public reactions to both county and municipal policy would provide useful baselines. The survey was done on a shoestring and was the writer's first experience in survey design and administration. About 300 interviews seemed feasible, and the author decided to work in the most and least competitive counties, attempting fifty interviews in each of six municipalities. The choice of municipalities in Bucks was clear, since only two communities there had been selected for study; in Delaware the selection depended on differences in social rank and on specific comparisons (such as Marple and Springfield) that looked interesting.

Those interviewed were a random sample of registered voters who had lived in their communities for at least a year. They were selected by means of a table of random numbers from voter street lists. They received a letter from the president of PENJERDEL introducing and briefly explaining the study, following which interviewers telephoned for an appointment. This procedure minimized infringement of privacy and probably lowered the response rate most significantly in communities normally prone to low response rates whose residents were more likely to be persuaded by direct confrontation than by formal appointment. The response rate was adversely affected by the fact that most of the interviewing was done during the summer (of 1963), when vacation schedules interfered with availability of the interviewees and with our ability to follow up many letters immediately, as well as by discrepancies between street lists and telephone directories resulting from spotty precinct work and removals after publication. Besides those (1) actually interviewed, the response rate depends on persons who (2) refused a direct interview but consented to answer a few questions over the telephone (designed to check on the characteristics of refusals), (3) refused completely, and (4) were classed as unavailable because, for whatever reason, no contacts could be made. The response rate recorded, overall and for each community, is the percentage that category (1) forms of the sum of categories (1), (2), and (3). In these terms, it is a low response rate.

As to the characteristics of *non*interviewees, the telephone interview data reveal that they have a somewhat lower occupational status than do the respondents in all townships except Ridley, and substantially less membership in local organizations in all townships as well as substantially less ability (or willingness) to mention any local issues or

TABLE B:1
Response Rate

	Selected	Inter- viewed	Phone Inteview	Complete Refusal	Not Avail- able*	Rate (percent)
Radnor	82	45	11	10	16	70
Marple	90	50	15	13	12	65
Springfield	81	51	11	7	12	74
Ridley	98	45	26	14	12	52
Bristol	104	50	4	20	30	67
Middletown	85	37	10	16	12	51
Total	540	278	77	80	94	62

* In Bristol the "Not Available" category is large because the interviewing—for reasons of personnel—had to be accomplished in a short time during the height of the vacation season. Thus, more letters were sent, and some people not reached during the shorter period have been arbitrarily allocated to "Not Available."

problems. Educational level was not collected for nonrespondents. As one would expect, the more participative persons tend to be self-selected for interviews. It may well be that outright refusals were still lower in occupational status and participation than those who consented to telephone interviews.

The resultant sample overrepresented high income and occupational levels, as may be seen when census and sampling distributions are compared (see Tables B:2 and B:3).

Oddly, Bistol Township (the lowest of all in social rank) was most satisfactorily sampled, according to this comparison, and Middletown least so. Apart from selectivity in the response rate, it may be that voter registration (as a population) is not fully representative of the more general population, that misreporting or poor interviewer classifications of occupation or misreporting of income in either the survey or census help account for disparities. Occupation is more poorly represented than income, suggesting that interviewer judgments may not have jibed sufficiently with census classifications: interviewers relied on the census breakdown in the publication, *General Social and Economic Characteristics;* but the more detailed census enumerator's breakdown was not employed.

Other distributions—e.g., age and sex—were not out of line. The distribution of party preference (on a question similar to that normally asked by the University of Michigan Survey Research Center) and of party registration (obtained from the street lists directly) may be of interest; the latter was representative within the limits of expected sampling error (see Tables B:4 and B:5).

Several points about interpretation of the survey data may be helpful to the reader. The first is a table of sampling error from which he may read the range of a distribution in percentage points, for a sample of size N, that may be expected with 90 percent probability to approximate the parent population of the sample. The tables include a "one-tailed"

TABLE B:2
Occupation (in percent of total)

	Professional		Managerial		Clerical		Sales		Craftsmen, etc.		Operatives		Private Household		Service		Laborer	
	C*	S**	C	S	C	S	C	S	C	S	C	S	C	S	C	S	C	S
Radnor	22.5	35.5	20.4	44.4	7.4	4.4	12.4	11.1	10.7	2.2	8.1	0.0	1.1	2.2	6.5	0.0	4.5	0.0
Marple	24.2	28.0	19.9	26.0	7.3	10.0	13.9	18.0	18.6	14.0	8.7	2.0	0.2	0.0	3.0	0.0	1.4	0.0
Springfield	26.1	45.0	19.1	11.7	7.4	9.8	14.3	11.7	18.5	17.6	8.4	0.0	0.0	1.9	2.0	1.0	1.3	0.0
Ridley	12.8	20.0	7.7	24.4	8.5	11.1	7.5	4.4	30.0	31.1	21.8	4.4	0.1	0.0	3.7	4.4	3.0	0.0
Bristol	12.1	12.0	7.7	14.0	8.1	16.0	7.3	14.0	27.6	18.0	26.5	6.0	0.0	0.0	3.6	2.0	5.4	18.0
Middletown	24.6	35.1	14.3	18.9	7.5	2.7	9.3	10.8	21.9	18.9	13.8	8.1	0.3	0.0	2.3	2.7	2.3	2.7

TABLE B:3
Incomes (in percent of total)

	Under $4,000		$4,000–$4,999		$5,000–$7,499		$7,500–$9,999		$10,000–$14,999		Over $15,000	
	C	S	C	S	C	S	C	S	C	S	C	S
Radnor	10.9	0.0	4.7	4.4	17.7	8.8	14.4	20.0	22.6	40.0	29.7	22.2
Marple	7.1	0.0	5.5	0.0	23.1	20.0	28.3	34.0	26.4	36.0	9.6	8.0
Springfield	4.9	0.0	2.7	1.9	23.2	9.8	26.7	35.2	31.4	37.2	11.1	11.7
Ridley	10.2	4.4	8.0	11.1	40.5	28.8	23.7	44.4	16.0	8.8	1.6	2.2
Bristol	10.7	2.0	9.8	6.0	41.8	38.0	24.9	38.0	10.9	12.0	1.9	2.0
Middletown	8.2	0.0	6.0	10.8	33.8	16.2	24.0	21.6	21.5	37.8	6.5	5.4

* C = Census.
** S = Survey.

TABLE B:4

Party Preference (in percent of total)

	Republican	Independent	Democratic
Radnor	62.1	26.6	8.8
Marple	38.0	46.0	16.0
Springfield	50.9	33.3	15.6
Ridley	35.5	37.7	26.6
Bristol	32.0	22.0	44.0
Middletown	32.4	24.3	43.2

TABLE B:5

Party Registration (in percent of total)

	Republican	No Party	Democratic
Radnor	86.6	—	13.3
Marple	70.0	4.0	26.0
Springfield	76.4	6.0	17.6
Ridley	73.3	2.3	24.4
Bristol	44.0	—	56.0
Middletown	40.5	—	59.4

test of differences between sample proportions appropriate in cases where there is theoretical reason to expect the difference, and a "two-tailed" test appropriate when such expectation is lacking. The tests numbered II and III may be used, for example, in assessing the sig-

TABLE B:6

Sampling Error

I. Approximate Sampling Error at 10 Percent Probability

Sample percentage	SAMPLE SIZE					
	300	200	100	75	50	25
50 percent	5	6	8	9	12	17
30 or 70 percent	4	5	8	8	11	15
20 or 80 percent	4	5	7	8	9	13
10 or 90 percent	3	4	5	6	7	10

II. Sampling Error of Differences Predicted in Advance
(for percentages between 35 and 65 at 10 percent probability)

Sample size	100	75	50	25
100	9	10	11	14
75		10	12	15
50			13	16
25				18

III. Sampling Error of Differences Not Predicted in Advance
(for percentages between 35 and 65 at 10 percent probability)

Sample size	100	75	50	25
100	12	13	14	18
75		13	15	19
50			17	20
25				23

nificance of a sample difference between two townships in proportions of yes-no responses to a question.

Often in the text (especially in Part V) statements are made— appropriately guarded, I hope—about the relation of social or economic indices, such as income, education, or occupation, to some other, dependent, variable such as attitude, opinion, or behavior. Unless noted, these statements rest on statistical significance of differences at the 10 percent level (generally regarded as a very lenient test), for counties or for the total survey. Such is not the case for individual municipal breakdowns, where small numbers tighten the statistical tests extremely, and where tendencies are cited if they are consistent among municipalities from which they were expected. Linear or continuous correlation techniques were not employed; instead, all inferences are drawn by breaking each variable into (usually) two classes and constructing tables for which tetrachoric coefficients or chi-square tests were used. Of the basic socioeconomic variables, education was broken between high school graduation and any college experience; occupation between professional and managerial groups on the one hand and all others in most cases, but occasionally between white- and blue-collar employment (which gave a less even division, overall); income in most cases at $10,000. The breaks occur at high levels, but these levels were necessary for a good distribution in fourfold tables in the total sample (though they were either too high or too low for good distributions in all municipalities).

All this should put the reader on guard against uncritical reliance on the survey results. I have tried to use them conservatively, in at least three ways: (1) by depending on them most heavily where there is reason to believe they understate a distribution or relation (as in the lack of knowledge about county affairs, or lack of participation); (2) by employing only responses to questions that seem, internally and from interviewer reports, to have worked well and that hang together in clusters about a general topic so that cumulative effects may be discerned and weighed; and (3) by interpreting them in most cases as indicative of tendencies and differences rather than as descriptive of a universe in any precise sense.[1]

In the summer of 1965 a second survey was taken to explore differences in civic and political participation between large and small communities. The survey was done by Robert Hawkinson, a Swarthmore undergraduate (and by a few student interviewers), as part of a thesis by Hawkinson. Fifty interviews were taken in each of four communities: Radnor and Ridley Townships (which were also in the first survey), and Swarthmore and Glenolden Boroughs, which are communities of about 6,000 population, small in area. The contrasts between the two large communities and between the two small communities are set out in the first two tables of Chapter 21. Sampling and interview procedures, response rates, and data breakdowns were similar to those of the first survey.

Despite the brief remarks in the Introduction a further word is probably in order about the treatment of power or influence in this study. It is also integral to the study of political competition. Here, as in the survey, I have been interested in tendencies and differences rather than in a precise description of any particular distribution of power in any particular community; in fact, that is all one can explore with the methods extant. I think it is enough for this comparative study. I have accepted *both* Robert Dahl's proposed tests of power and burden of proof *and* the mobilization of bias, contextual notion of Bachrach and Baratz, but I have sought to spell out the latter as much as possible in terms of specific interests and resources, as well as treating tradition and ideology.[2] What is often termed the reputational approach was employed in limited degree. In most interviews in the counties and in all municipal interviews informants were asked approximately the following question:

> It is often said of American local communities and governments that —no matter who is elected to office—there is a small group of people who are regularly influential in policy. Would you say that is true of ——————?

This general question was followed up as to individuals and organizations, and fields of policy. The overall results for the counties are reported in Chapter 19, and for the municipalities, in Chapter 21. One interesting tendency was for politicians automatically to interpret the question as referring to elective or, at least, party leadership, so that it was often necessary to broaden their frame of reference explicitly; businessmen were especially likely to interpret it in more conventional private power structure terms, whether or not they answered it affirmatively.

Besides the limited reputational approach, the chapters in Part IV rest on more historical detail than could be reported, with special attention to the origins of programs and sources of influence on decisions. Besides the case histories, considerable data were gathered for the last fifteen years on such points as organization and board memberships (their overlap and continuity), on tenure and turnover of public office, and on election and registration trends, but none of them, in their details, seemed sufficiently interesting or critical, as they turned out, to merit tabular presentation, though they certainly figured in descriptions and influenced conclusions.

NOTES

1. Introduction

1. Chester County, which does not abut on Philadelphia and is the most rural county in the metropolitan region, was omitted because of its slower growth and its lower legal status as a fourth-class county.

2. "The longer one frets with the puzzle of how democratic regimes manage to function, the more plausible it appears that a substantial part of the explanation is to be found in the motives that actuate the leadership echelon, the values that it holds, in the rules of the political game to which it adheres . . .". V. O. Key, Jr., *Public Opinion and American Democracy* (New York: Alfred A. Knopf, 1961), p. 537.

3. Nelson W. Polsby, *Community Power and Political Theory* (New Haven: Yale University Press, 1963), p. 117. I am using the term *structuralist* for what Polsby calls the "stratification theory" of power, for reasons apparent in the text. Other literature about this issue is cited in Appendix A.

4. Peter Bachrach and Morton Baratz, "The Two Faces of Power," *American Political Science Review*, 56 (1962), 947.

2. Three Centuries of Settlement

1. J. H. Battle, *History of Bucks County, Pennsylvania* (Philadelphia: A. Warner & Co., 1887), p. 280.

2. Ibid., p. 284.

3. Frederick Tolles has described the growing division between the urban and rural Quakers in *Meeting House and Counting House* (Chapel Hill: Univ. of North Carolina Press, 1948), and the bucolic Germans had little to do with Philadelphia. Urban-rural differences are also described in Carl Bridenbaugh, *Cities in the Wilderness* (New York: Knopf, 1955), and *Cities in Revolt* (New York: Knopf, 1955), and in Carl and Jessica Bridenbaugh, *Rebels and Gentlemen: Philadelphia in the Age of Franklin* (New York: Reynal and Hitchcock, 1942). The mixed economic and political identifications of the suburbs in the late eighteenth century appear in Theodore Thayer, *Pennsylvania Politics and the Growth of Democracy, 1940–1776* (Harrisburg: Pennsylvania Historical and Museum Commission, 1953), p. 131.

4. E. Digby Baltzell, *Philadelphia Gentlemen* (Glencoe, Ill.: Free Press, 1958), Ch. 9.

5. Nicholas B. Wainwright, *History of the Philadelphia Electric Company, 1881–1961* (Philadelphia: The Company, 1961), pp. 132–33.

6. Bureau of Statistics, Department of Internal Affairs, Commonwealth of Pennsylvania, *Employment by Broad Industry Groups and by County for Selected Years, 1919–1961* (Harrisburg: The Bureau, 1963).

7. Charles Palmer, *A History of Delaware County, Pennsylvania*, I (Harrisburg, Pa.: National Historical Association, Inc., 1932), p. 116.

8. On the evolution of larger lot sizes in the county, see James G. Coke and Charles S. Liebman, "Political Values and Population Density Control," *Land Economics* 37 (1961), 347 ff.; they argue that the pressure for larger lots has come from suburban officials (presumably responding to residents' preferences in part) rather than from developers.

9. Baltzell.

10. Gladys L. Palmer, *Philadelphia Workers in a Changing Economy* (Philadelphia: Univ. of Pennsylvania Press, 1956), esp. pp. 51–52. See also Southeastern Pennsylvania Regional Planning Commission, *Four County Industrial Land and Facilities Study* and *Four County Industrial Land and Facilities Requirements* (Philadelphia: Institute for Urban Studies, Univ. of Pennsylvania, 1957).

11. These economic characteristics are described in ibid. and more recently in Regional Science Research Institute, University of Pennsylvania, *An Investigation of Location Factors Influencing the Economy of the Philadelphia Region* (Philadelphia: The Institute, 1966).

3. The County as Society and Community

1. See especially Robert C. Wood, *Suburbia: Its People and Their Politics* (Boston: Houghton Mifflin, 1959), Chs. 1–2.

2. On costs of political agreement see James Buchanan and Gordon Tullock, *The Calculus of Consent* (Ann Arbor: Univ. of Michigan Press, 1962). For suggestions about motivation and suburban differentiation see *inter alia*, Wood; Charles Thibout, "A Pure Theory of Local Expenditures," *Journal of Political Economy* 54 (1959), 416; O. B. Duncan, "Residential Distribution of Occupational Stratification," *American Journal of Sociology* 60 (1955), 493; Wendell Bell, "Social Choice, Life Styles, and Suburb Residence," in William Dobriner, ed., *The Suburban Community* (New York: G. P. Putnam's Sons, 1958), p. 225.

3. Oliver P. Williams, et al., *Suburban Differences and Metropolitan Policies* (Philadelphia: Univ. of Pennsylvania Press, 1965), hereafter referred to as the Fels Study.

4. The social rank index used in the Fels Study was obtained from census data on the proportion of professional, managerial, and sales workers among employed males and the proportion of municipal population over age twenty-five with some college education; these two were equally weighted, and the scale was standardized over all municipalities. It is derived from Eshref Shevkey and Wendell Bell, *Social Area Analysis* (Stanford Univ. Press, 1955). Any such scale is arbitrary, but some scholars might cavil at the weight given education by the seemingly stricter requirements set for this variable, or at either the inclusion of sales personnel or exclusion of clerical workers among the upper occupational categories. A related study of Delaware County real

estate development concluded that local large-lot zoning was of limited direct effectiveness in protecting the tax base, since housing prices still varied substantially within zones. Instead, interviews with local officials suggested that zoning was primarily intended to preserve social and esthetic values and was only incidentally invidious. James Coke and Charles Liebman, "Political Values and Population Density Control," *Land Economics*, 37 (1961), 347.

5. Cf. Williams et al., Ch. 2; and Leslie Kish, "Differentiation in Metropolitan Areas," *American Sociological Review* 19 (1954), 388, for overall measures, and William Dobriner, *Class in Suburbia* (Englewood Cliffs, N.J.: Prentice-Hall Spectrum Books, 1963), on local social diversity.

6. Communities can be ranked by the semi-interquartile range of family incomes or by the percentage of incomes at the extreme ends of the distribution, or by Gini coefficients of income distribution. The scale of occupations in the census can be weighted, and means and standard deviations can be computed from it and compared. The same process also can be used with educational levels (neither distribution is normal, of course). Occupational and educational levels can be divided into classes and the extent of concentration in one or more classes compared among communities. All these things were done for this study, but they are not reproduced here because of the inadequacies of each index and the fact that their most obvious implications can be simply stated in the text.

7. Thomas R. Dye, "The Local-Cosmopolitan Dimension and the Study of Urban Politics," *Social Forces*, 41 (1963), 239. Dye's study asked two of the three questions dealing with consolidation and zoning, which were discussed on page 32.

8. James G. Coke, "Stability and Change: Local Government in the Philadelphia Metropolitan Area," *Public Administration Review*, 23 (1963), 186.

4. Interests

1. Malcolm R. Eiselen, *The Rise of Pennsylvania Protectionism* (Philadelphia: Univ. of Pennsylvania Press, 1932).

2. Ann Hawkes Hutton, *The Pennsylvanian* (Philadelphia: Dorrance & Co., 1962), p. 136, mentions that Grundy's father had been "a persistent Harrisburg visitor in his lobbying efforts to improve the tax situation," namely, to repeal the state's capital stock tax, which was finally accomplished in 1889. In the later years Joseph Grundy joined his father in Harrisburg.

3. J. Roffe Wike, *The Pennsylvania Manufacturers' Association* (Philadelphia: Univ. of Pennsylvania Press, 1960), p. 29.

4. From a letter quoted in James H. Soltow, "Small City Industrialists in the Age of Organization," *The Business History Review*, 33 (1959), 181.

5. Ibid., p. 183.

6. Edward Cooke, "Research: An Instrument of Political Power," *Political Science Quarterly*, 76 (1961), 69–70. Cooke's thesis is that provision of research directed at economy and efficiency is a subtle but conservative force.

7. For descriptions of these organizations, see W. H. Brown, Jr., and C. E. Gilbert, *Planning Municipal Investment* (Philadelphia: Univ. of Pennsylvania Press, 1961), Ch. 6.

8. Edward C. Banfield and James Q. Wilson, *City Politics*, p. 25. They

heavily rely on A. Vidich and J. Bensman, *Small Town in Mass Society* (Princeton Univ. Press, 1958).

9. Ibid., p. 28.

5. Influence

1. Peter H. Rossi, "The Organizational Structure of an American Community," in Amitai Etzioni, ed., *Complex Organizations* (New York: Holt Rinehart & Winston, 1961), p. 301, and "Power and Community Structure," in Edward C. Banfield, ed., *Urban Government: A Reader in Politics and Administration* (New York: Free Press, 1961), p. 413; Robert Schulze, "The Role of Economic Dominants in Community Power Structure," *American Sociological Review*, 23 (1958), 3, and "The Bifurcation of Power in a Satellite City," in M. Janowitz, ed., *Community Political Systems* (New York: Free Press, 1961), p. 19; and Norton E. Long, "The Corporation, Its Satellites and the Local Community," in E. S. Mason, ed., *The Corporation in Modern Society* (Cambridge, Mass.: Harvard Univ. Press, 1959), p. 202. Also, see R. J. Pellegrin and C. H. Coates, "Absentee-Owned Corporations and Community Power Structure," *American Journal of Sociology*, 61 (1958), 413, for an opposite thesis.

2. Dahl, *Who Governs?* (New Haven, Conn.: Yale Univ. Press, 1961).

3. The principal sources are the late nineteenth-century county histories written for the national centennial. These are supplemented by newspaper, documentary, and biographical data in county historical societies. But the record is much less complete for our suburban counties than it was for New Haven, and one cannot be sure that the sample provided by historical accounts is accurate.

4. Philip S. Klein, *Pennsylvania Politics, 1817–1832: A Game Without Rules* (Philadelphia: Historical Society of Pennsylvania, 1940), p. 365.

5. In Delaware County the central place of the Delaware County National Bank, whose early directors included ancestors of men now professionally active in Chester, may conveniently be traced in Henry Graham Ashmead, *History of the Delaware County National Bank* (Chester [Pa.] Times Press, 1914).

6. The twentieth century urbanizing trend is traced in some detail for one community in Sidney Goldstein, *The Norristown Study* (Philadelphia: Univ. of Pennsylvania Press, 1961).

7. Early Pennsylvania law freely allowed branch banking, but this was restricted in 1850 to branches specified in banks' charters. After the National Bank Act of 1863 the U.S. Controller of the Currency for some sixty years interpreted the law to prohibit the establishment of branches by national banks, and into the early twentieth century Pennsylvania's attorneys General held that the silence of state law on the subject was also a prohibition. A state law passed in 1927 limited branches to those already existing, but in the same year Congress legalized National bank branches in states permitting branch banking. In 1933 the Pennsylvania law was amended to permit Philadelphia banks to establish branches by merger in any contiguous township of the first class or *de novo* in any such townships without banking facilities, and in 1935 this arrangement was extended from township to contiguous

counties and later broadened to allow new branches in communities without adequate banking facilities (1937). Such is essentially the law today. Pennsylvania Joint State Government Commission, *Branch Banking*, Harrisburg: 1957. The growth of concentration in commercial bank deposits in the five largest banks in the Philadelphia metropolitan area went from 31.6 percent in 1920 to 65.4 percent in 1934 to 85.1 percent in 1958, and it continued to increase after 1958. U.S. Congress, House of Representatives, Select Committee on Small Business, *Banking Concentration and Small Business* (Washington: Government Printing Office, 1960), p. 28.

6. The Old Organizations

1. See especially Harry M. Tinkcom, *The Republicans and Federalists in Pennsylvania, 1790–1801* (Harrisburg: Pennsylvania Historical and Museum Commission, 1950); Sanford W. Higginbotham, *The Keystone in the Democratic Arch: Pennsylvania Politics, 1800–1816* (Harrisburg: Pennsylvania Historical and Museum Commission, 1952; and Philip S. Klein, *Pennsylvania Politics, 1817–1832: A Game Without Rules* (Philadelphia: Historical Society of Pennsylvania, 1940).

2. Tinckom.

3. Cf., E. E. Schattschneider, "The United States: A Functional Approach to Party Government," in S. Neumann, *Modern Political Parties* (Univ. of Chicago Press, 1955), and V. O. Key, "A Theory of Critical Elections," *Journal of Politics*, 17 (1955), 3.

4. The lone exception occurred in Bucks in 1936 when Roosevelt barely prevailed: then the Bristol industrial area briefly undermined the local organization, and since that time organized labor and the Italian population in Bristol have been minor political forces.

5. Higginbotham, pp. 331–32, and cf. Klein, pp. 52–56.

6. Edward W. Hocker, "Montgomery County" in J. Bennett Nolan, *Southeastern Pennsylvania* (Philadelphia: Lewis Historical Publishing Co., 1943), p. 661.

7. Klein, p. 71.

8. The direct primary began in Crawford County, long before the Civil War. Most counties did not adopt it until much later, however; and it was not required by state law until 1913. None of the suburban Philadelphia counties used it until 1913.

7. Bucks County

1. Philadelphia *Inquirer*, November 4, 1954.

9. Delaware County, I

1. Samuel T. Wiley, *Biographical and Historical Cyclopedia of Delaware County, Pennsylvania* (Richmond, Ind., and New York: Gresham Publishing Co., 1894), p. 178. See also John W. Jordan, *A History of Delaware County*,

Pennsylvania, and Its People, III (New York: Lewis Historical Publishing Co., 1914), p. 1,018.

2. Obituary, Chester *Times,* May 3, 1907.

3. Chester *Times,* March 8, 1963.

10. Delaware County, II

1. McClure was the only local political leader with whom the writer sought an interview unsuccessfully. Repeated attempts were unavailing, but ill health was probably the reason. In the past McClure occasionally gave interviews to reporters and students, and I have had access to notes of several such interviews. See Robert Allen, "No Hurrah for McClure," *The Nation,* July 26, 1957.

2. Chester *Times,* June 2, 1957.

3. *The End of Ideology* (Glencoe, Ill.: Free Press, 1960), Chs. 7–8.

4. Gaeton Fonzi, "Delaware County: The Everlasting Hurrah," *Greater Philadelphia Magazine,* June 1963, 73.

5. Oliver P. Williams et al., in *Surburban Differences and Metropolitan Policies* (Philadelphia: Univ. of Pennsylvania Press, 1965), found the percentage of Republican vote in all suburban municipalities positively associated with social rank, except that Republican percentages were heavier in communities of lowest social rank than they were in lower-middle-class communities. Political competition occured most frequently in lower-middle-class communities.

6. It is reliably reported that, at one of McClure's frequent meetings with a group of county manufacturers, his nominee for Congress was criticized and alternatives suggested. This was the nominee for whom McClure had overruled the War Board in 1958. He is said to have abruptly closed the discussion by suggesting that the manufacturers stick to business and "leave the politics to me."

7. Booz, Allen, and Hamilton, *A Survey of Government Organization and Finances, Delaware County* (New York: The firm, 1962), pp. 17–18.

8. See Pennsylvania Economy League, *Exploration of the Adaptability of Local Governments in the Penjerdel Region, 1950–1962* (Philadelphia: 1963), p. 279.

11. Structure and Functions

1. Sidney Schulman, *Toward Judicial Reform in Pennsylvania* (Philadelphia: Institute of Legal Research, Univ. of Pennsylvania, 1962), pp. 59–65.

2. Ibid., p. 5.

3. On the early justices of the peace see Philip S. Klein, *Pennsylvania Politics, 1817–1832: A Game Without Rules* (Philadelphia: Historical Society of Pennsylvania, 1940), Ch. 3, for the nineteenth century and, for the eighteenth century, Theodore Bean, *History of Montgomery County, Pennsylvania* (Philadelphia: Evarts and Peck, 1884), pp. 324–27. On the local courts generally, see William H. Loyd, *The Early Courts of Pennsylvania* (Boston: Boston Book Co., 1910); and J. H. Battle, *History of Bucks County, Pennsylvania* (Philadelphia: A. Warner & Co., 1887), Ch. 5.

4. Thus began the mass of special legislation that, by the time of the Depression, made a jungle of the Pennsylvania poor laws, with widely varying methods among the counties and localities. See William C. Haffner, *Poor Relief Legislation in Pennsylvania* (Cleona, Pa.: Holzopfel Publishing Co., 1913); Calvin G. Bristol, *Treatise on the Poor Laws of Pennsylvania* (Philadelphia: T. & J. W. Johnson Co., 1889); Emil Frankel, *Poor Relief in Pennsylvania—A State Wide Survey* (Harrisburg: Pennsylvania Department of Welfare, 1925); Pennsylvania Department of Welfare, *Poor Relief Administration in Pennsylvania* (Harrisburg: 1934).

5. See Klein, pp. 13–14 for a description of the important local groups of the early nineteenth century, including the militia companies, which were then commonly powerful in local politics.

6. The history of local and county powers is reviewed in more detail in Pennsylvania Economy League, *Historical Development of Local Government in the Penjerdel Region,* Monograph No. 1 of the Penjerdel Governmental Studies (Philadelphia: 1961).

7. The state classification act was passed in 1899 at the request of A. J. Cassatt, president of the Pennsylvania Railroad and a commissioner of Lower Merion Township. The Pennsylvania had developed Lower Merion as a combined real estate and railroad venture, and sought authorization of suburban services and a means of forestalling incorporation of separate boroughs within the township. See E. Gordon Alderfer, *The Montgomery County Story* (Norristown, Pa.: Commissioners of Montgomery County, 1951), p. 232.

8. Counties may enact ordinances in certain fields—e.g., zoning, environmental health—but the power is dormant in the suburban counties.

9. Act 638 of 1961 abolished the separate Institution District in fourth-through eighth-class counties; but it still holds for third-class counties. Delaware County's legislators opposed extension of the Act to third-class counties for reasons I have been unable to ascertain. The main effect would have been to reduce the formal complexity of county government and consolidate two budgets into one.

10. Under the Municipalities Authorities Act of 1945 (Act 382) any local government may establish an authority with broad borrowing power for any of a wide range of purposes otherwise within local power by simply passing an ordinance. Authorities with lease-back arrangements are common.

12. Planning

1. James G. Coke, "The Southeastern Pennsylvania Regional Planning Commission—A Case Study in Organization for Metropolitan Area Planning" (diss., Univ. of Minnesota, 1956), p. 117.

2. Ibid.

3. See esp. Robert Mitchell, et al., *Accelerated Urban Growth in a Metropolitan Fringe Area* (Philadelphia: Institute for Urban Studies, Univ. of Pennsylvania, 1954).

4. Sec. 701 of the Federal Housing Act of 1954, as amended, provides federal aid up to two-thirds of the cost of planning studies for municipalities under 50,000 population. The funds are disbursed through the state Bureau of Community Development, and enable county planning commissions, by contract with localities, to do local comprehensive plans. Federal aid has lowered the

municipalities' share of the expense of such plans from, typically, 75 to 25 percent.

5. Bucks County Planning Commission, *A Comprehensive Plan for Bucks County, Pa.* (Doylestown, Pa.: 1961).

6. Coke, Ch. 4.

7. Fels Institute, Univ. of Pennsylvania, *Planning Measures and Controls in Southestern Pennsylvania*, (Philadelphia: The Institute, 1961).

8. Ibid., II. There Bucks and Delaware are reported to use cost reduction to promote redesign proposals in both the subdivision review and approval functions. As of 1960 about 65 percent of the plans (ten lots and over) submitted to Bucks' planning commission were altered significantly, with about 50 percent of the alterations adding more lots to the plan, and Delaware's history was similar. Subdivision control in Montgomery nearly died out after 1956.

13. Taxing

1. Interdependence costs are the net of external costs to the individual (harm from unregulated private action or adverse public action) and decision costs (of gaining public agreement on action). For these writers, collective action to limit government action is economically rational since, short of rules requiring unanimous decision, public expenditures on any function will usually lead to overinvestment in it judged by market standards. James Buchanan and Gordon Tullock, *The Calculus of Consent* (Ann Arbor: Univ. of Michigan Press, 1962). Significantly, most of the illustrations in their study are drawn in terms of property taxes and local government.

2. Indeed, for third-class counties equalization is prescribed "within the taxing district," which may mean either the county or the district of an individual assessor; no one knows for sure, but Delaware and Montgomery officials maintain it means the latter. See Act 236 of 1953. The basic law is in 72 *Purdon's Pennsylvania Statutes Annotated*, Sec. 5020.

3. See, e.g., Richard Ratcliff, *Urban Land Economics* (New York: McGraw-Hill, 1949), Ch. 14, and the review article by Clyde E. Browning, "Land Value Taxation: Promises and Problems," *Journal of the American Institute of Planners*, 24 (1963), 301.

4. Booz, Allen, and Hamilton, *A Survey of Government Organization and Finances: Delaware County* (New York: The firm, 1962), p. 52.

5. "Market value must be the price which a purchaser willing, but not obligated to buy, would pay an owner, willing but not obligated to sell, taking into consideration all uses to which property was adapted and might in reason be applied." *Appeal of Park Drive Manor*, 380 Pa. 134 (1955), and the recent Delaware County case, *Appeal of Baldwin Lima Hamilton Corp.*, 412 Pa. 299 (1963). Extractive or mining properties (important in Bucks and Montgomery) raise especially difficult problems: the standard is market value, but the factors in market value are exceedingly complex. Cf. *Appeal of Susquehanna Collieries Co.*, 338 Pa. 366 (1940).

6. "What the law requires is uniformity in taxation of real estate as a class, and to be 'comparable' for that purpose, properties need not be identical; nor need they necessarily be located in the same immediate neighborhood." *Buhl Foundation v. Board of Property Assessment Appeals and Review of Allegheny County*, 407 Pa. 567 (1962), a leading case in the field of assessment.

Hammermill Paper Co. v. City of Erie, 345 U.S. 940 (1953), held that an owner of property assessed for taxation at its full true value is entitled to reduction of assessment to the same percent at which owners of other property of the same class are taxed, even though such reduction departs from a statutory requirement that property be assessed at true value.

7. For instance, floating dry docks were held not within the prior statutes authorizing taxation in *Sun Shipbuilding Co. v. City of Chester,* 23 Delaware County 29 (1931). In 1911 machinery was exempted in Pittsburgh (Allegheny County) and in 1915 in Philadelphia. In general, however, the "assembled industrial plant" doctrine was law in Pennsylvania until the 1953 act exempted "machinery, tools, appliances, and other equipment ... contained in any mill, mine, manufactory or industrial establishment." 72 *Purdon's Pennsylvania Statutes Annotated,* Section 5453.201 (a). Leading cases on the earlier doctrine and later exceptions include *Patterson v. Delaware County* 70 Pa. 381 (1872); *Gulf Oil Corp. v. Philadelphia* 357 Pa. 101 (1947); *Jones and Laughlin Tax Assessment Case,* 405 Pa. 421 (1961).

8. For a comparison of state and local tax collections in the fifty states, see Tax Foundation, Inc., *Facts and Figures on Government Finance* (12th ed.; New York: Prentice-Hall, 1963), p. 150. See also Tax Study Committee, Commonwealth of Pennsylvania, *The Tax Problem* (Harrisburg, Pa.: The Committee, 1953 and 1955).

9. There are exceptions: school districts may pay a fixed salary rather than a commission, and many do; first-class townships may do likewise, but rarely do; and since 1961, the counties themselves may collect the personal property tax, but none of the three counties does so. In first-class townships the tax collectors' (treasurers') total compensation *from the township* is limited to $10,000 annually.

10. Bureau of Municipal Affairs, Pennsylvania Department of Internal Affairs, *An Analysis of Local Tax Collection Costs in Pennsylvania* (Harrisburg: The Bureau, 1958); Mitchell J. Hunt, "The Fee System of Tax Collection in Pennsylvania: An Unseen Hand in Your Pocket," *Tax Policy,* 26, Nos. 8 and 9 (1959).

14. Comparisons and Priorities

1. The calculations are based on real property taxes only, but the ratios of per capita county taxes to municipal and school taxes are not much altered by inclusion of personal property taxes unweighted by municipal population.

2. The means for the counties were: Bucks, $4,088, Montgomery, $4,188, Delaware, $4,111; the standard deviations Bucks, $1,130, Montgomery, $1,440, Delaware, $1,960. These computations are based on the State Tax Equalization Board's figures and, of course, ignore the effect of assessment equalization in Bucks: disparities in Montgomery and Delaware are not systematically associated with assessment differences.

3. Oliver P. Williams et al., *Suburban Differences and Metropolitan Policies* (Philadelphia: Univ. of Pennsylvania Press, 1965), Ch. 4.

4. According to the 1960 census the percentage of elementary school children in private schools was 41.9 in Delaware, 31.5 in Montgomery, and 29.4 in Bucks.

5. Including the four-mill county personal property tax in the figures does

not change the picture significantly even though Montgomery County is much more reliant on it. In 1962 personal property tax receipts per capita were: Bucks, $1.23; Montgomery, $6.82; Delaware, $1.98.

6. In 1963 the ratios of county employees to population were: Bucks County, 1:678; Montgomery, 1:516; Delaware, 1:425. The total county employee figures, slightly rounded, are Bucks, 450; Montgomery, 1,000; Delaware, 1,300. Here a comparison of Delaware and Montgomery probably renders factors of scale irrelevant. Average salaries (salary bill divided by number of employees) are Bucks County, $3,200; Montgomery County, $2,864; Delaware, $3,075. The salary bill has been figured from controllers' reports with some arbitrary assumptions applied equally to the counties, and therefore the figures quoted are a rough approximation. (Nothing else was available.) It includes some part-time employees and excludes elected officials.

7. Counties and municipalities have been authorized to establish and maintain libraries since 1917 and to levy a special tax for the purpose, which is not separately levied in Bucks, Montgomery, or Delaware, though it is in many municipalities. In 1951 state aid for libraries in third-class counties was fixed at 20 percent of county appropriations, not to exceed $4,000. The State Code (Act 188 of 1961) sets up regional, district, and local libraries under an elaborate system of state aid.

8. *Library Services in Pennsylvania: Present and Proposed*, a survey commissioned by the Pennsylvania state librarian (Harrisburg: State Library, 1958), p. 77. This survey was the basis of the new State Library code. It found public-library expenditures in Pennsylvania much lower per capita than those of surrounding states.

9. Ibid., and Drexel Institute of Technology, *A Survey of the Public Library Facilities in Delaware County, Pennsylvania* (mimeographed), 1961, p. 7. This survey was made for the county branch of the American Association of University Women. It found serious inadequacies in most of Delaware County's local libraries.

10. Pennsylvania State Library, *Pennsylvania Public Library Statistics for the Year 1961* (Harrisburg: 1963).

11. For a survey of the legal and administrative aspects, see N. S. Fisfis and H. Greenberg, "Note: Suburban Renewal in Pennsylvania," *University of Pennsylvania Law Review*, 111 (1962), 61.

12. Act 226 of 1935 required commissioners to create a mosquito-extermination commission whenever petitioned to do so by voters numbering 10 percent of those at the last election. The five commission members are appointed by the county commissioners, who may appropriate up to a quarter of a mill for their use. Later the petition device was abandoned as a means of starting the program, and separate commissions were no longer required.

15. Natural Resources and Recreation

1. On intergovernmental relations and planning in the Delaware River basin see Roscoe C. Martin, et al., *River Basin Administration and the Delaware* (Syracuse Univ. Press, 1960).

2. Bucks County Planning Commission, *A Comprehensive Plan for Bucks County* (Doylestown, Pa.: 1961), p. 18.

3. "The Board of county commissioners may appropriate money . . . to

aid [municipalities] in the construction or maintenance of sewers or sewage treatment works, where such . . . works have been first approved by the sanitary water board of the state Department of Health."

4. The standard is that of the National Recreation Association. For a critique, see W. H. Brown, Jr. and C. E. Gilbert, *Planning Municipal Investment* (Philadelphia: Univ. of Pennsylvania Press, 1961), esp. Ch. 11.

5. Government Consulting Service, Fels Institute of Local and State Government, Univ. of Pennsylvania, *Physical and Governmental Organization for Regional Sewage Facilities* (Philadelphia: The Institute, 1960).

16. Health and Welfare

1. In 1963 fifty-two of the state's sixty-seven counties qualified. The standards are not demanding: graduate social work degrees for supervisors and college diplomas for caseworkers; no standards (before 1963) for clerical personnel.

2. See especially Government Consulting Service, Fels Institute of Local and State Government, Univ. of Pennsylvania, *New Directions: Public Child Care in Pennsylvania* (Philadelphia: The Institute, 1962); and State and Local Welfare Commission, Department of Public Welfare, Commonwealth of Pennsylvania, *A Reallocation of Public Welfare Responsibilities* (Harrisburg: The Department, 1963), with background papers.

3. In 1961 state legislation (Act 414) expressly empowered counties to administer so-called preventive and protective services. The federal social security amendments of 1962 required universal county child-care services by 1975 as a condition of 3:1 grants (Sec. 523 of the Social Security Act as amended), and Pennsylvania Act 491 of 1963 followed through by authorizing the state Department of Public Welfare to operate an agency in any county which by 1968 is not "adequately serving the needs of children and youth" and to bill the county for the service. The federal amendments also encourage a closer relation (not precisely defined) between child welfare and aid to dependent children, which in Pennsylvania are now county and state functions respectively.

4. Act 315 of 1951.

5. Montgomery County Medical Society, *Health Survey Report* (Norristown: 1957); Delaware County District, Health and Welfare Council, Inc., *Delaware County Community Health and Hospital Study* (Media: The Council 1961). Other evidence of inadequacy of some local health services and broad disparities among them is contained in Pennsylvania Economy League, *Exploration of the Adaptability of Local Government in the Penjerdel Region, 1950–1962* (Philadelphia: 1963), p. 215 ff. and pp. 329–30. The disparities recorded in all these studies are based on variation in per capita expenditure, qualification of personnel, frequency of inspections, and scope and stringency of regulations.

6. In the narrative that follows, besides my own interviewing and documentary search, I am relying on Chapter 10 of Oliver P. Williams, et al., *Suburban differences and Metropolitan Policies* (Philadelphia: Univ. of Pennsylvania Press, 1965), and an earlier manuscript by Harold Herman; also the

Institute for Urban Studies, Univ. of Pennsylvania, *Accelerated Urban Growth in a Metropolitan Fringe Area* (Philadelphia: The Institute, 1954).

7. Herman, manuscript referred to in note 6.

8. Pennsylvania Economy League, p. 196 ff.

9. Montgomery County Citizen's Child Study Committee, *Child Welfare Services* (Norristown: 1962); Bucks County Child Welfare Study Committee, *Report to the County Commissioners* (Doylestown: 1962).

10. Montgomery County Citizens' Child Study Committee, p. 8.

17. Industrial Development

1. Act 635 of 1956 authorized state aid to local industrial development agencies, defined as "any nonprofit corporation, organization, association or agency which shall be designated by proper resolution of the governing body of any county." To many persons this implied that county funds could go only to a public county agency, and in 1957 an amendment specifically authorized county appropriations to private industrial development agencies (Act 267 of 1957). Act. 537 of 1956 required 6 percent unemployment for three years or 9 percent unemployment for eighteen months to qualify as a critical area. Then the state authority would provide 2 percent financing of 40 percent of a project if 50 percent were obtained from local commercial sources and 10 percent from local private contributions.

2. Southeastern Pennsylvania Regional Planning Commission, *A Regional Industrial Land and Facilities Study* (Bridgeport, Pa.: 1957). See also Institute for Urban Studies, Univ. of Pennsylvania, *Four County Industrial Land and Facilities Study* (Philadelphia and Harrisburg: The Institute, 1956); and the several reports of individual county planning commissions done as an integral part of this study.

3. Over the decade total national goods-producing employment declined slightly, industrial employment alone was roughly constant, while the service trades grew rapidly. Committee on Labor and Public Welfare, U.S. Senate, *The Nation's Manpower Revolution* (Washington: Government Printing Office, 1963), Part 1, Table VII, p. 282 ff, and *passim.*

4. The industrial employment decline of 1954–56 was 13.4 percent in Bucks and 8 percent in Delaware.

5. See note 2 above. These financial inducements have been used on four occasions between 1956 and this writing (1966).

6. Bucks County Planning Commission, *The Economic Pattern of Bucks County*, mimeographed, 1959, p. 131. In 1955 a survey by the Lower Bucks County Chamber of Commerce reported that 13,000 of the 24,000 industrial employees worked in three plants. Philadelphia *Inquirer*, March 18, 1955.

7. Eugene V. Schneider, *Analysis of Industry in the City of Chester* (Chester City Planning Commission, 1959).

8. As a third-class city, Chester conducts its own tax assessment for local, though not for county, purposes, and its overall assessment ratio is roughly double that in the county at large. In 1962 several Chester industries voluntarily agreed to a small assessment increase to help the city in its financial crisis.

9. Pennsylvania Economy League (Eastern Division), *Improved Transportation for Southeastern Pennsylvania* (Philadelphia: 1960).

18. Transportation

1. Cf. the mass-transit demonstration provision of the Housing Act of 1961, and federal support for the Penn-Jersey Transportation Study, later the Delaware Valley (planning) Commission. See also the other provisions of the Housing Acts of 1961, 1963, and 1965 designed to further regional planning, and the metropolitan concern manifest in the report of the Subcommittee on Intergovernmental Relations, Committee on Government Operations, U.S. Senate, *Intergovernmental Relations* (Washington: Government Printing Office, 1963). See also the statement of the Commission on Intergovernmental Relations in its *Report* (Washington: Government Printing Office, 1955) at pp. 171–72, that federal airport grants should be modified to stimulate airport development from a regional perspective.

2. Pennsylvania Economy League, *Improved Transportation for Southeastern Pennsylvania* (Philadelphia: 1960).

3. Reduction in condemnation costs became more doubtful after the decision of *Griggs v. County of Allegheny*, 369 U.S. 84 (1962), in which it was held that the noise, vibrations, and disturbance to occupants of a house from close overhead flight from an enlarged county airport were equivalent to a taking of property requiring compensation.

4. The Aircraft Owners and Pilots Association is the largest of several similar national groups. It is said to have about 40,000 members. For its position, see the testimony in *Federal Airport Act of 1959*, Hearings of a Subcommittee of the Internal and Foreign Commerce Committee, U.S. Senate (Washington, D.C.: 1959), p. 167 ff.

5. The National Airport Plan designates general sites as integral to an overall civil-aviation system and thus deserving of federal aid. Being on the plan probably confers relative immunity from damage suits and advantages in zoning contests, since it is evidence of intent to remain and to possibly expand.

6. See especially Joan I. Gotwals, "Decisions of the Urban Traffic and Transportation Board, 1953–56" (Ph.D. diss., Univ. of Pennsylvania, 1963). Like the earlier chapters, my account relies heavily on interviews.

7. Pennsylvania Economy League.

8. John S. Gallagher, Jr., *Public Transportation in Montgomery County* (Malvern, Pa.: The author, 1961).

9. Ibid., p. 75.

10. Philadelphia *Evening Bulletin*, March 6, 1960.

19. Power, Politics, and Policy

1. Perhaps the best short discussion of these alternatives can be found in Robert Presthus, *Men at the Top: A Study in Community Power* (New York: Oxford Univ. Press, 1964), Ch. 1.

2. The late Joseph Pew's estate was valued at $26 million (Philadelphia

Evening Bulletin, April 9, 1964). Half a dozen men in Montgomery have been able and willing to give without stint, both locally and on the state and national levels.

3. Robert Dahl, *Who Governs?* New Haven, Conn.: Yale Univ. Press, 1961), especially 12.

4. Cf. V. O. Key, *Southern Politics*, Ch. 14, for the argument that politicians' stake in their party's reputation, under organized two-party competition, tends to remedy the "get rich quick" politics typical of one-party factionalism. This consideration was at stake in the 1962 primary campaign of the Republican Alliance in Bucks County.

5. Thomas Dye, "The Local-Cosmopolitan Dimension and the Study of Urban Politics," Ch. 3.

6. See Robert E. Agger, Daniel Goldrich, and Guy Swanson, *The Rulers and the Ruled* (New York: John Wiley & Sons, 1964).

7. Cf. the discussion in Chapter 2 above. Some suggestions about the effects of local economic structure on politics (largely on political structure) may be found in William Form and Delbert Miller, *Industry, Labor, and Community* (New York: Harper & Bros., 1960), Part I.

20. Politics, Administration, and the Community

1. Cf. the summary description in Robert C. Wood, *Suburbia: Its People and Their Politics* (Boston: Houghton Mifflin Co., 1959), Ch. 5.

2. See especially Werner Z. Hirsch, "Expenditure Implications of Metropolitan Growth and Consolidation," *Review of Economics and Statistics*, 41 (1959), 232; and "Administrative and Fiscal Considerations in Urban Development," *Annals of the American Academy of Political and Social Science*, 352 (1964), 48.

3. Seymour Sacks and William F. Hellmuth, Jr., *Financing Government in a Metropolitan Area* (New York: Free Press, 1961); Robert C. Wood, *Fourteen Hundred Governments* (Cambridge, Mass.: Harvard Univ. Press, 1961; Oliver P. Williams et al., *Surburban Differences and Metropolitan Policies* (Philadelphia: Univ. of Pennsylvania Press, 1965).

4. Williams, et al.

5. Pennsylvania Economy League, *Exploration of the Adaptability of Local Governments in the Penjerdel Region, 1950–1962* (Philadelphia: 1963).

6. Ibid., p. 268.

7. Ibid., p. 182.

8. Ibid., pp. 273–74.

9. Ibid., pp. 272–74, and Sections G and H. Cf. the suggestion in Robert Presthus, *Men at the Top: A Study in Community Power* (New York: Oxford Univ. Press, 1964), Chs. 10–11, that some small communities are too pluralistic for public effectiveness. Here, however, the pluralism is less organized.

10. The evidence of administrative success and residential satisfaction in Springfield is more interesting because, in 1955, one of the earliest cost-factor studies concluded that the township's pattern of development was far short of optimal. See Adolph D. Oppenheim, *Cost Factors in Suburban Development* (Bridgeport, Pa.: Pennsylvania State Planning Board and Southeast Pennsylvania Regional Planning Commission, 1955).

21. Competition

1. On the township's earlier history see Arthur H. Jones, *Cheltenham Township: A Sociological Anaylsis of a Residential Suburb* (Philadelphia: Univ. of Pennsylvania Press, 1940).

2. For a more detailed evaluation of services and fiscal and administrative problems in Bristol, see Pennsylvania Economy League, *Exploration of the Adaptability of Local Governments in the Penjerdel Region*, 1950–1962 (Philadelphia: 1963).

3. Ibid.

4. Cf. Scott Greer, *Governing the Metropolis* (New York: Wiley, 1962), Ch. 5, for the view that social rank, ethnicity, and life style are the basic variables in suburban political behavior.

22. Participation

1. For a review of the voluminous literature see, e.g., Alvin Boskoff, *The Sociology of Urban Regions* (New York: Meredith Publishing Co., 1962), Chs. 8–9.

2. John Bollens and Henry Schmandt, *Metropolis* (New York: Harper & Row, 1965), pp. 225–26.

3. Cf. the following summary of a National Opinion Research Center survey of associational memberships: "These findings suggest that education is associated with a particular kind of orientation. A higher rate of membership in civic and service associations combined with a lower rate of membership in the other types (lodges and fraternal, church and religious, veterans and patriotic, social and recreational) seems to point to a more cosmopolitan' orientation among the less well educated." Murray Hausknecht, *The Joiners* (New York: The Bedminster Press, 1962), p. 81 and table on p. 90).

4. Cf. Greer and Orleans, "The Mass Society and the Parapolitical Structure," *American Sociological Review*, 27 (1962), 634. The authors find a wide network of voluntary organizations throughout the St. Louis metropolitan area that are available for political mobilization, and they also find that people most active in such local organizations are most active in politics, also. My data and observation suggest that this kind of mix of social and political mobilization occurs at the local level but with the difference that specifically civic, policy-oriented, largely middle-class (especially professional) activity tends to be separate from politics, which makes for an important difference between the political structures and the policy responsiveness of high and low social rank communities.

5. See, e.g., Herbert Gans, *The Urban Villagers* (New York: Free Press, 1962), especially Chs. 11–12; William Dobriner, *Class in Suburbia* (Englewood Cliffs, N.J.: Prentice-Hall, 1963), Ch. 2; and Bennet M. Berger, *Working Class Suburb* (Berkeley: Univ. of California Press, 1960). For speculation linking class cultures to forms of employment or positions in industrial organization, see Robert Presthus, *The Organizational Society* (New York: Alfred A. Knopf, 1962), especially Chs. 6 and 7.

6. These distinctions loosely follow those among material, solidary, and purposive incentive systems suggested by Peter B. Clark and James Q. Wilson, "Incentive Systems: A Theory of Organizations," *Administrative Science Quarterly*, 6 (1961), 129. I have adopted the language without meaning to stick to the distinctions, since I find the latter not at all sharp at the margins and sometimes in need of subdistinctions. Much the same comment applies to the literature of class-cultural differences, which is still highly impressionistic and is not improved in that respect by the present study.

7. Robert C. Wood, *Suburbia: Its People and Their Politics* (Boston: Houghton Mifflin Co., 1959).

23. Administration

1. Pennsylvania Economy League, *Exploration of the Adaptability of Local Governments in the Penjerdel Region, 1950–1962* (Philadelphia: 1963), *passim*, and especially the concluding chapter; Oliver P. Williams, et al., *Suburban Differences and Metropolitan Policies* (Philadelphia: Univ. of Pennsylvania Press, 1965), Chs. 4–6.

2. Williams, et al., Ch. 6; Pennsylvania Economy League, concluding chapter.

3. Cf. W. Hirsch, Ch. 20; John C. Bollens, *Exploring the Metropolitan Community* (Berkeley: Univ. of California Press, 1961), Part 4; Henry J. Schmandt and G. Ross Stephens, "Measuring Municipal Output," *National Tax Journal*, 13 (1960), 369; Harvey Shapiro, "Economies of Scale and Local Government Finance," *Land Economics*, 39 (1963) 175.

4. Pennsylvania Economy League, p. 359. Note that Radnor, Cheltenham, the two Middletowns, and Ridley, of communities considered here, were not on the PEL list.

5. Ibid., p. 362. Evaluations on specific services of these jurisdictions are scattered throughout Section F of this publication.

24. Political Democracy

1. Dillon's Rule is the judicial doctrine that statutes conferring powers on local governments shall be strictly construed, and that nothing shall pass by mere implication. Historically, Louis Jaffe concludes about England and America that "judicial control of official action, through citizen or taxpayer suits, has flourished when the seemingly more desirable system of [central] administrative control has been lacking. These suits have had their initial and fullest development in the control of local authorities." See Jaffe, "Standing to Secure Judicial Review: Public Actions," *Harvard Law Review*, 74 (1961) 1265. In local government the public concept recurs in the law as a means of preventing perversion of government to private purposes and protecting real property values; thus public use in condemnation, public purpose in taxation, and the trinity of public police power objectives in regulation.

2. Robert Dahl, *Who Governs?* (New Haven, Conn.: Yale Univ. Press, 1961), Ch. 12.

3. Ibid., Ch. 5.

4. Again, see Appendix B for information about the sample survey, which was taken in the summer and fall of 1963. The national samples referred to are those of the Survey Research Center of the University of Michigan. See especially Angus Campbell et al., *The American Voter* (New York: John Wiley & Sons, Inc., 1960), especially Chs. 6–7.

5. On the conversion theory, see Wood, Ch. 5; and, on Bucks County in particular, Edward Janosik, "The New Suburbia," *Current History*, August 1956.

6. On national trends, see Bernard Lazerwitz, "Suburban Voting Trends, 1948–56," *Social Forces*, 39 (1961), p. 29.

7. Gabriel A. Almond and Sidney Verba, *The Civic Culture* (Boston: Little, Brown & Co., 1965), especially Chs. 5–6. For a further expression of this view, with more emphasis on the socializing role of local government, see Almond, "Democracy and the New Nations," *Stanford Today*, Autumn 1964.

8. Ibid., Ch. 13.

9. Scott Greer, *Governing the Metropolis* (New York: John Wiley & Sons, Inc., 1962), Ch. 2.

25. Governmental Adequacy

1. It should be noted that most of the basic philosophical traditions in political theory point in both directions: e.g., some utilitarians may favor larger units for more efficiency and rationality, while others prefer small units for their voluntary aspects and approximation to the market system of choice; some "idealists" like the complex political process of large, diverse communities and the broader values they may provide, while others value homogeneity and direct participation for their presumed effects on community and individual. Different conceptions of *liberty* and *equality* are also at issue. See, e.g., Robert C. Wood, *Suburbia: Its People and Their Politics* (Boston: Houghton Mifflin Co., 1959); and the writer's "Two Academic Models for Remodeling Local Government," in L. K. Caldwell, ed., *Politics and Public Affairs* (Bloomington, Indiana Univ. Press, 1962).

2. See e.g., Maurice Stein, *The Eclipse of Community* (Princeton Univ. Press, 1960); Greer, "Individual Participation in Mass Society," in Roland Young, ed., *Approaches to the Study of Politics*, Evanston: Northwestern Univ. Press, 1956.

3. Scott Greer, *The Emerging City* (New York: Free Press, 1962).

4. See Werner Hirsch, "Administrative and Fiscal Considerations in Urban Development," *Annals of the American Academy of Political and Social Science*, 352 (March 1964), p. 48; and "Urban Government Services and their Financing," in Werner Hirsch, ed., *Urban Life and Form* (New York: Holt, Rinehart & Winston, 1963).

5. For a skeptical view of regional land planning, see Morton Grodzins and Edward C. Banfield, *Government and Housing in Metropolitan Areas* (New York: McGraw-Hill, 1958).

6. Pennsylvania Economy League, *Improved Transportation for Southeastern Pennsylvania* (Philadelphia: 1960).

7. Act 531 of 1963 mandates local school districts with a minimum pupil population of 3,000, subject to a few exceptions.

Appendix A. Theory

1. For one treatment of these relations, see Peter H. Rossi, "Power and Community Structure," *Midwest Journal of Political Science,* 4 (1960), 390.

2. See, for example, the writings of E. E. Schattschneider, *Party Government* (New York: Rinehart & Co., 1942); and *The Semi-Sovereign People* (New York: Holt, Rinehart & Winston, 1960).

3. Theodore Lowi, "Toward Functionalism in Political Science: The Case of Innovation in Party Systems," *American Political Science Review,* 57 (1963), 570.

4. V. O. Key, *American State Politics* (New York: Alfred A. Knopf, 1956), Chs. 1–3, 9.

5. V. O. Key, *Southern Politics in State and Nation* (New York: Alfred A. Knopf, 1949), Ch. 14, and Anthony Downs, *An Economic Theory of Democracy* (New York: Harper & Bros., 1957), Ch. 7.

6. Key, Ch. 14.

7. Princeton Univ. Press, 1959.

8. James Robinson and Richard Dawson, "Inter-party Competition, Economic Variables, and Welfare Expenditures in the American States," *Journal of Politics,* 25 (1963), 265.

9. On the coherence of state tax patterns in this study, see Richard I. Hofferbert, "The Relation between Public Policy and Some Structural and Environmental Variables in the American States," *American Political Science Review,* 60, (1966), 73. On federal grants for public assistance, see, e.g., Robinson and Dawson, "The Politics of Public Welfare," in Herbert Jacob and Kenneth Vines, *Politics in the American States* (Boston: Little, Brown & Co., 1965).

10. Gilbert Y. Steiner, *Social Insecurity: The Politics of Welfare* (Chicago: Rand McNally & Co., 1966), p. 29 ff.; and Glenn W. Fisher, "Determinants of State and Local Government Expenditures: A Preliminary Analysis," *National Tax Journal,* 14 (1961), 355, and "Interstate Variations in State and Local Government Expenditure," ibid., 17 (1964), 73.

11. Key, *American State Politics,* p. 17.

12. Charles R. Adrian, "Some General Characteristics of Nonpartisan Elections," *American Political Science Review,* 46 (1952), 766.

13. Eugene C. Lee, *The Politics of Nonpartisanship* (Berkeley: Univ. of California Press, 1960), and Charles E. Gilbert and Christopher Clague, "Electoral Competition and Electoral Systems in Large Cities," *Journal of Politics,* 24 (1962), 323.

14. Charles E. Gilbert, "Some Aspects of Nonpartisan Elections in Large Cities," *Midwest Journal of Political Science,* 6 (1962), 345.

15. E. H. Rhyne, "Political Parties and Decision Making in Three Southern Counties," *American Political Science Review,* 52 (1958), 1,091.

16. There are extensive reviews in Robert Presthus, *Men at the Top: A Study in Community Power* (New York: Oxford Univ. Press, 1964), and Robert E. Agger, Daniel Goldrich, and Bert E. Swanson, *The Rulers and the Ruled* (New York: John Wiley & Co., 1964).

17. Nelson Polsby, *Community Power and Political Theory* (New Haven: Yale Univ. Press, 1963). Examples of the community study tradition in this respect are Robert S. Lynd and Helen M. Lynd, *Middletown* (New York:

Harcourt, Brace, 1929), W. Lloyd Warner et al., *Democracy in Jonesville*, New York: Harper & Bros., 1949; Arthur J. Vidich and Joseph Bensman, *Small Town in Mass Society* (Princeton Univ. Press, 1958).

18. Chapel Hill, Univ. of North Carolina Press, 1953.

19. *Who Governs?* (New Haven: Yale Univ. Press, 1961).

20. Ibid., especially pp. 100–103.

21. Peter Bachrach and Morton Baratz, "The Two Faces of Power," *American Political Science Review*, 56 (1962), 947. See also their "Decisions and Nondecisions: An Analytical Framework," ibid., 57 (1963), 632. The term *mobilization of bias* is drawn by them from E. E. Schattschneider, *The Semi-Sovereign People* (New York: Holt, Rinehart & Winston, 1960).

22. Agger, Goldrich, and Swanson.

Appendix B. Method

1. Seymour Lipset, Martin Trow, and James Coleman, *Union Democracy* (New York: Doubleday Anchor Books, 1962).

2. Robert A. Dahl, "A Critique of Ruling Elite Theorites," *American Political Science Review*, 52 (1958), 563; Peter Bachrach and Morton Baratz, "Two Faces of Power," *American Political Science Review*, 56 (1962), 947.

INDEX

Administration, county, 119–20, 125, 157–58, 293, 313
Administration, municipal, 237–39, 246–48, 278–83, 285–87
Adrian, Charles R., 255 n.
Aged, home for, 80, 88, 175
Agger, Robert E., 329, 351 n., 355 n.
Agriculture, organized, 39
Aircraft Owners and Pilots Association, 197, 350 n.
Airports:
  as aid to industrial development, 197
  in Bucks County, 85, 197–98
  in Delaware County, 200–202
  in Montgomery County, 96 n., 198–200
Aldan, Borough of, 249, 252
  in table, 251
Alderfer, E. Gordon, 344 n.
Alliance, in Bucks County, 86, 88, 90
Almond, Gabriel A., 354 n.
Andrews, Adolph, 79 n.
Association of Second Class Township Supervisors, 180
Aston Township, 249, 257, 258–59, 279
  in table, 250, 282

Bachrach, Peter, 337, 338 n., 356 n.
Baltzell, Digby, 23, 338 n., 339 n.
Banfield, Edward C., 340 n., 341 n., 354 n.
Banking, 25, 35, 53, 56, 341–43
  and industrial development, 192
Baratz, Morton, 337, 338 n., 356 n.
Battle, J. H., 338 n., 343 n.
Bean, Theodore, 343 n.
Bell, Daniel, 114
Bell, Wendell, 339 n.
Bensman, Joseph, 341 n., 356 n.
Berger, Bennett, 352 n.
Blue Bell Conference, 72–73, 91
Booz, Allen and Hamilton, 343 n., 345 n.
  management consultant study
    on Delaware County, 120, 143
Bodley, John Justus, 84–86, 88, 198
Borough government, 235, 249, 252, 267,

286. *See also* Municipalities
Boskoff, Alvin, 352 n.
Boyer, Edward B., 85–86, 88, 180, 198
Boyer administration (Bucks), 87, 168, 180, 190–91, 215, 221
Bridenbaugh, Carl, 338 n.
Bristol, Borough of, 18, 54
Bristol Courier, 37, 68, 84
Bristol Township, 84, 258, 266, 279
  in tables, 32, 221, 223, 238, 266, 269, 271–75, 282, 334–35
Brown, W. H., Jr., 340 n., 348 n.
Buchanan, James, 142, 339 n., 345 n.
Bucks County:
  courthouse, 81
  early political history, 53–54, 64–65, 67–69
  early settlement, 11–14
  effects of development, 227–29
  industrial development, 15–23, 24–25
  recent political history, 77–90
Builders. *See* Developers
Business influence in county policy, 212, 213, 215. *See also* Chamber of Commerce; Manufacturers' Association; Pennsylvania Manufacturers' Association

Campbell, Angus, 121 n., 354 n.
Chamber of Commerce:
  in Bucks County, 189, 190, 213
    comparison, 39
  in Delaware County, 193
  in Montgomery County, 96 n.
Chadwick, Wallace, 106
Cheltenham Township, 252–53, 255, 262, 279
  in table, 250
Chester, City of:
  growth, 21–23, 99–100
  illegality in, 114–16
  and industrial development, 192–93
  as political base, 101–102, 106, 112–13
  and transportation, 207